THE HISTORY

OF THE

47TH (London) DIVISION

1914 - 1919

Photo by]   [*Elliott & Fry.*

LIEUT.-GENERAL SIR GEORGE F. GORRINGE, K.C.B., K.C.M.G., D.S.O.,
G.O.C. 47th Division, 1916-1919.

Frontispiece (facing title)

THE
47TH (LONDON) DIVISION
1914 - 1919

BY SOME WHO SERVED WITH
IT IN THE GREAT WAR

With a Foreword by
The VISCOUNT ESHER, G.C.B., G.C.V.O., P.C.

Edited by
ALAN H. MAUDE

LONDON :
AMALGAMATED PRESS (1922) LTD., LAVINGTON ST., S.E.

1922

Printed and bound by Antony Rowe Ltd, Eastbourne

To the Glorious Memory
of Comrades of the
Forty=Seventh Division
who fought and fell

"In chivalrye,
"In Flaundres, in Artoys, and
in Picardye."

A FOREWORD.

By the Right Hon. Viscount Esher, G.C.B., G.C.V.O.

MY intimate connection with the 2nd London, or 47th Division, as it came to be called, both as President of the County of London Association, under whose auspices the Division was raised, and as Honorary Colonel of one of its Field Artillery Brigades, accounts for my having been asked to write this foreword.

There are two other reasons why I am glad to have had the opportunity of placing in the forefront of this excellent record of the service of the 47th Division a few paragraphs expressive of remembrance and admiration for all ranks of that splendid fighting force.

Assisted by Sir Ian Hamilton, I never abated for a moment—from September, 1914, to March, 1915—my efforts to induce Lord Kitchener to send out the Territorial Force in organised divisions, pressing hard for the early dispatch of the 2nd London. And when the Division was first in the line, I took the earliest opportunity of visiting the Grenay sector, which a part of the Division was holding.

The 46th and 47th were the two first Territorial Divisions to fight in France. No divisions throughout the whole war have a more brilliant record. It is as the 47th Division, rather than as individual units of the County of London troops, that the London Regiments will hereafter be remembered, long after divisional, and perhaps regimental, organizations will have ceased to exist.

During the fateful years from 1906 to 1914, while Europe was engaged in arming to the teeth, a few far-seeing soldiers and statesmen appreciated the coming situation, when the defensive battles for which Home troops were being raised and trained would inevitably be fought overseas. Whether officers and men took the Imperial Service obligation or not, it was foreseen that the Territorial Force would be certain to fight side by side with the Regular Army somewhere between the French coast and the Rhine, and not at Pevensey or at Hastings.

It is to these men who foresaw and planned the British Territorial Force that the thanks of the victorious nations are largely due. The Territorial Force stood in 1915 between the dead Regular Army and the living Kitchener Armies that fought the Battle of the Somme and enabled the war to be ultimately won.

A few of these same far-seeing men and their younger successors have here and now a clear vision of the future.

The Territorial Force of pre-war days has accomplished its glorious mission. Like Nelson's old ships, it can, and should be, towed into Hamoaze.

The future opens up problems of national defence wholly different from those of the past. We have got to stow away the masts and sails.

If the old nomenclature, made famous in Flanders and France, of the 47th Division and its component units is to be retained, it will have to cover a defensive organization wholly different in personnel and in material and in type from that of 1914. The defence of London —-the heart of the Empire—requires vision and prevision quite as acute, but wholly different, from the old problem, which was solved so well. The naval, military, and, above all, the aerial conditions of future warfare are as different from the old as the modern conception of the universe is from that of Galileo.

The moral of this record of the exploits of the 47th Division is that the young men of London should not be asked " Go ye and do likewise," but " Go ye and train yourselves to do as well, but differently."

If the statesmen of Europe are blind enough to prepare for other wars, then let the preparation be on very different lines, suiting the fighting action of our people to the last word of science.

There was once a time when the flight of English arrows through the air destroyed the heavily-equipped conventional army of France. Just as the smaller units of the old London Regiments became merged in the London Divisions during the World War without loss of the old local association, so the famous numbers of the four London Divisions, notably the 47th, need not be lost when Air Brigades and Air Divisions take their place, if only the people at the War Office who decide these things show a little imagination and sentiment.

When Sir Douglas Haig or Allenby praised the 47th and 60th Divisions, every Londoner felt a glow of pride. The tradition of such glories should not be lost, and if Londoners should ever be called upon again to defend their free homes, even though the conditions of warfare are as different from those of 1915 as from those of 1066, the memories of the 47th Division, as recorded in these pages, cannot be allowed to lapse.

ESHER.

PREFACE.

This history is the work of many hands. It is based on official war diaries and narratives of operations. Each chapter has been written by an officer who, by reason of service on the Staff or in command of a battalion, had special knowledge of the operations chronicled. Proofs were submitted to units and to numerous members of the Division, with the result that many valuable additions and corrections were received. That a story built on these lines should lack something in continuity of style is inevitable, but it is hoped that any short-comings of this nature will be balanced by greater accuracy in detail.

It is impossible in a single volume to record all the occasions on which battalions or other units fought with special distinction, while countless acts of individual gallantry must of necessity pass unnoticed. All that has been attempted is to produce a plain narrative which will enable members of the Division to see in proper perspective the events in which they took part. Every effort has been made to secure accuracy and completeness. It will be understood, however, that in the condensing of such a mass of material some minor errors and omissions may have resulted, which lack of leisure and the undesirability of further delay in publication have made it impossible to rectify.

Sincere thanks are due to all—including the divisional commanders and divisional artillery and infantry brigade commanders, as well as many of humbler rank, both commissioned and non-commissioned —who have helped in the production of this history. I am especially deeply indebted to Major G. C. Turner, M.C., of Marlborough College, who not only did much of the initial work in collecting material, but has also written a large part of the text dealing with some of the most important operations. Others who have each contributed one or more chapters are Captain A. H. Chaytor, K.C., Lieut.-Colonel W. Parker, D.S.O., Major J. C. D. Carlisle, D.S.O., M.C., Lieut.-Colonel G. E. Millner, D.S.O., M.C., Captain A. H. Paterson, M.C., and Captain R. H. Unwin, M.C. The divisional artillery narrative, by Brig.-General Whitley, and the narrative of the operations in August and

September, 1918, by Lieut.-Colonel B. L. Montgomery, have also been of the greatest assistance.

The heavy task of preparing the maps has been undertaken by Major S. H. Fisher, M.C., A.R.I.B.A., formerly Adjutant of the Divisional Engineers. The photographs of battlefields, with the exception of four taken more recently and lent by Major P. H. Pilditch, were taken by the Divisional photographer shortly after the Armistice. Drawings from sketches made in the field have also been contributed by Captain L. Beaumont Tansley, M.C., and Lieut.-Colonel W. G. Newton, M.C., A.R.I.B.A.

Among others from whom I have received particular help are Mr. E. Whitbourn, formerly Chief " A. & Q." Clerk at Divisional Head-quarters, who has compiled the long list of honours from the original records, and the representatives of various services who have furnished notes on the special work of their departments.

The deepest debt of all is to Brig.-General Mildren, who has made the publication of this history possible, and to Mr. F. S. Stapleton, of the Amalgamated Press, and formerly of the 6th City of London Rifles, who has taken infinite pains in supervising the printing and publishing of the book so that it may be as far as possible a worthy memorial of the Division whose deeds it records.

A. H. M.

London.

   August, 1922.

NOTE.—*As all the infantry battalions in the 47th Division, with one exception, were battalions of the London Regiment, they are referred to throughout as they were familiarly known in the Division—6th Battalion, 7th Battalion, etc. A list giving the full titles of the units will be found at the end of the book. The title of the one exception, now the 4th Battalion Royal Welch Fusiliers, is spelt in the following pages as it was during the period of the war.*

CONTENTS.

CONTENTS.

APPENDICES.

ILLUSTRATIONS.

xvii

B

PORTRAITS.

MAPS.

LIEUT.-GENERAL SIR CHARLES ST. L. BARTER, K.C.B., K.C.M.G., C.V.O.
G.O.C. 47th Division, 1914-1916

Chapter I.

MOBILIZATION AND TRAINING.

WHEN the war broke out, in August, 1914, the British Army at home consisted of six Regular and fourteen Territorial Divisions. The garrisons abroad were equal to about six more Regular Divisions. The 2nd London Division, afterwards renamed the 47th Division, was one of the Territorial Divisions which had been formed in April, 1908, out of the old Volunteer force under Lord Haldane's scheme of reorganisation. Permanent Divisional and Brigade Commanders and Staffs had been appointed, twelve infantry battalions were posted to the various brigades, and a proper complement of artillery, engineers, and medical and transport services was allotted, or created, to give a real divisional organisation and, at the least, to enable it to be rapidly prepared for war whenever the need should arise. When that need did arise in August, 1914, and in spite of the very short periods of annual training, considerable progress had been made towards efficiency.

For two years before the war the Division had been under the command of Major-General C. C. Monro, who, later on, was to become commander of the First Army in France, Commander-in-Chief in the evacuation of Gallipoli, and then Commander-in-Chief in India. His G.S.O.1, in August, 1914, was Lieut.-Colonel .W. Thwaites, R.A., who retained that post throughout the whole war training of the Division, both in England and in France, till he was appointed to command the 141st Infantry Brigade in May, 1915, and who only left the Division in July, 1916, on his promotion to the command of the 46th (North Midland) Division in France.

The infantry allotted to the 2nd London Division consisted of twelve battalions of the London Regiment, forming the 4th, 5th, and 6th London Infantry Brigades. The original battalions were the 13th (Kensingtons), 14th (London Scottish), 15th (Civil Service Rifles), 16th (Queen's Westminsters), forming the 4th Brigade;

the 17th (Poplar and Stepney), 18th (London Irish), 19th (St. Pancras), and 20th (Blackheath), forming the 5th Brigade; the 21st (First Surrey Rifles), 22nd (The Queen's), 23rd, and 24th (The Queen's)—all with headquarters in South London—forming the 6th London Infantry Brigade. But on September 15th, 1914, the London Scottish were sent to France, and early in November the Queen's Westminsters and the Kensingtons were also sent to France, as separate battalions, for service with Regular brigades; and the 6th, 7th, and 8th Battalions of the London Regiment were brought in from the 1st London Division to fill the three vacant places in the 4th London Infantry Brigade.

The Divisional Artillery, on mobilization, consisted of the 5th, 6th, and 7th London Brigades, R.F.A., each having three four-gun batteries of 15-pounder B.L. guns, and the 8th London Brigade, having two four-gun batteries of 5-inch howitzers. Each brigade had an ammunition column, but there was no divisional ammunition column. Later on, the 2nd London Heavy Battery, R.G.A., armed with four 4·7 guns, was also attached to the Division.*

The Transport and the Brigade Ammunition Columns received horses and vehicles commandeered from civilian sources, and this proved the weakest spot in the organisation. Most of the wagons were heavy and clumsy, ride-and-drive harness was scarce, so that teams could not be used, and loads had to be cut down to what could be drawn by a pair of horses, driven from the box. The result was that the Transport and Ammunition Columns had no mobility, and had the greatest difficulty in surmounting Stanmore Hill on their way to their war stations near St. Albans, and the scenes there will not be soon forgotten by those who saw them. How successfully these drawbacks were overcome under Lieut.-Colonel C. F. T. Blyth, T.D., the O.C., A.S.C., and Senior Transport Officer, and the commanders of the various ammunition columns, will be seen in the next chapter.

The 5th and 6th London Artillery Brigades did their annual training in July, 1914, but the other brigades and the infantry battalions of the Division had only just reached their summer camps at Perham Down, on Salisbury Plain, when war broke out, and they were all recalled at once to London to complete their

---

* A full list of units composing the Division will be found in Appendix C.

mobilization and equipment at their various headquarters. By the middle of August they had all marched to their war stations in the district round St. Albans. The artillery occupied the country round Hemel Hempstead, Berkhampstead, and King's Langley, while the infantry brigades were grouped in and round St. Albans, Hatfield, and Watford respectively.

A detailed description of the training would merely be a repetition of that of other Territorial Divisions, and would have little interest at this date. Men and officers were all keen to learn their job and anxious to become soldiers ; and their Regular comrades—generals, staff officers, adjutants, and instructors alike—worked like slaves to prepare them for the work before them, and their best testimonial is the work of their Division when it came under the supreme test of war. The training was entirely progressive, and brigade and divisional training was not attempted until February, 1915, one month before the Division left for France. The thorough groundwork in platoon, company, and musketry training, though dull and wearisome at the time, proved invaluable later.

i.e. 14|15 March.

At the end of October the Division was selected as one of the Territorial Divisions to be taken complete to France. A Divisional Ammunition Column was formed under Major A. C. Lowe, D.S.O., and frequent brigade and divisional route marches were practised in order to ensure the complete mobility of the whole Division. A terrible wet winter from November to March, and great delays in obtaining equipment, telephones, transport, and material, and even the most necessary clothing for the men, added greatly to the discomfort of the troops and the difficulty of training them for war. Spells of trench-digging in the neighbourhood of Braintree and Witham, in Essex, at which each of the Infantry Brigades took a turn, made an almost welcome break in the monotony of life. But the men remained invincibly cheerful, and prepared to extract some fun out of every trifle, such as the great square town watering-carts lumbering along in the mud as battalion water-carts, and the commandeered ginger-beer wagons in the Transport, painted with THWAITES in huge gold letters, which the men pretended was the trade mark of our G.S.O.1. The assumption, to his lasting regret, was quite unfounded.

After the transfer of General Monro to the command of the 2nd Division in France in 1914, Major-General T. L. N. Morland commanded the Division for a short time, but in September, 1914, he was succeeded by Major-General Charles St. Leger Barter, C.B., C.V.O., who took the Division to France in March, 1915, and remained in command of it until the end of September, 1916. The artillery of the Division, from April, 1912, till February, 1916, was under the command of Brigadier-General Cecil Wray, M.V.O.

It was on General Barter and Lieut.-Colonel Thwaites, therefore, and as to the artillery upon General Wray, that the main burden fell of directing the preparation and training of the Division for war. Of course, many other officers assisted in the training, and as brigade commanders, staff officers, or commanders of units, did work of the greatest value to the Division. The Regular adjutants, too—all officers of over twelve years' service—and the permanent staff instructors, most of whom were left with the Division until after it had found its feet in France, worked ceaselessly for its efficiency. But, owing to the exigencies of the Service, many of these officers were changed from time to time to go to France or for other reasons, and it is quite impracticable to appraise their services, and unfair to attempt to do so partially. All that it is possible to do is to mention here some of those officers who, by the length of their service with the Division in England and in France, and the position they occupied, became very generally known to the whole Division, and form as it were landmarks in the memory of great numbers of those who served with them in the first two years of the war.

Such were the brigadier-generals commanding the three infantry brigades, General G. J. Cuthbert, of the 4th London Infantry Brigade, General G. C. Nugent, of the 5th, General the Hon. C. S. Heathcote-Drummond-Willoughby, and General F. G. Lewis, one of the first Territorial brigadiers, who succeeded him in the command of the 6th London Infantry Brigade. Such again were, on the divisional staff, our A.A. and Q.M.G., Lieut.-Colonel R. M. Foot, of the Inniskilling Fusiliers; our D.A.A. and Q.M.G., Major H. V. de la Fontaine, of the East Surreys; our D.A.Q.M.G., Lieut.-Colonel G. E. Pereira, D.S.O., C.V.O., of the Grenadier Guards; our A.P.M., Lieut.-Colonel C. B. Wood, of the Scottish Rifles; and such also was our Senior Supply Officer, Major W. Campbell Galbraith, and also Lieut.-Colonel Charles Newton Taylor, the Camp Commandant and Senior A.D.C. to the G.O.C.

AT GORHAMBURY, ST. ALBANS, 1914.

Major Sir L. Alexander, Lieut.-Colonel Thwaites, and
Major Collen.

Each of these served for a long time with the Division training in England, and also for a long time with the Division fighting in France, and each of them, not only for his work but also for himself, won a place in the affectionate remembrance of all his comrades. They had their peculiarities, too, which pleased us all the more. Colonel Foot had a passion for paper. He kept two soldier typists clicking away for him not only from morn till dewy eve, but often also from dim twilight to eleven at night, and he loved to have everything done decently and in order and in quadruplicate. The War Office and H.Q. of Third Army (of which the Division at St. Albans formed part) loved this, too, and insisted on our being taught the full rigour of the official paper game ; and there was an occasion on which nineteen separate minutes, each preserved in quadruplicate, passed to and fro between battery, brigade, C.R.A., Division, Army and W.O., and at last succeeded in making a saving of threepence upon the charge of two-and-sixpence for painting the name of a field battery upon a bicycle which had been bought for an orderly so as to save the construction of a costly telephone line from the brigade to headquarters.

De la Fontaine was our expert on King's Regulations and on the Manual of Military Law, books full of surprises and pitfalls for the Territorial officers in those days, and many of us have often had to consult him at divisional headquarters, where he used to work till nearly midnight, behind a pile of cigarette ends, and usually with an extinct cigarette in his lips. He left us in France in July, 1915, to command a battalion of the East Surreys, and was killed in action near Ypres, to the great grief of his old comrades of the 47th Division.

Colonel Pereira and Colonel Wood were both retired officers who had devoted their leisure to explorations in the interior of China, but they had never met each other until, after the outbreak of war, they found themselves posted to the 2nd London Division, and working in the same office in St. Albans. Colonel Pereira afterwards became O.C. 4th Royal Welsh Fusiliers, and a Brigadier-General in France, and Colonel Wood ultimately left us to take over the arduous duties of A.P.M. in the Mesopotamia Expeditionary Force.

Galbraith, now Lieut.-Colonel W. Campbell Galbraith, C.M.G., was the best supply officer that any division ever had. Always smiling and cheerful, he would undertake to do anything that was required, and would do it, or get it done. He organised wood cutting, charcoal burning, and vegetable growing on a large scale for the Division, when these last two things were quite novelties in the Army ; and it was the firm belief of our men that no other Division in France was so well and so punctually fed, or so well looked after in the way of supplies, as we were.

Colonel Charles Newton Taylor, formerly of the London Scottish, served as Camp Commandant at H.Q. and Senior A.D.C. to the Divisional Commander during the whole period of training in England and until August, 1917, in France, and was known to almost every officer in the Division, and counted as a friend by every one of them.

Two other officers we must mention here, though they only joined the Division after we got to France. Major B. F. Burnett-Hitchcock, D.S.O., Sherwood Foresters, joined us as G.S.O.2 in France on March 25th, 1915, and after a short absence as A.Q.M.G. of the IVth Corps, returned to us as G.S.O.1 on August 20th, 1915, and remained with us till June 15th, 1916, when he left us to become a Brigadier-General and D.A. and Q.M.G. of an Army Corps, and later a Major-General and Director of Mobilization at the War Office. It fell to him to work out and control the whole process of demobilization at the end of the war. Major N. W. Webber, R.E., joined us as G.S.O.2 in August, 1915, and remained with us until May 24th, 1916, when he left us to become G.S.O.1 of the 2nd Division, and later Brigadier-General and Chief Staff Officer of the Canadian Corps.

The officers in the battalions and other units were drawn from every class, profession, and business. Those of a single battalion may be taken as an example of all. The C.O., Lord Liverpool, was seconded when war broke out, and was serving as Governor-General of New Zealand. His place was taken by Lieut.-Colonel J. Harvey, formerly a captain in the Irish Guards. The only other field officer when we went to France was a distinguished civil engineer in the Egyptian service. The company and junior officers included an ex-M.F.H., two fellows or ex-fellows of colleges at Oxford and Cambridge, the secretary of a great London bank (later to become a Brigadier-General, C.M.G., and D.S.O.), several men in the Home Civil Service who had got firsts at Oxford (one of whom got the D.S.O. and M.C., another the D.S.O.), four barristers (one a K.C.), three solicitors, a schoolmaster, several business men, and seven or eight boys straight from the Universities. At least eight were old Etonians, including the adjutant, Tom Morris, of the Rifle Brigade (later killed in action when commanding a battalion of the Rifles), and also including both the sons of the last Chief of the Staff at G.H.Q. in France, Oliver and Micky Lawrence, both afterwards killed in action. No mess could be more delightful or more full of cheerfulness and fun, which was helped, rather than hindered, by the great variety of experience and training of the men whom the war had brought together. One had returned from Hong Kong across Siberia, one from Spain, one from Egypt, and one from Russia, at the outbreak of war.

The N.C.O.'s and men of this particular battalion were all in the postal service—telegraphists, porters, drivers, sorters, letter-carriers—so there was not the same variety in the ranks as one would find in the other units, where men of almost every conceivable trade or occupation could be found, and masters and clerks, managers and workmen, serving together as privates in the ranks.

Billeting in these early days was no unpleasant task. Every householder was anxious to take in some men, and to do everything in his power to make them comfortable. People were quite hurt if they did not have "a soldier" allotted to them, and districts took a pride in the particular battalion that happened to become their guests. This was illustrated in one village a few months later, when a Rifle regiment succeeded to billets that had been occupied by the London Scottish. Two village belles tried hard to attract the attention of two young officers of the new battalion, and when no notice was taken of them, one turned up her nose and said in a loud voice : " Black buttons, indeed ! And us that has had kilts here, too ! "

But even with all their willingness to take in men, there was not room enough in the houses, and every school-house, parish-room, and public building had to be requisitioned and filled to overflowing with the men of the various units. Men had to be crowded into open barns and sheds giving little protection from the weather. Later on the householders cleared out their rooms, and instead of providing comfortable beds for one or two men, they took parties of six and eight men to sleep upon the floor.

As time went on there were many false alarms of departure for France or farther afield. "Surprise movement stunts," devised to test our readiness, sometimes provided amusement as well as annoyance. A certain brigade on one of these occasions received orders during the afternoon to leave for France that night. The rest of the day was crowded with incident. One mess presented the footmen where they were billeted with the remains of a case of whisky; another pressed £5 into the reluctant palm of the butler. As to the fair sex there were heartrending scenes, and, under the stress of emotion, no doubt, more was promised than was strictly intended. All ranks, with baggage, having marched to their entraining stations, were back in billets by 4 a.m., and faced the following day with mixed feelings.

A great scandal arose in the first months of 1915 over the sale of rations. Village shopkeepers were seen to be openly selling tins of Army jam, and ration sugar, cheese, and so on, and on inquiry by the Third Army it was found that all over the areas occupied by the 2nd London, and also by the North Midland Territorial Divisions, quartermasters, quartermaster-sergeants, and even company officers, had been selling various portions of the ration, chiefly jam and sugar, but also pepper, and part of the fat off the meat.

Brigadier-General Harold Grenfell, the A.Q.M.G. of the Third Army at Easton, in Essex, was charged to make the strictest inquiry. A number of officers narrowly escaped instant arrest and court-martial. But the further the inquiry went the more clear it became that everything had been done honestly and in good faith, and in the best interests of the men, to save something for them out of the utter waste of rations that was going on. For the men were getting far more jam than they could eat, and were sick of the sight of "plum and apple," and also of cheese, which they hated. And they—or most of them—had plenty of pocket-money, and wanted milk with their tea (which was not then in their rations) instead of handfuls of brown sugar (which was). Also, the company cooks were inexperienced, and the great bulk of the meat was made into stews, and the bone and most of the fat was simply flung away as useless. Applications had been made again and again for leave to draw less rations, with or without allowance, but these were always refused, so officers were forced to collect the

EMBARKING AT SOUTHAMPTON.
Brig.-General Cuthbert and Lieut.-Colonel Foot in foreground.

OFFICERS OF THE CIVIL SERVICE RIFLES, MARCH, 1915.
LEFT TO RIGHT (standing) : Lt. J. C. D. Carlisle, Lt. F. W. Lewis, †Lt. L. Davies, †Sec.-Lt. Clark, †Lt. R. Chalmers, Sec.-Lt. G. C. D. Stevens, Lt. F. C. Oliffe, †Lt. A. Roberts, Lt. F. R. Radice, Lt. B. Barnes, Capt. H. M. Crofts, Capt. G. E. Stokes, MIDDLE ROW : Capt. G. A. Gaze, Capt. and Q.-M. W. H. D. Clark, †Capt. A. E. Trembath, D.C.M., †Capt. and Adjt. F. W. Parish, Col. A. M. Renny, Major H. V. Warrender, Capt. W. F. K. Newson, Capt. H. H. Kemble, Surg.-Capt. R. W. Branthwaite. FRONT ROW : †Sec.-Lt. B. Scott, Lt. G. C. Grimsdale, Lt. G. G. Bates. Lt. A. C. H. Benke, Lt. T. H. Sharratt.   † Killed.

wasted surplus rations and sell them for what they would fetch, and use the money as a fund to buy milk, currants to make puddings, and other additions to the men's catering.

However, before the inquiry was finished, orders came for both ourselves and the North Midland Division to go to France, and what happened after we left nobody knew and nobody cared.

Vermelles , 1915 .

Chapter II.
FESTUBERT, GIVENCHY, AND MAROC.

THROUGHOUT the winter of 1914-15 a number of Territorial battalions were serving in the trenches in France and Flanders, but serving as single units attached to brigades of the Regular Army. By March, 1915, the time had come for the Territorial Force to take the field, and serve in its own divisions.

The North Midland Division (afterwards the 46th) and the 2nd London Division led the way. To the former belongs the honour of being the first Territorial Force Division to cross to France, and they were instantly followed by the 2nd London. On March 9th and 10th, 1915, General Nugent's brigade, consisting of the 17th, 18th, 19th, and 20th Battalions the London Regiment, crossed from Southampton to Havre and moved up to Cassel, as the Division was destined for the Ypres salient. But the special request of its former commander, Lieut.-General Sir C. Monro, and the losses incurred at the Battle of Neuve Chapelle caused its destination to be changed, and the rest of the Division, as it arrived, was diverted to the Béthune area, and the brigade at Cassel was brought down to Allouagne in omnibuses, old friends of theirs taken from the streets of London. Each battalion occupied forty-two vehicles, and the vast procession of 'buses loaded with men in the shaggy grey or piebald goatskin coats, just served out to them, looked like a glorified " Wild West Show " rather than like British infantry going to the front, and caused great amusement to the men and to their comrades of the other units of the Division.

Arrived in the Béthune area, Divisional Headquarters were established at Marles-les-Mines, and the troops were billeted in the neighbouring villages, such as Auchel, Burbure, Allouagne, Ecquedecques, Raimbert, Ferfay, and later also Lapugnoy, Labeuvrière and Fouquereuil, names which were loved and massacred by the troops. To these places they returned again and again during the next year or so, and found a welcome from the villagers, which grew into a deep affection as time went on and men returned again to the same billets. In this area, too, the Division, sadly changed as regards personnel, was destined, after the Armistice, to spend the months of waiting for demobilization.

The Division now formed part of the Ist Corps, commanded by its old G.O.C., General Monro, which in its turn formed part of the First Army under Sir Douglas Haig. Preparations for taking over a part of the line began immediately. At first selected parties of officers and N.C.O.'s were attached to battalions of the 1st and 2nd Divisions serving in the trenches, and were replaced by fresh parties every few days. Later, three battalions at a time were attached to the 2nd Division, then in the line about Givenchy, and were replaced from time to time by other battalions.

Brigadier-General J. C. Wray, our C.R.A., had crossed to France on March 3rd, and by March 22nd the batteries had all arrived and were inspected by the Commander-in-Chief, General French, at Equighem. The Territorial artillery was still armed with the old 15-pounder guns, with two batteries of 5-in. howitzers, some which had been in action at Omdurman in 1898. As it was not thought advisable that any part of the fighting line should be covered by 15-pounders alone, it was decided to mix them with the 18-pounders, and our divisional artillery was scattered in separate batteries among the Regular brigades. In a very few days the newcomers had adapted themselves to the existing conditions of war, choosing carefully concealed positions along hedges and in woods, and observing a couple of miles ahead from ruined houses behind the trenches, such as Dead Cow Farm at Festubert, Le Plantin, Artillery House at Givenchy, the Cowl House at Cuinchy, and the buildings on the La Bassée road.

The 2nd London Heavy Battery, marching north to Ypres to be attached to the Indian Corps, was caught in the first great German gas attack. The men fought with their rifles, but were overwhelmed, and the guns, with " London " on them, were captured. When this was announced by the Germans there was very considerable anxiety in London, from the impression thereby created that the London Division had been at Ypres in the gas attack, and had been driven back to such an extent as to lose their heavy guns.

A COUNCIL OF WAR.
Major-General Sir C. Barter, Lieut.-Colonel Newton-Taylor,
and Lieut.-Colonel Thwaites.

Meanwhile, our remaining batteries were very short of ammunition. In April their allowance was three rounds per gun per day for the 15-pounders, and one round only for the howitzers. During May they carried out registering and wire-cutting for the Festubert battle ; and at Givenchy, on May 25th and 26th, the Division for the first time fought with the support of their own artillery. But the heavy rate of fire was too much for the old 15-pounder guns, and by the evening of May 26th eleven guns out of thirty-six were out of action.

As early as May 13th a French artillery group of 75's had been lent to the Ist Corps, and had been in action just north of the La Bassée Canal and near the celebrated "Tuning Fork" roads, while our Division was holding the line in front of them. And, later on, when the Division moved south to the Grenay sector, our artillery munitions were so short that we had to get the support of the French artillery, who lent us two heavy batteries and the 75's of the French 58th Division, of our friend General Bajolles. This French artillery was under Colonel Muller, a most enthusiastic gunner, whose greatest delight was " arroser les Boches." " Tuez les Boches, et encore tuez les Boches ! " he used to say, and the really marvellous quickness and efficacy with which his guns would come into action to support any infantry in the line or any working-party upon whom the Boches might open fire was the admiration and delight of our men. From the first he installed his own telephones direct from the infantry to the guns that were to support them, and the latter instantly began to " arroser les Boches " as soon as the Huns began to shell us. Up to that time Company Headquarters had to telephone to the battalion, battalion to infantry brigade, and in any special case that to the division, and so on back to the guns— a wearisome and disgusting routine of red tape, which was too often crowned by the reply that the guns could not possibly spare the ammunition, or by the belated firing of a few rounds.

Once after an inspection of the 75's Colonel Muller suggested to the C.R.A. that they should visit the new French anti-aircraft equipment. With this he was very much pleased, but he was much annoyed with the personnel. He said: "If you want to see drill, go and look at the English horse artillery. They have a rotten equipment, but do marvels with it. As for you, it is waste to give you anything up to date—you might as well give a monkey a razor."

But while we record the shortage of ammunition, the wearing out of the guns, and the artillery support given to the Division at first by regular batteries of 18-pounders, and later by the French 75's and heavies, it must not be thought that the infantry felt the slightest loss of confidence in our own artillery. They fully realised the handicap imposed by the lamentable lack of ammunition, but they saw that their batteries, when they had the good ammunition which we got later on, could shoot very well, even with an inferior weapon, and their pride in their own Territorial gunners was so great that they would have preferred to retain them even armed with 15-pounders, rather than have any outside artillery with 18-pounders. It may have been stupid obstinacy to refuse to see the merits of the better gun, but it shows the pride of the men in their own Division and every part of it. The gunners, however, were under no false illusions as to their handicap, and dreamt almost nightly of more up-to-date equipment, while French visitors to battery positions regarded with ill-concealed mirth and amazement " ces drôles de piéces," and displayed much sympathy for the sweating detachments who toiled at them.

The Higher Command must have thought our divisional artillery was doing good work, for from the time they reached the front, at the end of March, our Divisional Artillery Headquarters were kept continuously at work for over four months, and they went into rest for the first time at the Bois des Dames, in August, 1915, and at once began to train their men in the use of 18-pounders and 4'5 howitzers, which weapons, however, were not issued to them until the following November.

As the bulk of these pages must be occupied with the infantry a few incidents in the story of the artillery may be recalled here. The first effort of our divisional artillery was a very happy one. They were behind the 4th Guards Brigade at Givenchy, who suddenly called for supporting fire during the night. The guns were already laid on the right objectives, and they got their supporting fire in forty-five seconds from the call—a very good performance when one considers the then state of the communications.

The 13th Battery had all the bad luck—which would please the superstitious. During the Battle of Loos they had a defective carrier-ring, which resulted in the breech-block of a 15-pounder blowing out and igniting the non-metal-contained cartridges in the

BRIG.-GENERAL THWAITES, WITH COLONEL MULLER, COMMANDING FRENCH ARTILLERY IN THE MAROC SECTOR, 1915.

FESTUBERT CHURCH.
May, 1915.

WASHING DAY IN BILLETS AT CAUCHY, 1915.

LE PREOL
Headquarters of 47th Division at the Battle of Festubert, May, 1915.

Facing page 14

gun-pit. The Nos. 1, 2, and 3 were killed on the spot, but their No. 4 *ran* about 400 yards to get help for them, with no clothes and no skin left on him. He found the medical officer, and died ten minutes afterwards.

The same battery after Loos went into action just north of North Maroc. On two days running No. 1 gun-pit was hit by an 8-in. shell, which wiped out the whole detachment each time.

In the Grenay sector Lieut.-Colonel E. H. Eley most successfully concealed the 22nd Battery in the railway cutting south-east of Les Brébis, each 5-in. howitzer being placed between some abandoned railway trucks, and the intervals covered with tarpaulins, so that no break showed from the air. There was also a very cunningly sited position near Les Brébis station, with the guns between the scullery outhouses of a row of miners' cottages. This was first discovered by the 19th Battery, and afterwards nearly every battery in the Division had a turn there. These were the only British gun positions which were not found marked in the German maps captured at Loos.

Sometimes one got an amusing reminder of a man's previous occupation in civil life. The C.R.A., visiting a gun-pit of the 6th London Brigade, near the Tuning Fork, asked a question of the corporal in charge. He did not know, but would call the sergeant. Whereupon he bawled out : "Sergeant Green! Forward, please!"

To return to the Division round Marles-les-Mines and Lillers. On March 25th Major B. F. Burnett-Hitchcock, D.S.O., Sherwood Foresters, joined us as G.S.O.2. The training of our battalions in the trenches with the 2nd Division was continued until April 20th. Divisional headquarters were moved to Béthune, and on the 25th the Division went into the line. The 5th London (141st) Brigade took over the Festubert sector, and the 6th (142nd) the Rue de l'Epinette sector, from the Indian Division, the 4th London (140th) Brigade being in corps reserve. On the same day C squadron of King Edward's Horse, under Major E. V. Hermon, arrived from England to be our divisional cavalry. They, with the divisional cyclist company under Captain H. C. Leman, and later under Captain Norie, were used for every conceivable purpose, and more than once took their turn most efficiently in the trenches.

The Germans had just used gas with deadly effect at Ypres, so precautions against gas were hastily sought for. Strange pads and masks were served out in quick succession. The first gas-pad was a home-made affair, devised jointly by our medical and "Q" staff at Béthune, and was composed of a brown knitted "cap-comforter," folded into a pad to cover nose and mouth, and furnished with four long white tapes. This we were ordered to tie on our faces after damping the pad with a solution of carbonate of soda, if we happened to have such a thing about us, but if not then with another liquid which contains a certain amount of ammonia, and is obtainable even in the trenches.

Supply officers scoured the country searching for carbonate of soda, but the combined stocks of every chemist within reach went only a very short way to fill the need.   Soon more elaborate chemical masks were provided.   Gas experts visited the Division and lectured on the proper use of masks, and filled trenches with gas, through which the officers of the Division marched, headed by the G.O.C. and his headquarter staff, all duly muzzled with the latest appliances.

The men were thoroughly glad to get to France and to end the long period of winter training in the country round St. Albans, now remembered chiefly for so often having had to fling themselves flat in attacks over its muddy ploughs, and for the glorious flow of invective with which their errors used to be pointed out to them by the various generals and staff officers responsible for their military education, who now saw the results of their work.   For the men were now soldiers, proud of themselves, proud of their units, and proud of their Division.   The supply and transport and medical services worked smoothly and efficiently, and the men thought themselves better fed and better looked after than any division with which they came in contact, and they had the fullest confidence in their leaders.   And they deserved that confidence, for it was a surprising sight to see, for instance, the long lines of transport, manned entirely by Cockney drivers, men who had never lived in the country or been out of sight of a gas-lamp, toiling steadily through the darkness, in mud and pouring rain, and delivering their loads with unfailing regularity and punctuality to every unit of the Division.

The men considered themselves fortunate, too, in their trench training in the front line, for they found in the 2nd Division, under Major-General Horne—now General Lord Horne—some of the best battalions in the Service, including the 4th Guards Brigade,

GIVENCHY.

THE BRICK STACKS, GIVENCHY.

Facing page 16

with whom many of our battalions double-manned the firing-line, and learnt from their regular comrades to keep their trenches clean, repaired, and strong, and all the various duties of a battalion in the firing-line. And later on, in July, 1915, when one of the first " Kitchener's Army " divisions—the 15th (Scottish) Division that fought so well and suffered so heavily at Loos—came up to take over a sector of the line for the first time, they themselves—the 47th London—were selected to give to the new " K " division the same instruction in the duties of the firing-line as they had received from the 2nd Division and the 4th Guards Brigade.

At the same time selected parties of officers of the 15th Division attended our Divisional Bomb School of Instruction at Nœux-les-Mines to learn something of the very crude bombing of our Army in 1915.

About twelve different types of bombs and rifle-grenades were then more or less under trial, and new experimental bombs came out almost every week. All were pretty bad, and the Army in France, during the summer of 1915, fought mainly with the Battye bomb. It was a rough iron casting about the shape and size of a small glass tumbler, with oblong lozenges cut in the outer surface to facilitate bursting into small pieces. A plug of hard wood, having a hole bored for the insertion of the fuse and detonator, was hammered into the mouth of the tumbler, above the bursting charge, which was ammonal. The fuse was lit by a lighter, got from the French coal mines, looking like two cardboard thimbles one inside the other, and the fuse was inserted in the inner one. To light it the outer thimble had to be pressed down and twisted on the inner one, which then lit the fuse. This burnt (from three to five seconds, according to its length) down through the hole in the wooden plug, and so ignited the detonator, which, in turn, exploded the bursting charge. But accidents were of constant occurrence, and our bombing-parties were frequently knocked out by their own bombs. Even in the bomb schools we had repeated premature bursts. The lighter was intended for long fuses, not three and five seconds lengths, but three or five minutes fuses, as used in the coal mines.

Sometimes possibly the powerful flash from the lighter forced its way down through the hole in the plug beside the fuse, but what was no doubt the chief cause of the constant accidents was only discovered in July, 1915, namely, that the men who fused the bombs used often to receive a fuse too thick to go readily into the detonator or the lighter, and instead of stripping the insulating tape only from either end of the fuse, to save time, and without consulting their officers, they used to strip whole lengths of fuse, yards long, and then cut it into short lengths so that the part going through the plug also was left naked, and if there was the slightest looseness in the hole round the fuse the flash was apt to be carried on the naked surface of the fuse right down to the detonator, and if it did not enter the detonator it probably lit the ammonal which set off the detonator.

After repeated accidents the 47th Divisional Bomb School, in July, 1915, discovered the cause of these failures, and, undoubtedly, this discovery saved many lives of our men, as measures were taken throughout the whole Army to prevent similar accidents in future. Soon, however, the Mills bomb, with its automatic system of lighting the fuse as the bomb was thrown from the hand, was perfected, and was made in sufficient quantities to do away altogether with the home-made bomb, where the bomber had to unwind a sticky tape, pull out a safety nail, and then (with the fingers of his *left* hand, fingers always clumsy and often cold and wet, and frequently nervous in addition) take the cardboard lighter, wobbling on the top of two inches of pliable fuse and secured to the bomb with a bit of wire, to twist the upper thimble on the lower one to light the fuse. Small wonder if fatal accidents were common, and brave men thought the risks from our own bombs were far more than from those of the enemy.

On May 9th, and again on May 15th to 18th, 1915, great attacks were made by the First Army, and heavy fighting took place at and north of Festubert on the immediate left of our Division, but the attacks in each case failed to break through.

Our 7th Battalion was ordered to support the right of the 7th Division on May 15th, and for several days' fighting was under the orders of the G.O.C., 2nd Infantry Brigade. The London front was heavily shelled by the Germans, and for the three days, May 16th to 18th, we suffered three hundred and twenty casualties in killed and wounded.

On May 11th the name 2nd London Division, which, to avoid confusion with the 2nd Division, had already been changed to

FESTUBERT VILLAGE.

BATTERY POSITION AT FESTUBERT.

Facing page 18

" London Division," was again changed to 47th (London) Division.
The 4th, 5th, and 6th London Infantry Brigades became the 140th,
141st, and 142nd Infantry Brigades ; but the artillery, field ambulances, and R.E. field companies retained their old names.

On May 24th to 27th the Division took part in the Battle of
Festubert, holding the line Festubert, Le Plantin, Givenchy. The
German trenches opposite Le Plantin, about the points known
as J 1 and J 2, had been taken by the 10th Canadians, who handed
them over to Strathcona's Horse. The latter made repeated and
most gallant attacks with great loss on the rest of the German
trench extending southwards and ending in a strong point at J 3.

The Canadians were directed to attack another very strong
position known as K 5, and the 8th London Battalion took over
from them, on May 23rd and were directed to take the remaining
trench, including J 3, the possession of which was needed to secure
the left flank of an attack to be made by our 142nd Brigade from
Givenchy, north-east towards Chapelle St. Roch. In repeated
attacks by the 8th the trench up to J 3 was taken, bit by bit, but
J 3 itself was not taken until the morning of the 26th, after its
garrison of the 91st Prussian Guard Reserve and its machine-guns
had considerably harassed the left flank of the 142nd Brigade's
attack the night before.

The attack by the 142nd Brigade on the German trenches, known
as the " S " bend, north-east from Givenchy, was to be made at
6.30 p.m. on May 25th, and was to precede an attack by the Canadians
farther north at 9 p.m. ; and it was the first big attack in which
the Division took part.

From the trenches on the left, near Le Plantin, the present
writer saw that attack by the 142nd Brigade. The 21st Battalion
was in support, and the first advance was made by the 23rd and
24th London Battalions, who swept across the open ground just
like a field-day attack at St. Albans, and at once captured, with
comparatively small losses, the German trenches opposite to them.
But they then encountered a fierce and deadly enfilading fire from
the German guns, and particularly from a heavy battery posted
near Auchy-les-la-Bassée, far to the south and out of reach of
the guns of our Division.

Later on these would have been dealt with by other guns which
could reach them, but in those days there were no counter-batteries,

and no corps artillery, and each division had to rely upon the guns posted behind it in its own divisional billeting zone. Supports were brought up, including the 20th Battalion, which was then in divisional reserve, and desperate efforts were made to extend our gains, but tremendous losses were suffered by the men crowded in the captured trenches. Nothing could be done to keep down this enfilading fire, and by the following morning much of the captured trenches had been knocked to bits and had to be abandoned, but a considerable part of their front line was retained and taken into our own trench system.

In this attack Lance-Corporal Leonard James Keyworth, of the 24th Battalion, won the first V.C. of the Division for most recklessly and persistently standing up on the German parapet and throwing bombs into their trenches in the course of a long and desperate bombing attack, in which Corporal Keyworth himself threw about one hundred and fifty bombs, and out of the seventy-five men engaged no fewer than fifty-eight were killed or wounded.*

He got his V.C., but many more of the 24th deserved one. One of their youngest subalterns, Lieutenant F. Chance, lying mortally wounded on the edge of some sloping ground, refused to let his men bring him in, and waved them back again and again, because from where he lay he could see that when they got to him they ran great risk of being shot down.

The 142nd Brigade suffered severe losses in this affair, and by the evening of the 26th their fighting strength was reduced to 1,225 in all. The Germans had been seen registering on their own trenches, and there can be little doubt that they were fully prepared for our attack. By means of their microphones they were able to listen to our trench telephones, and are now known to have done so. But their use of microphones was not even suspected at this time, although they frequently used to hail newly-arrived battalions by name within an hour of their taking over the firing-line. A sort of spy mania infected the minds of our authorities, who were content to put down all these occurrences to information conveyed by spies from behind our lines, although both the microphone and the tapping of messages by induced electric currents were facts well known to every scientist.

---

* Lance-Corporal Keyworth afterwards died of wounds received at Loos.

Lance-Corporal L. J. KEYWORTH, V.C.,
Late 24th Battn. London Regiment (The Queen's).

From time to time our Higher Command turned their attention to various devices for winning the war. The personal appearance of the troops attracted their attention. The following is quoted from Ist Corps Routine Orders dated April 12th, 1915:

"Moustaches—

"It is observed that of late the provisions of King's Regulations regarding the shaving of the upper-lip have been disregarded. . . . Any breach of these regulations will be severely punished in future."

The most farcical apologies for a moustache were adopted, cut as close as nail-scissors would clip them. We never heard of any punishment. Perhaps that was not strange in an army whose King wore a beard, whose Prince of Wales, with clean-shaven face, was then serving with them, and whose greatest wars, from Wellington's backward, had been fought clean-shaved. Before long formal permission was given to shave the upper lip if you liked.

On April 20th, 1915, the order was issued that "Batteries in action are not to hang their washing up in the vicinity of the guns."

Later the vocabulary of the troops received attention at General Headquarters. Slang expressions were no longer to be used. Such "slang" words as "dug-out" and "bomb" were forbidden. Instead, the words "splinter proof" and "grenade" alone were to be used in future.

Shortly after this a corps commander paying a flying visit to the trenches reached the lines of a certain company. "Where is Captain Smith?" asks the attendant C.O. "He is asleep, sir. Been out all night with a working-party." Just then Captain Smith appears, rubbing his eyes. "I am sorry they sent for you, Captain Smith," says the G.O.C., in his kindest tones. "You were in your dug-out, weren't you?" "No, sir." "What!" says the general. "Do you tell me you were *not* in your dug-out?" "No, sir," says Smith. "We have no dug-outs now, sir. I was sleeping in my splinter-proof."

Some visiting generals gave great delight to the troops. One general—whose name we could give—found it difficult to follow his trench names on the map. Going round the firing-line of breastworks at Festubert with a major of the Canadians he kept on asking, "What is this place called?" "What is this?" At last they came to a low bit, under fire from the German snipers, and particularly unhealthy. " Ah ! And what place is this ? " says the general, looking over the parapet. " This," said the exasperated major, " is the place where you are going to put your head down and run as fast as God will let you, or you'll get a bullet in your backside."

On May 31st, 1915, General Nugent, commanding the 141st Infantry Brigade, was killed by a stray bullet, and Lieut.-Colonel Thwaites was appointed to command this brigade. His place as G.S.O.1 of the Division was taken by Lieut.-Colonel the Hon. W. P. Hore Ruthven, C.M.G., D.S.O., Scots Guards (now Lord Ruthven), who had previously served as D.A.A. and Q.M.G. with the Division in peace-time. However, on the formation of the Guards Division, Colonel Ruthven went to them as G.S.O.1, and Lieut.-Colonel B. Burnett - Hitchcock became G.S.O.1 of the 47th Division on August 20th, 1915.

Meanwhile, early in June the French handed over to our army the line from the La Bassée Canal southward to Lens, and the 47th Division, on June 2nd, took over the Vermelles sector (" Y "), and later on the " X " sector, opposite Loos, and the " W " sector, from Loos to the French front opposite Lens, and in one or other of these sectors they spent the summer, having divisional head-quarters most of the time at Verquin, and working hard at strengthening and improving the trench system and digging a new front line in " X " sector, running northward from the Loos road and considerably nearer to the German trenches. Later on they were to do the same thing in " W " sector, as part of the preparations for the attack on Loos. The Divisional Artillery Headquarters during this time were in the mine buildings at Les Brébis.

As we were always so near the French army, and had several times had the help of their artillery, and as our G.O.C. and most of his staff could speak French, it came about that we saw a great deal of the French generals and their staffs, and many warm friendships grew up, and the most cordial relations existed between us all. Throughout the autumn and winter of 1915 a frequent exchange of visits and hospitality took place between our staffs and the French generals and their staffs, and particularly General Curé, of the IXth French Corps d'Armée, General Bajolles, of the

JUNE 18TH, 1915.
In the trenches at Maroc on the centenary of
Waterloo. Captain Kennedy, Captain Ruthven,
and Lieutenant Eastwood, with riflemen of the 21st
London Regiment and some French neighbours.

MAROC CHURCH, 1915.

58th Division, and General Sir Georges Lefèvre, of the 18th Division, who had received the K.C.M.G. for his timely support of our troops earlier in the war.

The kitchens on both sides were made to put out their utmost efforts for these merry dinners, and although the French cooks in general left ours far behind, yet we had one dish, the soldiers' suet and currant pudding, which, perfectly cooked and masquerading as "*Duff aux Soldats*," was always welcomed, and completely demolished by the French guests.

Thus it happened that on June 18th, 1915, the hundredth anniversary of the Battle of Waterloo, the 47th Division was holding the right of the British line and working in close liaison with our French Allies. A snapshot taken in the trenches near Maroc on that day and reproduced in this volume, shows a group of officers and riflemen of the 21st Battalion (1st Surrey Rifles)—among them Brigadier-General Kennedy, then adjutant of the battalion—with some men of a neighbouring French regiment.

LOOS FROM BATTALION HEADQUARTERS, JANUARY, 1916.

GERMAN FRONT LINE AND DOUBLE CRASSIER, LOOS, FEBRUARY, 1916.

Chapter III.

THE BATTLE OF LOOS.

AT the end of August the Division took over from the 15th
(Scottish) Division the W sector, which it had left
at the beginning of the month. This sector extended
from the Maroc-Puits No. 16 road (exclusive) northwards to the
Béthune-Lens road (exclusive). Schemes were by now well
in hand for an offensive on a grand scale, and no time was lost
in making the necessary preparations. The existing front line
was not suitable for the attack opposite Loos ; it lay in a concave
curve north of the Double Crassier, and diverged, to a distance
of some 700 yards, from the enemy front line. A new line was,
therefore, dug in the form of a chord across the arc of the old line,
joining up the heads of long saps pushed out into No Man's Land.
Work on this trench—about 1,500 yards from end to end—was
started on August 27th by the 141st Brigade, under R.E. direction.
Every night a battalion was brought up by bus from Noeux-
les-Mines and marched to the scene of operations. It was a relief
to get these large parties clear of the square in Les Brébis, for
it was the rendezvous of all kinds of transport at dusk, and the
tall spire of the church made it a well-known target for German
guns.

Some remarkably good work was put in by the infantry and
R.E. on these new trenches. The front line was deep and well
traversed, and in alternate bays special recesses were made to
receive gas cylinders. An assembly trench was also dug 50 yards
behind, fitted throughout with hurdles to assist the assaulting
infantry in climbing out of the trenches, and many connecting
saps were cut. Under supervision of the 2/3rd London Field Coy.,
R.E., over two miles of trenches were dug in three weeks. Luckily,
the enemy allowed the work to be carried on almost unmolested.
and there were amazingly few casualties among the working or

the covering parties which the trench garrison of the 142nd Brigade supplied. Other preparations were made on an unprecedented scale. Dumps of all kinds were built and filled; a system of " keeps " was completed along the old support line; advanced headquarters were made and a water-supply system was arranged.

The telegraph and telephone cables were laid mostly in communication trenches, but where these did not serve they were in some cases buried about one foot to preserve them from traffic and splinters. Artillery lines were laid on the south and west sides of trenches and R.E. lines on the north and east to avoid confusion. Use was made of an electric power cable buried 2 ft. 6 in. deep and connecting the mines at Les Brébis and Le Maroc. For the approaches to artillery observation posts in the notorious " Artillery Row " at North Maroc rabbit netting was used in some cases, to reduce to a minimum the danger of having communications cut by shell-fire.

On September 18th the first gas-cylinders were carried into the front trench. It was our first sight of these horrid objects, though dark rumours and trial trips into gas-filled trenches had prepared us for the shock, and we handled them with a certain holy dread. They were extraordinarily awkward things to carry up a long and narrow communication trench. Slung horizontally on a pole, they stuck at a sharp corner, and they were abominably heavy. They eventually became by familiarity most unpopular with the troops.

On this and the following nights, however, they were safely stored and packed with sandbags in their appointed bays, and the garrison were left to trust that the skill of the experts, and the unwariness of the enemy, would keep the secret safe until the day. The successful conveyance of the cylinders into the trenches was largely due to the efforts of Captain H. R. A. Hunt, the G.S.O.3, who organised and looked after the whole business.

The work of carrying up these cylinders and putting them in the parapet was performed by the 15th Battalion, who had been specially drilled and trained for the work under Captain Hunt's supervision. It was completed on the night of September 19th, and the 15th Battalion returned to Haillicourt by omnibuses early on the morning of the 20th.

During this period of preparation a novel form of training for the attack was initiated by the 47th Division. Ground in rear

WATER TOWER O.P., VERMELLES.

BATTERY POSITION AT VERMELLES.

Facing page 26

resembling the objective allotted to the Division was marked out
by flags and tracing tapes so that every trench and noticeable
feature was shown on the ground. The units detailed for the
assault were trained over this course, so that every officer and
every man knew exactly what his duty in the assault was to be.

These rehearsals were complete in every detail ; assembly for
assault through the complicated trench system, advance of waves,
reinforcements of bombs and ammunition, and evacuation of
casualties were all practised.   A thorough reconnaissance of the
enemy's trenches was carried out by all leaders down to platoon-
sergeants. Each was provided with a panorama sketch of his
own front. The value of this preparation was proved by the immediate success of the assault at a cost of fewer casualties than
were incurred by any other division.

The Division had at its disposal its own four Field Artillery
Brigades (three with 15-pounders and one with 5-in. howitzers),
several regular field batteries attached from other divisions, and a
few heavy batteries. The mass of the heavy and siege artillery
was under the direct control of the IVth Corps.

Four days' bombardment preceded the attack. It was good to
hear and see. The constant sharp reports of guns, from the light
mountain battery, a few hundred yards back, to 60-pounders,
and the slow bustle of the howitzers, mostly of the lighter calibres,
but occasionally a 9·2 or 15-in. lumbering across like a L.C.C.
tram and ending in a mass of red or black dust and smoke in the
valley below—all very stimulating after months of enforced economy
in ammunition. Aeroplanes were up all day, single machines
working for the guns, and large formations that set out on their
reconnaissance into the sunrise behind Loos. For the first three
days the wind was easterly and the artillery observers were much
hampered by the dust and smoke from our own shell, which was
blown back by the wind and made observation extremely difficult.

But the Boche seemed to be singularly little impressed by our
activity. He was not in any way excited by a demonstration
on the 22nd, in which the garrison tried to look as if they meant
to attack by blowing whistles, showing rows of bayonets, and
trooping like a stage crowd round island traverses, waving scaling-
ladders as they went.

On the nights of the 23rd and 24th, the 141st and 140th
Brigades relieved the 142nd Brigade in W3 and W2 sectors.

The former sector extended from the Grenay-Loos road (exclusive)
to the northern limit of W sector, and W2 extended southwards
from the Grenay-Loos road to opposite the south-east corner of
South Maroc. The relief on September 23rd was carried out in a
violent thunderstorm, which made the guns sound foolish in com-
parison, and filled the trenches with a foot of water. At the same
time, final preparations were pushed on, almost the last work being
to throw bridges across the forward trenches to allow the passage
of cavalry and guns in the hoped-for break-through on the 25th.

Behind the lines activity was extraordinary, reaching its climax
on the night before the battle, when it took one battalion nearly
nine hours to get from its billets in Noeux-les-Mines to the position
of assembly for the attack. The roads forward of this village were
packed with transport after dusk. Supporting divisions were
coming up. Supply and ammunition convoys moved in endless
procession to their various units and dumps. All available billets
were filled to the utmost, and every foot of cover and much open
ground was crowded with horse-lines and parked transport.
Every estaminet in Mazingarbe and Les Brébis was packed during
business hours with troops, laughing and singing. White wine
and watery beer may be poor cheer, but rumour and expectation
made up for that.

Gas had not previously been used by the British Army, and
our commanders were very shy of it before the battle. The wind
might be unfavourable, and, if so, the plan of attack would have
to be altered at the last minute. At a corps conference on the
24th it was decided that unless the wind were suitable for gas
the 47th Division would attack without it. Shortly before zero,
however, the officer in charge of our gas operations reported that
the wind was blowing southerly at about one mile per hour. The
order was given to carry on.

On the morning of the 25th the extreme right of the British line—
W1 sector—was held by the 21st and 22nd Battalions, whose
left flank was to be the pivot of the whole attack. On their left
—in W2 sector—was the 140th Brigade, and on the left again
—in W3 sector—the 141st Brigade, which joined the right
flank of the 15th Division. The remaining units of the 142nd
Brigade were in reserve in the Grenay line.

At 5.50 a.m. zero the gas and smoke operations started. The
gas was worked by the Special Coy., R.E., and the smoke by a

BETHUNE : VIEW LOOKING TOWARDS THE LINE FROM THE CHURCH TOWER, 1915.

THE DOUBLE CRASSIER, LOOS.

company of the 4th R.W.F. (Pioneers). On the 47th Division front the gas went fairly well. The cloud rolled slowly forward, and its effect was apparent from the lessening force of the enemy rifle fire. Nearly all the cylinders were emptied, and our own casualties in letting off gas were few, owing entirely to discipline and obedience to orders regarding the wearing of smoke helmets in the advanced trenches before the attack.

Forty minutes after zero the infantry attack began. On the right a gallant army of dummy figures, worked with strings by the 21st and 22nd Battalions, made progressive appearances in the smoke-cloud, and did their duty in attracting a fair share of fire. The real attack started opposite the Double Crassier, and north-wards of this point line after line of men left our trenches. In outward appearance they were hardly more human than the dummies farther south—strange figures, hung about with sandbags and bandoliers of ammunition, with no caps, but smoke-helmets on their heads rolled into a sort of turban, with the mouthpiece nodding by way of ornament over their foreheads. Each line went forward at quick time down into the valley and was lost in the smoke. It is a splendid proof of the thoroughness of the practice of the attack and previous reconnaissance that, in spite of the thick smoke, direction was kept all along the line.

The 7th Battalion advanced on the Double Crassier, the west end of which, with the trench running just under it, was their first objective. Their second objective was some 400 yards of the German second line north of its junction with the Crassier. The 6th Battalion attacked on their immediate left the first and second German lines. The 8th Battalion was in close support, and the 15th in brigade reserve. Both the 6th and 7th Battalions reached the first line without many casualties ; but it was strongly held, and the garrison seemed to have been frightened rather than incapacitated by our gas, which had mostly drifted across to the 141st Brigade front. The wire in front of the second line was a more serious obstacle, and both battalions had many casualties here ; later in the day the 8th Battalion was sent forward to reinforce them. A counter-attack came early against the 7th. The enemy tried to work round the end of the Crassier and eject them from the front line, but Captain Casson's A Company successfully met every attempt, and, with the help of the 8th Battalion grenadiers, established a firm position on the

Crassier. The whole of the 140th Brigade objectives were captured by 8 a.m., together with some 300 prisoners and three machine-guns.

Out of eighteen officers who took part in the attack the 7th Battalion lost fourteen, ten of whom were killed. Captain Casson was among the latter, and his gallant company was cut to pieces, but he had, by a very bold piece of soldiering, held the German counter-attack till reinforcements arrived.

The 141st Brigade, on the left, had farther to go. Their attack was led by the 18th Battalion, whose objective was the German second line from the Lens-Béthune road (where they joined the 6th Battalion) to Loos Cemetery. Two battalions followed them abreast, the 20th on the right and the 19th on the left, and passed through the 18th Battalion when the latter had attained its objective. The 20th were to capture important points south of the village—a copse and chalk-pit, a small enclosed " garden city," and a crassier (slag heap) running south-east towards Lens from the Tower Bridge ; the 19th attacked the cemetery, the southern edge of the village itself, and the Pylons, or " Tower Bridge." The 17th Battalion was held in reserve.

The 18th started off, kicking a football in front of them. No Man's Land was easy going, and difficulty began at the first German line. It was here that the leading waves suffered most severely. The second line was reached well up to time, and was found to be strongly wired, but, fortunately, it had few defenders. On the right the 20th pushed on to the " garden city," which fell into their hands. A Company, under Captain G. Williams, successfully fought their way to the Chalk-pit. Here they captured two field-guns, which were standing a few weeks later in London, on the Horse Guards Parade. A line was established northwards from the Chalk-pit to join up with the companies on the Loos Crassier. The 19th Battalion, in the meantime, had a hard fight for the cemetery, where a trench was cut actually through the graveyard, but they won their way through and on to the village, where they joined the 15th Division in clearing houses and cellars.

Here Lieutenant F. L. Pusch, of the 19th, who was killed in action later in the war, did particularly gallant work, for which he was awarded the D.S.O. He led a party of bombers, and in one house, which he entered alone, he captured seven prisoners, after being badly wounded in the face by one of them.

Another act of gallantry, which also won the D.S.O., was performed by Major E. B. Blogg, of the 4th London Field Coy., R.E. Beneath the church tower of Loos the enemy had laid mines. Under heavy shell-fire Major Blogg went in and cut the fuse, thereby saving many lives.

The 19th Battalion finally reached their last objective, the Tower Bridge. Lieut.-Colonel C. D. Collison-Morley was killed soon after leaving our trenches at the head of his battalion, and the 19th was put under the orders of Lieut.-Colonel A. B. Hubback, of the 20th Battalion, who so had charge of the whole front line of the 141st Brigade.

Soon after nine o'clock all objectives had been captured by the Division except the western end of a narrow spinney which ran south-west from the Chalk-pit, which the 20th Battalion had taken. This contained a network of trenches, and its very plucky defenders held us up for the next forty-eight hours.

The remainder of September 25th was spent in consolidating. Local counter-attacks were met and beaten off on the Double Crassier, in the spinney, and on the south-east edge of Loos, largely by the concentration of artillery fire previously arranged in anticipation of this counter-attack.

During the night the Pioneers linked the southern point of the captured trenches with our old line, thus completing the defensive flank which it had been the task of the 47th Division to secure. Units of the Division had sent back as prisoners 8 officers and 302 other ranks, and had captured 3 field-guns. For the measure of success attained our casualties had been light, amounting to about 1,500 all ranks.

Both before and after zero the enemy's artillery fire was surprisingly slack considering the warning he must have had. Loos itself, however, soon became a regular shell trap, and an intermittent but very accurate shelling of the Loos-Béthune road caught many wagons and limbers, and left them smashed on the road, while such mules as escaped wandered about in a state of bewilderment for days.

The position of the Division was comparatively simple throughout the Loos operations. It gained its objectives within a few hours of zero, and was subsequently concerned with keeping the position it had won. But north and east of that position a battle of desperate and complex character raged from September

25th to 28th, and it is impossible to appreciate the value and difficulty of the work of the divisions without noting roughly the progress of the general engagement.   On the 25th the 15th (Scottish) Division had, with great gallantry and in face of heavy loss, captured that main part of the village of Loos which lay north of our line of attack, and had pushed on over the crest of Hill 70, with their left flank uncovered east of Puits No. 14 bis., on the Lens-La Bassée road.   In the north things had not gone so well, and their neighbours could not get up to cover the 15th Division left flank.   In spite of the fine start, therefore, their forward position was found to be untenable, and the evening of the 25th found them holding a precarious position on the reverse slope of Hill 70, with a left flank resting on the Bois Hugo.

A farther advance had been planned for September 26th, and the 47th Division had been warned to be ready to follow up a general advance by the IVth and XIth Corps.   As a part of this scheme, with a view to improving and prolonging the defensive flank of the main advance, troops of the 15th Division, reinforced by a brigade of the new 21st Division, made an attack on Hill 70 and the high ground south-east of Loos at 9 a.m.   But by this time the Germans fully realised their danger, and the attack met with determined resistance and fearful loss.   As the day wore on, our line on Hill 70 moved back, and the force of troops to hold it was seriously weakened.   Farther north, also, the main eastward push had been similarly punished.   Brand-new troops, hurried forward to their first battle, and ignorant of the country, had advanced bravely, and met with overwhelming loss, especially of their leaders.

In face of this situation, and the inevitable confusion and un-certainty it involved, the position of the Division, and of Brigadier-General Thwaites' 141st Brigade, was not easy.   He held the least stable position of the line.   All his battalions had had hard fighting, and must be kept continually on the alert to meet counter-attack.   His left flank was unprotected except by a swaying battle on the open ground between Loos and Hulluch, a battle which was going, apparently, not at all in our favour.   The withdrawal of the 15th Division had, in fact, left a gap of about a mile between the left of the 141st Brigade and the 1st Division near Hulluch. Our line from the spinney to the Loos Crassier was intact, held by the 20th and 17th Battalions, but the north of the village lay open to

MAJOR-GENERAL SIR WILLIAM THWAITES, K.C.M.G., C.B.
Commanding 141st Infantry Brigade, 1915-1916.

attack. In support, just west of the village, was the 18th Battalion, and early in the afternoon the 23rd Battalion was sent forward to prolong this second line northwards to the Loos-Vermelles road. The west end of the spinney, it will be remembered, was still in the enemy's hands, but General Thwaites told Divisional Headquarters that he must have the spinney bombarded with heavy guns before he could launch his bombing attack to drive the enemy out.

It is hard enough to follow the course of these operations in retrospect ; at the time it was impossible to do so. Wild rumours came in from all sides ; small bodies of men came by, saying that they were the only survivors of their units ; waves of men moving back over the sky-line to the north were described now as prisoners being brought back, now as our own men retiring. But the one thing that General Thwaites made clear to his C.O.'s, who, in turn, impressed it upon their officers and men, was that they must hold their positions at all costs. Major S. J. Lowe, Brigade Major, 141st Infantry Brigade, and Major A. C. Gordon, 5th London Brigade, R.F.A., together with Lieutenant Young, 20th Battalion, who was killed, distinguished themselves in carrying out these orders under heavy fire.

During the afternoon General Thwaites had moved his own advanced headquarters from Le Maroc to the remains of a house at the " Valley Cross Roads " on the outskirts of Loos. This ruin was so exposed that when night fell it was found inexpedient to use even a shaded light. The reception of messages from Divisional Headquarters by telegraph was therefore impossible, and the telephone had to be used instead until daylight returned. Through these headquarters the Division had to transmit messages later on for the 1st Brigade in Loos, which was temporarily under the orders of our G.O.C., and for the 3rd Cavalry Division (also in Loos), who had no other telegraphic communication with the IVth Corps for some time.

In the first line there was some brisk bomb-fighting, but shelling was nowhere heavy on our front (it is probable that the Lens batteries had been moved back hastily on the 25th) ; the difficulties were the extraordinary sense of uncertainty and the fatigue of troops who had been fighting or working continuously for thirty-six hours.

During the afternoon the situation was eased by the arrival of the 6th Cavalry Brigade, which relieved the remnants of the

E

15th Division and became responsible for the line north and east of Loos and for the defence of the village. The Guards Division similarly took over from the XIth Corps (the 21st and 24th Divisions) farther north. At the end of an anxious day of terribly costly fighting, fresh troops were holding an ill-defined defensive line, and waiting for an opportunity to renew the attack. The 47th Division had maintained its position only by constant effort, and night brought no rest from the work of consolidation.

On this same day, September 26th, the French had had considerable success in the Champagne, where 14,000 prisoners had been taken, and farther north General Foch's Tenth Army had captured Souchez, the scene of bitter fighting throughout the summer.

The attack of the Guards Division on September 27th was timed for 4.50 p.m. At the same hour it was arranged that the 20th Battalion, supported by a company and the bombing platoon of the 23rd and troops of the 19th, should clear the enemy from the west end of the spinney. This operation was entirely successful. A preliminary bombardment prepared the way, and the assaulting troops, led by bombers, smothered the garrison in the maze of trenches which had been the centre of an obstinate resistance and a perpetual menace for the last two days. With the capture of the spinney the last outstanding piece of the 47th Division's objective was taken. The heavy and accurate bombardment of the copse at long range by Major Pollard's howitzer battery contributed largely to the success of the operation.

No one who saw it can forget the advance of the 3rd Guards Brigade to attack Hill 70, as they moved in artillery formation across the open ground down into the Loos Valley. The Welsh Guards, in action for the first time, and the 4th Grenadiers led the attack, and passed through our support line on their way to Hill 70 ; the supporting battalions halted in our lines during the night. The enemy shelling had gained in strength during the day, as guns were brought back after our first attack was held, and the battalions met with heavy shrapnel-fire as they came forward down the slope. But they moved on in perfect order, and the sight of them did more than restore confidence that had been shaken by the confusion of the previous day. On Hill 70 the Guards met with strong resistance, and suffered very heavily from machine-gun fire on the crest of the hill. They finally consolidated a line well up the slope. On the left the 2nd Guards

Brigade had rushed, but were unable to hold Puits No. 14 bis, and held a line running through the Chalk-pit on the Lens-La Bassée road. A second attack in the Puits on September 28th gained no further ground.

At this point our attack came to a standstill, as did that of the French on our right, and a rearrangement was made of the troops in the line. On the night of September 28th-29th the 142nd Brigade relieved the 141st Brigade, who, after four days spent in the most critical part of the divisional front, were withdrawn into reserve at Le Maroc. The 140th Brigade extended their line to include the old W1 sector, which had not moved. On the night of September 29th-30th the 142nd Brigade lengthened their line outwards and relieved the Guards on Hill 70. On their left the 12th Division came up to relieve the Guards Division. On September 30th the 140th Brigade were relieved by the 152nd French Division, which became responsible for the line as far north as the Béthune-Lens road. This was a fine division, very strong, and magnificently equipped, and it was good to see them come marching along the Harrow Road to take the place of our men, who were tired and battle-stained, and very glad of the chance to wash and sleep.

The 142nd Brigade held the line for three days. During this time, Lieutenant Baswitz, bombing officer of the 22nd Battalion, with some bombers, explored some dugouts in No Man's Land on Hill 70, and brought back six Guardsmen and two Germans, who had been there in forced alliance, the Englishmen for three and the Germans for four days. Lord Cavan wrote sending the thanks of the Guards Division for this exploit.

The Brigade Signal Office in the cellar of a house in Loos was blown in, two infantry runners being killed and several sappers badly knocked about. Communication with the Division was restored within ten minutes.

The telegraph communication between Division and Brigade was well maintained. Lines were laid from brigades to battalions and in some cases to companies as soon as the front line settled down. Visual signalling was not much used on account of the exposed position of headquarters. The motor-cyclists did very good work on the exposed road from Le Maroc to Loos. Communication between the Division and the IVth Corps was maintained with difficulty owing chiefly to the devastating effect of wagons moving in and out of their transport lines during the night.

On the night of October 1st the French relieved the 142nd Brigade, taking over the whole Loos sector, which they held until the 47th Division relieved them there in January, 1916.

For the next few days the Division was in corps reserve, resting and refitting in villages south-west of Bethune.

Comparatively little was said in the newspapers about the part played by the London Division in the Battle of Loos. The characteristic which most strongly impressed the popular fancy was the fact that in these operations the New Army was first employed on a large scale. Moreover, the actual attack is apt to give most scope to the imagination of the war correspondent, and the attack of the 47th Division got quickly home to clearly-defined objectives. And the main share of prisoners and spoils of war did not come our way. But the Division performed a distinct and important function in the general scheme. It was the hinge upon which the attack swung, and its own attacking brigade formed the southern flank of the salient which marked the British advance.

Once captured, a position must be held, and this is apt to be the hardest part, for conclusion of successful attack is not rest, but work and defence against all comers.

At the end of November, shortly before he left France, Sir John French inspected the 142nd Brigade at Lozinghem, and to them, as representing the Division, he expressed in the strongest possible terms his appreciation of the value of the Division's performance, the success of which, he said, had definitely assured him of the safety of a most vulnerable point in the field of operations.

Chapter IV.

WINTER IN THE LOOS SALIENT.

THE Division had only a few days' respite after the Loos fighting, for the battle was not yet over, and, as our losses had been comparatively light, we were held ready to take part in further operations. But a few days gave time to make good the deficiencies of equipment and clothing, which were considerable. The quartermaster's store is always an important place ; after a fight it is the hub of the universe, and the storemen, sometimes envied for their safety rather than admired for their industry, show that they have to work hard for their living.

At the end of September the 4th Battalion, Royal Welsh Fusiliers, which had already been in France for nearly a year, joined the Division as pioneer battalion. This fine Territorial battalion had its headquarters at Wrexham, and was recruited chiefly in Denbigh and Flintshire. After hurried training at Northampton, it embarked for service in France on November 5th, 1914, with a strength of 29 officers and 850 other ranks.

After a short period of active service training, the battalion joined the 3rd Brigade, 1st Division, and was involved in much hard fighting at Festubert, Givenchy, Neuve Chapelle, and Richebourg. It had suffered heavy casualties, including the loss of the Commanding Officer, Lieut.-Colonel F. C. France-Hayhurst, who was killed when leading his men into action at Richebourg, before it was converted, in September, 1915, into a pioneer battalion.

The fact that almost all the then remaining warrant officers, non-commissioned officers, and men were skilled miners no doubt largely weighed with those who decided on the change, and the excellence of the pioneer work during the attachment of the battalion to the 47th Division testifies to the wisdom of the Higher Command in their selection.

On October 5th the Division moved forward to the Noeux-les-Mines area.   On the 8th, at 3 p.m., the expected German counter-attack developed all along the line from the Double Crassier to the Hohenzollern Redoubt.   The 140th Brigade was sent to Mazingarbe, and placed under the orders of the 1st Division ; the other brigades stood by in their billets, ready to move at half an hour's notice. The counter-attack was most successfully repulsed at every point; with great loss to the enemy.   The character of the fighting is shown by the fact that the IVth Corps alone used 9,000 grenades in two and a half hours.

Meanwhile, further offensive operations were planned. Sir Henry Rawlinson (G.O.C. IVth Corps), in his inspections of the 141st and 142nd Brigades on October 9th, had ominously expressed his conviction that they would maintain their reputation in any future efforts they might be called upon to make, and it soon became known that the Division's next objective was the village of Hulluch.   The IVth Corps operations were to consist of two parts.   First, a local operation by the 1st Division to capture the line of the Lens-La Bassée road in front of Hulluch, and, second, a general attack in which the 47th Division was to capture the village.   The 142nd Brigade, which had been in support during the previous operations, was to attack this time.

On the day of the 1st Division attack, October 13th, the 140th Brigade was moved forward by the 1st Division to trenches near Bois Carré, west of the Loos-La Bassée road, ready to support the attackers ; the 142nd Brigade was in trenches near Le Rutoire ; and the 141st Brigade in billets at Mazingarbe.   The Pioneers (4th R.W.F.), who had been working for the 1st Division for the past week, had returned to us, and were followed by a letter of thanks from the 1st Division for the excellent work they had done. The attack started with a gas and smoke discharge at 1 p.m.   The 1st Division reached, but could not hold, their objective, and, after heavy loss, were left holding the line from which they started. In the north some ground was gained at great cost, and on this afternoon the 46th Division captured the line in the Hohenzollern Redoubt, which we came to know well two months later.   On the following day the 140th and 141st Brigades relieved the 1st Division in the front line.

The 20th Battalion (141st Brigade) took over the front line from the 1st South Wales Borderers (3rd Brigade) with A Company on the left. This company's headquarters, together with battalion headquarters, were in the Chalk-pit.

The trenches were in a very much damaged condition. The front line trench in front of the estaminet by the Chalk-pit was completely blown in and could not be held at all in daylight. It was completely restored before A Company was relieved.

Many hundreds of smoke-bombs and " ball "-bombs were found in the trenches. These were collected and placed for safety against the forward side of the Chalk-pit, which was there some 30 or 40 feet deep. By some extraordinary piece of bad luck this had no sooner been done than the enemy burst a shell right on them. The whole dump went up and burnt furiously for two hours or more, in spite of the heroic efforts of R.S.M. Muir and others to put the fire out. The atmosphere in the Chalk-pit, it is alleged, was rendered doubly pungent by the language of Lieut.-Colonel A. B. Hubback, commanding the 20th Battalion, whose headquarters were in the lime-kiln in the Chalk-pit.

Seeing clouds of smoke issuing from the quarry the enemy put down an intense bombardment of our front and support lines, which completely cut all communication with the rear and combined with the exploding bombs from the dump to make the Chalk-pit a particularly unhealthy spot for some time.

The artillery were kept busy during this period, and hardly a day passed without a heavy bombardment of the Bois Hugo or other likely assembly places for a counter-attack. On these occasions our unfortunate infantry never had to wait very long for the Boche reply.

Meanwhile, the 142nd Brigade was left in support, and went back, a battalion at a time, to Mazingarbe to practise the attack on Hulluch on a flagged course, a rather discouraging business in view of the events of October 13th.

All ranks eagerly participated in this training, which the French Command observed with deep interest, and many valuable suggestions were made by all ranks at the conferences. The rank and file, particularly, realised the value gained, which carried out the spirit of combined training by ensuring that every man knew what was expected of him. The project, however, was abandoned within a few days, and our active operations of 1915 had come to an end.

The sector of the line which we held for the next month was remarkably unpleasant. It formed the middle sector of the whole salient which marked the Loos advance, and ran, roughly, parallel to the Lens-La Bassée road northwards from the Loos sector, which the French held, falling back north-west towards the quarries on our left. Our line lay well down the forward slope towards Hulluch, and could be, and was, enfiladed by guns from behind Hill 70 on the right, and from the cover of the mining villages of St. Elie and Haisnes on the left. Long communication trenches led down the slope, exposed to enemy observation. The Boche held a strongly-mined and well-established line along the main road in front of Hulluch, and perpetually harassed us in our exposed trenches. But our worst enemy was the weather. The attack on September 25th had marked the end of the fine autumn weather ; heavy rain fell frequently during the following three weeks, and the end of October began the November soak. The sector had hitherto been looked upon as the jumping-off ground for further attacks, and work had been done from that point of view ; it fell to us to organise it for trench warfare. The old German front system lay about 1,000 yards behind the line and forward of this there was no dugout accommodation. The front line had been designed for a gas-attack, and the special recesses, over-weighted with sandbag revetments, collapsed and filled the trench. Our predecessors, in want of better cover, had gone in extensively for under-cutting the parapet. With perpetual rain most of these cubby-holes kept falling in, and anyone who used them for shelter ran the risk of premature burial. There was hardly any wire in front of the line, and every night parties staggered out with coils of barbed wire and French concertinas. We were grateful to the Boche for a captured store of screw pickets—the first we had seen—which were soon reproduced as a regular R.E. store. Again, the communication trenches were in an awful state. A tangle of derelict telephone cables caused the ungodly—carrying a rifle and a couple of boxes of bombs or other such trifle—to blaspheme not a little, and when this was cleared away the mud remained, often eighteen inches or two feet of it. Up these trenches—Haie, Posen, or Vendin Alley—all daylight traffic must come.

Under these conditions it is easy to see that there was no lack of work for R.E. and pioneers, and any infantry available for carrying and digging. The actual trench garrison were responsible for maintaining their own dwelling-place, and, after being worried by day by " pipsqueaks," coming from apparently impossible directions, they started at dusk wiring and clearing the worst landslides from the trench. Their least uncomfortable time was after the job of work was done, when a group of men, who were lucky enough to have one, could gather round a brazier, under a tent of waterproof sheets, and get some sort of clammy warmth before " stand-to."

Regimental transport men, too, and ration-parties are likely to remember the Hulluch sector. Stores of all kinds, rations, S.A.A. and bombs, and R.E. material were brought up across country from Vermelles to Lone Tree. This tree, while it stood, was the only prominent object on the slope, about 1,800 yards behind the front line. It had been useful as an aiming mark for our guns before the advance, and was cut down when it was found that the enemy put it to a like use. Here, in the mud, stores were unladen, and carrying-parties made their rendezvous. Double teams, starting early, had difficulty in reaching the dump by ten o'clock. Their visit was enlivened by stray rifle and machine-gun bullets, and in the rain and darkness the business of delivering the goods could not be got through in a few minutes. It was a different scene from the meetings on a fine summer evening in Maroc, when the latest rumour from refilling-point could be discussed in peace and quiet. The fate of ration-parties from the front was even worse. They left the line at about 6 p.m. ; they were lucky to get away from Lone Tree by 10.30, and after stumbling across shell-holes and trenches, they delivered a few sandbags full of sodden food to an unappreciative C.S.M. in the early hours of the morning.

At this period of the war the administrative arrangements for the feeding of troops in the front-line system were crude, and much had to be learnt before we arrived at a relatively high state of efficiency in this essential branch of staff work, on which the health, comfort, and fighting efficiency of the troops so much depend.

During this winter a great advance was made in artillery methods. The long-expected 18-pounders replaced the ancient 15-pounders, with which the batteries had hitherto been armed. The supply of ammunition, especially of high - explosive shells, improved, and henceforward the infantry could expect an offensive and defensive artillery support unhampered by any serious shortage of shells.

Then, too, the increasing use by the enemy of armour-piercing shells and the open and unsheltered character of the ground led to a notable development in the construction of defensive positions. The old rows of sandbags and foliage gave place to tunnelled dug-outs and covered gun-pits.

The absence of high ground or houses behind the front line brought into vogue the custom of trench observation, which, though it may not always have been satisfactory from the gunnery point of view, had the important result of bringing artillery officers and men into personal contact with the infantry, to the advantage of both arms.

We made the acquaintance of two new pieces of equipment during this period. The first was the " boot, gum, thigh." A few pairs were distributed among battalions in the line " for trial and report, please," and runners and visiting officers from battalion headquarters dragged foot after foot through the mud of Posen Alley, wondering whether they would not rather have wet feet, after all. But the gum-boot was a real boon to men who had to stand for hours in mud and water, provided that they had the chance to get into a dry place from time to time and ventilate their feet. The other new weapon of defence was the steel helmet. At first only a few were issued to sentries and officers and N.C.O.'s on duty in this line, but their use was so apparent that they were soon a regular part of the fighting man's equipment, in spite of the unfavourable report on them by a senior officer on the ground that they were unbecoming.

Communication in this sector was very difficult. Brigade headquarters were almost as far forward as those of battalions ; the lines were long and exposed to shell-fire and damp.

On November 6th the Lord Mayor of London paid a visit to his citizens in the Hulluch sector, and was taken as far forward as the reserve battalion in the old German line near Posen Station.

The rule in the IVth Corps during the winter was two months in the line and one month in corps reserve for each division. The 47th Division was relieved by the 1st Division by November 15th, and went back to the familiar Lillers area—Auchel, Allouagne, Burbure, and all the other villages which seemed in those days to like us as much as we liked their estaminets. A month of rest and mild training followed, varied by a divisional route march, the first and last of its kind, which took us from our comfortable

COMMANDANT ROSSET, A WELL-
KNOWN FRENCH GUNNER, WITH
BRIG.-GENERAL THWAITES.

IN THE LINE NEAR LOOS.
NOVEMBER, 1915.

SITE OF HOHENZOLLERN REDOUBT, 1918.

billets to villages in the direction of Bomy, where rations arrived about midnight, and some of us tried to combine a late breakfast with an early start, rather to the disadvantage of the former. The expedition, however, was said to have been a valuable piece of training for the staff.

Apart from the casualties suffered by the Division in the Battle of Loos, the ensuing month of trench warfare had taken its toll of 900 all ranks killed and wounded. Many men, too, were evacuated sick in those days of "uncivilised" war. Reinforcements to replace these losses came very irregularly, and some battalions were much below strength. This variation was the result of causes too complicated to be examined in detail. Some units were more fortunate than others in their recruiting areas and in their recruiting organisation. Many men sent out in drafts in those last days of the voluntary system were found to be physically unfit to stand the strain of war, though there were middle-aged men and boys among them who nobly played the part of fitter men who had yet to be called up. A welcome addition came to the Division in November of the 1/3rd and 1/4th London Regiment, two experienced battalions which were at the time much reduced in strength. The 1/4th Battalion was attached to the 140th Brigade, and the 1/3rd to the 142nd Brigade. A party of the latter was soon detached to run a divisional draft training depot at Vaudricourt under Lieut.-Colonel Howell, the remainder being attached to the 23rd Battalion. After sharing the hardships of two months in the trenches with us, these battalions left the Division in February to join the 56th (London) Division, which was then forming.

At the end of the second week in December the Division relieved the 15th Division in the north sector of the Loos salient, which included the quarries and the Hohenzollern Redoubt. The legacy of the awful fighting which had taken place in these trenches on and after September 25th, in the shape of half-buried bodies and a general atmosphere of mortality, alone made this part of the line almost uninhabitable, and there were other disadvantages. Near the quarries a precarious hold was maintained by us on some rising ground in front of our main line by two long parallel saps which ran across to the German line. We held these saps and piece of trench joining their heads, and so completing the Hairpin. We also held a piece of Essex Trench, which continued the top of the Hairpin southwards. An equally high value was set on this position by our Higher Command and by the Boche. The former looked upon it as a valuable tactical point ; the latter as a piece of their front-line system insolently occupied by the enemy. The day after the Division took over the line the enemy raided Essex Trench. This raid, and another, was successfully repulsed by the 18th Battalion, who had three anxious days defending the position. Their success in doing so earned the praise of the Corps Commander (Sir Henry Rawlinson). A few days later the Boche renewed his efforts, and succeeded in bombing the 15th Battalion out of some twenty yards of Essex Trench. Two counter-attacks, which cost the 15th Battalion and bombers of the 18th Battalion fifty casualties, failed to regain the captured ground. Our hold on the Hairpin was less secure after this misadventure, and work was at once put in hand to protect it by a new fire trench on the southern flank. This was to be effected by Russian saps, driven just underground, and broken through when complete, and on these saps the R.E. and Pioneers worked at top pressure for several nights. But our real danger lay farther underground. The infantry had previously reported sounds of mining under the Hairpin. Experts visited the spot, and pronounced their fears groundless—a report which reassured the authorities rather than the garrison, who are apt to be fussy about such things. When miners of the R.W.F. heard the same sounds the question was taken more seriously. The garrison of the top of the Hairpin was reduced, the Russian saps were abandoned, and a new scheme was started of joining the legs of the Hairpin nearer to its base.

At tea-time on December 30th the Hairpin was blown up, and with it we lost many of Captain Woolley's B Company of the 22nd Battalion, and most of the bombing platoon. A number of men, fortunately, were not buried by the explosion, but were cut off and became prisoners. At the same moment the enemy opened a remarkably heavy bombardment on our front line, causing many casualties to the garrison, knocking in the trenches, and levelling with the ground the local communication trench. Throughout this anxious half-hour the 22nd and neighbouring battalions maintained a steady rifle and machine-gun fire in the new craters, and no Boche infantry attack developed. A party of seamen from the Grand Fleet on a visit to the front were in the line with the Brigade. They were surprised to find that the sea has no monopoly of mines. They also showed us that sailors can fight on land as well as at sea, and did useful work manning a machine-gun, the crew of which had been knocked out. The support battalion was hurried forward to relieve the 22nd, and everyone worked hard to clear the battered trenches. In the morning high mounds of chalk were seen to command our front line, and the Boche was occupying the new trench across the Hairpin which we had so conveniently dug for him. Three days later the Dismounted Division relieved us, and we moved south to take our old Loos sector from the French.

The Division had spent a thoroughly "windy" month, full of excursions and alarms, during which our first Christmas in France had passed unobtrusively. The 142nd Brigade, indeed, had been lucky enough to be in billets in Sailly-Labourse and Verquin at the time, but of them at least one battalion had been favoured with a special Christmas Day alarm, and a battalion mess Christmas dinner was laid when the order came to march off to a new billet. The brigades in the line had to make the best of a muddy job, and were enlivened by a little extra activity on the part of our guns, just to show the Boche that any attempt at fraternisation would be severely discouraged. Many batteries fired 300 rounds apiece during the day, by way of a Christmas present for him. Mines and counter-mines, hurricane bombardments, and mud— liquid, penetrating mud that flowed in over the top of knee-boots and sent many men down the line with trench feet—these are among the chief memories of Christmas, 1915, our first Christmas at the war.

We relieved the French 18th Division at Loos on January 4th, 1916. On completion of relief, their commander, General Sir Georges Lefèvre, K.C.M.G., under whose command we had passed, wrote the following letter to the divisional commander :

"At the moment of handing over command of the 47th British Division to Major-General C. Barter, C.V.O., C.B., Chief of this Division, I wish to inform this General Officer of my great admiration for the manner in which every service of his Division has been working during relief operations, and for the superb attitude of his troops in every circumstance.

"The 18th French Division leaves the Loos sector with regret, but knows that it cannot be in better hands than those of the 47th British Division, who captured it."

On the return home of Sir John French at the end of 1915, Sir Douglas Haig, who succeeded him as C.-in-C., handed over the command of the First Army to Sir Charles Monro. The new army commander had been our divisional general at the outbreak of war.

The Loos sector had become considerably more habitable since we had left it. The French seem to aim at comfort in their trenches rather than at the smartness which we try to bestow on our firebays when circumstances do not allow us to spend our spare energy by polishing buttons. They are more naturally soldiers and need less the artificial encouragements that have come to mean so much to us. Their dugouts are apt to have a pleasant domestic air, sometimes combined with a touch of drawing-room elegance, which makes their inmates forget to consider how much cover lies above their head. Ours generally miss this amenity, and resemble the cave-dwellings of primitive man at their worst, and, at their best, an efficient and compact cabin between decks.

Loos had been much ruined during our absence, and no overground accommodation remained. The best cellars were the battalion H.Q. in the post-office, and the spacious rooms under a farmhouse on the western edge of this village, which were used as an advanced dressing station, manned by the 6th London Field Ambulance. Boche shells had knocked the top off one of the pylons of the Tower Bridge.

The bulk of the artillery went into positions in and around Grenay, where the still intact cottages of Maroc gave a welcome improvement in observation. The practice of pushing up guns close to the trenches began to be carried out, and a gun of the 19th London Battery was brought into action in the fosse at Calonne, not more than 300 yards from the front line, to shoot laterally at the railway triangle east of Loos. Although searched for by every type of missile, including trench-mortar bombs, the gun remained in action for several weeks, until the battery left the neighbourhood.

Some batteries were engaged in counter-battery work, and poured an immense amount of ammunition on to the battery positions, billets, and communications in and around Lens. At last it could be felt that in weight of metal we could at least hold our own, and even carry out the precept that it is more blessed to give than to receive.

Mining operations again demanded our most serious attention. Our predecessors had driven a long tunnel under the north arm of the Double Crassier, and a great pile of excavated chalk proclaimed this enterprise to all the world. But more secret and urgent

LOOS CRASSIER, WITH BROKEN PYLONS.

HARRISON'S CRATER, FROM SNIPER'S HOUSE, LOOS.

Facing page 46

work was going on farther east, where the line crossed the Lens-Béthune road, and on January 23rd our miners successfully blew up a large mine, the visible result of which was Harrison's Crater. The 21st Battalion was holding the line at this point ; they had considerable casualties from the explosion which destroyed our own trenches, but they successfully occupied the near lip of the crater. The difficult work of consolidation was undertaken by the 4th London Field Coy., R.E., who lost a number of men in the effort, and later by the 2/3rd Field Coy.   A fortnight later we blew a mine to improve our position on the east edge of the spinney south of Loos.   By way of retaliation the Boche blew a mine near Harrison's Crater, which undid the work we had done to consolidate it.   Within a few days, on February 14th, we were relieved by the 1st Division, and went into corps reserve.   On February 17th the Division was transferred (on paper) to G.H.Q., in which supposedly blissful state it remained for a whole week.

The last week of January, like that of the preceding month, was a very " windy " time.   January 27th is the anniversary of the Kaiser's birthday, and it was feared that his loyal subjects would mark the day by some special exhibition of *schrecklichkeit*. To meet this contingency reserve battalions were moved forward in readiness.   But nothing beyond a very lively " artillery duel " took place on our front.   Gas was a constant cause of anxiety. Defensive apparatus of all kinds was elaborated.   " Gas alert on " or " gas alert off " was regularly reported, and opened a new drain from the supply of Government stationery.   Gas practices were regularly held in the trenches, a sort of game in which the platoon commander blew a whistle and everyone put on his clammy smoke helmet, and snorted like a grampus through a rubber spout for the next few minutes.

Elaborate defensive work was undertaken in the Loos sector. One notable achievement was the construction in a remarkably few weeks by the 4th Royal Welsh Fusiliers (now commanded by Lieut.-Colonel G. Pereira, C.B., D.S.O., the first D.A.Q.M.G. of the Division) of a tunnel through the Loos Crassier.   This greatly strengthened the support line, that had hitherto run right over the Crassier in a very exposed position.   It was now possible to walk along the support line without journeying over the top of the Crassier ; thus a great saving of time was effected and considerable overhead protection provided.

In addition to our own Pioneers, the 11th Hants. (Pioneers) Battalion was working for the Division. We also had attached to us a brigade of the 16th (Irish) Division, who learnt trench routine from us, and supplied large working-parties. During January, 1916, several changes in command took place in the Divisional Artillery. Brigadier-General E. W. Spedding succeeded the C.R.A., Brigadier-General J. C. Wray, who went home sick and was transferred to the 57th Division, and Major M. Muirhead succeeded Major D. J. C. E. Sherlock as Brigade-Major, R.A.

Photo by]   *[Lambert Weston.*

BRIG.-GENERAL J. C. WRAY, C.B., C.M.G., M.V.O.
C.R.A. 1912-1916.

Facing page 48

Chapter V.

VIMY RIDGE AND SUMMER, 1916.

THE Battle of Loos and the subsequent winter mark the end of a period in the history of the war. They also constitute a link with the new developments that first had full play with us in the Battle of the Somme. In the early days of trench warfare the rifle had been the most effective weapon. The infantry had borne the burden of attack and defence. Machine-guns and artillery, immensely effective as they proved themselves to be, were not yet of sufficient strength to be more than weapons of opportunity.

A change came gradually. Increased weight of artillery enabled the infantry to count on support which had perforce been reckoned an occasional luxury before. Battalion machine-gun sections, each with four Vickers guns instead of the old two heavy Maxims, were formed into brigade companies, and the whole came by-and-by to be co-ordinated by the Division under the senior machine-gun officer. Lewis guns became more numerous, and it was hard for the battalion commander to keep a supply of trained men to meet the increase. Loos, a bombers' battle, had established the necessity of a great supply of bombs. The old stove-pipe trench mortar—*varium et mutabile semper*—was to fade away before the Stokes mortar, which we used first in April. Each weapon had its busy enthusiasts, and everyone became a specialist in 1916. The cry of "back to the rifle" was not yet heard. And the main cause of these changes was the greatly increased supply of men and materials. The new Ministry of Munitions had got under way under Mr. Lloyd George, and the Military Service Bill became law in January, 1916.

The armies of our Allies and of our enemies developed likewise. But the Boche was still ahead of us, and the new methods first appeared in the storm that broke at Verdun on February 21st.

On that fateful day the Division was grazing in the pastures of G.H.Q. reserve—cold comfort, for the ground lay deep in snow, and brigades sent successively for training to the Bomy area found it impossible for the next fortnight to accomplish much in the way of training. As a result of the pressure on the French at Verdun the British Army took over the sector held by General Foch's army southwards from Loos. The 47th Division was restored to the IVth Corps, and on March 16th Major-General Barter assumed command of the Souchez sector, which we had taken over from the 23rd Division, who had relieved the French a few days earlier.

A noteworthy change in the Division at the beginning of February was the departure of Lieut.-Colonel R. M. Foot, the chief of our " Q " Staff since mobilisation, who left us to go home to the new 62nd Division, and the appointment as A.A. and Q.M.G. of Lieut.-Colonel S. H. J. Thunder, whom we were lucky enough to keep until after the Armistice; his great knowledge of the Division became invaluable in times of constant change.

The Carency and Souchez sectors, which the Division now held, included the commanding Lorette Spur, the valley of the Carency, and the west slope of the northern spur of the Vimy Ridge. Near the crest of this spur the French had maintained a precarious footing, and the foremost position was a line of detached posts, accommodated in grouse-butts. Behind our forward system of trenches lay the long Zouave Valley, along which the Boche could put down an almost impassable barrage. He overlooked our front trenches from the Pimple—a little eminence at the extreme north of the Ridge; we had magnificent observation from the east point of the Lorette Spur of the ground behind his line, and of the country east and north for many miles. (Observers from this point saw the Loos Tower Bridge fall on the afternoon of April 16th.)

Reserve units and wagon-lines were in billets in Villers-au-Bois, the Servins, Camblain L'Abbaye, Estrée Cauchie (commonly known as Extra Cushy), and in huts in the woods of Bouvigny and La Haie. It was pleasant, rolling country, very pretty in spring-time, and a welcome change after a winter in the black mining district.

On a preliminary reconnaissance of the area, Major E. B. Blogg, D.S.O., R.E., commanding the 4th London Field Coy., R.E., was

MILDREN CRATER

6TH LONDONS—VIMY—1916.

Facing page 50

mortally wounded by a rifle bullet. His death was a great loss to the Engineers and to the Division.

We found the new area very peaceful at first. The enemy, used to a policy of "live and let live," exposed himself very freely, and made efforts at friendly conversation. The 18th Battalion unbent so far as to give him "The Times" in answer to a request for news. One or two deserters came over to us. His trench-mortars, however, worried us from the first, though we pointed out that this was inconsistent with the conciliatory attitude of the infantry, and retaliated by energetic sniping. As time went on, and the Saxon division in this sector was relieved, the Boche became more and more aggressive, and the first peaceful weeks only served to conceal great activity underground. The 176th (Tunnelling) Coy., R.E., under Major E. M. F. Momber, were allotted to the divisional area. They found the enemy's work well advanced, and were confined to operations mainly defensive.

The first German mine went up on April 26th. The 140th Brigade were about to relieve the 141st Brigade at the time, but the danger had been anticipated, and a supporting company of the 6th Battalion was sent up in advance. Our front line was broken by the explosion, but the crater was immediately seized, and the near lip consolidated. Rifle-fire from the 17th and 18th Battalions protected the consolidation, and prevented any counter-attack. The crater was called New Cut Crater. On the 29th our miners blew a camouflet some hundred yards north of this, which detonated a Boche mine, and formed Broadridge Crater. By way of retaliation, the enemy sprang a third mine between the two. This destroyed part of the front line, and the 6th Battalion suffered over eighty casualties from the explosion and subsequent very heavy bombardment ; but, under Colonel Mildren's command, the crater was successfully occupied, and the new line through Mildren Crater ran roughly where the old line had been.

Just south of these operations the mining situation suddenly became critical. No fewer than eleven German galleries were suspected, and our front line was in imminent danger. The 176th (Tunnelling) Coy., R.E., started counter-mining, and the work was pushed on with all possible speed. Increased shifts of miners worked all night May 2nd-3rd, burrowing forward from old French listening galleries ; large parties of the 141st Brigade brought up timber, and every available man from the trenches carried soil from the mine-shafts. The 21st Battalion were occupying the area affected (A section, Carency sub-sector) and were warned to be ready to seize the craters; they were to be helped in the work of consolidation by the 2/3rd London Field Coy., R.E. At 4.45 p.m. on May 3rd four mines were fired, and our guns opened an intense bombardment, to pay back with interest what the 6th Battalion had suffered so heavily three days before. After the bombardment the 21st Battalion parties rushed forward, and held the far lips of the craters. The R.E. and Pioneer detachments then came up, and the night was spent consolidating the near lips. Excellent progress had been made by dawn, when the infantry withdrew to the new positions. Three big craters had been formed, and were named, from right to left, Momber, Love, and Kennedy Craters, after the tunnelling company, field company, and battalion commanders concerned. A fourth mine blew back and only just broke the ground. The whole operation had been very successful, and everyone played up splendidly in the emergency.

Major Momber wrote in his report to the Division: "The infantry assisting us all worked themselves dead beat, and I wish to express my thanks for the way they assisted us. I think the whole of this work, done in the time available, must constitute a record."

The situation was thus eased on our front; but the enemy was continuously aggressive, worrying the front line with many "minnies," and the whole of the forward area with frequent bombardment. Immediately south of us he did some successful mining, and the 25th Division were blown out of a part of their line in the Berthonval sector. They counter-mined, and on May 15th put up a string of mines and reoccupied their line. On May 19th this troubled sector was taken over by the 140th Brigade, who handed over to the 23rd Division the pleasantest part of our line, the Lorette defences.

Our new piece of front was not a satisfactory inheritance. Lately the scene of destructive mining, it was in a bad state of disrepair. No wire covered the front or support lines; the front line consisted of disconnected posts, isolated by day; there were no shelters of any kind in the front system. Altogether it was a position ill-equipped to counteract the increasingly aggressive efforts of the enemy, who lost no chance of inflicting casualties on our unprotected troops. His trench-mortars were more than

COBURG TRENCH, VIMY RIDGE.

VIMY RIDGE CRATERS.

Facing page 52

usually active on the 19th and 20th, and on the latter day there was a heavy bombardment from 5 a.m. to 11 a.m. of the trenches near Ersatz Alley. The 141st Brigade, however, managed to relieve the 142nd Brigade on this day in the Carency sector, now the left section of the divisional front. The night was quiet, and was spent in hard work on the new sector.

On Sunday, May 21st, the German guns started work early. All the morning the trenches in both brigade fronts were persistently shelled. At 3.40 p.m. the bombardment became intense, and a barrage on Zouave Valley—the first " box barrage " which we had experienced—practically cut all communication with the front. During the next four hours the trenches south of Love and Momber Craters were pounded mercilessly, and the garrison, especially those in the shelterless trenches of the Berthonval sector, suffered terribly. The battery positions had their share, too, and four guns were knocked out. At 7.45 p.m. the shelling was lifted off the front trenches, and fell with increased violence on Zouave Valley and farther back, especially on gun positions. At the same time the German infantry attacked, with their right flank on Love and Momber Craters, across the whole 140th Brigade front, into the line of the 25th Division. They came over in great force, and the weight of the attack fell upon the 7th and 8th Battalions, who had lain for four hours in unprotected trenches, under a bombardment far heavier than any we had ever known before. These battalions with the troops on their right were driven out of the front trench, across two supports, into a line half-way down the slope.

The 7th Battalion, on the right, made a local counter-attack as early as 8.40 p.m., but it was not in sufficient strength to recapture any ground. The attack on this sector was effectively held up by a block established in Old Boot Street, a very gallant action led by Captain L. E. Rundell. Night fell upon the confusion caused by the attack. Many of the survivors of the bombardment in the front line were captured—among them Captain G. Portman and Captain G. N. Clark, of the 8th, together with Captain F. M. Davis and Lieutenant Brooks, of the 7th, who had held the front trenches till 7.45 p.m.—and, until the first lull came at about ten o'clock, it was extremely difficult to get any accurate idea of the situation. Communications were broken, and the battalion commanders concerned found it impossible to co-ordinate their arrangements for counter-attack. At 2 a.m. on the 22nd a company each of the 15th and 18th Battalions made an effort at the junction of the brigade fronts, but without success.

Captain H. B. Farquhar, who led the 15th Battalion company, was wounded and missing. Lieut.-Colonel A. Maxwell, of the 8th, was wounded during the night, and the remnant of his battalion came under the command of Lieut.-Colonel Warrender, of the 15th, who relieved them before dawn. As soon as it was light, Major Whitehead, in the absence of Lieut.-Colonel Mildren, of the 6th Battalion, reconnoitred the right front, and fixed on an old French trench as the best line of resistance. This was successfully occupied and consolidated by the 6th and 7th Battalions on the evening of the 22nd. Throughout these operations the 140th Brigade was commanded by Colonel Faux, of the 7th Battalion, while Brig.-General Cuthbert acted as divisional commander, General Barter being on leave.

The 20th Battalion was holding the right of the 141st Brigade line, including the craters, and joining the 140th Brigade at Ersatz Alley. The top of this communication trench had been the centre of the bombardments, and was practically obliterated. The right company (A Company) held up the first attack, Captain Young directing the rifle-fire in the line. After a fight they were driven back into the support trench.

Captain Young was able to bring the three platoons of A Company back over the top with very little loss owing largely to the very gallant action of Sec.-Lieutenant Lomas, D.C.M., the Battalion Lewis-gun officer. The latter, by himself, took a gun into the open over the top of the support-line and covered the retirement of the company. He was killed shortly afterwards.

The enemy in his first rush got into the craters held by B Company. Their commander, Captain Taylor, was acting as adjutant at the time, but on hearing of his company's plight, he went forward and organised a counter-attack, which drove the enemy from the craters. Unfortunately, both he and Captain Young lost their lives in this action. Lieut.-Colonel W. H. Matthews, of the 20th, unable to counter-attack in view of the situation on his right, established a defensive flank by means of blocks in the lines forward of that to which the 140th Brigade had been driven back.

In this he was greatly assisted by Captain G. Williams, M.C. (officer commanding A Company), who now took command of

GRANDE PLACE, LILLERS.

SOUCHEZ.

Facing page 54

B Company in addition to his own, and maintained the position in the support and reserve lines, and successfully defended the exposed right flank. Captain Williams, whose conduct won him the then rare distinction of a bar to his Military Cross, was severely wounded on the following evening. His company, which had gone on to the Ridge 120 strong a few days earlier, left it with only 17 remaining. The honours it had won included a Military Cross (C.S.M. W. H. Davey), two D.C.M.'s (Ptes. Martin and Andrews), and five Military Medals.

The exact position of the right flank of the 141st Infantry Brigade being now in some doubt, Major B. C. Battye, the Brigade major, at great personal risk, undertook a close reconnaissance and was able to locate it. For this service he was awarded the D.S.O.

Two companies of the 18th Battalion reinforced the 20th during the night of May 22nd. Brig.-General Thwaites was wounded on the night of the 23rd, and Lieut.-Colonel Tredennick, of the 18th Battalion, took over temporary command of the 141st Brigade.

The 142nd Brigade had been brought up from reserve on the afternoon of May 21st. By evening it was in the support system along the Divisional front. The C.R.E. (Lieut.-Colonel S. D'A. Crookshank), who was at advanced Brigade Headquarters at Cabaret Rouge on the same afternoon, organised the R.E., who were in billets thereabouts in an old French line on the forward slope looking across Zouave Valley. During the night 21st-22nd the 2nd Division moved forward from Corps Reserve, and its 99th Brigade was placed at the disposal of the 47th. Units of the 2nd Divisional Artillery also reinforced our artillery. On the night of the 22nd the 142nd and 99th Brigades relieved the 140th Brigade and a part of the 20th Battalion, and were ready to counter-attack on the following day.

Our own counter-attacking battalions on the evening of May 23rd were the 21st and 24th. The 24th Battalion (Lieut.-Colonel G. A. Buxton-Carr) was not supported on their right. On each flank of their attack was a communication trench held as a sap by the enemy, who could enfilade any advancing troops. Bombers were sent forward to deal with these, but they made no progress, and the battalion was held up. The 21st (Lieut.-Colonel H. B. Kennedy), on the left, went ahead and recaptured the old line north of Ersatz Alley, where they stayed for an hour, and did great execution among the enemy whom they found in the trench and dugouts. But no troops came up on their right, and they were compelled to come back to their starting-point. Nothing was left to show for this gallant and costly action beyond a few yards of our old front line, where the block was moved southwards to include in our line its junction with Gobron communication trench. Seven Military Crosses were awarded to members of the 21st Battalion for gallantry in this action—probably a record number for one battalion in a single operation.

The strain which these operations threw on the medical services was a heavy one. When the 47th Division took over the Souchez Sector the 5th London Field Ambulance relieved the field ambulance of the division holding the line. The Advanced Dressing Station was established at Cabaret Rouge, a collecting and car post at Point " G," at the end of the Cabaret Trench, and the Main Dressing Station was about three miles behind the line in some huts used as a hospital by the French during their occupation of the sector. This place was officially known as Quatre Vents.

It was admirably suited for a M.D.S., and later on in the campaign, when similar stations had to be established and maintained by the R.A.M.C. in the devastated areas, visions of Quatre Vents would rise like some haunting mirage. At first things were fairly quiet, and working-parties were out fixing water points in the Zouave Valley and collecting material from the derelict huts, horse standings, etc., in the area; with this the accommodation at the M.D.S. was considerably enlarged and improved. The time and labour expended on these building operations, at first entered upon with the spirit that usually pervaded what were considered unnecessary fatigues, were soon to be amply repaid.

On Sunday, May 21st, a number of casualties began to arrive at the M.D.S., and an incessant stream, which rapidly increased in numbers, continued to flow in during the next four days. The total number dealt with exceeded 1,500, all of which were fed, the majority redressed, and many operated upon. It will thus be seen that the accommodation and R.A.M.C. personnel were taxed to the utmost.

On the night of May 25th the 6th Brigade relieved the 141st and 142nd Brigades, and on the 26th the 2nd Division took over command of this sector and the 47th Division was in reserve.

The Vimy fighting cost us 63 officers and 2,044 other ranks killed, wounded, and missing. At that price we were taught the necessity to arrange our defence in greater depth to meet new methods of attack with increased weight of artillery. Our own guns adapted themselves quickly to new conditions, and the Divisional Artillery between noon on May 21st and 4 p.m. on May 24th fired over 32,000 rounds, which must have taken their toll of casualties on the other side. It seems doubtful now whether our risky position near the crest of the ridge was worth holding at such cost, when a strong position on the high ground near Cabaret Rouge, with the same observation from the Lorette Heights, was available. The magnificent spirit which refuses to yield to the enemy any ground, however useless, is worth much; but were the Higher Command justified in incurring the resulting losses ?

In this sector the communications were very good indeed as far forward as Cabaret Rouge, but they were never reliable in the Zouave Valley, most of which was hidden from German observation, and therefore constantly visited with very searching shell-fire. During the heavy fighting it could not even be crossed by runners. The smoke and dust frustrated the most carefully planned visual signalling.

From Cabaret Rouge to Villers-au-Bois (Brigade Headquarters) two cables were buried five feet deep by cavalry lent by the Corps and superintended by officers of the Divisional Signal Company— at a later date at least forty lines would have been put in such a trench, but at that time cable of the sort required for burying was very scarce. These lines held throughout with one interval when they were broken by a 9·2-in. shell. The repair did not take long.

The batteries, especially those in and near Carency, suffered heavily from the accurate German counter-battery fire.

The situation of the Artillery was complicated, not only by the fact that the batteries were in the midst of relieving those of the 25th Division, but by the four brigade ammunition columns being in course of disbandment. From this time onwards the supply of ammunition to battery wagon lines was to be carried out by the Divisional Ammunition Column.

After the trying days on the Vimy Ridge the Division was resting for about a fortnight in the Bruay-Diéval area. At the end of this period the Lord Mayor of London (Sir Charles Wakefield) visited us. The official photographer followed in his wake, and several pictures of the incidents of his visit are in the Imperial

War Museum. At this time also General Thwaites returned from hospital, cured of his wound.

On June 12th we began to move up the line again, this time to the Angres sector, where we stayed for a month. It was a peaceful time, but for an elaborate programme of bluff operations which ushered in the Battle of the Somme. The artillery did most of the demonstration, but infantry also played a part in the form of raids, a new kind of amusement invented by the Canadians up north. The first divisional raid was done by the 19th Battalion near the Bully Crater in the Angres sector, the prelude to many successes achieved later by the Division in these enterprises. It was preceded by a discharge of gas, for which some 1,300 cylinders had been brought up in Army Service Corps wagons with old motor-car tyres fitted to their wheels.

Two raiding-parties with blackened faces reached the Boche trenches successfully, secured a live enemy for purposes of identification, and killed others. Sappers of the 4th London Field Coy., R.E., went over with the party, each carrying thirty slabs of gun-cotton in a pack for demolitions. One of them found the dugout he wanted to blow up occupied, so set a fuse to his pack and bowled it down the steps of the dugout.

The battalion signallers took over a telephone line and maintained communication with Battalion Headquarters from the enemy trench during the whole raid.

The next raid, undertaken by the 15th Battalion, on the night of July 3rd-4th, was less successful. It was remarkable from the fact that the enemy put down a " box barrage," the second of our acquaintance, on the piece of trench attacked. This failed in its object of catching the raiders, but kept them from getting nearer than bombing distance from the trench. During the raid Lieutenant G. L. Goodes' 140th Trench Mortar Battery did notably good work. They fired 750 rounds in half an hour, although two mortars were knocked out and four gunners wounded.

A 22nd Battalion raid on July 8th was a more elaborate affair. It consisted of two acts. First, a discharge of smoke on the Souchez sector was succeeded by a raid in the Angres sector by sixty infantry and four sappers. The party reached their objective, but found no Germans in the trench. Dugouts were bombed, and some demolition done. Some hours later, in the early morning, the second raid started with a discharge of smoke and gas along

[*Imperial War Museum.*

THE LORD MAYOR'S VISIT, JUNE, 1916. A GROUP AT DIVISIONAL HEADQUARTERS.

FRONT ROW: Col. Evelyn Wood, D.S.O. (Secretary, City of London T.F. Association), the Lord Mayor of London (Col. Sir C. C. Wakefield), Major-General Sir C. Barter, Major R. S. McClintock (G.S.O. II).
SECOND ROW: ——, Lt.-Col. C. Newton-Taylor (Camp Comdnt.), Capt. H. I. Nicholl (D.A.A. and Q.M.G.).
BACK ROW: Lieut.-Col. S. H. J. Thunder (A.A. and Q.M.G.), Capt. J. C. D. Carlisle (G.S.O. III.), Capt. R. O. Schwarz (D.A.Q.M.G.).

the Angres sector.   A raiding-party followed, but were met with all kinds of fire—artillery, trench-mortar, and machine-gun.   Only a few individuals reached and bombed the trench, which they found strongly manned.

Undoubtedly many such enterprises were spoilt by the fact that the Boche frequently overheard our telephone conversations on his listening sets.   Many months later we learnt from a captured document that he had on one occasion heard our Town Major of Villers-au-Bois announce to a front-line battalion that he would have billets ready for them after their relief that evening.   That we were dimly aware of such danger was shown by the first adoption of fancy names for units in March, 1916.   At first there was some sort of system about the names—e.g., the 141st Brigade specialised in stationery, paper, string, etc., while the Train was jam, and the Signal Company was cable.   But later the names became purely irrelevant.   Nabob's staff-captain once rang up his Nurse, and was put on in error to Oily.   The Division, and, consequently, the G.O.C., was often given a Christian name.   At one time it was Fanny, but this was supplanted by the more dignified John.   Last of all, in 1918, the great co-ordinators at G.H.Q. brought their minds to bear on the subject, and every unit in the Expeditionary Force had a separate and meaningless combination of four letters, a scheme which had the single good result of making one chary of using the telephone at all.   Mercifully, at all times of real stress in operations it was assumed that the Boche was too busy to listen to us, and it was possible to call things what they were without the fear either of unintentional treachery or of a F.G.C.M.

It was, however, in this sector that a few " Fullerphones " were first issued to the Division.   These telegraph instruments defy any listening sets, and afforded a much-needed feeling of security to commanders in the " danger area."   There were at this time only enough of them available to work between battalions and brigades. During the winter of 1916-17 they were multiplied to an extent which permitted of their use between companies and battalions.

During June and July, 1916, several well-known figures left the Division. Early in July Brigadier-General W. Thwaites left the 141st Brigade to command the 46th Division.   He had nursed the 47th Division in early days as G.S.O.1, and had commanded the 141st Brigade since May, 1915.   A few days later

Brigadier-General G. J. Cuthbert was appointed to command the 39th Division, and left the 140th Brigade, which he had brought out to France. This is not the place to assess the great value to the Division of these two commanders ; the story of their brigades must speak for them. No one who served under them will be ignorant of it, and each left behind him a fund of anecdote which will keep his memory green. Brigadier-General Lord Hampden succeeded to the 140th Brigade. After a month, during which Brigadier-General R. J. Bridgford was in command, Brigadier-General R. McDouall came to the 141st Brigade. The General Staff, too, suffered change, for during June Lieut.-Colonel B. Burnett-Hitchcock and Major N. W. Webber, R.E., who had so successfully worked together for the divisional commander during Loos and onwards, left us. Before the war was over they were together again, but at a more wearisome job, in charge of demobilization at the War Office. They were respectively succeeded by Lieut.-Colonel J. T. Weatherby as G.S.O.1 and Major R. S. McClintock, R.E., as G.S.O.2.

The Royal Naval Division, which had been learning from us the ways of war on the Western front, relieved us on July 18th, and we returned for a short spell to the Carency and Berthonval sectors, now delightfully quiet. Before we left, the R.E. and Pioneers were able to join up the "grouse-butts" into one continuous trench. The 141st Brigade was temporarily attached to the Royal Naval Division as divisional reserve, and remained in billets round Bouvigny-Boyeffles. At the very end of July we handed over to the 37th Division, and marched away to train for the Somme.

In the Angres sector we had seen the last of flowery trenches and pleasant, deserted villages, with fruit and vegetables, a little way behind the line. Vimy had shown us the devastated result of concentrated shelling ; such desolation was soon to be our normal dwelling-place.

Chapter VI.

THE BATTLE OF THE SOMME, 1916.

CONSIDERABLE reinforcements came to the Division during June and July, 1916. Men from different parts of the country now came to our London battalions under the new scheme by which drafts from training depots at home were posted at the Base, and sent where they were most needed. But the spirit of the Division did not change, and each unit had a strong enough character and tradition to absorb any reinforcement that came its way.

It was a strong Division that started marching southward on August 1st. We had hot summer weather for the journey, and started early each morning from our billets to get our marching done before the heat of the day—a pleasant rest during the afternoon and evening in a quiet country village, a night under the sky in a green orchard, breakfast at sunrise, and on the road again. The 142nd Brigade did all its marching by night. Five days' march brought us to the St. Riquier area, where the Division spent a fortnight. These were pleasant days, with training early and late to avoid the heat of midday, and plenty of opportunity for everyone to get fit and for battalions and companies to get to know themselves with that feeling of unity which is of priceless value at all times, but most of all in action. Billets were good, the people very friendly; it was a good war when one strolled about listening to the band on Sunday afternoon, or joined an expedition to the neighbouring town of Abbeville, not yet devastated by the bombs of enemy aeroplanes.

Towards the end of the period the Artillery carried out some open warfare training close to the field of Crécy.

On August 20th the Division started moving forward via Ailly-le-Haut-Clocher and Villers-Bocage to Baisieux, where it became part of the IIIrd Corps. The brigades were billeted round Bresle,

Franvillers and Lahoussoye, and spent the next three weeks in training for the attack. On September 1st the 140th and 141st Brigades started rehearsing the High Wood battle on a flagged course. Representatives of the Division were introduced to the great secret of the moment, and hope of the future, the Tank.

The Divisional Artillery had been in action since August 14th, when they relieved the 23rd Divisional Artillery in support of the 15th Division. The batteries were in position in Bottom Wood and near Mametz Wood, with some farther east near Montauban and in front of Caterpillar Valley, and they knew the ground over which the Division was to operate, very thoroughly. They had been engaged in closely supporting the 15th (Scottish) Division in its gradual encroachment on the fortified village of Martinpuich, and had had a full share of casualties, especially among observing officers and signallers, during local attacks and in the constant " area strafes," in which both sides indulged freely.

Between September 10th and 12th we relieved the 1st Division in the High Wood sector. We walked into a new world of war. We passed through Albert for the first time, under the Virgin, holding out her Child, not to heaven but to the endless procession below. Fricourt, where the line had stood for so long, was now out of range of any but long-range guns, and we could see freshly-devastated country without being in the battle. All round the slopes were covered with transport of all kinds, and whole divisions of cavalry waiting for their opportunity. Farther forward in Caterpillar Valley heavy howitzers stood in the open, lobbing their shells over at a target miles away. Up near the line by Flat Iron Copse and the Bazentins the ground was alive with field-guns, many of them hidden by the roadside and startling the unwary.

All these things, later the commonplace of a successful " push," were new. But we never saw anything quite like High Wood. It had been attacked by the 7th Division on July 14th—just two months before our arrival—and had indeed on that day been entered by a party of cavalry. But it had been an insuperable obstacle to subsequent attacks, and the trench which we took over ran through the centre of it, leaving more than half still in Boche hands. As for the wood, it was a wood only in name— ragged stumps sticking out of churned-up earth, poisoned with fumes of high explosives, the whole a mass of corruption. But

ALBERT CATHEDRAL, 1916.

there was life enough in the trenches and below ground. Outside the wood the country was a featureless wilderness. Here is a description written at the time :

" Imagine Hampstead Heath made of cocoa-powder, and the natural surface folds further complicated by countless shell-holes, each deep enough to hold a man, and everywhere meandering crevices where men live below the surface of the ground, and you will get some idea of the terrain of the attack."

The absence of natural landmarks must always be borne in mind, for it explains what might seem to be instances of confusion and bad map-reading in the progress of the operations.

The attack of September 15th was conceived on a grand scale. It was hoped that the breaking of the German third line, which was then holding us up, would constitute a decisive victory after the costly and indecisive fighting of the previous month. Many fresh divisions, of which we were one, were brought up for the occasion, and great hopes were placed on the effect of the novelty of the Tanks. Three corps were engaged, of which our own, the IIIrd Corps, was on the left flank. The function of the IIIrd Corps was to form a defensive flank on the forward side of the ridge on which Martinpuich and High Wood stand, to cover the advance northwards of the XIVth and XVth Corps on our right. The 47th Division was on the right of the IIIrd Corps, thus linking the north-easterly movement (swinging north) of the IIIrd Corps with the northerly movement of the XVth Corps. It will be seen how the obstacle of High Wood, which delayed our advance for a time, while it went forward on both sides, made this task particularly difficult. The Division attacked on a two-brigade front. On the right was Lord Hampden's 140th Brigade, with the 7th Battalion clear of High Wood and joining the New Zealand Division, and next on the left, attacking up the east side of the wood, with two companies clear of it, came the 15th Battalion.

The 141st Brigade, under Brigadier-General McDouall, with the 17th Battalion on the right and the 18th Battalion on the left, was faced by the wood all along its front. On the left came the 50th Division. Our attack had three objectives : First, a line clear of High Wood ; second, the Starfish Line, down the forward slope ; third, on the right the strong Flers Line, where the 140th Brigade were to join up with the New Zealanders, falling back to join the 141st Brigade in a communication trench, Drop Alley, whence the final objective was prolonged westwards along Prue Trench in the valley. On the right the 8th Battalion were to pass through the 7th and 15th, and capture the Starfish Line, and the 6th Battalion to pass through them again to the Flers Line. On the left the 19th and 20th Battalions were to capture and consolidate the second and third objectives. The 142nd Brigade, under Brigadier-General Lewis, was in reserve about Mametz Wood, ready to move forward at zero to Bazentin-le-Grand, where it would be immediately in support of the attacking brigades.

Zero was at 6.20 a.m. The troops attacking High Wood were at once engaged in heavy fighting. Four Tanks accompanied the attack, but could make no headway over the broken tree-stumps and deeply-pitted ground and were stuck before they could give the help expected from them. The infantry, thus disappointed of the Tanks' assistance, were also deprived of the support of the guns, which were afraid to fire near the Tanks. The 17th and 18th Battalions and half the 15th Battalion had a desperate fight for every foot of their advance. The enemy met them with bombs and rifle-fire from his trenches, and machine-guns from concrete emplacements, still undamaged, mowed them down. With the second wave of attack the 19th and 20th Battalions and part of the 8th joined the fight, and during the morning five battalions were at once engaged in the wood. Casualties were very heavy. Among many others fell Lieut.-Colonel A. P. Hamilton, of the 19th Battalion, who called all available men to follow him, and went up into the wood to try to restore order to the confused fighting. A little later Major J. R. Trinder, of the 18th, was killed. At eleven o'clock General McDouall arranged with Lieut.-Colonel A. C. Lowe, R.F.A., for a new bombardment of the wood. At the same time the 140th Trench Mortar Battery succeeded in beating its previous record of concentrated fire. Its efforts finally demoralised the German garrison, who began to surrender in batches, and before one o'clock High Wood was reported clear of the enemy. On the flanks, meanwhile, our progress had been faster. Tanks had been a great success with the division on our right, causing dismay to the garrison of Flers, and our own right flanks had gone forward with the New Zealanders—the 7th Battalion fighting their way to the first objective, a part of the 8th Battalion to the Starfish Line, and the 6th Battalion beyond this again. Some few got as far as the Flers Line, though this could not be held, and it was found later

TWO BATTALION COMMANDERS.
Lieut.-Colonel A. P. Hamilton, M.C., 19th London Regt.
(killed at High Wood) ; Lieut.-Colonel W. H. Matthews, D.S.O.,
20th London Regt.

Facing page 64

that their forward positions were in the Cough Drop, a group of trenches in a valley west of Flers. As these units of the 140th Brigade went forward, they suffered more heavily from the exposure of their left flank, and the 6th Battalion especially lost many men from enfilade machine-gun fire, and there were only two officers and about one hundred other ranks of the attackers left to occupy the Cough Drop. On the left, similarly, the 50th Division went forward and occupied their second objective, but their right flank was exposed, and they could not hold their ground.

On the afternoon of the 15th our situation was that High Wood was captured after desperate fighting in which the 141st Brigade had become so much disorganised from loss of leaders that it was temporarily formed into a composite battalion under Lieut.-Colonel Norman, of the 17th. The work of establishing a line on the first objective clear of High Wood was started by a mixed party under Captain H. S. Read, of the 20th Battalion. On both flanks, meanwhile, the attack was going ahead, but was endangered by the gap opposite High Wood. Three battalions of the 142nd Brigade had been sent forward during the morning and placed at the disposal of the attacking brigades; only one battalion, therefore—the 22nd —remained in divisional reserve, and nearly all that was engaged in the necessary work of carrying up ammunition. The capture of the Starfish Line, however, was considered essential, and at about 6 p.m. the 21st and 24th Battalions attacked with this object, under command of Lieut.-Colonel Kennedy. On the right the 21st Battalion at great cost attacked the Starfish Line, and captured the Starfish Redoubt itself, but their attempt to get on farther to the Cough Drop did not succeed. The 24th Battalion, attacking from the wood, met such heavy fire that they did not get to the Starfish Line, but dug themselves in about 200 yards in front of the first objective of the 141st Brigade. Only perfunctory artillery preparation could be arranged for this attack, and the assaulting troops suffered fearfully, the 21st Battalion having only 2 officers and 60 other ranks left unwounded out of 17 officers and 550 other ranks who attacked. The night was spent in consolidating the ground along the divisional front.

During the afternoon some of the batteries began to move up in support, the first being the 19th London Battery, under Major Lord Gorell, who brought his battery up into the shell-hole area immediately behind High Wood.

G

Accompanied by Major Marshall, of the 18th Battery, Lord Gorell made a brilliant reconnaissance of the divisional front, and was able to report the line actually held that night by our troops, together with much other valuable information. For these distinguished services Lord Gorell was awarded the D.S.O.

With the object of securing the junction of the IIIrd and XVth Corps, we were ordered to make good a ridge running northeast from High Wood to a point above the villages of Flers and Eaucourt l'Abbaye. This involved the capture of the Cough Drop—a lozenge-shaped group of trenches just under this ridge— and a communication trench, Drop Alley, which ran from it northeast to the Flers Line, and the Flers Line itself, forward of its junction with Drop Alley, on to the ridge. Three companies of the 23rd Battalion, with one company of the 22nd, were detailed for this job, under command of Lieut.-Colonel H. H. Kemble, of the 23rd. They attacked at 9.25 on the morning of September 16th. The Cough Drop presented no difficulty, for the 6th Battalion were found to be already in possession, but the trenches round it were effectually cleared of the enemy. The attack, however, went beyond its objective, misled by the discovery that this objective was already held by the 6th Battalion, and heading straight for the strongly held Flers Line. Aeroplanes reported our men in the Flers Line, and even in Eaucourt l'Abbaye, and these may have been parties of the 23rd ; if so, they were cut off before they could establish connection with supporting troops, for they never returned.

It was considered imperative to get a footing in the Flers Line where it was joined by Drop Alley, and on the evening of the 17th orders were issued to the 140th Brigade to effect this. But that day steady rain had begun, making bad conditions far worse, and it was decided to postpone this operation until dawn of the 18th. A mixed force of the 8th, 15th, and 6th Battalions, under Lieut.-Colonel Whitehead, of the 8th, then attacked, and succeeded in occupying both the Flers Line and Drop Alley to within 50 yards of the junction which the enemy still held. Earlier on the same morning two companies, one each from the 23rd and 24th Battalions (under Major T. C. Hargreaves and Captain Figg), had attacked and occupied a part of the Starfish Line west of the Starfish Redoubt, which the 141st Brigade and the 24th Battalion successively failed to take on September 15th. This night attack was guided by a

GUN POSITIONS NEAR THE STARFISH.

CROSS ROADS, WEST OF LONGUEVAL, AND DELVILLE WOOD.

Facing page 66

lamp fixed forward of the objective by Lieutenant W. G. Newton, adjutant of the 23rd Battalion. The Boche counter-attacked soon after the trench was gained, and succeeded in bombing our men almost back to the Redoubt. When we attacked again we found the trench deserted—a typical instance of the enemy's clever and bold methods. Very gallant and devoted work had been put into the consolidation of the Star-fish Line on the night of the 17th-18th by a large working-party consisting of two sections of 2/3rd London Field Coy., R.E., and two companies of the Pioneers. This party, suffering many casualties on their way up, worked on the trench from the Redoubt to within 100 yards of the centre of the enemy's resistance on the left. During the work a strong patrol, under Major S. G. Love, R.E., and Lieutenant D. J. Williams, R.W.F., passed behind the enemy beyond this strong point. The party withdrew just before the attack mentioned above, on the morning of September 18th. With their experience, it was later planned, on Major Love's suggestion, that a party of the 4th R.W.F., under his command, should again attack the enemy's strong point. The Corps, however, ordered instead a retrenchment round this point to join up with the 50th Division on our left, which was completed by the Pioneers on the following night.

On September 19th we were relieved by the 1st Division, the 140th Brigade fighting to the last, repelling a counter-attack by which the enemy, for a while, won his way down Drop Alley, almost as far as the Cough Drop. The Divisional Artillery, Engineers, and Pioneers were left in the line under the 1st Division, and the 19th Battalion remained forward for a few days to clear the battlefield.

Such a bald account as the foregoing attempts no more than to give a general idea of the progress of the operations, to suggest to those who took part in them the significance of events which, at the time, they almost certainly did not appreciate. It cannot in any way represent the strenuousness, the wonderful heroism, the appalling discomfort and weariness of those days. Battalions went in fit and strong, full of confidence to take their part in the great British offensive. They came out, a few days later, a handful of men, muddy and tired out. Four days' fighting cost the Division just over 4,500 officers and men in casualties, and it is notable that those battalions (the 23rd, the 21st, and 6th) lost most heavily which had been in the open, under the German machine-gun fire and artillery barrage. Every battalion went into battle magnificently—wave after wave, just as at the last rehearsal when every detail is perfected. The lines of dead later bore mute testimony to the quality of our men and their training. That the momentum of the attack was spent in High Wood is no wonder, and the difficulty of making good the delay afterwards can but emphasise the value to the enemy of the position we had won. There are several divisional memorial crosses in High Wood. The 47th Division gained no higher honour than that its cross should stand among them, and that it should bear the latest date.

The heavy losses incurred in the capture of High Wood, and the delays which occurred later in the prosecution of the attack by the 47th Division, as also by the division on its left, were mainly due to the unfortunate decision regarding the disposition of the IIIrd Corps Tanks in the area of the 47th Division—a decision which was taken in opposition to the urgent representation, more than once expressed to higher authority by the Divisional Commander after personally visiting High Wood in conjunction with the Brigadier concerned, that the Tanks could not move through the wood, owing to the insurmountable nature of the obstacles inside it. Had the Tanks been placed outside the wood, as urged by Sir C. Barter, they could have materially helped the attackers in the wood. As it was they were the cause of the infantry being obliged to attack the wood without artillery assistance. A whole brigade was, in the event, practically put out of action, and the whole operation, including that of the division on the left, was thrown out of gear.

The communications between Division and Brigades at Bazentin were very bad, chiefly owing to the fact that, although Fricourt Farm had been prepared as advanced headquarters, Divisional Headquarters (on the Army Commander's advice) remained to the south-west of Albert. This necessitated very long lines, subject to severe shell-fire between Fricourt and Bazentin, and to even more persistent interruption by traffic between Albert and Fricourt. The greater part of this stretch was occupied by horse-lines, across which the telegraph-lines had to pass. If cables were laid on the ground they were soon trampled into the mud, while the airline poles were broken down by wagons. Nothing but " permanent lines " could stand, and their erection required time and heavy

material. In front of Brigade Headquarters the lines held fairly
well. The ground was favourable for visual signalling, but this
means failed in the attack, owing to the forward station being
knocked out by shell-fire.

By September 21st the Division was back in the Baisieux area
—the brigades at Henencourt, Bresle, and Millencourt. The
remainder of the month was spent resting, refitting, and absorbing
fresh drafts, by addition of which the net loss to the Division after
the High Wood operations was reduced to 111 officers and 1,471
other ranks. The new men, however, could only have the most
hasty training with their units, and the deficiency of experienced
officers placed a great responsibility on those that remained in our
second appearance on the stage of operations.

On September 28th Major-General Sir Charles St. L. Barter,
K.C.B., C.V.O., left us. He had commanded the Division since
our early days of training at St. Albans. He brought us out to
France, watched us in the first months of apprenticeship, directed
us to victory at Loos, and guided us through a difficult winter and
through the anxious days of Vimy. He trained the Division for the
Somme, and saw it spent in a harder fight than any before, the
capture of High Wood. Under the command of Sir Charles Barter
the fine tradition of the 47th London Division was firmly established,
a tradition which was ever enhanced, as fresh opportunities came,
under our new commander, Major-General Sir George F. Gorringe,
K.C.B., C.M.G., D.S.O., who succeeded him after a few days'
interval, during which the Division was commanded by Major-
General W. H. Greenly.

The 141st Brigade went up first to take over the line from the
1st Division. They were in by dawn on September 29th. A
further advance was intended, in which our objective was the
village of Eaucourt l'Abbaye, a group of houses round the old
abbey buildings, reputed to have extensive cellars, lying low, at the
point where a short valley, from the direction of High Wood,
turns at a right angle north-west towards the Albert-Bapaume
road. Eaucourt l'Abbaye, therefore, is commanded by higher
ground on every side except on the north-west. Before the attack
it was desirable to push forward along the Flers Line on to the high
ground south-east of the village. The 18th Battalion were ordered
to do this. Their first attempt on September 29th was unsuccessful,
but on the next day they gained the ground required.

The attack on Eaucourt l'Abbaye started at 3.15 p.m. on October 1st. The attacking battalions, from right to left, were the 19th, the 20th, and the 17th. The 18th Battalion was in support, and, farther back, the 23rd, placed under orders of the 141st Brigade. Two Tanks co-operated, but had to start from cover some distance behind the infantry, and could not reach the village till at least an hour after zero. The right two battalions entered the Flers Line without difficulty. But their further advance was held up by persistent machine-gun fire from the west corner of the abbey enclosure. The Tanks later silenced these guns, whereupon the 19th and 20th Battalions rushed through the village, and established a line to the north of it. This position was most successfully held by troops under Lieutenant L. W. Needham, of the 20th Battalion, who held on under most difficult conditions until our line was established round Eaucourt l'Abbaye. On the left of the attack the 17th came up against uncut wire in front of the Flers Line ; some of them got through this, but not in strong enough force to hold the line, and they were bombed out. Again, therefore, our troops on the right had gone forward and occupied their objective, but their position was menaced by an unprotected left flank, and a gap was left on the right of the 50th Division in the Flers Line. To put this right the 23rd Battalion was ordered to attack the Flers Line, and to push on through the village to join up with the 19th and 20th Battalions. This operation was planned for 5 a.m. on the 2nd, just before dawn, but owing to the dark, wet night, the battalion was not assembled until 6.25 a.m., when it attacked in broad daylight. The advancing waves were cut down by machine-gun fire from the flank, and the attack achieved nothing.

On the following day, at 3.35 p.m., two companies of the 18th Battalion attacked up the Flers Line successfully, got through Eaucourt l'Abbaye, and completed the circuit of our troops round the village. It was later discovered that we might have made good our line on the night of October 1st without trouble, for the German battalion which had met the 141st Brigade attack was expecting relief that night, and left before their relief arrived. The enemy quickly found this out, and rushed up a battalion from support. Two companies came up to occupy the Flers Line opposite Eaucourt l'Abbaye ; one tried to go east of the village and was stopped by our barrage and the fire of the

MEMORIAL CROSS IN HIGH WOOD.

BUTTE DE WARLENCOURT.

forward troops of the 141st Brigade ; the other came west of the village through the gap, and occupied their trenches just in time to meet the attack of the 23rd Battalion next morning. They were helped to save the situation by a dark night of pouring rain and our ignorance of newly-gained ground which we had hardly seen by daylight.

The capture of Eaucourt l'Abbaye brought several of the batteries over the High Wood ridge into a little valley beyond the " Starfish," where they maintained a precarious existence for the remainder of their stay on the Somme, and helped to cover the gallant but unsuccessful attacks of the 47th, and later of the 9th Division, on the Butte de Warlencourt.

On October 4th the 140th Brigade took over the line from the 141st Brigade in preparation for another general attack. On the next day the 6th Battalion gained an important point by occupying the old mill 500 yards west of Eaucourt l'Abbaye.

The IIIrd Corps attack of October 7th was on a three-division front. On our right was the 41st, and on our left the 23rd Division, both our familiar neighbours later in " The Salient." The main German line of defence opposite us was the Grid Line, running north-west from Gueudecourt to Warlencourt, and including the Butte de Warlencourt, an ancient mound of excavated chalk, about 70 feet high, cunningly tunnelled by the enemy, and used as an observation post from which machine-gun and artillery fire from positions echeloned in depth was directed with devastating effect on the western slopes up which our men had to advance. Anticipating an attack on this important line, the Germans had dug a new trench across our front over the high ground north of Eaucourt l'Abbaye, westward into the valley. This trench—named Diagonal —was the first objective of the 140th Brigade ; their final objective was the Grid Line, including the Butte itself. The 8th Battalion was to secure Diagonal Trench, the 15th and 7th (in order from the right) were to push on to the final objective ; the 6th Battalion was in support. The attack was at 1.45 p.m. on October 7th. The whole attacking line came under very heavy fire from Diagonal Trench, the garrison of which were apparently armed with automatic rifles. On the right some progress was made, and a line was established along the sunken road leading north-east from Eaucourt l'Abbaye to La Barque, where a mixed force of the 15th and 8th Battalions was organised and commanded by Captain G. G. Bates, of the 15th. On the left the companies of the 8th, followed by the 7th Battalion, tried to advance down the slope, forward of the mill, and met, in addition to fire from Diagonal Trench, the full force of the enemy artillery and machine-gun fire, cleverly sited in depth, so as to bring a withering cross-fire to bear along the western slopes leading up to the Butte and the high ground to the south of it. From across the valley the enemy had magnificent observation of the ground leading to our objective, and made full use of it.

Not a man turned back, and some got right up under the Butte, but they were not seen again. Parties dug themselves in where they could, and a post was located on the next day by an aeroplane half-way up the road towards the Butte. The only permanent gain, however, on the left, was a few posts pushed out from the mill, which were established as strong points, to keep in touch with the 23rd Division, who advanced along the line of the main road, and succeeded in capturing the ruined village of Le Sars. The 140th Brigade suffered very severely in this operation, and on the following day were relieved of the left portion of their line by the 142nd Brigade. But it was found to be impossible to relieve the 6th Battalion detachment in the advanced posts, which were left in their unenviable position until the 142nd Brigade attacked past them.

Our relief by the 9th Division was impending, and it was hoped to improve the position on our left before we handed over. With this object the 142nd Brigade made another attempt on October 8th to seize Diagonal Trench, and, if successful, were to assault the Butte. At 9 p.m. the 21st and 22nd Battalions made the attack, after one minute's intense bombardment. The 21st Battalion advanced to within 200 yards of Diagonal Trench without a casualty. Then, all at once, the full force of machine-guns was turned on them with dreadful effect. It seemed that the short bombardment had warned the enemy to be ready just in time. On the left, three companies of the 22nd entered Diagonal Trench without great opposition. But it was found to be a position untenable by day, and our success was limited to the establishment of several strong points, some 100 yards short of the objective. Only in this, their last operation, did battalions of the 142nd Brigade attack under command of their own brigadier, General Lewis.

On October 9th the 26th (South African) Brigade relieved the 140th and 142nd Brigades in the line. The Division had finished its part in the summer fighting of 1916. Our total loss in casualties on the Somme was 296 officers and 7,475 other ranks killed, wounded, or missing. At this price we had borne our share in the successful advance of the IIIrd Corps, moving the line forward nearly three miles, and capturing, on the way, two German defence systems of prime importance. We were the last to fight in High Wood, and the first to break ourselves against the high ground in which stood the Butte de Warlencourt. Although attacked successively by three other divisions, the Butte was not captured until the enemy left it in his general retirement at the end of February, 1917. The Divisional Artillery remained in action for a few days longer and, together with two brigades of the 1st Divisional Artillery, supported the unsuccessful attack of the 9th Division on the Butte on October 12th. After this they were relieved in the line and assembled in the Behencourt area preparatory to marching northwards.

During the Somme operations every branch of the Division had been taxed to the uttermost. The artillery were continuously in action from the middle of August under new and exhausting conditions. Guns were crowded forward in positions which offered little or no cover and accommodation, and were kept constantly at work firing at difficult targets, or providing hastily-prepared barrages for local operations. Difficulty of transport hit the artillery harder than any other branch of the Service. As the weather grew worse, the few forward tracks were almost lost in the general morass, and convoys from batteries and divisional ammunition column had to plunge, up to the axles in mud, over the shell-torn ground that lay between the head of the made-up roads and their gun positions. Before they could get back to their open lines they must take their place in the solid train of traffic, moving slowly along the winding " German road " that led back from Bazentin towards Fricourt. Conditions had changed remarkably since 1915. On the night after Loos, transport could use any road right up to our front line. Nearly a fortnight passed after September 15th, 1916, before a single mule track was got through over the High Wood crest.

The long distances over which the infantry carrying-parties had to struggle every night with supplies of ammunition and food were a heavy strain on the brigade in reserve. At this stage the use of pack animals and limbered wagons for the supply of the forward area was still in its infancy.

The R.E. and Pioneers had the work of consolidation after each advance—a long march over heavily-shelled wilderness, followed by work under the worst conditions, black wet nights, heavy ground, constant chance of coming upon some little enemy stronghold that had survived our last assault. There was, besides, the work of clearing communication trenches, of making forward tracks and tramways, arranging water-supply, and so on—the provision of all the ways and means of life in an uninhabitable region, and, not least, the bringing forward of all material necessary for their work.

Fricourt Farm formed the local habitation of Divisional Headquarters during the attack on Eaucourt l'Abbaye and subsequent days. At the start communication with brigades at Bazentin was well maintained. As the enemy were pushed back the shelling in the " Valley of Death " between the farm and Bazentin diminished in intensity. But as soon as that occurred the inevitable artillery wagon-lines made their appearance, mushroom-like, during the night. Men lit fires in the trenches under the cables; heavy armoured cable was found in one case doing extra duty as a picket-line for horses; the linesmen of the New Zealand Division on our right, mistaking our lines for theirs, broke in on the conversations of staff officers with remarks from the consequences of which they were preserved only by their extreme remoteness and complete incognito.

On several days when the road to Bazentin was drying up after rain the mud became so sticky that the motor-cyclist despatch riders stuck in it and the despatches had to be carried by mounted orderlies. On the day before the last relief, however, the Corps had extended their permanent route nearly as far as Bazentin—a very good performance—and communication troubles became normal again.

The divisional medical arrangements for the Somme battle opened up a new departure in the collection and evacuation of the sick and wounded. Hitherto the plan adopted had been for two field ambulances each to be responsible for a section of the front with the third in reserve running a depot for divisional sick not requiring evacuation. This was now changed. One field

A SCENE ON THE SOMME FRONT, 1916.

ambulance, reinforced by the bearer sections and horse and motor ambulances of the other two, was now to become responsible for the front, while the other two with their remaining personnel were established at Franvillers and Millencourt, where depots were opened for sick and convalescents.

The 5th London Field Ambulance formed an advanced dressing station at Flat Iron Copse, which was shared with a New Zealand and the 2/3rd Northumbrian Field Ambulances, the main dressing station was formed at Bottom Wood, while a corps collecting station was formed at Fricourt, which, from its position, found itself doing duty for the corps on the right as well, soon after the beginning of the battle. During four days over three thousand cases passed through this station alone.

While here the field ambulance received an unexpected visit from the Prime Minister, who chatted with the wounded and took a lively interest in their various experiences, remarking on the general high spirits that prevailed ; before leaving, Mr. Lloyd George expressed to Captain Clark his approval of all that he had seen.

As the operations progressed and the advanced dressing station was moved forward to the Cough Drop, a bearer relay post was established near the corner of High Wood, while the post at High Alley became the main dressing station and headquarters of the field ambulance. Here the horse transport had their lines of necessity by the side of four batteries of heavy howitzers, with a 9·2 battery in rear. Interesting events were predicted when all the batteries opened out, as was their custom at dusk, but when that time arrived the least concerned of all were the horses.

An enterprise which earned the gratitude of many was a field ambulance post, established on the side of High Alley, where hot tea could be obtained for the asking, night or day. Large numbers of men, worn out, wet through and ready to drop, eagerly availed themselves of the opportunity, and went on their way refreshed and with a renewed interest in life, even if the flavour of the tea was sometimes overcome by that of the chloride of lime in the water.

The field ambulances worked under conditions of the utmost difficulty owing to the impossibility, during the greater part of the battle, of using wheeled transport farther forward than the main dressing station at Bottom Wood. During the first phase, wounded had to be carried by hand from the dressing station at High Alley

to that at Flat Iron Copse, and often as far as Bottom Wood—
a journey sometimes taking five or six hours. The absence
of landmarks, and the difficulty of locating regimental aid-posts
established by the battalion M.O.'s during the advance, added to
the bearers' troubles.

For the attack which began on October 1st, the Cough Drop,
now accessible by day and providing excellent shelter, was selected
for the advanced dressing station. There was a wonderful
German dugout—it seemed wonderful to us then—built as an
aid-post, with three entrances in the side of a bank. It
provided accommodation for some seventy stretcher cases. The
dugout was destroyed owing to a chapter of accidents on
October 2nd. To quote an account written by a lance-corporal
of the R.A.M.C. (in private life a musical critic of distinction):
"Deep in the bowels of the Cough Drop, in the dressing-room,
someone played the fool with a Primus stove—you don't
realise the number of imbeciles in a supposedly sane community
till you see men playing the fool with Primus stoves. Someone
else went to throw water over the blaze, but the supposed
water was paraffin. The well-timbered dugout caught fire.
Everyone escaped; there was nothing else to do. An immense
quantity of stores was destroyed, but far the worst was that this
precious haven, where, in emergency, so many wounded could be
housed out of harm's way, had 'gone west' for good."

On the same day Captain S. Clark, who was temporarily in
command of the 5th London Field Ambulance, was killed by a
German sniper while searching for a wounded man reported to be
lying somewhere in the forward area.

It was for gallantry on this occasion that the Military Cross was
won by the Rev. David Railton, then a chaplain attached to the
141st Brigade, and afterwards Vicar of Margate. Mr. Railton
was the owner of the famous " Padre's Flag," the Union Jack which
was used at the funerals of many men of the 47th Division in the
field, and which was used on Armistice Day, 1920, at the funeral
of the Unknown Warrior.

At the Armistice Day service in 1921 the flag was solemnly
dedicated and placed above the grave of the Unknown Warrior in
Westminster Abbey. Representatives of the 47th Division were
chosen to place it in position at the dedication ceremony. The
flag was put to many uses in the Division, from serving as the cover

of a rough Communion table to helping to decorate the stage at concerts behind the line.

The mistaking of paraffin for water, when the two-gallon petrol can was the only receptacle in use for every kind of liquid, except rum, was pardonable. At least one other serious accident occurred from the same cause in the big German dugout at Bazentin-le-Grand which, during the first attack, served all three brigades as advanced headquarters. A major, who was acting as liaison officer from the neighbouring New Zealand Brigade, found himself presented with a whisky-and-paraffin—the divisional soda-water factory was not then in being. The supply of water as the line advanced and the stock of petrol cans became exhausted was a matter of the greatest difficulty. Forward of Bazentin-le-Grand Wood, where large tanks were filled from time to time by water-lorries which had to take their turn in the endless stream of traffic on the German road, every drop of water had to be man-handled. Weary carrying-parties struggled through the slime with two petrol cans full—something over 40 lb. of water—and returned dead beat, only to be sent back with another load.

All the supply services were kept at high pressure. The 19th Divisional Supply Column, which had already borne the strain of battle with its own division for some time, instead of being relieved with the 19th Division, was exchanged for our own column, and was kept working day and night under almost impossible conditions. The congestion of troops, and scarcity of roads—fewer and worse as they approached the line—threw a severe strain, too, on the Divisional Train and Ordnance personnel, the regimental stores, and first-line transport. The congestion and the frequent shelling of Albert railhead, where several divisions were loading, made the supply situation at times most complicated, and it needed great devotion to duty on the part of all concerned to ensure the regular supply of rations to the fighting troops.

On October 10th the brigades were at Albert, Franvillers and Lavieville. Here they had valedictory inspections by the IIIrd Corps commander (Lieut.-General Sir W. Pulteney), and on October 14th they entrained at Albert for a journey northwards.

On the same day the Divisional Artillery, having been relieved in the line, assembled in the Béhencourt-Fréchencourt area, preparatory to marching to join the Division in the Second Army area.

In a farewell message to the Division, General Sir Henry Rawlinson, Commanding Fourth Army, wrote as follows :

The operations carried out by the 47th Division during the Battle of the Somme have been of material assistance to the Fourth Army, and I desire to congratulate all ranks on their gallantry and endurance.

The capture of High Wood and the trenches beyond it on September 15th and 16th was a feat of arms deserving of high praise, whilst the attack and capture of Eaucourt L'Abbaye on 1st, 2nd, and 3rd October, involving as it did very hard fighting, was a success of which the Division may be justly proud. The Divisional Artillery has rendered excellent service in supporting the infantry attacks and in establishing the barrages on which success so often depends.

I regret that the Division have now left the Fourth Army, but at some future time I trust it may be my good fortune to again have them under my command to add to the successes they have won at Loos, at High Wood, and at Eaucourt l'Abbaye.

NEAR SHRAPNEL CORNER, YPRES, DECEMBER, 1916.

Chapter VII.
THE YPRES SALIENT, 1916-1917.

ON October 14th the infantry of the Division marched into Albert from their billets in Laviéville and Franvillers to entrain for the North.

There were some anxious moments, as trains were late and fresh columns kept converging on the station approach, where time was whiled away by the music of the London Irish pipers. Albert was still within artillery range of the German guns, but this unpremeditated concentration passed unnoticed, and the last train, containing part of the 141st Brigade, got away in due course.

Their progress was not rapid, various rumours circulating to account for the delay. As the transport had all gone before by march route permission was given for the iron ration to be consumed. The delighted faces of some of the men on the receipt of this information showed clearly that they had exercised intelligent anticipation and were faced with a foodless future of unknown duration, for estaminets in Albert were few and far between. However, as the trains crawled slowly towards Amiens, undamaged villages came in sight, and at each halt parties slipped away to purchase eggs and bread, and if the train started again in their absence, walked after it and caught it up. The Divisional Staff were most helpful, walking ahead of the train as it approached Amiens and purchasing ample supplies at the station.

After passing that congested spot progress was more rapid, and after a journey that occupied some thirty-four hours to cover the thirty-six miles, the Division went into excellent billets round Pont Remy and Longpré, to be occupied, alas ! for a few hours only. The following day units marched back into the pleasant Somme Valley and re-entrained for the North, passing through the hospital areas round Etaples.

On October 16th Divisional Headquarters were established at Hooggraaf, near Poperinghe, and arrangements were made to take over the Bluff sector from the left brigade of the 2nd Australian Division, and the Hill 60 sector from the right brigade of the 4th Australian Division. Meanwhile, the Division was arriving from the South, the 140th and 142nd Brigades reaching the Boeschepe area on the 17th, and the 141st Brigade the Steenvoorde area on the 18th.

The Divisional area west of Ypres was a dull and depressing slice of country, almost dead flat, intersected by *beeks*, or ditches, with a few somewhat squalid clusters of houses at intervals, and covered with frequent hut-camps that required incessant labour to keep them drained and habitable. As time progressed these grew and multiplied, together with new railways, heavy and light, dumps, horse lines, heavy battery positions, " sausage " balloon stations, and all the impedimenta of the war of position. An excellent arrangement was that by which units coming out of the line always went to the same camp, and thus came to regard it as theirs, taking more pride in its upkeep and amenities generally than if they had been only casual occupants.

Except for the occasional delights of Poperinghe the Division was dependent on itself for the necessary relaxation when out of the line. Its own excellent " Follies " and the corresponding units of its neighbours provided constant entertainment, culminating in the very successful revue of Christmas, 1916. Good playing fields were deficient in that closely cultivated country, where grassland was almost unknown and the best field became a slippery morass in wet weather.

A captured artillery map, which gave the Second Army Intelligence Department much invaluable information as to the exact location of enemy battery positions, was less accurate with regard to ours, but showed every hutted camp with unpleasant accuracy. As most of these were under direct observation from the enemy's observation posts on the Wytschaete-Messines Ridge, the only wonder is that they were left so long in peace, serious shelling of the back areas being almost unknown until April, 1917.

Farther east and to the south of Ypres the country, though still flat, was much more picturesque, and was dotted with country houses, small and large, with what had been delightful gardens and

LILLE GATE, YPRES.

CLOTH HALL, YPRES.

Facing page 80

well - wooded approaches. Though, much knocked about the majority were still habitable.

Coming to the line itself, the ground sloped gently upwards to a low ridge, the possession of which, it was no secret, was regarded by the Second Army as vital to the retention of the whole sector, the spur in the south-east part of Ravine Wood, the Verbranden-molen Spur, the Bluff and Zwartelen Spur (north of the railway) being specially valuable. That this view of the tactical situation was shared by the enemy was shown by his heavy attack on the Canadian Corps in the previous June, the repulse of which cost our oversea comrades over 8,000 casualties. A repetition of this was constantly before the minds of the Army Commander and his Staff. This accounts for the fact that the Divisional front was relatively narrow, extending from the Ypres-Comines Canal (exclusive) on the right (Bluff sector) to the Zwartelen Spur, north of the Ypres-Comines railway (inclusive) on the left (Hill 60 sector), a frontage of 2,300 yards.

This required a garrison of two brigades, with four battalions for the front and support lines in the Bluff, Ravine, Verbrandenmolen and Hill 60 sub-sectors, with two battalions in local reserve at railway dugouts and Woodcote House, and two farther back at Swan Château and Halifax Camp, the remaining brigade being out of the line in Ottawa, Devonshire, Ontario, and Vancouver camps. The front line from the right included the large group of mining craters, mostly of enemy origin, at the end of the cutting that carried the Canal across the ridge, the earth embankment (or Bluff) being tunnelled to provide covered communication with the craters and dugout accommodation for part of the garrison.

To the north the line, partly breastwork, partly trench, con-tinued just below the crest in front of the Ravine and the wrecked village of Verbrandenmolen to the second cutting through the ridge through which the railway ran. The left was overlooked and in places enfiladed or taken in reverse by the low eminence of Hill 60, which was in enemy hands. In spite of the greatest care, casualties were constantly occurring from enemy snipers.

North of the railway the defences were of a most elaborate nature, as great mining activity had been going on for twelve months, and we had now a very large mine dug right under the hill and ready for the coming Battle of Messines.

H

The guarding of this treasure involved two systems of underground defences, the infantry being responsible for the high level as well as the surface, and the tunnellers for the low level workings. In case the enemy's countermining activities should necessitate the premature explosion of the big mine, a special local operation, involving the attack and capture of Hill 60 and the adjoining sectors, was ready to be brought into operation at very short notice.

To the north of the hill the ground sloped down to a swampy valley, so that a continuous line became impossible and a series of posts approached only at night over the open took its place, with a strong point at Battersea Farm in support.

Touch was maintained with the Division to the north by means of night patrols. The ground, especially at the Bluff, where mining activities had unearthed a series of quicksands, was very soft and swampy in wet weather, No Man's Land being quite impassable to either side. Drainage was very difficult when the ground became waterlogged. It almost appeared that water in those parts had the faculty of draining uphill. Much good work had been done in the previous six weeks by the Australians, but much additional shell-proof accommodation was required to make the defence secure.

The artillery were arranged in two groups, one in Ypres and one in the Railway Dugouts. The batteries went into positions which had been occupied on and off for years, such as Brisbane Dump, Doll's House, Trois Rois, Lankhof Farm, and some east of Ypres. They were all well known to the enemy, and in fact nearly all well in view from their high ground, but there were no others better, so it was a matter of making the best of it and strengthening the pits as much as possible. The appearance of any of these positions after a heavy bombardment by 5·9-in. and 8-in., however, made one sadly conscious of the fact that they existed almost on sufferance. Indeed, it was always a marvel that the enemy did not knock them out more often than he did.

At 8 a.m. on October 19th, Major-General Gorringe took over command, the 140th Brigade taking over the Bluff and the 142nd Brigade the Hill 60 sectors. The Canadian tunnellers, however, remained, being relieved at intervals by the Australians. Mining activity on both sides was considerable, though not of the strenuous nature to which the Division was accustomed on the Vimy Ridge. Our tunnellers claimed to have the upper hand, and subsequent events proved that this contention was fully justified.

No sooner was the Division installed than the enemy proceeded to celebrate their arrival by a little mining activity at the Bluff. At 6 a.m. on October 22nd they blew two or three mines near craters C and D, the 6th Battalion with their usual luck being the garrison at the time. Our posts in C and D craters were buried by the explosion, the two craters being practically blown into one, and some men were also buried at the eastern end of B crater. A new and separate crater, known as E, was also formed to the north of D.

No attack was made by the Germans when the mines were blown, but about 9 a.m., when the 6th were digging out the buried men, some Germans came across with a machine-gun from their trenches, which were only some fifty yards from C and D craters. The 4th Australian Division, on the south side of the Canal, fired at the raiders and inflicted some casualties, but they bombed our men and mounted their machine-gun in such a position as to command the interior of B crater. Our men escaped through the tunnel to A crater, but failed to reoccupy B, owing to the fire of the hostile machine-gun. The tunnel was therefore blocked, and trench mortars were turned on to the Germans who were occupying the eastern lips of C and D craters.

The situation remained unchanged until night, when our men reoccupied B crater, and found no trace of the Germans in any of the others. The lip between B and C and D craters was consolidated in such a way as to command the interior of the two latter.

On October 23rd the G.S.O.I., Lieut.-Colonel Weatherby, D.S.O., went sick, and was replaced by Lieut.-Colonel A. J. Turner, D.S.O., from the Second Army. Colonel Turner was the second distinguished cricketer to join the Divisional Staff, for we already had Captain R. O. Schwarz, of " googly " fame, as D.A.Q.M.G.

In the year during which he served on the Divisional Staff—from March, 1916, to March, 1917—" Reggie " Schwarz made many friends in the Division, and his unfailing cheerfulness and winning personality was a considerable asset to the hard-worked " Q " staff. It was with deep regret that we heard of his death in hospital a short time after a severe attack of bronchitis had sent him down to the base in 1917.

The weather had now turned colder and rain was frequent. The "trench strength" of the Division was 264 officers and 8,481 other ranks. The Division having settled down, the usual process of reminding the enemy that there was a war on began on October 30th by an organised bombardment of the enemy's front and support lines opposite the Bluff, considerable damage being done.

On November 4th the Duke of Connaught inspected the 18th Battalion (London Irish Rifles), of which battalion he was Honorary Colonel, and the Commanding Officer, Lieut.-Colonel B. McM. Mahon, M.C., was presented to him. The same day our miners succeeded in blowing in an enemy gallery that had been driven under our front line, and the mining situation became easier. The enemy's trench-mortars having devoted considerable attention to Marshall Walk, and a good deal of damage having been caused, a pre-arranged scheme of immediate retaliation was introduced which succeeded in largely abating the nuisance.

On November 18th the first frost occurred. Reinforcements, especially of officers, had been steadily trickling in, so that by the 25th the "trench strength" had increased to 352 officers and 8,635 other ranks.

The 1st Canadian Tunnelling Company, on December 11th, blew a large camouflet in rear of the enemy's gallery, which was threatening C and D craters, and on the following day they broke into this from our own workings, occupying 500 feet of enemy workings, which contained much mining material and two dead Germans. No prisoners were, however, captured.

The enemy bombarded the whole Divisional front on December 15th. This was followed by the S O S going up on the 23rd Divisional front on our left at 4.25. This signal was mistaken for our own, with the result that both artilleries expended much ammunition before the situation again became normal.

Two days later a patrol of one N.C.O. and one man returning from Glasgow to Berry post was captured by the Germans, the N.C.O. subsequently escaping and returning to our lines. Next day a ticklish operation was successfully performed by the tunnellers, who blew a large camouflet at Hill 60 without detonating the large mine. On December 21st the Commander-in-Chief inspected

BRIG.-GENERAL VISCOUNT HAMPDEN, K.C.B., C.M.G.
Commanding 140th Infantry Brigade, 1916-1917.

in the rain the 18th, 19th, and 20th Battalions, chatting informally
with many officers and men, and expressing himself as much
gratified with the appearance and steadiness of the units under
unfavourable conditions.

On the following day a raiding-party of the Civil Service Rifles
succeeded in entering the enemy's front line between the Bluff and
the Shrine after a two minutes' bombardment.   The trenches were
found to be considerably damaged and several dead and wounded
Germans were found.   Owing to their violent resistance none of the
enemy was brought back alive, but the raiders accounted for about
a dozen Germans, and a shoulder-strap identified the troops opposite
as belonging to the 416th Regiment of the 204th Division, which
agreed with our existing information.   The losses of the raiders
were two other ranks missing, believed killed, and two officers
and nine other ranks slightly wounded.

During the night of the 23rd-24th a series of patrols went out along
the Xth Corps front.   One near the Bluff encountered a party of
about twenty of the enemy and drove them off with bombs.
Another south of the railway cutting was fired on and lost three
men, but much useful information was gained as to the condition
of the enemy's wire, his method of holding his trenches, and the
state of No Man's Land.

Meanwhile the 141st Brigade, which had the good fortune to be
in Divisional Reserve, made the most of their opportunity of
celebrating Christmas.   With vivid recollections of 1915 and the
Hohenzollern Redoubt, they determined to go while the going was
good, and company dinners started officially as early as the 21st.
The hutted camps proved invaluable for this purpose, as many of the
larger huts were just large enough to have a complete company
packed into them before dinner.   Their removal afterwards was
not always so simple.

The supply of turkeys was insufficient to provide everybody with
this seasonable delicacy, but an excellent substitute was found in
the shape of roast pork, which could be obtained locally " on the
hoof." Dinners in camp had this further advantage over cele-
brations in " Pop," that the dispersing revellers were spared the
well-meant but sometimes embarrassing attentions of the A.P.M.
and his zealous assistants.   Mess carts had scoured the country
as far afield as Bailleul and Hazebrouck to such good purpose that

the resultant menus would have been no discredit to many a London restaurant, though the cooks were without almost everything in the way of apparatus that a chef is supposed to want. The troops in the line were less fortunate, the enemy bombarding fairly heavily, and causing considerable alarms, damage, and casualties. The signallers had to repair one buried cable in thirty places and then lay a new one.

Two changes occurred in the command of infantry brigades on December 28th, Brigadier-General F. G. Lewis, C.M.G., commanding the 142nd Infantry Brigade, went sick, and Lieut.-Colonel H. B. P. L. Kennedy, D.S.O., commanding the 21st Battalion, took over temporary command. Brigadier-General R. McDouall, D.S.O., commanding 141st Infantry Brigade, went on a month's leave, handing over to Lieut.-Colonel W. C. W. Hawkes, commanding 4th Battalion R.W.F. (Pioneers).

The year closed quietly, the only disturbance being a little celebration at midnight, arranged by the gunners. First one round of 9·2-inch, a pause ; nine rounds of 6-inch, a pause ; one round of 8-inch, a pause ; and then seven rounds from the 60-pounders to ring in 1917. The infantry added five rounds rapid as their contribution.

January 1st was marked by a heavy enemy bombardment of the whole Divisional front which did considerable damage to our trenches, blowing in the entrance of North Street tunnel to crater A. All indications pointed to a raid, but none took place, and by 6.15 p.m. things had become quieter. At night mild excitement was caused by the circulation to units from Divisional Headquarters of details of the New Year Honours and Awards, which covered the period March to September, 1916, and thus included the Somme operations.

For some days the enemy had been shelling the back areas in a desultory fashion, and on the 4th an unpleasant reminder of the possibilities of the new German field-gun was given by a direct hit on Swan Château by a 77-mm. shell which burst in a room occupied by runners of the 17th Battalion, killing one and wounding eleven. The enemy's artillery and trench-mortar activity, combined with the effects of rain and snow, made the maintenance of our trenches most laborious and difficult. The earth, especially near the Bluff, had the consistency of porridge, and revetting was necessary by means of " A " frames, corrugated iron, and expanded metal. These latter, in their turn, when damaged by artillery fire, were very difficult to clear away.

When it is remembered also that all troops on duty were equipped " boots, gum, thigh," that these had to be changed at least once in each twenty-four hours and carried to and from the drying-rooms, that water had to be brought from a considerable distance, and that the Divisional Commander had given strict orders that all troops on duty in the front system were to be supplied with either a hot meal or a hot drink every four hours, it will be appreciated that a tour in the front-line was no period of ease and leisure. Added to this, the evacuation of casualties, both killed and wounded, was a laborious business that absorbed the services of a number of men, so it is not surprising that a constant state of guerrilla warfare existed between the Staff and the battalions as to the discrepencies between " trench strengths " and the numbers who actually paraded for " work."

Major-General Gorringe's insistence on hot food was, however, fully justified by results, the numbers evacuated sick being surprisingly small in view of the, at times, appalling weather conditions. Casualties from " trench feet " also, as compared with the previous winter, dwindled to quite small proportions, thanks to the precautions recommended and enforced.

On the 15th the Division suffered a heavy loss. Major Lord Gorell, D.S.O., when returning from observing for his battery, was mortally wounded by a shell in Marshall Walk. A pre-war Territorial officer of high professional attainments, and at times almost reckless courage, his loss was universally mourned.

As the enemy's artillery activity showed unpleasant similarity to that displayed previous to his attack on the Canadians the preceding June, the Army authorities considered a similar operation probable, and measures were taken to counter it. On January 16th these took the form of a mixed intense and deliberate bombardment by the Divisional Artilleries of the 47th, 23rd, and 41st Divisions, the Corps Heavies, and the Army " Circus." The enemy's retaliation caused considerable damage ; the Battalion Headquarters in Larchwood Tunnels was blown in, and the orderly-room sergeant of the 6th Battalion was killed. The artillery observation post in the Bluff craters was also blown in by a shell which killed Lieutenant Duffus and his telephonist.

Poor visibility on the following day put a stop to the bombardment. Several days' snow and frost followed. On the 25th the enemy shelled the 142nd Brigade Headquarters at Bedford House, obtaining direct hits with 8·2-in. on the mess and the brigade major's dugout. The Staff had prudently retired to the cellars, and suffered only the total loss of the sweet course.

Hard frost continued during the early days of February, the thermometer falling to zero on the 2nd. This made all work, except wiring existing trees and pickets, almost impossible, and since the water froze as it percolated into the trenches, it seemed only a matter of time before the garrisons on both sides would be lifted to ground level. On February 9th, during a burst of mutual artillery activity, a green light was seen to go up near the Ravine. As all wires to this sector had been cut, and this was at the time our S O S signal, it was naturally assumed to indicate an enemy raid, and the Divisional and Corps Artillery promptly responded. When communication was restored, it appeared that the light was a German one, apparently fired in anticipation of a raid by us.

On the 14th the enemy were very active against our back areas, the Café Belge and Brisbane Dump being heavily shelled. Poperinghe was also shelled by a long-range gun. From now on the front-line infantry began to feel real sympathy for the Transport, as the latter were frequently shelled on the way up with rations, which they nevertheless always contrived to deliver sooner or later. Owing to the heavy demand for R.E. material and ammunition, convoys from the Divisional Ammunition Column, Train, and Engineers, as well as from the Field Ambulances and Supply Column, were trekking night after night over the shelled roads through Vlamertinghe and Ypres, and the task of the military police in controlling the never-ending stream of traffic in the darkness was no light one.

Throughout the desolate winter months the 4th Royal Welsh Fusiliers were constantly engaged in the work of improving and maintaining trenches, dugouts, and trench tramway communications in the forward area.

The narrow-gauge tramway tracks running forward from Woodcote Farm Junction to the Bluff and Ravine received unusual attention from the enemy during the spring months of 1917. The cutting of big sections of line was of almost daily occurrence, but

CAFE BELGE, NEAR DICKEBUSCH, 1918

BLUFF CRATERS, YPRES.

Facing page 88

the Pioneer breakdown gangs dealt with every emergency, and on no occasion was the nightly flow of engineering stores, rations, and ammunition to the front-line interrupted for long.

A small party of the enemy attempted to raid the 6th Battalion on February 18th near the top of Hedge Row, but they were observed and fired on. Two were killed and several wounded, including the leader, an uncommunicative feldwebel, who was captured with gunshot wounds through both hands. A wounded private was also brought in and proved to be much more talkative. Both belonged to the 65th Reserve Infantry Regiment.

Later on another party succeeded in entering our trenches near the same spot, and in the inky darkness approached a Lewis gun which had been fixed to fire on a gap in the enemy's wire. The team were busy lifting out the gun to fire on the raiders and mistook the latter in the trench for our own men, so that the enemy succeeded, after badly wounding the corporal in charge and another man, in getting away with the gun, but without any prisoners.

The outstanding event of this winter in the Ypres salient was the raid carried out by the 6th Battalion on February 20th, 1917. The raid was planned and rehearsed long before its actual execution ; in fact, it was reported that the proprietors of any estaminet in Poperinghe were prepared to tell you the date, time, and personnel of the projected operation for some months before it took place. If this was so, either the German Intelligence Service had deteriorated or the accuracy of the information was doubted, because when the raid was eventually carried out after a week's wire-cutting, extending, it is true, over a wide area, the prisoners admitted that they were completely surprised by the attack.

The plan was to raid the enemy trenches in the map-square I.34 in daylight, with the object not only of inflicting casualties, capturing and destroying war material, dugouts, machine-gun and minenwerfer emplacements, but of gaining information in regard to the hostile front system and its garrison, and also to look for, and, if found, to destroy any mine-shafts in the vicinity, to search for gas-cylinders, and to destroy a light gun which had been the cause of considerable annoyance to us, and had been located not far behind the German third line.

Zero was fixed at 5 p.m. with the idea of ensuring more efficient control and taking advantage of the dusk to cover the withdrawal of the attackers an hour later.

The troops employed consisted of four companies of Lieutenant-Colonel Mildren's 6th Battalion, with six Lewis guns, one officer and twenty sappers of the 520th Company, R.E., and one officer and four other ranks of the 2nd Australian Tunnelling Company, making a total of twenty officers and six hundred and forty other ranks. With the object of deceiving the enemy as to the actual point of the attack, a dummy raid by the 22nd Battalion of the 142nd Infantry Brigade, who were holding the Hill 60 sector, was arranged to precede the actual raid, a small mine being fired in No Man's Land five minutes before, and a second two minutes before zero.

The firing of the first mine was to be followed by a barrage of field-guns and 2-in. trench-mortars, which lifted at zero to form a box barrage in rear of the craters until zero, plus ten minutes. Trench junctions and strong points behind the line were bombarded by howitzers and 2-in. trench mortars, and smoke-bombs were fired at Hill 60 and the Caterpillar. Various coloured rockets were fired behind our lines. Other coloured rockets were collected in the Bluff craters and were fired in salvos, six, nine, and twelve minutes after zero, while the 41st Divisional Artillery kept the high ground south of the Canal under heavy fire throughout. Finally, Stokes mortars were borrowed, for over eighteen were in position to barrage the enemy's front-lines on the actual front to be raided, most of which was too close to permit of wire-cutting by the 18-pounders. The usual artillery and machine-gun co-operation was arranged, and smoke-grenades and trench-mortar smoke-bombs were used to isolate the raided portion of the enemy's lines and prevent accurate enfilading fire being brought to bear from the high ground on their side on either flank.

This plan worked out admirably The enemy was evidently very nervous of the situation at Hill 60, and as this had been included in the previous wire-cutting, mistook the dummy raid for the real one, as his counter barrage was prompt, and, of course, descended upon almost empty trenches, the garrison, with the exception of the minimum number of sentries, having been withdrawn into the tunnels. The firework display from the Bluff also contributed, as another barrage descended on that area. The hurricane bombardment of the eighteen Stokes mortars not only cut the enemy's wire, but forced the garrison of the

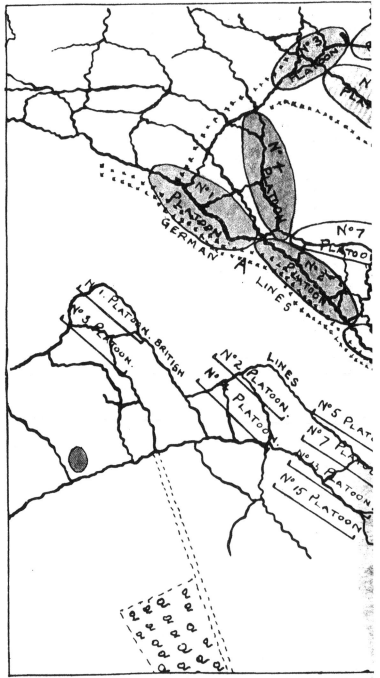

Rough sketch of plan of attack issued to officers and N.C.O.'s of the Londons for the assault which took place on the German lines at 5 p.m. February 20th, 1917.

Each platoon was allotted its task as indicated by the numbered ovals,

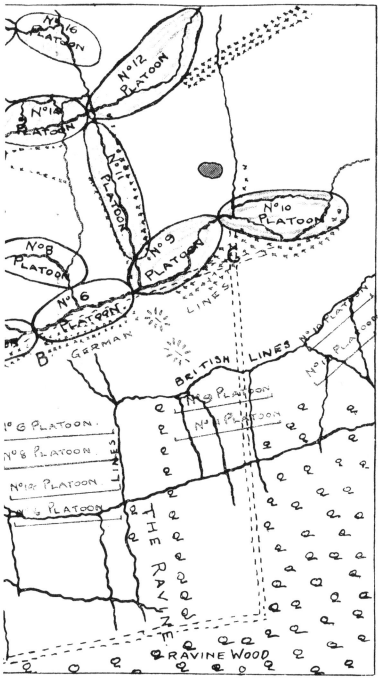

ssaulting troops forming up as shown. The ground had been carefully studied
om aerial photographs and personal observation. The careful training of the
oops and the enthusiasm of all ranks overcame the very great difficulties of
ie assault, and resulted in the outstanding success of the operations.

front-line either to get into their concrete dugouts or stop outside and be killed.

In consequence, the attackers met practically no hostile fire when going over. They captured the front-line almost without resistance, the hostile machine-guns in their concrete recesses not being ready for action. The only officer captured in the raid was found in one of the dugouts, which was solidly built and almost undamaged. He proved to be the officer in command of the sector, and had been caught on an ordinary tour of inspection without a revolver or even a stick. He was a brave man, and it was only the lack of something to do it with that had prevented his putting up a fight. The intermediate line, which did not appear to be used, was badly flattened out, and the main support line was also badly damaged and yielded a considerable haul of prisoners. There were no gas-cylinders, and only one mine-shaft was discovered, which was destroyed.

The light gun was not found. Enemy dugouts and machine-gun emplacements were wrecked by firing mobile charges in them, and this very nearly caused us severe casualties, as during the noise and confusion of the raid the R.E. Company had the greatest difficulty in diverting triumphant raiders returning dragging machine-guns and other loot from the neighbourhood of dugouts containing a fizzling charge of ammonal. The withdrawal was carried out according to plan, the red rockets that were fired behind our lines proving a useful guide and signal. Other rockets of a different colour were being fired north and south of the actual signals.

The total results were : One officer and one hundred and seventeen other ranks captured, two of whom died in our trenches ; two heavy and three light machine-guns and large quantities of documents, maps, and papers. A large number of the enemy were also killed or wounded when escaping to the rear. A great deal of destruction was carried out in the enemy's trenches at a total cost of eleven other ranks killed, three died of wounds, two missing, with four officers and fifty-six other ranks wounded, a total of seventy-six. The number of prisoners broke all existing records, and was never equalled in a raid by a single battalion during the whole of the war. The large number may be attributed to the fact that the enemy were largely surprised, while the attacking troops had few casualties going over, and also succeeded in cutting off the bulk of the garrison of the enemy salient. The official German account of this extraordinarily successful raid, circulated to the German Press of February 22nd, 1917, was as follows : " Strong English patrols which attempted to advance after exploding mines on both sides of the Ypres-Comines railway were checked by our barrage fire. Some few did reach the German lines, but were driven out again, losing prisoners. It is significant that the unwounded English prisoners captured here were so absolutely intoxicated that it was impossible to interrogate them."

On February 25th three officers' patrols of the 141st Infantry Brigade went out, but encountered no enemy patrols, and reported that all was quiet and the enemy's line was not strongly held. Two days later the 39th Division—commanded by our old friend General Cuthbert—relieved the 23rd Division on our left. Next evening another mutual " scare " occurred, both the 6th London in the railway sub-sector and the enemy sending up the S O S during a bombardment. The 6th had one officer and twenty other ranks hit, and one Lewis gun knocked out. As raids and bombardments by both sides were of almost nightly occurrence on the Corps front, these incidents admit of easy explanation, the lines being so close together that the putting down of a hostile barrage naturally led the infantry on the spot to assume that a raid was taking place, or about to do so.

On March 15th the enemy, suspecting that the railway was being used to bring up timber and stores, heavily bombarded the neighbourhood of Zillebeke Halt, destroying the track for some three hundred yards to the west of that place. On the 23rd the 142nd Infantry Brigade moved back from Divisional Reserve to the training area at Tilques. Early next day a hostile aeroplane flying low was successfully engaged by a Lewis gun of the 20th Battalion and crashed behind the enemy support line, where it was ultimately destroyed by our artillery. Following on a very heavy trench-mortar bombardment which blew in all the tunnelled entrances in the craters, the enemy succeeded in entering them, but subsequently withdrew without securing any prisoners.

Several organised bombardments of the enemy lines were undertaken during this period, and it was determined to repeat the raid of the 6th Battalion. The 18th Battalion were selected for this, and were taken out of the line for training, their place in

1-6 April

the Hill 60 sub-sector being taken by the 20th Battalion. The preliminaries were similar to those of February, but on this occasion the enemy was better prepared. He brought up a battalion of storm troops into close support, and his artillery preparations were more complete. The London Irish were shelled on their way up to the line, losing one of their company commanders, Captain Fairlie, badly wounded by shrapnel. When they went over, the enemy promptly put down a " nut-cracker " barrage on both front-lines and brought up his reserves.

The result was something very like a pitched battle in the enemy reserve-line, casualties on both sides being heavy. The state of the ground was very bad and caused delay, and the continued enemy barrage forced the returning raiders to deviate to both flanks. The net results were eighteen prisoners taken, many of the enemy killed, and dugouts and emplacements destroyed. Our casualties were about one hundred and sixty all ranks, including Sec.-Lieut. M. E. Thomas, commanding the detachment of the 517th Coy., R.E., who accompanied the raiders, wounded. That evening an enemy aeroplane bombed Divisional Headquarters.

On the following day the reorganisation of the Divisional front began. The 23rd Division took over the Hill 60 sub-sector from the 141st Infantry brigade, relief being complete by 2.15 a.m. on April 9th. Hardly had the newcomers settled than the enemy opened a heavy artillery and trench-mortar bombardment of their new sector, also shelling the Dickebush and Brisbane Dump road with gas-shells. At 7 p.m. he raided Hill 60 sub-sector, after disabling many of the garrison with carbon monoxide trench-mortar bombs. The Germans penetrated into the " high level " underground defences, and a confused struggle, in which infantry and Australian tunnellers co-operated, took place. Extraordinarily little damage was done in the circumstances, one bomb being thrown into the Company Headquarters, which was empty, and another into the dynamo which supplied the electric light for the tunnels, without disabling it.

That evening the 7th Battalion took over the Spoil Bank section south of the Canal from the 41st Division, relief being complete by 2 a.m. on April 10th. This southward move took the Division astride of the Canal, which was a serious obstacle to counter-attacking troops. The move also obviated the cutting of the

Divisional front in two by the barraging of the railway cutting, which now formed the north boundary. On the night of the 14th-15th a patrol of the 7th Battalion, south of the Canal, lost its way and was captured.

This period was marked by great artillery activity on our part, with considerable enemy retaliation. On April 12th the 142nd Brigade, who had returned from the training area, relieved the 140th Brigade on the right. The 141st Brigade then moved out, returning on April 26th. On the 20th our artillery supported the 41st Division, who were being heavily shelled, following this up with a raid. The command of the Divisional Artillery had been taken over at the end of March by Brigadier-General E. N. Whitley, a Territorial officer who had already won distinction with the West Riding Division, and a brother of the present Speaker of the House of Commons. Two months earlier Major the Hon. H. G. O. Bridgeman had joined the Division as Brigade Major, R.A. Both these officers were destined to remain with the 47th until the end of the war, Major Bridgeman being promoted to command a brigade in November, 1918.

In the early hours of April 24th the enemy attempted to raid the centre battalion of the 140th Brigade, but were driven off by Lewis-gun fire. This was repeated on the following morning near the Ravine, but the left battalion again succeeded in driving the enemy off.

On the 29th the enemy shelled the Reninghelst-Ouderdom road with a 4·7-in. naval gun, one shell landing on the parade-ground of the 141st Brigade reinforcement camp and wounding two men. From this period the whole of the Divisional area was intermittently shelled, and the strain on the troops was proportionately increased, no one being able to count on uninterrupted rest when out of the line. The constant whistle of our shells going over and the enemy's retaliation proved most trying even to those whose nerves were the strongest. On April 30th the enemy exploded a pile of trench-mortar ammunition at Brisbane Dump and did considerable damage, and a fire occurred in the Battalion Headquarters in the tunnels in the Bluff.

Chapter VIII.

THE BATTLE OF MESSINES.

IT was a great relief to all ranks when the long damp nights started growing shorter, and the trenches and country in general began to show us that spring had arrived and that summer was coming.

We soon began to realise, however, that as well as summer other things were in the air. More minute investigation of the enemy's lines, and more frequent work by our aeroplanes, gave us the idea that operations were pending. In addition to the regular visits to the forward areas by our Divisional Commander and his Staff, Staff officers of higher formations showed even more interest than usual in our positions and those of the enemy opposite to us.

Well as the secret was kept, there was that indefinable something in the air which made us think that at no very far distant date we should be called upon to carry out some form of offensive operations.

At this time, May 1st, the Division formed part of the Xth Corps of the Second Army, and was holding the front from the Bluff Craters, on the Ypres-Comines Canal, as their right boundary to a point a few hundred yards north of the famous Hill 60. Two brigades were in the line, and one in reserve in hutted camps near Ouderdom.

For many weeks both our own miners and those of the enemy had been actively at work on our front, especially at the Bluff Craters and about Hill 60.

There were many alarms of enemy mines being blown at Hill 60, and our own large mine, actually under the German lines at this point, was often in danger either of being discovered or fired prematurely by us to prevent discovery. A special scheme was, therefore, arranged in the event of the blowing of this mine being necessary at short notice, and the brigade holding the left sector of the line had many anxious moments. Fortunately, however, this great mine of ours was never discovered until the day when we ourselves made very good use of it.

Several weeks before the actual details of the offensive became known to the front-line troops our artillery had started organised destructive shoots on various points in the enemy's lines and on his communications, and as usual this provoked retaliation on our back areas. On May 6th the 21st Battalion at Halifax Camp had to move their quarters owing to shelling, though they were in the resting brigade.

About the middle of May the details of the "Second Army Offensive," as the operation was termed, were pretty thoroughly known by all concerned, and orders were issued accordingly, informing us that the object of the attack was to capture the dominating Messines Ridge, from which the enemy had for many months had splendid observation of our lines and back areas.

Each corps in the Second Army was given its objective. To our Corps, the Xth, was deputed the task of capturing about 6,000 yards of front to a depth of about 1,000 to 1,500 yards, which included the heavily entrenched position known as the Damstrasse on the right, the White Château, both banks of the Ypres-Comines Canal, Hill 60, and Battle Wood, on the left.

Three Divisions attacked on the Xth Corps front, the 41st, 47th, and 23rd, from right to left respectively. To the 47th Division fell the lot of attacking astride the Ypres-Comines Canal. The Divisional Commander decided that the 140th Infantry Brigade (Brig.-General Kennedy) should attack on the south, and the 142nd Infantry Brigade (Brig.-General Bailey) on the north side of the Canal. Two battalions of the 141st Brigade were placed under the command of the attacking brigades, the 17th Battalion operating with the 140th Brigade and the 20th with the 142nd Brigade.

The approximate disposition of the infantry of the Division at the actual date of the attack is shown in the map.

To reach these positions the various battalions had to carry out several more or less rapid moves.

During the first fortnight of May our gunners were steadily pounding away at the enemy's defences and starting to cut his wire.

HILL 60, YPRES.

THE WHITE CHATEAU, HOLLEBEKE.

Facing page 96

To the 141st Infantry Brigade fell the duty of holding the Divisional front before the operation, and they did valuable work in preparing trenches, dumps of rations and ammunition, and many other things for the final day.

The enemy's artillery had by now (May 19th) become much more active, and both our trenches and our artillery positions came in for some heavy shelling at times.

The two attacking brigades were given opportunities for re-hearsing their attacks, and had a few very pleasant days in the Steenvoorde area at the end of May. How useful and important was this training over taped-out courses was shown on the day of the attack, when both officers and other ranks found the enemy's trenches almost identical with those that had been laid out for them to practise over.

The splendid devotion to duty shown by our Air Force in taking photographs of the enemy's positions was of the greatest possible use to us in locating and putting on the maps any difficulties in the way of hidden wire and machine-gun emplacements which had to be overcome in our advance. We learnt many useful things, too, from our divisional intelligence summaries, which enabled us to go direct to good dugouts in the enemy's lines, where company and battalion headquarters could be established.

On June 1st our bombardment of the enemy's trenches and the cutting of his wire became intense, and on June 4th the attacking troops began to get into their allotted positions.

Divisional Headquarters moved up from Hooggraaf to Winnipeg Camp, 140th Infantry Brigade Headquarters to Spoil Bank, and 142nd Infantry Brigade to the Bluff Tunnels.

It speaks very well for the sometimes maligned Staff that the concentration marches of all troops of the Division were carried out without a hitch, and every unit was in its allotted position by 5 p.m. on June 6th. Every effort had been made by the Divisional Commander to ensure the comfort of the troops during the trying hours immediately preceding the attack, and success rewarded his efforts on their behalf.

At these times there are bound to be halts on the roads up to the trenches, when such large bodies of troops and transport are moving over badly shelled roads and newly-made cross-country tracks, but everybody felt that he was being given every chance to arrive

at his appointed place as fresh as possible.   Great efforts were made
to keep the actual date and hour of the attack secret, and it appeared
from information obtained from prisoners afterwards that these
were quite successful.

The principal features of importance to be captured on the
Divisional front were (a) on the 140th Brigade front, the White
Château and stables, and the portion of the Damstrasse trench
opposed to them ; (b) on the 142nd Brigade front, the two Spoil
Banks and the Canal Bank.

Never before had the Division been in better spirits or more
confident of success.   Only to hear our artillery firing over our
heads was to know that we were going to receive splendid support
from our gunners, not only in accuracy but in weight of shells.   Our
battery areas seemed to grow guns every few yards—large and small.

" Z " day, as the day of the attack was known, was finally fixed
for June 7th, and zero hour for 3.10 a.m.   By 2.30 a.m. every man
was in his place, absolutely ready and heartened up by a good hot
breakfast.

During the night of June 6-7th the front line troops had cut gaps
in our own wire entanglements to let our attacking troops assemble
in No Man's Land.   Positions of battalions were as follows :

140th Infantry Brigade	On the right	8th Battalion.
	On the left	7th Battalion.
	Support	15th and 6th Battalions.
142nd Infantry Brigade	On the right	24th Battalion.
	On the left	22nd Battalion.
	Support	23rd and 21st Battalions.

A section of Tanks was allotted to the 140th Infantry Brigade to
assist in the capture of the Damstrasse and the White Château and
stables.   Of the four Tanks actually engaged, one was ditched 200
yards north of the château, and two others near the stables.

During the winter our miners had prepared a series of large mines
to be exploded in conjunction with this attack, and these were to be
fired at zero hour.   The nearest to our Divisional front were the
ones at St. Eloi, on our right, and our friend under Hill 60 and the
Caterpillar on our left.

At zero hour (3.10 a.m.) on June 7th, immediately after the
explosion of the great mines, and supported by fire of unprecedented

accuracy and weight, our attacking infantry stormed the enemy's front-line trenches.

To one who saw the dull glare of the exploding mines and the continuous flashes of our guns, and heard the rumble of the explosions mingled with the crash of the shells and rattle of the machine-guns, this zero hour will always remain a very vivid recollection. The ground trembled with these vast subterranean explosions, and the debris hurled high into the air could be seen against the grey dawn of the morning sky.

In such a setting did the men of the 47th Division attack their objectives in the Battle of Messines. These objectives, with one exception, were all safely in their hands on that day by the appointed hours.

From the beginning the attack went well. Opposition was met with and overcome all along the line. Hostile machine-guns came into action, and were destroyed, as seemed best to those on the spot, great initiative and daring being shown by subordinate commanders in this respect.

On the right the 7th and 8th Battalions of the 140th Brigade went forward with splendid dash and overcame all obstacles until the White Château was reached. Here the attack was held up temporarily. But our men were not to be denied, and at the third attempt, in which Lieutenant J. F. Preston, 7th Battalion, especially distinguished himself, the last of a determined party of the enemy were at last forced to surrender, and the most difficult part of this brigade's task was finished. The 6th and 15th Battalions, which were detailed to pass through the 7th and 8th to complete the attack, had a difficult task to carry out, but reached their final objectives to the scheduled time, reorganised, dug themselves in, and held every foot of ground they had captured. The 6th Battalion had to pass through the vicinity of the Château stables to avoid what had been reported to be an unfordable stream, take ground to the left, deploy to the right, and get into their assigned position in time to move forward at the appointed hour. Led by their fearless commander, Lieut.-Colonel Mildren, they carried out this trying operation under heavy fire without incurring many casualties. It was a brilliant piece of work by this brigade, which, besides taking four officers and 278 other ranks prisoners, captured ten machine-guns and one minenwerfer.

The 140th Brigade suffered in casualties :

	Killed	Wounded	Missing
Officers	7	32	1
Other ranks	157	752	47

Among the many gallant officers and men who fell during the day was Captain W. E. Ind, M.C., Adjutant of the 15th Battalion, who was mortally wounded during the attack. As an able officer and a very gallant gentleman, his loss was keenly felt throughout the Division.

At the same time the 142nd Brigade attack was proceeding well up to time, and the leading battalions, the 24th and 22nd, gained all their objectives, and were ready to pass the 23rd and 21st through their lines when these latter advanced for the second phase of the operation.

The 23rd Battalion, who had to cross the Canal and take trenches on the south side to connect up with the 140th Brigade troops, encountered considerable opposition, and only after hard fighting managed to reach and hold their final trenches. Their left, however, had become exposed, as the 21st Battalion on their left had been held up short of the triangular Spoil Bank by hostile machine-guns concealed in the Spoil Bank, and in spite of the most gallant efforts could not get forward. On the left of the 21st Battalion again the troops of the 23rd Division were having difficulty in clearing the enemy out of Battle Wood, and this rendered their left flank also exposed.

As soon as definite information was received from the 21st Battalion that they could not capture the triangular Spoil Bank, Brigadier-General Bailey decided to make a fresh attack on this strong point with troops of the 20th Battalion, as both the Divisional and Corps Commanders were particularly anxious that the whole of our objectives should be in our hands by night-fall.

Heavy artillery was turned on to the Spoil Bank during the afternoon, and at 7 p.m., supported by a strong artillery barrage, three companies of the 20th Battalion, who had been sent up from reserve, attacked.

While these companies were forming up, however, they had been heavily shelled, and the moment they advanced they met with a particularly heavy fire from the hostile machine-guns concealed in the Spoil Bank. Although some progress was made, the attack was eventually held up without gaining its objective. Later, this obstinate resistance point of the enemy was captured by troops of the 141st Brigade.

Casualties in the 142nd Brigade during these operations amounted to :

	Killed	Wounded	Missing
Officers	11	28	—
Other ranks	167	833	48

The prisoners taken by the 142nd Brigade numbered two officers and 151 other ranks, in addition to four heavy machine-guns, two light machine-guns, and two trench-mortars. Lieut.-Colonel H. H. Kemble, commanding the 23rd Battalion, was mortally wounded while supervising the forming up of his battalion for their advance. His loss not only as a commanding officer, but as one of the oldest members of the Division, was very much felt. He came to France as second in command of a company in the 15th Battalion, and had been with the Division the whole time since its landing.

It would be impossible here to give a detailed account of the various duties performed by the other units of the Division— Artillery and Engineers, the Pioneer Battalion, the R.A.M.C., the Supply, Transport, and Signal Services, and others—one and all performed their tasks in the same gallant and devoted way as the attacking infantry. Great use was made of our machine-guns, both individually and in batteries, for putting up both offensive and protective barrages. Signal detachments attached to both artillery and infantry went forward with some of our most advanced troops in order to set up rapid communication. Their efforts were, in most cases, very successful, as throughout the whole battle news was transmitted back very rapidly and with extreme accuracy. During the day of attack a special captive balloon was detailed to receive messages by lamp, direct from the front-line battalions, in case of communication being impossible by any other means.

No account of any operation can be complete without mention being made of the battalion and brigade runners. A more devoted and determined set of men cannot be imagined. Their esprit de corps was wonderful, and during June 7th their reputation for gallantry was only enhanced. No matter how heavy the enemy's barrage or how deadly his machine-gun fire, our runners managed to find a way through to deliver their messages.

Another very efficient arm of the Division was our trench-mortar batteries, who took part in the initial barrage on the 142nd Brigade front, at points where our trenches were too near to those of the enemy to enable effective artillery fire to be brought to bear. One Stokes mortar detachment fired no fewer than 120 rounds in the three minutes of the final bombardment.

Throughout the whole operation the infantry found that our artillery fire was wonderfully accurate, and the advancing troops were able to keep within thirty yards of our creeping barrage without danger to themselves. The difficulties of finding battery positions, far enough advanced to enable the guns to cover our infantry to the limit of their advance, were very great, as also was the supply and storage of ammunition at the gun positions. As on all other occasions, though, Brigadier-General Whitley, the C.R.A., and the officers and men under his command performed wonders in this respect, as was shown by the fine support which they gave the attacking troops. One 18-pounder battery alone, during the twenty-four hours from the beginning of the attack, fired no fewer than 6,000 rounds, which means that each detachment must have lifted approximately ten tons, and this in spite of being shelled.

On June 9th the 141st Brigade relieved the 142nd Brigade north of the Canal, and the latter brigade was withdrawn to support positions for reorganisation.

On June 13th the Division was relieved by units of the 24th and 41st Divisions, and moved back into the Westoutre area for a well-earned rest.

Thus ended, for the Division, the Battle of Messines. As a battle it had many aspects, but chief among them, perhaps, was that it was a carefully studied attack, after infinite preparation, from a well-organised trench system against an equally well-entrenched enemy. Never before had our artillery superiority over the enemy been so great, and the successful results achieved by this operation were the outcome of months of planning by all formations down to the smallest details.

The artillery, with their positions mostly " given away " by huge ammunition dumps and furious firing, came in for weeks of the heaviest shell-fire they had yet experienced, especially in Zillebeke, at Bedford House, and in St. Eloi (" Dead Man's Gulch "). Casualties were numerous and new guns frequently in demand.

The horses also during the whole of the summer suffered severely, gun teams and ration and ammunition wagons being frequently knocked out on the shell-swept roads at night. The scene at Shrapnel Corner or any other main cross-roads on any morning was more than enough to make all real horse lovers fervently hope that the big wars of the future would be waged without their aid. They received no rewards and were allowed no " nervous break-downs," but it is certain that most of them suffered from fear of shell-fire very acutely.

The total casualties suffered by the Division during the Battle of Messines were :

	Killed	Wounded	Missing
Officers	21	76	1
Other ranks	359	1764	82

Ypres from Railway Dugouts   December 1916.

Chapter IX.

MENIN ROAD AND WESTHOEK RIDGE.

THE Division remained only three days in the Westoutre area, and on June 13th moved back into comfortable billets round Blaringhem for rest and training after the strenuous time in the Battle of Messines. Divisional Headquarters and the 141st Infantry Brigade were quartered in Blaringhem village, the 140th Infantry Brigade at Ebblinghem, and the 142nd Infantry Brigade at Sercus.

It was a tremendous relief to be in proper billets again, with green fields round us, and not to have the continuous noise of the guns in our ears at night, and before our eyes the desolate shell-marked ground at which we had been looking for the last nine months. It was a change which all units of the Division fully appreciated, and reorganisation and training were started with a will as soon as everybody had had some much-needed sleep and been able to get rid of some of the accumulated mud of the salient. The weather was all that could be desired. Hot sun during the middle of the day, with cool mornings for work, and warm evenings for recreation of all kinds.

Musketry training was begun at St. Martin-au-Laert, and our reinforcements and men from units who had remained at the reinforcement camp during the fight were quickly absorbed. This was the first occasion on which an organised reinforcement camp was used by the Division, and the results obtained showed us the wisdom of this new arrangement.

On June 26th Divisional aquatic sports, organised by Lieut.-Colonel Galbraith, were held in the canal at Blaringhem, and were a great success. They were enjoyed not only by the members of the Division, but also by a great gathering of the local inhabitants who came from all the villages round. In fact, the Blaringhem rest area and the all too short time we spent there will always remain a pleasant memory to those who were there, and when orders were received on June 27th for the Division to start moving up to relieve the 41st Division in the area round Ridge Wood, it was with genuine regret that we quitted our hospitable billets.

The march up to the forward area was uneventful, the Division passing through Meteren and so into the salient once more. On June 29th the 142nd Infantry Brigade relieved the 124th Infantry Brigade south of the Ypres-Comines Canal, and took over roughly the ground which had been captured by the 140th Infantry Brigade on June 7th.

Many German concrete dugouts had been converted for use at unit headquarters in the captured lines, and the enemy was extremely active with his artillery all round the famous White Château. He was using quite a number of gas-shells, too, which made our stay in these trenches anything but a peaceful one. Much work remained to be done to complete the consolidation and reorganisation in depth of our newly-won position.

Patrols were active, both our own and the enemy's, and hardly a night passed without some small encounter taking place, most of which resulted in our favour and in the capture of several prisoners.

On the night of July 3rd-4th the 141st Infantry Brigade took over the line north of the Canal, and the front of the 142nd Infantry Brigade was reduced by the taking over of their right battalion front by troops of the 19th Division.

A good piece of work by a strong fighting patrol of the 7th Battalion was carried out on July 9th, which resulted in the capture of ten Germans at Forêt Farm, a fortified point in the enemy's outpost line. Our artillery put down a heavy barrage on the farm, which eventually caught fire, and Sec.-Lieutenant Goldsburg, who was in command of the patrol, took full advantage of this fact, not only to make his captures but to inflict heavy loss on the enemy as they retired.

Fighting patrols of the 6th and 8th Battalions also did very useful work in attacking enemy posts, and carrying on the principle of giving the Germans opposite to the Division no rest. One specially good minor operation was carried out by Sec.-Lieutenant Sampson and thirty men of the 6th Battalion, who, advancing very closely under an artillery barrage, completely surprised the enemy in Oblique Trench, and captured twenty-nine prisoners.

On July 25th, after just four weeks of holding the line, the Division received orders for relief by the 41st Division, and so ended a tour of duty chiefly memorable for its night patrol work, several small but very successful raids, and heavy gas-shelling of both trench and back areas by the enemy.

After being relieved by the 41st Division, we moved back only as far as the Westoutre area, as the Division was in Xth Corps reserve for eventualities in the offensive of the Second and Fifth Armies, attacking in conjunction with the French troops farther north of Ypres, which was launched on July 31st. This offensive met with considerable success, and by August 8th the Division received orders to move back into the Wizernes area for a further period of training and reorganisation.

The 140th Infantry Brigade had to be left behind, when the Division moved back, to undertake certain work on defences, and also to be in close support of the Xth Corps front in case of emergencies ; but on August 15th they were relieved from these duties, and rejoined the Division after their extra stay in the unpleasant forward areas.

On August 16th the Division was transferred from Xth Corps, Second Army, to XIth Corps, Fifth Army. This change showed us that before long we should probably be called upon to go into the line somewhere east of Ypres to take part in the Fifth Army offensive, which was still in progress, and gradually gaining ground over the waterlogged and desolate country in the neighbourhood of the Westhoek Ridge, whose acquaintance we were shortly to make.

On August 17th the Division, less Divisional Artillery, 140th Infantry Brigade, and 4th R.W.F., moved up by tactical train to the IInd Corps area, preparatory to relieving the 8th Division on the night of August 18th-19th, in the front-line defences between the Westhoek-Zonnebeke road and the Ypres-Roulers railway.

During the winter we had all seen much of Ypres on our way up to the trenches, but we were now to become more intimately acquainted with it and its wonderful ramparts, the Menin Gate, Hell Fire Corner, and many other well-known landmarks. We were also to get to know the sensation of marching up the Menin

BIRR CROSS ROADS, NEAR YPRES.

Facing page 106

.

road on a pouring wet night, with its mass of transport, its mud, and the enemy's shells trying to prevent any horse, wagon, or man arriving at his destination that night.

Gas-masks were in constant use, and everybody became an expert in the rapid adjustment of these valuable items of our kit. The journey through Ypres, too, was always a trying time for troops moving up the line, as frequent halts were necessary in the narrow street ways, and it was very seldom that some part of the poor, battered town was not being shelled. But the traffic control was most efficient, and the Military Police seemed always to be standing at their allotted corners, no matter how hot the shelling was, ready to help with all kinds of information, military and otherwise.

We found our old friends of Loos, the 15th (Highland) Division, on our left when we went into the line, and on August 15th this Division attacked with some success, and our front-line troops pushed forward posts in conjunction with their advance to the line of the Hanebeek, a small stream, which our shelling had turned into an absolute morass.

The rain was our chief enemy in these trying days, when to get off the duckboard tracks often meant sinking up to one's knees in the sodden ground. It seemed to rain every day and every night, and on the night of August 26th there was a perfect deluge, which filled every shell-hole—the ground seemed to consist of little else—with water up to the brim, and made the roads and tracks more difficult than ever.

Offensive operations under these climatic conditions were extremely trying, the deep dugouts often being inches deep in water, and anybody in possession of a concrete German pill-box was much to be envied. Derelict Tanks were to be seen in all directions, and generally the state of the forward areas was anything but pleasant.

Communications were extremely difficult, as we had no buried cable systems to rely on, and wires laid over the open were continually being cut by the enemy's shell-fire or damaged by the weather. Trenches, as such, were practically non-existent, and a series of fortified shell-holes with occasional pill-boxes acted as our defences. Practically all communication up to the front line was over the open, and in many cases under enemy observation, so that visits to the front line by day were not joy trips. Pigeons were of great use in sending back messages, and our infantry made frequent use of flares for showing their positions to our areoplanes when other means of communication failed.

On August 30th the IInd Corps, of which we formed part, was transferred to Second Army, and on September 3rd the Division was relieved in the line by the 25th Division. During this tour of duty our right was on the high ground in front of Inverness Copse, where we joined up with the 23rd Division. The enemy's observation from the vicinity of Polygon Wood and the high ground towards Hollebeke enabled him to bring accurate artillery fire to bear on any movement by day in the forward area, but the Division had advanced the front line at many points, and considerably improved our line for any troops which might have to make an attack from it. The enemy opposite to us was only holding a series of outpost positions very lightly, with the main body of his troops in rear in natural features, such as woods and small valleys, and this made it difficult for our artillery to inflict much damage on his front-line troops, as their positions were continually moving. The state of the ground, too, was greatly in the enemy's favour, and with a little wire and a few fortified shell-holes his position was not an easy one to attack except on a wide front.

On relief by the 25th Division, the 142nd Infantry Brigade moved to Steenvoorde on September 5th, and the 141st Infantry Brigade to the Busseboom area. The 140th Infantry Brigade had been in Divisional reserve in the Winnipeg Camp area, where it remained.

Brigades only remained in these areas for a very short time, for on September 8th, 9th, 10th, the 140th and 141st Infantry Brigades moved up and relieved the 25th Division, and on September 10th the G.O.C., 47th Division, assumed command of practically the same front as was held by the Division before, but under the orders of the Ist Anzac Corps, to which we had been transferred on September 5th from IInd Corps. Our main task was now to make the preparation on the front of the Anzac Corps for the offensive timed for September 20th, in which they were taking a leading part. This included the construction of several cross-country tracks in the forward area, and a road and trench railway track to Bellewarde Ridge. The heavy enemy shelling by night and their good observation by day made this extremely difficult, but the Royal Welsh Fusiliers, then under command of Lieut.-Colonel W. H. Matthews, succeeded in carrying through this work up to time by adopting the principle of spreading their men out in pairs at intervals of some twenty yards or so.   Thus they were able to work in broad daylight in an area directly under enemy observation without attracting his attention and with but few casualties.

The 142nd Infantry Brigade moved up into reserve in camps around Dickebusch.   Our orders were to keep up a continuous pressure on the enemy in the hope of inducing him gradually to give ground, and we were continually carrying out small raids at night, not only to keep up the offensive spirit of our men, but to break down the already weakening moral of the enemy.   One very successful raid was carried out by troops of the 7th Battalion, commanded by Lieutenant B. N. Cryer, against a German strong post near Inverness Copse, at dusk, on September 15th.   This enemy post was on the top of, but just over the crest of the high ground at Inverness Copse.   During previous attacks by the IInd Corps it had held out stoutly and resisted all previous attempts to capture it. It formed a small but dangerous salient into the front we took over, and from it withering fire had been brought to bear during previous attacks on our troops in their attempts to seize the high ground at Inverness Copse.   To ensure a good start for the leading waves in the next attack it was imperative for us to gain possession of it and thus straighten out our front line.

After carefully studying the ground for several nights before, by means of patrols, the raiding-party, under cover of a hurricane artillery barrage, rushed the post, killed ten of the enemy, and captured thirty-six prisoners and a machine-gun, with comparatively light casualties.   This operation earned the troops concerned the praise of the Army and Corps Commanders, who considered it a really first-class piece of work.   An enemy counter-attack against this newly-established post, which had been consolidated, was driven off early on the morning of the 16th, with heavy loss to the enemy, but the gallant Cryer, to the regret of all, was killed.   In his memory the captured post was named " Cryer Farm."

There were many other offensive incidents of this nature, some successful, others unsuccessful, but the Division advanced its line considerably during this tour in the trenches, and handed over much newly-won ground when it was relieved by troops of the 1st and 2nd Australian Divisions on September 16th to 18th.   It had been a trying time for all troops in the forward area, and it was with relief that the infantry moved back into camps in the support area, and thence to the Eecke area, for an easier spell. The artillery once more were left behind in action, and did not rejoin the Division until its rest was ended.

On September 21st the Division started entraining at Godewaersvelde, Caestre, and Cassel, for transfer to General Horne's First Army farther south, where on arrival it came under orders of the XIIIth Corps (Lieut.-General McCracken), and remained for a few days in villages round Marœuil before taking over a quiet sector of the line from the 63rd (Royal Naval) Division.

To say that the Division was sorry to leave the Ypres salient would not be true, but on leaving it could look back on many successful operations carried out, many weary months in which we held intact the front of line entrusted to our keeping, and much useful knowledge obtained as regards all branches of a soldier's training. We considered ourselves experts at all kinds of drainage systems, even to making liquid mud and water run up hill, apparently, under the careful and never-failing instruction of the Divisional Commander.

That the services of the troops of the Division were appreciated, not only by our own Commander, but by the Army and Corps Commanders under whom we served in the salient, is testified by the following order issued on September 22nd, as we were about to quit the Second Army :

The following extracts from letters received by the Divisional Commander from General Sir Herbert C. O. Plumer, G.C.M.G., G.C.V.O., K.C.B., A.D.C., Commanding Second Army, and from Lieut.-General Sir W. R. Birdwood, K.C.B., K.C.S.I., K.C.M.G., C.I.E., D.S.O., Commanding 1st Anzac Corps, are forwarded for information and communication to all concerned :

1. *From General Sir Herbert C. O. Plumer, G.C.M.G., G.C.V.O., K.C.B., A.D.C.*

" Before your Division leaves the Second Army I should like to express to you, and to ask you to convey to all Commanders and Staff, my appreciation of the excellent work the Division has done and of the way in which they have carried out all the duties assigned to them.

" They have taken part in a highly creditable manner in an important offensive operation, they have carried out some successful raids, and have throughout the whole period maintained their positions efficiently.

" I am sure they will do well wherever they may be sent, and I wish you all the best of luck."

2. *From Lieut.-General Sir W. R. Birdwood, K.C.B., K.C.S.I., K.C.M.G., C.I.E., D.S.O.*

" I must write, however, to thank you again so very much for all the real cordial and great help which you have given us while your Division has been with me. All my people have recognised this so very fully, and we are one and all most grateful to you for it. If you will let your Brigadiers and Regiments know this, and how gladly we shall welcome the opportunity of having the 47th Division with us again one of these days, I shall be grateful.

" I went round this morning to see what I could as to how things were going on, and was delighted to see the real progress which has been made in every direction."

The Divisional Commander, in publishing the above, desires to express to all under his command his grateful thanks for the loyal help and support which he has at all times received from them, and his high appreciation of their gallantry and devotion to duty since taking over command of this Division.

One and all have carried out the duties with which he has entrusted them in a highly creditable and soldierly manner.

He congratulates them most sincerely on the splendid record and successes which they have achieved, both in the various operations and in the different branches of work, no matter how difficult or dangerous, which they have so devotedly carried out during the past eleven months in the Ypres salient—a record of which they may indeed well feel proud.

(Signed) S. THUNDER, Lieut.-Colonel,
September 22nd, 1917. A.A. & Q.M.G., 47th (London) Division.

St Pierre Church _ Ypres _ Jan 1917

Chapter X.

OPPY AND GAVRELLE.

THE hope indulged in for many a past month of a change of scenery from the dreary wastes of Flanders, and the dream of rest billets which might justify their name in back areas which enemy aeroplanes would not bomb every night without respite, of trenches which were not merely connected shell craters, and of villages which, though evacuated by their inhabitants, might still bear some resemblance to the normal haunts of men, were at last to be realised.

It was a cheery Division that detrained in the vicinity of Marœuil, near Arras, and relieved the 63rd (R.N.) Division (including the 28th London Regiment—the Artists Rifles—old comrades of the 2nd London Division) on the Gavrelle-Oppy front, with headquarters at Victory Camp, Ecurie. Up till a short time previously the XIIIth Corps front had been an uncommonly active one, but at the end of September, 1917, all was quiet, and, with a view to providing the maximum of comfort and health for man and beast during the coming winter, both in the line and back areas, a scheme of work was initiated under Corps instructions, and was forthwith put into operation. The trench system taken over by the Division was an extensive one. Dug deep in the rich loam some distance down the forward slope, it required an enormous amount of labour for its maintenance in winter.

The system adopted in the line was that of a series of defended localities, strong posts from half a mile to three-quarters of a mile apart, garrisoned at first by platoons, and intended when finished to be garrisoned by companies. The gaps in the line of posts were covered by artillery and machine-gun fire from the rear. Orders were issued that no attempt should be made to maintain lateral communicating trenches between these posts, the necessary labour

Photo by]   [*Lambert Weston.*

MAJOR-GENERAL G. J. CUTHBERT, C.B., C.M.G.
Commanding 140th Infantry Brigade, 1914-1916.

and material not being available. About half a mile in rear of the posts ran the line built by our predecessors, and known as the Naval and Marine Trenches, while behind that again lay the Red Line. In rear of this rose a prominent ridge behind Bailleul village, which made it possible for our forward areas and the enemy trenches to be under complete observation.

While this system of forward posts certainly enabled work to be concentrated with a gain in time, labour, and material, it had the disadvantage of affording a series of admirable targets to the enemy artillery and trench-mortars, especially in the case of those posts situated on commanding and consequently relatively high ground, as, for instance, Mill Post, or those forming a distinct salient in the line of posts, as, for instance, Bradford Post. This system was no doubt only intended to be employed during the winter months, a modern version of the old-time " winter quarters," and as such it possessed not only the advantage of economy of forces already referred to, but had the added advantage of practising all ranks in the infantry units in constant patrolling in the open or semi-open between the posts.*

In the back areas much useful work was carried out by the construction of drainage schemes, the erection of cook-houses, the improvement of huts used for billets and the building of horse standings, but, as was almost invariably the case during the whole war, all work done was on the point of completion just in time to be enjoyed by our successors, for the Division appeared ever to be fated to move on before enjoying the fruits of its labours.

Although all ranks set to work at once with the determination to get on with the job, progress, except in the back areas, was slow, owing to the constant retaliation to our shelling, the bad weather, and dark nights, which made working-parties in the line of small avail ; the most useful work was done by the actual trench garrisons. The enemy artillery were peaceably inclined during the early weeks of the Divisional tour, but when our Divisional Artillery came into the line, after having stayed on in the Ypres salient for a short

---

*These posts were, unfortunately, held by the British garrison in March, 1918, at the outbreak of the German offensive, when they were simply treated as bullseye targets and received specially accurate fire, the entire garrisons being put out of action. (See " History of the London Rifle Brigade," page 226.) This confirmed the fear of the critics at the time of their construction, that when the " winter garden " period was reaching an end, the opportunity would be lacking to construct a fresh system of defences capable of resisting a possible attack by the enemy.

K

time, they began to " strafe " the enemy on every possible occasion with their usual promptitude.

Not since the Division had left Vimy Ridge, when the observation from Notre Dame de Lorette rendered it possible to initiate retaliation under almost ideal conditions, had there been such opportunities for artillery and infantry co-operation ; it was again possible to economise the time taken by artillery liaison officers with infantry units in sending back reports, batteries frequently being able to retaliate when necessary on enemy trench-mortar emplacements almost before the enemy bombs hit the British lines. The infantry of the Division always held the opinion that whenever their own artillery supported them, liaison was as complete as possible, and invariably supported the tendency of the Divisional Artillery to make the war as unpleasant as possible for the enemy, even though the penalty of retaliation (prompt or deferred) was the inevitable consequence. How frequently were requests sent to artillery for retaliation when in fact the enemy's fire was actually retaliation for that of our own gunners.

There was never any intention, however, on the part of the Division to give the enemy a rest, and as soon as our own artillery took over they started wire-cutting, to enable a series of raids to be carried out in conjunction with similar or larger enterprises on other fronts. The enemy was well wired in ; the artillery gave necessary attention to that matter. The British lines were also well wired in, so much so, indeed, that in some sub-sectors infantry battalions were under the necessity of cutting lanes through their own wire during their first tour in the line so as to furnish an exit to their patrols. A novelty at this time was the supply of smoke and incendiary shell to field-guns. The former gave promise of most useful results, but the latter, though wonderful to look at on a dark night and warranted " to set fire to a trench-board under a foot of water," were of more doubtful effect, and were later little used.

The first organised " hate " in this sector took the form of a discharge of 710 gas projectors into Oppy village on October 11th at 3 a.m., shortly after, or perhaps during, a relief by the enemy division opposing us. Apart from minor patrol engagements, our first raid was carried out by a party of the 17th Battalion London Regiment at 3.30 a.m. on October 18th north of the Arras-Gavrelle road.

Bailleul and Field Artillery Camp from Mont Noir . September 1917.

Frequent raids by divisions on the flanks during the ensuing fortnight, further gas projections, the activity of our patrols and the policy of constant annoyance to the enemy had some visible effects, for desertions from the enemy became more frequent, showing that his moral was becoming affected to some extent.

The chief event of the Divisional tour on this front took place on the afternoon of November 4th, in the form of a combined raid over a flagged course on a frontage of about 1,000 yards and a depth of about 500 yards immediately south of the Arras-Gavrelle road by two companies each of the 23rd Battalion London Regiment (Major T. C. Hargreaves, D.S.O.) and the 24th Battalion London Regiment (The Queen's) (Lieut.-Colonel G. E. Millner, D.S.O.). In all about 500 of all ranks were engaged, including attached R.E., with explosives for demolitions, specially trained for the purpose by Major S. G. Love, D.S.O., R.E.

The raiding companies moved out of the line four days before the attack to train for the event at St. Aubin. The remaining companies took over the line as a composite battalion under the command of Major T. O. Bury, 4th R.W.F., and made all the necessary preparations on which success must largely depend, including continuous Lewis-gun fire on the gaps made by the artillery in the enemy's wire, in the course of reported practice barrages, cutting twenty-four gaps in our own wire, labelling these, fixing guiding marks and making steps in the fire bays. Similar tactics were carried out by the other divisions on the flanks, so as to keep the enemy guessing.

Before the event every officer and man had patrolled No Man's Land, so as to become familiar with the ground.

At 4.30 p.m. every man was in his assembly position when rockets of every description were sent up on the whole Corps front. This so puzzled the enemy that his barrage was dispersed, spasmodic and ineffective. Our artillery barrage was excellent, so accurate, indeed, that our men were at one time unable to get at the fleeing enemy. Major F. G. Stapley, R.F.A., was actually in the line and afforded invaluable assistance throughout the operations. Triplicated wires running by alternative routes enabled communication between each of the raiding companies and advanced battalion headquarters and thence to brigade headquarters to be maintained uninterrupted.

THE MILL, GAVRELLE.

The enemy front-line was carried within five minutes of zero hour, and his support-line five minutes after that. The enemy was overwhelmed and offered little resistance. The garrison, including a large working-party, probably numbered about 150 or 200 men. Of these over 100 were killed, and fifteen, belonging to the 459th Infantry Regiment, 236th Division, were captured, along with four heavy machine-guns, a number of light machine-guns, and two trench-mortars. In the half-hour that the raiders spent in the German trenches over nine dugouts were destroyed or set on fire (in some cases with their garrisons, who would not come out of them) together with numerous stores and ammunition. One man accounted for nine of the enemy single-handed ; one officer for four or five. The small number of prisoners captured, as compared with the number of enemy killed, is explained by the receipt of news shortly before the raid that some enemy bombing aeroplanes flying over South London had killed the relatives of some of the men. In fact, a notice-board was left in the raided area : " We'll teach you to bomb London." Our casualties were very slight : 23rd London, 9 other ranks killed and 32 wounded (including one officer) ; 24th London, 2 other ranks killed and 10 wounded (including 2 officers).

Everybody was very much pleased with everybody else, including the Army, Corps, Division, and Brigade commanders. General Horne himself attended a special parade of the units who carried out the raid and specially praised their work, as well as that of the staff of the 142nd Infantry Brigade, under Brigadier-General Bailey, who were responsible for the preparations.

The much-discussed " winter post scheme " came into full operation on November 19th, by which date orders had been received for relief by the 31st Division and concentration in the Aubigny area. Our destination was the XVIIth Corps, Third Army, and active operations on the Cambrai front, where General Byng launched his attack with Tanks on November 20th, were the magnet to which we were being drawn.

" Bedford House ", Ypres , 1917.

Chapter XI.

BOURLON WOOD.

"TOO good to last!" There spoke the cheerful pessimism of the "other ranks" when they heard that another move was imminent. For we had begun to assume a certain permanence in our positions on the Oppy front, and to regard them as affording the promise of a quiet winter broken only by a merry Christmas.

But by the beginning of November the field-kitchen, most fertile handmaid of rumour, was busy with strange stories of a journey to the far south. The censor was troubled with letters that made indiscreet reference to ice-cream and barrel-organs. The wise men, with whom the instinct of prophecy never dies, spoke of our transference to the Italian front as a matter of certainty.

Speculation was rife not so much as to our share in the tactical operations to be undertaken there, but rather as to the amount of transport available, the chance of good billets, and the opportunity for leave. For a few days every thought was of Italy. But soon the news of the retreat of the Italian Army was balanced by that of a great advance on the Cambrai front, and we began to realise that we might be destined for battle in a far less distant field.

On November 19th the 31st Division, who had been holding the line on our left, threw in their reserve brigade to take over our front trenches, while the positions in rear were occupied by troops of the 21st Division, returning from the Ypres Salient. We said good-bye with some regret to the security of the sunken road, to the wooden cities that were growing by the side of the Arras-Lens Road, to the gay haunts of Amiens, and the sixty-five estaminets at Marœuil. For the next ten days we travelled in a semi-circle, north-west and west and south-west of Arras, until, on November 25th, we crossed the Bapaume-Peronne Road, and then moved due east towards the new battlefield. During this time Captain J. C. D. Carlisle (whose advancement had been rapid and well deserved) was appointed G.S.O.2 of the Division.

The movement of the division was not an easy one for the officers or men. In order to become mobile, the transport of every unit had to be lightened. Surplus stores were dumped at Acq—so generously that twenty-two lorries were subsequently employed in removing them to Albert. Cherished plans for Christmas which had involved the purchase of pigs and geese, the erection of a soda-water factory, the assembling of all luxuries which had become necessaries at this time, were all recast by this sudden turn of destiny. Valises were reduced in many cases to 35 lbs., spare suits of khaki, and football boots rooted from old hiding-places on the limber ; comfort gave way to mobility.

For a week the Division moved almost daily. Motor-omnibuses were only once available, and then but for one brigade ; the roads were congested with other troops and transport moving in and out of the battle. As a result the men marched long distances and suffered many hardships. The weather was intensely cold, and the billets where units rested for the night were not always proof against the rain and sleet. For many this was the first glimpse of the country which the enemy had devastated before his retirement in the previous winter. We had seen the indiscriminate wreckage which the fury of the Somme battle had wrought upon woods and grassy slopes ; we had endured the clammy mud of the Ypres Salient, where country that could never have been very beautiful was furrowed with trenches, pitted with shell holes, and fouled by the devil's embroidery of barbed wire. But here we faced a new order of desolation, complete and organised.

Village after village had been wrecked in order that the country might not be habitable for the troops that followed the retreating enemy. The ground was barren, the only landmark a ruin rather larger than the others.

In all these facts there was something to depress the soldier
as well as to fatigue his body.   But the spirit of the men
prevailed.   The Territorial is a soldier by choice, but not by
taste.   He does not like war, and the ways of the Army
are not to his fancy.   But the Londoner finds an inconsequent
happiness in the trifles and details of life, extorting comedy
from a rissole and farce from a "little black hat," so that
for the greater part of his day he forgets he is in the Army.

Thus it fell out that though the call to battle was sudden,
and the way to it not an easy one, all ranks entered the
field with brave and determined spirit.   Football was played
on the dry ground by Barastre when three days' hard marching
lay behind them and action faced them on the morrow.

The Division left the XIIIth Corps and First Army on November
22nd, and were posted to the XVIIth Corps in the Third Army
for two days.   They then passed to the IVth Corps for three days,
and on November 27th came under orders of the Vth Corps, who
were responsible for the operations in Bourlon Wood.   The position
here was extremely critical.

In order to make the situation clearer it is necessary to go back
a little and trace the events which produced the first battle of
Cambrai.

In the spring of 1917 the Germans found their position on the
Somme untenable in view of the successes gained by us in the
summer of 1916, and they retired to their newly-constructed
Hindenburg Line, methodically blowing-up every building and
cutting down every fruit-tree in the country they abandoned.

No cultivation had gone on in this devastated area for the past
two years, and the country now looked like open chalk downs
covered with rough grass.

The Hindenburg Line had been laid out with the greatest of care
to utilise all commanding ground, and had been most elaborately
fortified with deep dugouts, belts of wire many yards thick, and
well-built gun-pits, but in leaving the large Havrincourt Wood,
whose front edge was within 1,000 yards of their line, the enemy
gave us the chance of collecting a large force completely concealed
from observation.

In the spring of 1917 our troops, following up the retiring
enemy, found themselves up against this heavily-wired and

continuous line of entrenchments which comprised all the high ground west of Cambrai.

After pushing back the enemy into his trench line, little was done all the summer beyond making certain preliminary arrangements of light railways and roads suitable for an attack on a large scale. The sector from Mœuvres, where the Drocourt-Queant switch-line joined the Hindenburg Line through Havrincourt, Trescault, Gonnelieu, and Honnecourt, was left particularly quiet, and the enemy's whole attention was devoted to the Ypres salient, where battle raged incessantly after July 31st.

Suddenly, on November 20th, without the slightest warning or sign of preparation, we opened an attack on the Hindenburg Line between Hermies and Gonnelieu, supported by an immense mass of tanks which swept through all the belts of wire and over trenches twelve feet deep, so that at the end of the four days we had formed a great salient four miles in depth, reaching to the old Canal de l'Escaut at Marcoing and spreading northwards along the ridge of Bourlon Wood and southwards along the ridge which runs from Bois Lateau to Gonnelieu and looks steeply down to the canal about Banteux.

This newly-won territory is characterised on the north by the wide valley between Flesquières and Bourlon Wood, but on the south is divided into much narrower and steeper valleys separated by high ridges like the fingers of an outstretched hand pointing towards Cambrai. Gonnelieu and the Bois Lateau crown the most easterly ridge, La Vacquerie the next, which we afterwards called Welsh Ridge, with Gouzeaucourt and Villers Plouich lying in the valley to the west of it; then came Highland Ridge, with Beaucamp behind it, and most westerly of all the ridge from Queen's Cross to Trescault, behind which lay Gouzeaucourt Wood and the ruined village of Metz-en-Couture, a place of great importance, as all the roads into the salient passed through it.

The enemy had lost valuable ground in Bourlon Wood and village. Its retention by us threatened his line to the north, enabling us to observe and enfilade his trenches as far as Oppy and Gavrelle. From the high ground at Bourlon Wood, too, we had excellent observation of Cambrai and the intervening country, as well as of that to the north towards Douai.

In consequence, attack and counter-attack had followed each other almost without cessation for a week, the village changing hands each day. The casualties on both sides had been heavy ; the issue still hung in the balance.

When the Division took over the Bourlon Wood Sector at 10 a.m. on November 29th, the greater part of the wood was still in our hands, the British line running from west to east a mile to the north of the Bapaume-Cambrai Road. We relieved the 62nd Division on the night of November 28th-29th, the three dismounted regiments of cavalry, who were reinforcing them, remaining with us for twenty-four hours.

This relief was not carried out without considerable difficulty, owing to heavy shelling by the enemy, who continually barraged all approaches to Bourlon Wood. The guides were late, but the relieving battalions, led by Lieut.-Colonel Mildren, commanding the 6th Battalion, pushed on without waiting for them and completed the relief at the cost of several casualties.

The 141st Brigade took the right sub-sector, with the 140th Brigade on the left, and the 142nd in reserve in the Hindenburg Line. The 62nd Division, acting under orders from the Corps, insisted on the whole of the 141st Brigade being sent into Bourlon Wood to relieve their brigade. In protest against this Major-General Gorringe urged that to crowd seven battalions (four of 141st Brigade, one of 140th Brigade, and two of dismounted cavalry) and forty-seven machine-guns into the wood, which already contained one battalion of the 59th Division on the right, would only invite excessive casualties without increasing the adequacy of the defence. For a wood in modern warfare is more safely held by rifle and Lewis gun posts, suitably placed on the forward edge of the area under some sort of cover, and machine-guns in depth outside the wood, with a fair field for fire and observation, than by a mass of units struggling in the undergrowth, half-blinded by the gas that clings to every bush.

The protest was overridden, and on the night of November 28th-29th seven battalions were all in position in the wood. The enemy bombarded heavily with gas-shells during the night, and the 141st Brigade suffered many casualties. On the following morning the command of the sector passed to

our Division, whose advanced Headquarters were in Havrincourt
Château, and steps were taken to thin out the troops in Bourlon
Wood so that, by the 30th, only four battalions remained
there (one of the 140th Brigade and three of the 141st
Brigade), with twenty machine-guns, the remainder being sited
in depth, in positions whence they could bring effective direct
fire on the ground on our left and on both flanks of
Bourlon Wood.

The disposition of the battalions on November 30th will be
observed in Map VII, the second position of the 20th Battalion
being that taken up on the reduction of the garrison in the
wood. The 7th Battalion was lent to the 2nd Division on
our left in order to help them to hold their line. Later
in the day it was recalled to the assistance of its own brigade,
and the 23rd Battalion took its place near the canal, and
held the front line for a few hours.

The artillery covering the front held by the 47th Division consisted
of the 62nd Divisional Artillery and the 40th Divisional Artillery,
and the batteries were all well forward on the ground between
Havrincourt and Graincourt. The positions were more suitable
to the continuance of the attack than to defence, and if the enemy
had been successful in capturing the ridge on which Bourlon Wood
stands, and establishing observation posts, the situation of the
artillery would have been precarious, as all the gun positions would
have been overlooked.

Command of the artillery covering the Division passed at
noon on November 30th to the C.R.A., 47th Division.

On the right of the 47th Division the line was held by the 59th
(North Midland) Division, commanded by Major-General C. F.
Romer, and on our left was the 2nd Division, commanded by Major-
General C. E. Pereira.

The 56th (London) Division, which lay beyond the 2nd, was, like
the 47th, composed almost entirely of London Territorials. It was
formed from the 1st London Territorial Division and included
our three battalions—the 13th (Kensingtons), the 14th (London
Scottish), and the 16th (Queen's Westminsters)—which had preceded
the 2nd London Division to France, while we had the 6th (City of
London Rifles), 7th (Royal Fusiliers), and 8th (Post Office Rifles)
which had joined us at St. Albans from the 1st London Division.

On the morning of Friday, November 30th, the enemy made a counter-attack in force, directed chiefly against the haunches of the new salient, and he renewed his efforts to recapture the wood. Our troops found themselves in circumstances peculiarly unfavourable for defence. The trenches, when taken over, were barely 4 ft. deep ; there was no wire, and few tools. In the sector held by the 24th Battalion there were no trenches at all. The support trenches were not continuous ; the trees obscured the situation ; the gas hung in the thick undergrowth. Efforts had been made during the twenty-four hours of our occupation to get wire set out in front, and the trenches fire-stepped and dug to 6 ft. in depth. The enemy had shelled heavily during the night, but the guns rested before dawn, breaking out again about 8.30 a.m. into a heavy bombardment of our lines from Mœuvres, in the west, to Fontaine Notre Dame, in the east. Meanwhile, Bourlon Wood was treated to an intense gas-shell bombardment.

Our artillery replied with equal violence of fire, and the duel continued till ten o'clock, when the enemy were observed to be advancing in two waves over the crest of the hill 2,000 yards to the east of Mœuvres. At the same time the enemy was occupying the village of Mœuvres and threatening the exposed left flank of the 6th Battalion. Three hostile balloons were seen in position over Bourlon village throughout the day, and aeroplanes flew unchecked along our lines directing the fire of the enemy upon our positions. The front line of the battalions on the left was continuously harassed by the enfilading fire of a field-gun from Bourlon village on the right, and a small man-handled gun on the left.

Heavy casualties resulted among the defending troops. The enemy continued to advance in waves from Quarry Wood in a southerly direction, but their advance was checked for a while by the accurate fire of our artillery and machine-guns. The latter were arranged in batteries of four, thus facilitating control, and giving a heavy volume of fire with a maximum of surprise. The enemy advancing were thus enfiladed from positions north of the sugar factory, and the attack driven westward. Soon after midday the enemy were seen retreating in disorder over the crest of the hill. It was agreed by all observers of this stage of the battle that it was the disposition of our machine-guns which saved our line.   The two batteries on the left of Bourlon Wood fired westward and enfiladed the advancing enemy, while the frontal fire of the three batteries near the sugar factory, and a fourth battery on the left, caught each wave as it appeared over the crest of the hill.

About 2 p.m. the enemy assaulted again after a heavy bombardment of our lines on the west of Bourlon Wood.   The right flank of the 2nd Division, on the left of our 6th Battalion, gave ground at the same time, and the enemy drove in a wedge between our left flank and the right of the 2nd Division.

A gap formed between the 6th Battalion and the 15th Battalion, and the enemy forced our left flank to a position a few hundred yards in rear.   Lieut.-Colonel Mildren, commanding the 6th Battalion, thereupon counter-attacked with his reserve company, reinforced by all the runners, signallers, and orderlies at Battalion Headquarters, and restored the line.

At 5 p.m. another counter-attack was made by two companies of the 8th Battalion, together with the remnant of the 6th Battalion, and a line was established on higher ground, which was held without incident that night.   The 15th Battalion had, however, been forced to yield a little ground.   Lieut.-Colonel Segrave formed up A Company, reinforced it with all his headquarters personnel, and led a counter-attack, regaining a considerable part of the lost ground.   When dusk came communication with the troops on the left was re-established, and a quiet night ensued.

Meanwhile, attacks against the 141st Brigade on the right were launched by the enemy, but were broken up before they reached our trenches by our Lewis gun and rifle fire, supported by the artillery and machine-guns.   The hostile bombardment which preceded them was very severe, and the 19th Battalion suffered many casualties from gas, their strength being ultimately reduced to 9 officers and 61 other ranks.[*]

---

[*] " During the afternoon a strong hostile attack was made upon the 141st Brigade, on the right of the 47th Division.   For some days the German artillery had been steadily pouring gas shell into Bourlon Wood, until the thick undergrowth was full of gas.   Many casualties were caused to our troops, and gas masks had to be worn continuously for many hours.   None the less, when the enemy attacked, he was again hurled back with heavy loss.   A distinctive feature of the defence was the gallantry of the Lewis gunners, who, when the attack was seen to be beginning, ran out with the guns in front of our line, and from positions of advantage in the open mowed down the advancing German infantry."—From " The Story of a Great Fight," issued by the General Staff, February, 1918.

While our troops were holding Bourlon Wood against such odds, the enemy had broken through to the south of us and captured the village of Gouzeaucourt. They approached at one time to within a mile of our refilling point, east of Metz-en-Couture. The Divisional Train received orders to cease issuing supplies and to withdraw to Neuville Bourjonval, where Rear Divisional Headquarters were established. Advanced Divisional Headquarters were in Havrincourt Park.

Meanwhile, the 235th Brigade, R.F.A., which was about to come into action on our divisional front, was diverted and sent to the south of Havrincourt Wood to support a counter-attack on the part of the Guards Division.* Although the Guards had only recently come out of action, after experiencing severe casualties, this sudden counter-attack was brilliantly successful, and the village was retaken. The Guards expressed their warmest appreciation of the promptness with which our gunners had come into action from the line of march, and for the accuracy of their fire on points which they had had no chance to register beforehand.

It was a hard day for the 47th Division. More than eighteen months had passed since we had been on our defence. We were fighting in unknown country which we had had little opportunity to reconnoitre, and communications were extremely difficult, the S.O.S. being at times the only signal that did not fail. Our casualties were heavy :

              6th Battalion .. 13 officers and   369 other ranks.
             15th Battalion .. 11   ,,   ,,   288   ,,   ,,
            141st Brigade .. 69   ,,   ,, 1,939   ,,   ,,

It was subsequently ascertained from prisoners that the enemy had intended to attack simultaneously from the north and from the east, and so drive us from the Bourlon Salient. In some quarters it was maintained that the main attack was the one from the north which our troops faced, and that the attack from the east, though more successful on the issue, was originally intended as a feint to distract our troops from the main operation in Bourlon Wood. Whatever the relative strength and importance of the two attacks may have been, the one from the east did not meet with

---

* The work of the Artillery in these operations is described on pages 137 to 141.

so stout a resistance, and the enemy advanced as far as Gouzeaucourt very quickly, capturing men and guns in large numbers, and menacing our communications in the rear.

But the honour of the London troops was worthily upheld. Ground was only yielded under extreme pressure, counter-attacks were immediate, determined, and successful. Those who suffered from the intense fire and the suffocating gas will look back upon the day with horror not unmixed with pride.

In thanking the 47th Division for the " magnificent defence of the important position entrusted to them," Sir Douglas Haig wrote :—

Though exposed throughout the day to the repeated assaults of superior forces, they beat off all attacks with the heaviest losses to the enemy, and by their gallant and steady conduct contributed very largely to the security of the Divisions engaged on the whole front of attack.

The line on the north and north-west of Bourlon Wood could not be regarded as a permanent position. There was higher ground in front of us still to be regained. From defence we must turn to attack.

The 140th Brigade was ordered to retake the original line held before the attack on November 30th. Two companies of the 8th Battalion on the right, and two companies of the 7th Battalion on the left, advanced at 8.10 p.m. on the evening of December 2nd under cover of artillery fire. Simultaneously the 2nd Division on our left advanced their right flank. The 7th Battalion experienced some opposition in the form of heavy machine-gun fire, and sustained heavy casualties. The 8th Battalion were more fortunate, encountering no organised line of enemy resistance, but fighting with small parties in shell holes. Both battalions reached their objectives, consolidated, and held them, thus restoring the line as first taken over by the Division. In this advance of 300 to 400 yards, 52 prisoners and 18 machine-guns were taken. Officially described as a " minor operation," colloquially dismissed as " a good show," it was in reality an effort at a time when troops were tired, which reflected great credit and produced valuable results.*

---

* The following message from the Army Commander, dated December 3rd, 1917, was forwarded by Lieut.-General Fanshawe the same day :

G.O.C., V. A.C.

Will you please convey to the G.O.C., 47th Division, my very best congratulations on their excellent achievement last night.

This operation was of the greatest value to the situation and reflects the greatest credit on those who carried it out.   J. BYNG (General).

BOURLON : SUGAR REFINERY ON BAPAUME-CAMBRAI ROAD.

BOURLON WOOD FROM THE SOUTH-WEST.

The third task of the Division was the evacuation of Bourlon Wood and the withdrawal to the Hindenburg Line. This is not the place in which to discuss at any length the reasons which caused the higher command to favour a withdrawal. It is, however, obvious from a study of the map (see Map VII) that our retention of the southern half of Bourlon Wood was likely to prove a very uncertain and expensive proposition. The Hindenburg trenches running north and south, and facing the enemy, offered a far better line of permanent resistance for the winter. A withdrawal from one position to another, however obvious the advantages it may offer, demands two necessary factors—a considerable amount of detailed staff work, and a very real confidence in the moral of the men.

It was decided that our Division should withdraw, with the 2nd Division on our left, and the 59th Division on our right during the night of December 4th-5th from the wood to the Hindenburg support line, a total distance of nearly 5,000 yards. The 142nd Brigade had taken over the Bourlon Wood Sector on December 3rd, so upon them fell the main burden of withdrawal. To the 140th Brigade was allotted the task of providing an outpost line between Graincourt and La Justice, which was to be held for twenty-four hours in order to cover the withdrawal of the 142nd Brigade and to allow them time for the consolidation of their new positions.

The 4th R.W.F. were responsible for establishing and garrisoning four strong posts in front of the Hindenburg Line at places marked " S.P." on the map. A brigade of the 62nd Division came forward and held this section of the Hindenburg Line while our troops were retiring from the wood, as a precautionary measure against any attempt of the enemy, should they learn of our withdrawal beforehand, to hasten its progress. The withdrawal involved the moving back of all the batteries behind the Havrincourt-Flesquières ridge, and this was carried out successfully on the night of December 4th. As soon as the withdrawal was completed, the 40th Divisional Artillery was relieved by the 77th Army Brigade, R.F.A. The 62nd Divisional Artillery was not relieved by our own gunners until December 11th.

At 11 p.m. on the 4th, the battalions of the 142nd Brigade began to withdraw, leaving in each case two or four platoons to hold

L

an outpost line through the wood. They reached their new position in the Hindenburg Line without incident, the enemy apparently having no idea that we were in process of withdrawal. The platoons left behind in the wood fired Verey lights and rifles at normal intervals, and assisted a body of Royal Engineers in the destruction of dugouts, derelict tanks, and useful material which could not be carried back. Signallers recovered the cables as far as possible, and elsewhere cut them and insulated the ends, to hinder their use for overhearing.

So far as time allowed, contrivances to delay and injure the enemy in his re-occupation of the wood were set in position, and trip-wires hidden in the undergrowth. At 4 a.m. these small bodies of infantry evacuated the wood and rejoined their units in the new line without loss. The last to quit the wood were the Engineers, who destroyed such of the enemy guns as had not been salved, and rendered uninhabitable the catacombs in Graincourt.

More would have been done in the way of destruction if greater notice could have been given. But the Division only received orders to evacuate on the morning of December 4th, and the orders only reached battalions at 4 p.m. on the same day for a withdrawal to be effected seven hours later.

Throughout November 30th and the following days our field ambulances carried out the evacuation of the wounded under great difficulties, but with unwearying gallantry and marked success. The 4th Royal Welsh Fusiliers especially distinguished themselves by carrying up ammunition through the gas-infected area, working hard all night in improving the line and carrying back all wounded who remained in the aid-posts and advanced dressing-stations in Bourlon Wood at dawn.

By 4.30 a.m. there were no British troops left in the wood. Before 10 a.m. it was again occupied by the enemy. At dawn on December 5th the 142nd Brigade were holding the main line, the R.W.F. occupying the four strong points 1,000 yards in front of them, while the 15th Battalion held covering positions to the west and east of Graincourt. The strong points were to be a permanent feature of the defence, but the positions of the 15th Battalion were only temporary, and the order for their evacuation was received on the night of December 5th-6th.

The 15th Battalion was only 200 strong at this time, and still suffering from the effects of gas poisoning, but inasmuch as the 141st Brigade was practically out of action, and the 140th Brigade seriously weakened, they were the only troops available for the holding of the Graincourt-La Justice Line. They were insufficient to garrison the village of Graincourt, as well as the high ground on both sides of it, and were therefore posted on the higher ground to cover the flanks of neighbouring divisions.   A and B Companies, on the left of the village, received the order to retire and did so at 5.30 p.m.   During the day the enemy had made several attempts to enter Graincourt, but they were beaten back by machine-gun fire, and our positions on the left were maintained.   A certain number of Germans did filter through to the village, which was then bombarded by our guns with good effect.

On the right, however, the position grew more serious as the day advanced.

At dawn on the 5th, Sec.-Lieutenant Aylmore had taken a Lewis gun and team to a position marked "L.G." on the map, to cover the withdrawal of C and D Companies.   Unfortunately, before the order to withdraw reached the companies, the outposts of the division on our right had been driven back, and the enemy began to envelope the right of the 15th Battalion. They had received a warning order beforehand that if after the night of December 5th-6th it was impossible to hold their position, they were to withdraw to the southernmost of the four strong points.   When the enemy faced them in front and rear they cut their way through with great spirit, Sec.-Lieutenant Lacey giving the order "make for the sun."

It was now about 4 p.m., and the sun guided them at length to the strong point.   But before they reached there they fought hard against an enemy that pressed on all sides at once. Sec.-Lieutenant Lacey was brought in wounded. Sec.-Lieut. King was last seen tending a wounded sergeant. He and Major Warne, Captain Burtt, Sec.-Lieutenant Potts, and Sec.-Lieutenant Houslop were all fighting in the rear of the withdrawal, and were captured by the enemy.   Sec.-Lieutenant Chambers, of the 140th Machine-gun Company, and his team were also wounded and captured after doing brave work with their gun.

It had been impossible to communicate what was happening to Sec.-Lieutenant Aylmore and his gun team in their isolated position. They also had been surrounded by a force of 150 to 200 Germans.   After firing the gun for some time they were enveloped and compelled to retire.   On their way they encountered several parties of the enemy and used their one gun with effect.   They surprised some of the enemy in the act of digging, and fired on them.   The Germans attacked with shovels and wounded one of the team in the back.   On they went, an officer, three men, a wounded man, and a gun, fighting all the way, arriving at last at the same strong point.

So ended the withdrawal, the last stage being as full of daring and incident as anything in the whole chapter of the Cambrai battle.   The 15th Battalion suffered heavily, but they could recall no episode in France or Belgium so full of fire and spirit as this refusal of their troops on the outpost line to surrender to an enemy that had already surrounded them.

The four strong posts were handed over by the R.W.F. to parties of the 142nd Brigade on December 5th, and were held without incident till the 9th.   On the early morning of that day the enemy made a determined attack on Post No. 2 (*vide* Map VII), which was garrisoned by Captain A. W. Durrant (23rd London) and ninety men.   The enemy assembled 400 strong in a trench 200 yards in front of our post, and soon after 7 a.m. attacked across the open.   They were beaten off by rifle fire.   Other tactics were tried.   Taking advantage of cover offered by the sunken road and disused trenches, they bombed their way forward and gained a footing in the south of the post.   The garrison countered and drove them out, re-establishing their communication with the 21st Battalion on the right by 8.30 a.m.

But at 9 a.m. the enemy again succeeded in bombing their way into the post, this time bringing a light machine-gun with them.   A wedge was driven into the small garrison, and Captain Durrant was left with only thirty men in the centre of the post, the remainder of his company being forced to join the 21st Battalion on their right.   The machine-gun prevented the arrival of reinforcements ; the S.O.S. signal received no answer.   At 11 a.m. an attempt was made by the enemy to reach the centre of the post.   Captain Durrant

shortened his line, concentrated his thirty men, and held up
the attack. Two hours later the 21st Battalion counter-
attacked, but insufficiency of troops and the hostile machine-
guns rendered the effort fruitless. The artillery behind us
began to bombard the post, and Captain Durrant was compelled
to retire. He and his little force crawled back under the
wire and, by dusk, were in the comparative safety of our
trenches. His pluck in holding to his post so long, and his
judgment in retiring at the last possible moment, were subsequently marked by conferring on him the D.S.O.

These three phases of our share in the Battle of Cambrai—
a stout defence, a successful attack, and a skilful withdrawal—
formed a complete test of the powers and moral of the
Division. In this narrative no judgment can be attempted
of the conduct of affairs by the Higher Commands.
Posterity will doubtless find someone to blame for that costly
acquisition and retention of ground from which withdrawal
was found to be necessary but a few days later. We may
rest assured that the 47th Division has no need to defend
its share in the operations. Orders to do difficult things at
short notice were received and obeyed. We lost no ground
that we did not retake. A special message of congratulation
and thanks was received from the Commander-in-Chief, and
in forwarding it to the units of the Division, the Divisional
Commander added these words :

" England, and London especially, may well be proud of
you."

The Division was considerably below full strength when
it entered the battle, and during the operations the casualties were
enormous.

The 19th Battalion suffered particularly heavily. Fifteen officers
and over 600 men took up a position in the wood. Ten officers were
sent down gassed, five died within a few days, and the battalion
left the wood with a strength of five officers and sixty-five other
ranks. Of these, only one officer and between twenty and thirty
of the men remained a few days later, the others being sent to
hospital suffering from the effects of gas.

Where so many of the brave have fallen, it is invidious
to think that one is missed more than another. But it was

unusually tragic, even in the bitterness of war, that Lieut.-
Colonel Adrian G. Gordon, D.S.O., who had led the 235th
Brigade R.F.A. with such skill and courage on November 30th,
should have been killed on December 12th by a chance shell in
front of Havrincourt,* and that so gallant a young officer as
Captain L. E. Rundell, M.C., of the 7th Battalion, then acting
staff-captain of the 140th Brigade, should have fallen on
December 10th.

Both brigades of the Divisional Artillery were throughout
the early days of December constantly in action and under
fire, the men in the battery positions living in shell holes in
bitter weather, rain alternating with frost, and the drivers
working day and night in bringing up ammunition and moving
waggon lines.   The 235th and 236th Brigades R.F.A. rejoined
the Division on December 11th, but on the relief of the
infantry on December 16th they remained in action, covering first
the 59th and then the 17th Division, until the 47th again took over
the line early in January.   An account of the Brigades' adventures
while detached from the Division will be found below.

The Royal Engineers played many parts.   They were
responsible for the demolitions during the withdrawal, and did
much in little time.   One party of them returned to Graincourt
after it had been partially occupied by the enemy to make
further demolitions, and on meeting Germans, destroyed them
also.   Some acted as stretcher-bearers on November 30th, others
as reinforcements to the 15th Battalion when they were hard
pressed on the same day.   Throughout the battle the devotion of
the sappers to whatever duty they were called upon to undertake

---

* Major E. R. Hatfield, D.S.O., who had served with a battery of the
Division since mobilisation, was seriously wounded by the same shell. The
following letter was received by General Gorringe from General Fielding, who
was commanding the Guards Division when our artillery supported their
counter-attack on November 30th :

"December 2nd.

"Dear Gorringe,—I write to tell you that I had two brigades of artillery
sent to cover me without a C.R.A., and I had therefore to make one of them
acting C.R.A.   His name was Lieut.-Colonel Gordon, commanding 235th
Brigade, 47th Division.   He had a difficult job to do, having no staff; but
he did exceedingly well, and had a great grasp of the situation—full of ideas
and very sound.   In my opinion well fitted for C.R.A. of a division.   I
should like you to thank him for his services, and to tell him that they were
much appreciated.—Yours sincerely,

G. FIELDING."

"Guards Division."

was conspicuous and among their commanders Major S. G. Love won especial distinction in these operations.

The work of the R.A.M.C. was made more difficult by the circumstances of the battle. The gas in Bourlon Wood hung in the trees and bushes so thickly that all ranks were compelled to wear their respirators continuously if they were to escape the effects of gas. But men cannot dig for long without removing them, and it was necessary to dig trenches to get any cover from the persistent shell-fire. Throughout November 30th there was, therefore, a steady stream of gassed and wounded men coming to the regimental aid-posts. Their clothes were full of gas, and as the medical officer could not dress wounds without removing his respirator, he, too, felt the effects. No fewer than seven medical officers went to hospital gassed as the result of this dilemma. During the afternoon the few roads that led into the salient became so congested that the motor ambulances returning for more cases could not reach the dressing-stations. Wounded were sent by horse ambulance and limber and the broad-gauge railway in order to avoid congestion.

The disposition of the front and the consequent lines of evacuation caused the old practice of having two field ambulances clearing the line again to be resorted to. Under this scheme the 4th London Field Ambulance became responsible for the left, and the 5th London Field Ambulance for the right front.

During this battle the chain of evacuation took a new turn, for after treatment at the advanced dressing-station, cases were transferred direct to the Corps main dressing-station. The collection of the wounded presented features of extraordinary difficulty. As a general rule, the walking wounded cases are greatly in excess of the stretcher cases, and are dealt with fairly rapidly; but in this instance, as the majority of the walking wounded were blinded by the gas, their collection and evacuation made as great a demand on R.A.M.C. personnel and vehicles as it would have done if all had been stretcher cases. Every form of vehicle was impressed, and even empty water-carts carried their quota.

One of the most pitiful sights of the war was to see the long queues of forty to sixty temporarily blinded men linked up, slowly wending their way through the wood guided by R.A.M.C. orderlies.

In the first twenty-four hours of the battle 4,700 casualties passed through the dressing-stations. The route along which the wounded had to be evacuated passed through an area heavily and continuously shelled with both H.E. and gas shell, for the enemy persistently barraged the approaches to Bourlon Wood. Three of the ambulance drivers were killed, and the R.A.M.C. suffered 70 casualties. Rarely have the medical services of the Division been called to face more sudden, difficult, and perilous tasks.

As an inevitable result of driving this narrow salient into the enemy's front without having adequate troops available to relieve the pressure by attacking elsewhere, all communications became difficult. The few roads which existed were intermittently but heavily shelled, especially at night, with the inevitable result of long delays and considerable casualties among both men and animals. All these difficulties were cheerfully overcome by the transport services.

The Signal Company also was faced with great difficulty in maintaining communications. Visual signals and pigeons often were the only means.

The enemy attacked twenty-four hours after the Division had taken over the line and before any serious improvement in communications could be effected. At the time there was one line to each infantry brigade and only one line serving six artillery brigades ; no lines nor any power-buzzer communication to battalions, in spite of the fact that this chalky country was ideally suited to the latter.

Divisional Headquarters, under canvas at Havrincourt Château, were out of communication with the Corps for most of the time during the first few days. The heavy shelling round Havrincourt and the absence of communication trenches, with the addition of several stretches behind battalion headquarters which were exposed to machine-gun fire, made the maintenance of lines very difficult when they were laid. The retirement on December 4th eased matters considerably for the signal service.

The 4th Battalion R.W.F. were on their way from Bertincourt to Trescault, when the enemy attacked on November 30th. The roads were blocked and under heavy fire, but the companies plodded through, and on arriving at Havrincourt were sent forward to garrison the Hindenburg support line. The

FLESQUIERES, NOVEMBER, 1917.

next few days and nights were times of strenuous and continuous work. They carried ammunition up to Bourlon Wood each evening, stayed to dig communication trenches, to put a firestep in the front line, to consolidate the trenches we regained on December 2nd, to salve a German railway and its rolling-stock, finishing their night's work by carrying back the wounded. This was the nightly programme till December 4th, when they went forward to the four strong points. These they put in some state of defence, and then held them against the attacks of the enemy till they were relieved on December 6th. The Battle of Cambrai was a great episode in the history of the regiment. Fear and fatigue were conquered by spirit and discipline.

The officers and the men in the trenches surpassed themselves, rations were not so good as they had been a month before, there was little shelter from the weather, much work to be done, and the nights long and cold. Wearily, cheerily they crawled to the slow trains that took them back beyond Albert for a snowy Christmas. But what happened there must form the subject of another chapter.

    *   *   *   *   *   *

The 47th Divisional Artillery, whose movements have hitherto been only briefly outlined, played no less important a part than the rest of the Division in repelling the German counter-attacks of November 30th and the succeeding days. The story of their share in the operations is told in the following narrative by the C.R.A., Brigadier-General Whitley :

On the early morning of November 30th the enemy made a counter attack in force to recover his lost Hindenburg Line, the chief weight of the attack being directed against the haunches of the salient where our new front line joined the old.

As has already been told, the attack on the north faces of the salient, though made by five German divisions, was beaten off, thanks to the splendid steadiness of our 47th Divisional Infantry, and those of the 2nd and 56th Divisions on their left. The front of the salient towards Cambrai was also held intact by the 29th Division, but on the southern face of the salient the 55th and 20th Divisions were driven in, and before noon the Germans had overrun Bois Lateau, Gonnelieu and Villers Guislains, and had entered

Gouzeaucourt and Gauche Wood. If they succeeded in pushing forward to Queen's Cross they would look into Metz and thus command the bottle-neck on which the whole of the troops in the salient depended.

Fortunately, the Guards Division, which had been relieved on the previous day in the northern part of the salient, had only gone as far back as Fins, and was now turning about and marching up to Queen's Cross.

Our two Artillery Brigades (the 235th and 236th) had spent the last four nights on the site of the village of Bus, crowded into accommodation that was only built to hold half their number, and were engaged in calibrating some of their guns on the ranges at Fricourt in the old Somme battlefield, while parties of officers were out reconnoitring the German guns which had been captured in the advance on November 20th, and were now to be brought into the IVth Corps Headquarters at Villers-au-Flos.

At 9.30 a.m. a Staff car from the Corps brought an order to the 235th Brigade R.F.A., to "stand to" ready to move in any direction. Lt.-Colonel Gordon was out reconnoitring, but the adjutant of the Brigade, Captain S. T. Davis, rode at once to Corps Headquarters and received orders to march immediately to Neuville Bourjonval, where they would report to G.O.C. Guards Division.

The 236th Brigade R.F.A. (Lt.-Colonel A. H. Bowring) were awaiting the return of several of the guns from the ranges, and did not get orders to move till late in the afternoon.

The 235th Brigade were on the move in ten minutes, the colonel had got back, and with his Staff rode ahead to the Guards Division, whom he found at Metz. The infantry were not yet up from Fins, and the roads were filled with wounded soldiers, gunners carrying dial sights and other gun stores, and transport streaming back in a considerable confusion. The Brigade was ordered to go into action covering Gouzeaucourt, and, for the first time for many a long month, carried out the procedure laid down in Field Artillery Training for quickly reconnoitring and taking up a position, just outside Metz.

The men were full of spirit, and our batteries cheered as they drove up into action, the only troops in that part of the field who were facing the right way. It was now after 2 p.m., and as information was scanty, the adjutant of the Brigade was sent forward to find out the situation. He rode over Highland Ridge and down into Villers Plouich, in spite of rifle-fire, and satisfied himself that the enemy were at any rate not advanced across the valley towards Queen's Cross. An hour later he found the Guards Infantry assembling about Queen's Cross to attack Gouzeaucourt. The attack was supported by the 235th Brigade R.F.A., and was completely successful, but an attempt to push on and recapture Gonnelieu was beaten back with serious casualties to the Guards.

Prisoners reported that the German attack was to be renewed the next day, and the 235th Brigade, who alone were covering the Guards Division on a front of three miles, had a busy night harassing all likely approaches and advancing in succession to new positions just below the crest of the Queen's Cross-Trescault Ridge in front of Gouzeaucourt Wood.

During the night November 30th-December 1st the Guards Divisional Artillery arrived, and went into action under Lt.-Colonel Gordon's command, the 75th Brigade R.F.A. behind Gouzeaucourt Wood, and the 76th near Heudecourt. The 235th Brigade, R.F.A., was led during this period, when Colonel Gordon was acting C.R.A. to the Guards Division, by Major A. J. Cowan, D.S.O., of D/235th Battery.

On the morning of December 1st the enemy did not resume his attack from Gonnelieu, and the day was spent by 235th Brigade R.F.A. organising the position and settling down.

The 236th Brigade R.F.A. received orders late in the afternoon of November 30th to move up as soon as their guns arrived from Fricourt, in support of the 20th Division, who had been driven off the Gonnelieu-Lateau Wood ridge and were holding somewhat precariously the Welsh Ridge about La Vacquerie. At 4.30 a.m. on the 1st the 236th Brigade moved off, and just as dawn was breaking crossed the Queen's Cross-Trescault Ridge, just north of the 235th Brigade. They came into action on the forward slopes above Villers-Plouich, looking across to La Vacquerie at only 3,000 yards range.

During the day the enemy tried hard to get forward from Lateau Wood to La Vacquerie, but the observers of the batteries were able to get their guns on to these attacks and broke them up. The enemy supported his attacks with artillery fire, and the barrage came forward as far as the battery positions of the 236th Brigade, causing some casualties, as every one was in the open without cover, except a very few shallow trenches.

On December 2nd the C.R.A. of the Guards Division took over command of the artillery covering his infantry, and Lieut-Colonel Gordon became Group Commander, with headquarters at the south-east edge of Havrincourt Wood. Meanwhile, the enemy persisted in attacking La Vacquerie, five batteries of the 20th Divisional Artillery were added to Lieut.-Colonel Bowring's command, and protective barrages were called for frequently.

Down in Villers Plouich a quantity of ordnance stores had been collected as well as provisions, and any spare time the batteries had was well spent in salving part of these stores.

Fighting for La Vacquerie continued, the battery positions were becoming known, and on December 5th, A/236th Battery (Major W. Cooper, M.C.), and D/236th Battery (Major Duncan, M.C.), were withdrawn to the Beaucamp Valley, while Brigade headquarters moved back to a chalkpit east of Havrincourt Wood. This day the Germans finally got possession of La Vacquerie Farm which commanded the positions of the batteries still in the Villers Plouich valley, and by the 8th, B/236th Battery (Major W. J. Barnard, M.C.), and C/236th Battery R.F.A. (Major Carey-Morgan) were withdrawn under heavy shell-fire to positions behind the Queen's Cross-Trescault Ridge near the Brigade headquarters.

Meanwhile, 235th Brigade R.F.A. had been relieved by the 9th Divisional Artillery, and after one night in waggon lines at Fins had moved up to the north of 236th Brigade R.F.A. in Boar Valley, the valley in which Beaucamp stands, facing almost due east.

On December 11th a triangular exchange of artillery was arranged between 32nd, 36th, and 47th Divisions, under which our own 235th and 236th Brigades R.F.A. rejoined the 47th Division in the Havrincourt-Flesquières sector after a short but very arduous battle.

The discomfort of officers and men in the battery positions, living in shell holes in bitter weather, rain alternating with frost, with almost continuous firing, was rivalled only by that of the drivers, with their horses always in the open and kept in incessant work, bringing up ammunition at night to the guns and changing the position of waggon lines by day. The 236th Brigade, for example, placed their waggon lines on December 1st behind Gouzeaucourt Wood, but were shelled out on the 6th, and went to the west of

Metz, thence to Fins three miles further south, to Bertincourt five miles to the north, and finally back to Bus, being much worried during the whole period by enemy bombing.

It was the nearest approach which the Brigades had had to moving warfare, with most of the impedimenta of trench warfare discarded, the Brigade office established in a shell hole and paper limited to the ordinary signal message pad, but throughout the whole battle the batteries showed themselves ready to accept novel conditions and quick to grasp essentials.

DIVISIONAL CHRISTMAS CARD, 1917.

Designed by Rfn. C. R. Stanton, 21st London Regt.

Chapter XII.

REST AND REORGANIZATION.

CHRISTMAS, 1917, was spent by the greater part of the Division, except the artillery, under tolerably comfortable conditions. The brigades were billeted in villages behind Albert—the 140th round Ribemont, the 141st round Bouzincourt, and the 142nd round Laviéville. The Divisional canteen did a big business in pork and turkeys and such other delicacies as could be obtained, and everybody settled down to enjoy a peaceful Christmas after the stress of the past month.

There was little rest, however, for the transport. A heavy snowfall and continued frost had made the roads and places almost impassable, and the long journeys with supplies to outlying villages, together with the insatiable demand for fuel, meant a long day's work for the Divisional Train and Supply Column.

During this period the original Supply Column of the Division, the 47th, which had accompanied it from England, was restored to it for good, the system of changing over the mechanical transport with every change of area having been found unsatisfactory.

Brigade training began directly after Christmas, but it soon became clear that a return to the line was imminent. On December 29th orders were issued for the Pioneers and two field companies to move up to the Vth Corps area on New Year's Day. On the following day the enemy attacked on the Vth Corps front, and the 142nd Brigade was moved up by train at a few hours' notice. On January 4th it relieved the left brigade in the Flesquières sector, which was already covered by our own Divisional Artillery. In a raid on the 24th Battalion on January 6th, one prisoner was taken by the enemy.

Meanwhile, the whole Division had been transferred from IIIrd to Vth Corps. Divisional Headquarters left the château of Baisieux on January 6th for the Nissen huts of Neuville Bourjonval; on the 7th the 141st Brigade, who had moved into the Bertincourt area two days earlier, took over the right brigade front of the 17th Division, and Sir George Gorringe took over the command of the whole Divisional front. The 140th Brigade remained in the rest area until January 10th, when they rejoined the Division at Bertincourt.

Intense cold, followed by a thaw which rendered the trenches almost impassable, added greatly to the hardships of the troops in the line. Except for normal artillery activity, however, the days passed quietly. It was decided to evacuate the Havrincourt-Premy salient, including Dago Trench and Premy Switch, and this was done on the night of January 14th-15th.

The evacuation of the salient by the 140th Brigade involved a demolition of eight dugout systems, with twenty-four entrances, and in making these uninhabitable and otherwise making things as uncomfortable as possible for any Germans who might seek to take up their abode there, 1,505 slabs of gun-cotton, and 108 gallons of petrol or paraffin were used.

Work on the Beaucamp-Trescault-Hermies line was begun on January 24th, and a working party of 300 infantrymen was employed on it daily. A great deal was done by all arms in preparing rear lines of defence. Batteries were arranged in depth; anti-tank guns were placed on the Flesquières Ridge, and alternative systems of communication from front to rear were practised.

The Chaplain-General (Bishop Taylor-Smith) visited Divisional Headquarters, which were now established in Ytres, on January 26th, and on the Sunday officiated at a church parade of the 140th Brigade.

A 47th Divisional memorial cross was erected at Eaucourt l'Abbaye on February 3rd, 1918, when Major L. Boosey, of the 22nd Battalion, the senior officer present, read the following words of dedication :

We set up this memorial to the honour of our brave comrades who fell in the battle of Eaucourt L'Abbaye on October 1st, 1916. Their names are too many to repeat, but not one of them shall be forgotten. For in the face of a powerful enemy they continued to go forward, giving their lives for England and for London, for all they loved best at home.

Peace has come to this village ; its trees and houses shall grow again. So we have placed a cross on the place where our soldiers fell, as a sure sign that they, too, rest in peace, and have the certain hope of a glorious resurrection in Jesus Christ, our Lord.

BRIG.-GENERAL W. F. MILDREN, C.B., C.M.G., D.S.O.
Commanding 141st Infantry Brigade, 1917-1919.

A memorial cross was also erected in High Wood in commemoration of those who fell in the successful attack of September 15th, 1916.

Two important changes in organization, which were being put into effect throughout the British armies in France, resulted in great changes within the Division during the next few weeks. These were the reduction of the strength of infantry brigades from four battalions to three, and the combination of the four machine-gun companies into one machine-gun battalion.

The reorganisation of the infantry resulted in the loss to the Division of the 6th Battalion (City of London Rifles), the 7th Battalion, and the 8th Battalion (Post Office Rifles). These three City battalions, which had joined the Division some months before it embarked for France, had played a leading part in most of the big operations in which it had been engaged, and their loss to the Division was a heavy one. They were ordered to join the 58th (London) Division, where they were to be amalgamated respectively with the 2-6th, 2-7th, and 2-8th Battalions, London Regiment, which were already serving there. A large proportion of their personnel, however, was retained with the 47th, and was sent as drafts to other units of the Division. The 6th Battalion, for example, received orders to dispose of its personnel as follows : 14 officers and 250 other ranks to the 2-6th Battalion London Regiment; 8 officers and 250 other ranks to the 1-15th Battalion, and 6 officers and 170 other ranks to the 1-18th Battalion. The 8th Battalion sent its headquarters and 200 men to the 2-8th; 7 officers and 250 men to the 1-24th, and 8 officers and 300 men to the 1-17th.

As might be expected, there was no little heartburning over the question who should be taken and who should be left. There was much making of nominal rolls (in triplicate), much hurried transferring of indispensable clerks and mess-servants at headquarters who were suddenly found to belong to one of the doomed battalions, and much quiet horse-coping and camouflaging of transport and equipment.

At last the tangle was more or less straightened out, and on February 2nd the Divisional and Brigade Commanders bade farewell at Bertincourt to the headquarters and nucleus detachments of the " Cast-iron Sixth," the " Shiny Seventh," and the Post Office Rifles as they left in omnibuses to join the 58th Division.

M

The 47th Division owed to these " lost tribes " several dis-
tinguished commanders and Staff officers who remained with it,
among them Brigadier-General Mildren, a former Commanding
Officer of the 6th, who had succeeded Brigadier-General Erskine
on January 2nd, 1918, in command of the 141st Brigade ; Lieut.-
Colonel (afterwards Brigadier-General) Maxwell, of the 8th, and
Lieut.-Colonel C. Salkeld Green, of the 7th, while others, such as
Lieut.-Colonel W. B. Vince, afterwards returned to us.

In the war diary of the 8th Battalion the closing entry, written
almost three years after the landing of the unit in France, runs
as follows :

> The battalion is gone, and its officers and men scattered abroad. But the spirit
> of the battalion—that spirit which carried it through over two and a half years of
> hard fighting—will always remain in the hearts of those who have served in and for it.
> *Hæc olim meminisse juvabit.*

To fill the gap thus made in the 140th Brigade, the 17th Battalion
was taken from the 141st Brigade and the 21st Battalion from
the 142nd. The new order of battle, therefore, was :

140th INFANTRY BRIGADE.
(BRIGADIER-GENERAL H. B. P. L. KENNEDY, D.S.O.)

15th Battalion, London Regiment (Civil Service Rifles).
17th   ,,   ,,   ,,   (Poplar and Stepney Rifles).
21st   ,,   ,,   ,,   (First Surrey Rifles).

141st INFANTRY BRIGADE.
(BRIGADIER-GENERAL W. F. MILDREN, C.M.G., D.S.O.)

18th Battalion, London Regiment (London Irish Rifles).
19th   ,,   ,,   ,,   (St. Pancras).
20th   ,,   ,,   ,,   (Blackheath and Woolwich).

142nd INFANTRY BRIGADE.
(BRIGADIER-GENERAL V. T. BAILEY, D.S.O.)

22nd Battalion, London Regiment (The Queen's).
23rd   ,,   ,,   ,,
24th   ,,   ,,   ,,   (The Queen's).

The reorganisation of the machine-gun companies took place
towards the end of the month of February, which passed without
incident of importance on the Divisional front. An enemy raid

on the front of the 17th Division on our left and a great increase
of patrol activity, however, were among the many indications that
the expected German offensive would not be long delayed.

On February 22nd and 23rd the Division was relieved by the
63rd (Royal Naval) Division. The 141st Brigade went back to
Lechelle, and the 142nd to Rocquigny. The machine-gun companies
were also concentrated at Rocquigny under the Divisional machine-
gun officer, and at midnight on the last day of the month the 47th
Battalion, Machine-gun Corps, officially came into being. Its first
commanding officer was Lieut-Colonel H. J. N. Davis, D.S.O., who
was succeeded a few weeks later by Lieut.-Colonel Wyndham
Portal, D.S.O., M.V.O. The latter, who had previously commanded
the Household Battalion in France, remained with the Division
until after the Armistice.

Another change in the Divisional Staff had taken place a few
days earlier, when Lieut.-Colonel A. J. Turner was appointed to
command a brigade of another division. He was succeeded as
G.S.O.1 by Lieut.-Colonel C. M. Davies, D.S.O.

On February 27th the 4th Royal Welsh Fusiliers, like other
Pioneer battalions, was reorganised into three companies instead
of four.

In some of the artillery units also reorganisation was in progress.
From December onwards the water supply for wagon lines was so
small that the Divisional Ammunition Column, with the exception
of the S.A.A. Section, was sent right back to Pont Noyelles and
Querrieu Château, half-way between Albert and Amiens. Here
preparations were made for the reception of 150 Indian native
drivers, with a view to replacing a similar number of British.

The three medium trench-mortar batteries were reorganised as
two batteries each of six 6-in. Newton mortars, X-47 under Captain
J. G. Blaver, and Y-47 under Captain A. L. Hope. In addition
to the preparation and occupation of positions in Flesquières,
from which they could support the infantry in our existing line,
positions were prepared and manned in some of the rear lines.

On March 7th the Divisional Artillery was relieved, and the
whole Division was out at rest together for the first time since
1916.

Training in the field, in which all arms combined, and musketry
on the range at Le Transloy, interspersed with gymkhanas, boxing,

and football matches, occupied the first three weeks of March. Just outside the village of Bus an excellent racecourse had been laid out by a division which had previously been in possession of that desolate area. The jumps—which were vigorously shelled by the Germans later during their advance, under the impression that they were gun positions—were still in good repair, and two most enjoyable gymkhanas were held there on March 9th and 16th.

Meanwhile, the shelling of back areas, and the bombing by night, became daily more persistent. On March 12th, Divisional Headquarters, in the remains of the château at Ytres, was heavily shelled. Captain Arthur Gorringe, the camp commandant, and a brother of the Divisional Commander, who had won the affection of all with whom he came into contact during the short period of his service with the Division, was seriously wounded in the hand.

Sunday, March 17th, was the third anniversary of the Division's first landing in France. A special service of thanksgiving, remembrance, and self-dedication was held in the evening in the large theatre at Lechelle. So many of the original members of the Division desired to attend that it was impossible to accommodate them all, but the theatre was crowded with representatives from every unit of the Division. The Divisional Commander and his Staff were present. The service was conducted, and an address was given, by the Senior Chaplain, the Rev. A. E. Wilkinson, M.C., and the music was provided by the band of the 19th Battalion.

On the same day orders were received for the Division to relieve the 2nd Division in the La Vacquerie sector, south-west of Cambrai, on the right flank of the Third Army. The 2nd Division, as well as the 63rd (Royal Naval) Division had suffered heavy casualties during the recent gas-shell bombardment by the enemy. Its replacement in the line at this stage by the 47th Division, which had been in training as a counter-attack division for the right flank of the Vth Corps and the Third Army, was a change of Corps plan which had far-reaching results.

Chapter XIII.

THE RETREAT FROM CAMBRAI.

ALTHOUGH the big German attack was expected in March, 1918, the exact day and hour when it should be launched was not known. The night of March 20th-21st was quiet. This was not unusual as, with the exception of aeroplane bombing raids and an artillery bombardment early every morning, the enemy had of late refrained from great annoyance in the forward positions at night. The world, however, woke up at 4.15 a.m. on the 21st to excessive noise of shells and guns. Alert sentries sent up the S.O.S., and our artillery soon replied. " The usual morning strafe," said someone, and snoozed down into his blankets again. His composure was short-lived, however, for the enemy fire increased in intensity, and gas-shell was fired in particularly heavy concentrations; heavy trench mortars joined in with a nasty, thick, methodical bombardment of our front line posts and sapheads, long-range guns sent high-bursting shrapnel over the headquarters and villages miles behind the line. The staffs turned out—in pyjamas first—and telephones were soon busy. It was soon realised that this was no ordinary bombardment, and that at last the great attack had come.

The 47th Division, part of the Vth Corps (Lieut.-General Sir E. A. Fanshawe), had relieved the 2nd Division in the La Vacquerie sector on March 19th and 20th. The 141st Brigade took over the left front on the night of the 19th-20th, and the 140th Brigade were to hold the right front from the night 20th-21st. The 142nd Brigade was in reserve. On our left was the 63rd (Royal Naval) Division (Major-General C. Lawrie), also in the Vth Corps. On the right was the 9th (Scottish) Division, temporarily commanded by Brigadier-General H. H. Tudor. This division was in the VIIth Corps (Lieut.-General Sir W. N. Congreve, V.C.), and formed part of General Sir Hubert Gough's Fifth Army.

The important factor in these dispositions was that the 47th Division was on the extreme right of Byng's Third Army, and the task of defending the flank of the army fell to the 47th.

The front line which the Division took over was on Welsh Ridge, the left sector of it being on the reverse slope. Observation was bad. The reserve line was on Highland Ridge, some 2,000 yards behind, and from this an excellent field of fire was obtainable. Between the two ridges was the narrow Couillet Valley, which, with its steep sides, was a regular gas-trap. Here the troops of the 2nd Division in support had suffered severely from gas-shell on March 18th and 19th.

Thus it happened that on the very day when the German offensive began the 2nd Division, which had suffered heavy casualties and was comparatively weak in strength, went into Corps Reserve, while the 47th Division, which was not only stronger in numbers and fresher, but had for the past week or two been undergoing special training as a counter-attack Division, took its place in holding the line.

According to orders, the command of the La Vacquerie Sector was to pass to Major-General Sir G. F. Gorringe, our Divisional Commander, at 6 a.m. on March 21st, but in view of events, he assumed responsibility for the front at five o'clock—after the bombardment had started, and before the scheduled time for taking over had arrived. The divisional relief was not yet complete. We had the 2nd Divisional Artillery still with us, and only part of the Machine-gun Battalion had been relieved. This state of things was inconvenient, for misunderstandings and delay may often arise when units are strange to one another. Throughout the whole of the next anxious days the work of the 2nd Division units with us was excellent and deserving of the greatest credit ; their loyalty and eagerness to assist and obey orders of commanders strange to them (our C.R.A. and O.C. Machine-gun Battalion took over command during the day) left nothing to be desired.

Our own artillery, whose wanderings are briefly described elsewhere, left the Division on March 21st, and moved northwards. They were not restored to it until May 22nd. The field artillery covering the sector held by the 47th Division at the opening of the attack consisted of the two brigades of the 2nd Divisional Artillery—the 41st Brigade R.F.A. under Lieut.-Colonel Barton, and the 36th Brigade R.F.A. under Lieut.-Colonel Goschen, the 34th (Army) Brigade R.F.A. under Lieut.-Colonel Parry, and the 87th Brigade R.F.A., from the 19th Divisional Artillery, under Lieut.-Colonel Peel. The 36th Brigade, R.F.A., was transferred to the 63rd Division on the night of March 22nd-23rd. On March 23rd the remaining three brigades were affiliated respectively to the 142nd, 140th, and 141st Infantry Brigades, and acted in conjunction with them during the greater part of the retirement.

Meanwhile, our men in the front line were having a horrible time. It was not, apparently, the enemy's plan to launch a massed attack on our front. He seemed to rely on the main attack farther south, assisted by strong and continual pressure on our immediate front, to force us out of our positions. The bombardment grew more intense, and by nine o'clock we had suffered heavy casualties. The gas-shell was especially deadly, and for hours our men had to wear their masks, and while thus handicapped, continually to repel the enemy's fighting patrols. Later in the day the enemy advanced under a smoke screen, and only after repeated efforts and wearing our troops down by trench-mortar fire and gas did he succeed in gaining one or two isolated positions in our front line. Local counter-attacks by the 18th and 19th Battalions drove back the enemy, who had in some places reached our second-line trench—a very fine piece of work after the drubbing they had received from the enemy's guns and mortars.

Reports received showed that the enemy had made progress on our right and had occupied the front-line system of the Division on our right. On the left the 63rd Division had had similar experiences to our own, and had also held their ground. Farther north, Doignies had been lost, and it became evident that if more progress were made against the corps north and south of us, the 47th and 63rd would be forced to fall back. The 4th R.W.F., the Pioneer Battalion, had been ordered up to Metz from Lechelle, and the remainder of our Machine-gun Battalion, which was back at Rocquigny, had come forward into reserve. Such was the situation in the evening.   The Division could well feel proud that the front was still intact, especially in the light of the terrific bombardment.   Reports showed that, in spite of a day under continual fire, the men were still confident and in good spirits.

During the night the situation on our flanks became worse. At 7.48 p.m. the 47th and 63rd Divisions were ordered to leave their front line and take up a position along the Highland Ridge, in accordance with the prearranged plan of the Third Army.

This withdrawal under the nose of the enemy was made unknown to him and without mishap.   The signal service had remained good throughout the day, the buried cable being the strength of the system.

Eleven prisoners had been taken, and these stated that the objectives of the attack were unlimited.   So we were to expect another hard day.

The night was quiet.   Hostile artillery was evidently busy taking up new positions, and firing was spasmodic.   As soon as daylight appeared, the enemy crept cautiously forward, only to find the position vacated.   Strong patrols were pushed out down the southern slopes of the Welsh Ridge to discover our whereabouts, and many endeavours were made to reach our positions, but our machine-guns, Lewis-gun posts, and snipers had been well placed, and all day the enemy was prevented from crossing the Couillet Valley.   Our position, and the fine obstinacy of our men, gave us an opportunity of inflicting heavy casualties.

Again and again the Germans tried without success to get across to Highland Ridge.   The situation gave encouragement to the infantry, who had no doubt of their ability to hold the position indefinitely.   But south of us things were going badly.   As early as 7.30 a.m. the Divisional Commander realised the danger on our right flank, caused by the withdrawal of the 9th Division.   During the morning the situation became more and more dangerous, and this was represented to Vth Corps.   By midday the 9th Division was already back on its second system (*i.e.*, our Metz Switch system) and an extension of our right was necessary.   The R.W.F. were ordered to occupy the Metz Switch on the right of the 142nd Brigade.   The situation was becoming an anxious one.   The right of the 140th Brigade was already in the air, although the position of the Pioneer Battalion formed an echelon, and thus prevented the enemy from cutting in behind our front system. During the afternoon things on our right grew still worse. The Fifth Army were rapidly falling back, and at 4.10 p.m. a Staff officer from the 9th Division reported that they were leaving their second system at 4.30 p.m., and in the evening intended to retire behind Fins.

This, of course, made our Highland Ridge position quite impossible. Orders had been issued for a withdrawal that night to the second system, which the 142nd Brigade was to hold. The 141st Brigade was to pass through and concentrate west of Metz, and the 140th Brigade was to occupy the Metz Switch as far as Fins, so as to form a long defensive flank, and, if possible, get into touch with the 9th Division. This difficult operation was very successfully carried out, and considering the continuous pressure of the enemy and the uncertainty of the situation of the 9th Division, was a very creditable performance. Mention, however, must be made of the splendid stand made by the 18th Battalion on the Highland Ridge. As soon as dusk fell the Germans attacked from Villers Plouich. The London Irish stood calm and, by rifle and machine-gun fire, beat off the enemy, who left many dead and wounded before our trenches. A second attack was launched. This, too, was unsuccessful. A third and a fourth time the enemy attempted to reach our position, but each time he was repulsed with great loss. The men of the 18th, anxious to convince the German he was trying an impossible thing, counter-attacked and cut off the hostile attacking party, and then proceeded to annihilate it. Seven Germans were spared and brought in as prisoners. Not one escaped.

It was clear by the evening that not only must we give up the ridge, but the second system was also rendered untenable, and as soon as the 140th and 141st Brigades were in their allotted positions the 142nd returned to the trenches covering Metz, known as the Metz Switch. The Divisional frontage was now 8,000 yards. The trenches were only half dug, and there was little wire. The artillery were moving to new positions, and a protective barrage during the night was out of the question. No sooner had all preparations been made to defend this long line than the 9th Division reported they would have to leave their position in front of Equancourt before daylight. This left the 47th Division holding a four-and-a-half-mile front from Metz (inclusive) to Fins (exclusive), with an exposed right flank, and the enemy advancing in a north-westerly direction. Should the enemy succeed in turning the flank, the disaster would be incalculable. By 10 p.m. the Germans were in Fins. A Company of the Pioneer Battalion (now under the command of Brigadier-General Kennedy of the 140th Brigade), hastened to strengthen the end of the line ; No. 11 Motor Machine-gun Battery, which had that day been attached to the Division, was sent there, too, and, with the help of an additional section of our own machine-gunners, covered all the western and northern exits of the village. The map (No. VIII) shows the position at 10 p.m. on March 22nd, and illustrates how the Division changed front and defended the right flank of the Third Army that night on the line of the Metz Switch. The 99th Brigade of the 2nd Division was placed under the command of the 47th Division at 10.30 p.m., and ordered to advance from Ytres and reinforce our right. This brigade never reached or established connection with the 140th Brigade on this line of defence, however. It was very much reduced in strength, having suffered heavy casualties in the gas bombardment a few days earlier.

Communications had become worse, as we were getting off the front network of telephone lines, and much had to be done by means of runner and despatch-rider. During the day much visual signalling had been done, the 140th Brigade keeping up communication all day with the Metz exchange by this means. The 15th Battalion, on the extreme right, had an anxious and heavy task to perform, and the fact that no Germans filtered through the gap throws great credit on the way in which the patrols and machine-gunners did their work that night. One of the officers attached to the 140th Brigade Headquarters (Lieutenant H. A. Gilkes, M.C.) went out alone to Dessart Wood and brought in two German prisoners, a piece of work typical of this gallant young officer, who won the rare distinction of three bars to his Military Cross.

All the other services of the Division were also in the picture. The Field Companies, R.E., which were working all over the divisional area when the attack started, were, after many difficulties, now concentrated behind the Metz Switch.

A little note in the official records reads : " A.D.M.S. reports communication established with all battalions.   Aid-posts all clear by 4.30 p.m."   Those who were with the Division on March 21st and 22nd and the following days know that to get the wounded dressed and away to safety on such occasions implies hard work, continuous devotion to duty, and the highest efficiency.

Not one machine-gunner was idle ; all were in position along and immediately behind the Metz and Dessart Switches. The artillery no sooner took up a position to support the infantry than the situation changed, and guns had to be moved. All through the night and day guns were moving from position to position, laying out the lines of fire, only to find when all was ready that new situations necessitated new moves.   A good deal of firing was done on the enemy roads at night, but the constant changing prevented combined firing programmes.

It is well to pause here, for after that night the nature of the operations changed.   From now on the fighting was more open. Co-ordination became more and more difficult, communication more hazardous.   Up to this point we had been prepared to defend for a long period every position taken up.   It was known that the enemy had penetrated the Fifth Army front, but how far he had progressed was not known.   One expected at any moment to hear that the limit of retirement on our right had been reached.   Each successive position to which the 47th Division had been ordered to withdraw had been organised in depth with a view to defence, and there we had been prepared to stand. But the operation was vaster than we knew, the enemy's success more penetrating than we could have imagined, and from now on the task of the Division was not to hold definite positions to grim death, but to keep the enemy's advance in check, and at all costs to prevent him striking in behind us, thereby cutting off our troops and subsequently rolling up the flank of the army to which we belonged.

The 142nd Brigade, acting as rearguard to the Division, withdrew during the night 22nd-23rd to the Metz Switch, having the 63rd Division on their left and two companies of

the R.W.F. on the right.   Dawn of the 23rd found the 140th
Brigade with its right flank exposed, and a nasty gap had been
made more dangerous by the further retirement of the 9th
Division from Equancourt to Manancourt.   The Germans were
now seen west of Fins ; their machine-guns were thus able
to enfilade our right battalions.   The situation was again
growing impossible, and the withdrawal to the Green Line
(an old line of German trenches running east of Etricourt
and Ytres) was inevitable.   The 141st Brigade was ordered
to occupy this line with two battalions ; the third battalion,
with the R.E. Companies attached, were to face south and
form a connecting-link between the Green Line and the right
of the 140th Brigade.   The 140th and 142nd Brigades were
then to fall back to the high ground west of Ytres and covering
Lechelle.   The enemy had evidently realised the situation,
and now made desperate efforts to get through the gap and
behind the 140th Brigade, and it was due to the prowess of the
15th and 18th Battalions and R.E. Companies that he was prevented from doing so.   Heavy fighting took place.   The enemy
advanced, supported by trench-mortar, machine-gun, and artillery
fire ; close fighting ensued, in which one company of the 15th
was surrounded and, unfortunately, never extricated.   The
R.E.'s, under the fine leadership of Major S. G. Love, D.S.O.,
proved that they were as good fighters as they were engineers.
There is no doubt that the frustration of the enemy's plan
of rolling up our line from the position to which he had penetrated
on our right rear on this occasion saved the Division and the right
of the Third Army from disastrous results.

Meanwhile, the enemy had not confined his efforts to this
sector alone.   All along the Metz Switch, determined attacks
were launched.   The line was not strongly held owing to the
length of front the Division was occupying.   Heavy casualties,
too, had further reduced our powers of resistance.   A very
determined onslaught was made on the position held by the 23rd
Battalion near the Metz Cemetery.   Dense masses of Germans
had been seen at eight o'clock advancing a mile away.   Machine-
guns opened fire, and even at this range inflicted many casualties.
The two companies of the R.W.F. which were on the right of the
23rd had been ordered to reinforce the exposed flank of the 140th

Brigade, thus leaving a gap of 300 yards between the 23rd and 21st Battalions. The attacks of the enemy prevented this gap being filled, although gallant attempts to do so were made by the 21st Battalion, who suffered thereby many losses. The 23rd Battalion threw out a defensive flank and prepared to withstand the enemy. The vacated trench was soon occupied by him, and he proceeded to open heavy fire on our men. Captain Brett, who commanded the 23rd Battalion in this position, sent a fighting patrol along the trench to try and get in touch with the 21st, but the enemy was in too great numbers, and well supplied with bombs.

The Germans continued to advance, but still the 23rd Battalion held on, and prevented the enemy from getting possession of this piece of high ground on the right flank. This state of affairs lasted until the zero hour for the prearranged retirement of the 142nd Brigade arrived. The defence of the Metz Switch by the 23rd London Regiment under Captain Brett stands out in the history of the retreat as one of the most gallant and determined examples of refusal to give way before strong and well-nigh overwhelming attacks. Four waves of the enemy attacked the trenches ; counter-attack followed attack ; our artillery supported with continual heavy fire, and the Germans lost heavily. When the hour arrived for the 23rd Battalion to withdraw from the trenches, they did so in their own way, in their own time, and unmolested by a defeated and disheartened foe.

In the afternoon the 140th Brigade retired from the Dessart Switch to the high ground east of Lechelle, but leaving some men on the right of the front in the Green Line. Near Lechelle they were joined by elements of the 99th Brigade, of the 2nd Division, who then assisted in checking the enemy's advance from the south-east.

These troops of the 140th Brigade who had withdrawn were collected at Four Winds Farm about 2.30 p.m. on March 23rd. As they were being got into line across the Lechelle aerodrome the enemy attacked the troops of the 9th Division south of the Rocquigny-Manancourt road and forced them back. The Berkshires, of the 99th Brigade, who were on the right of the 140th Brigade, were also compelled to fall back, but halted on the continuation of the line held by the 140th. The enemy advanced over the ridge from the direction of Etricourt, but was stopped by the small force which had been collected on the aerodrome.

This force consisted largely of odd headquarters details, and totalled about 300 men from different battalions of the 140th Brigade, of which the greater part was still in the Green Line. It stood firm in its position in the open near Four Winds Farm until 7.30 p.m., when the enemy attacked under a heavy barrage and drove our troops back. It was here that Captain R. de Saumarez, who had recently been appointed Staff Captain of the 140th Brigade, was killed while passing up ammunition. The troops were reformed in the valley near Lechelle Wood and withdrew to the Rocquigny area.

The 142nd Brigade retired from the Metz Switch area, but were closely followed and harassed by the enemy. Near Vallulart Wood the brigade made a stand, but the enemy were in great strength, and our men, tired after the strenuous fighting in the morning, were forced to fall back on Ytres. All day the artillery had been in action, covering the infantry's withdrawal. Batteries "leap-frogged" back to new positions west of Ytres. The heavy trench-mortar batteries had buried their weapons, and the personnel were now used as runners and observers, and worked on temporary lines of defence.

It was a hard day, March 23rd. On our left the 63rd Division was also holding the enemy, and touch was always maintained, but on the right there was ever danger—for the Fifth Army continued to retire faster and farther, ever widening the distance between our junction with the 63rd Division on our left and the left of the 9th Division to the South.

The enemy again remained quiet during the night, except for spasmodic artillery fire. As the 141st Brigade had been ordered to take up a new line east of Le Mesnil, it was essential that the 142nd Brigade should fall back to the west of Ytres. The 23rd Battalion had already proceeded westwards, and the 22nd and 24th Battalions were about to follow, when the startling rumour reached them that the Germans were in Bus. A hurried consultation between the commanders took place in Ytres, and it was decided to make for Rocquigny via Bertin-court, and so to circumvent Bus. It might mean cutting a way through the German line, for it looked as if these two battalions had been cut off. Advanced guards were thrown out, and all through the night the men marched, expecting at any moment to run into the enemy, anxiously approaching first Bertincourt then Barastre. It would not have surprised them if enemy machine-guns had opened on them at any point ; the Germans might have been anywhere about them. But they got through without mishap, and Rocquigny was entered at 7 a.m. of March 24th. It is still a mystery how the Germans got into Bus that night. That they were there there is no doubt, for reports came from many sources that our troops had been fired on from the village. The only explanation is that an enemy patrol must have filtered through from the south-east. But, however simple the explanation now, it does not diminish the tension and anxiety of that eerie march through the night of the 22nd and 24th Battalions.

For three days the troops of the 47th Division had been fighting and marching, digging and manœuvring without ceasing. From now on the operations were of a still more open nature. The men adapted themselves well to the new conditions, and Lewis gun and rifle fire were very effectively maintained throughout. The men were still unshaken, but tired. There had been no sleep ; food had been eaten when and how it could. Casualties had been heavy, and many men had become separated from their units. The consolidation, therefore, of a definite line of defence was a practical impossibility.

Dawn of March 24th found the 141st Brigade in line by Le Mesnil. The 140th had withdrawn from Lechelle Aerodrome, where they had harassed the enemy's advance from Etricourt. The 142nd were marching into Rocquigny. Divisional head-quarters was at Combles and moved early to Les Bœufs ; the 9th Division was back at Bouchavesnes, thus leaving our right still exposed. We were in touch with the 63rd Division on the left, and the 17th Division was reported to be coming up to fill the gap between us and the 9th Division.

The Germans wasted no time after darkness had disappeared, but advanced in some strength towards St. Pierre Vaast Wood, and, meeting with no opposition, pushed on to Combles and thence in the direction of Morval. A glance at the map will show the precarious position of the 47th Division, and will account for subsequent events.   Massed attacks were made against the position round Mesnil where the 141st Brigade offered a stout and well-maintained resistance.   Fighting was severe, hand-to-hand encounters taking place in Loon Copse. The 51st Brigade (17th Division), which had arrived about 6 a.m. on the right of the 141st Brigade, was forced to retire, and the enemy advanced round our flank on Rocquigny. The 21st Battalion of the 140th Brigade, and the 20th Battalion of the 141st Brigade, under Lieut.-Colonel F. R. Grimwood, still held on, however, and kept the enemy at bay east of the village all the morning.   Attack after attack was repulsed with a vigour that must have surprised the enemy, and it was not until 2 p.m. that most of our men left the village.   Lieut.-Colonel G. Dawes, D.S.O., M.C., commanding the 21st, with a few headquarter details, remained in Rocquigny until 3.30.

The remains of the 20th Battalion held the line in front of Rocquigny alone after the rest of the 140th and 141st Brigades had left.   The enemy were round their right flank and in the village behind them, but the 63rd Division were holding the line to the left, and they decided to protect the right flank of that division as long as they could.   The 20th manned both front and rear of the shallow trench and were heavily engaged, suffering many casualties.   The Battalion was under direct artillery fire from Mesnil.   At 4 p.m. the 63rd Division unexpectedly retired, and the 20th Battalion were left practically surrounded.   They then fought their way back towards Le Transloy, but were under close-range fire from three sides and very few of the battalion reached Le Transloy at dusk.   Lieut.-Colonel Grimwood and his Adjutant were entirely cut off and captured.   The remnant of the battalion from Le Transloy joined the 141st Brigade at High Wood.

The advent of the 51st Brigade on our right eased matters considerably, and it was no doubt due to its presence and resistance that the rest of our Division was able to get away safely and reassemble by Le Transloy.

Meanwhile, the advance on Morval threatened the Les Bœufs-Guinchy Road, along which all the divisional transport was moving.   The R.E. Companies and Pioneers under Major Love and Major J. H. Langton, 4th R.W.F., were ordered to defend this road until the transport should have passed.   Here

Photo by]   [Langfier.

Brig.-General H. B. P. L. KENNEDY, C.M.G., D.S.O.
Commanding 140th Infantry Brigade, 1917-1919.

Facing page 160

the Germans received another surprise, for our men, admirably placed, took advantage of the targets offered, and hundreds of the enemy were mown down by rifle and machine-gun fire. The Motor Machine-gun Battery joined this gallant force later on, intensified the resistance, and increased the slaughter.

The 34th (Army) Brigade R.F.A., which was under the orders of Brigadier-General Whitley, our C.R.A., supported this rearguard, and got some good shooting over open sights at the enemy as they attempted to advance from Morval and from Leuze Wood.

All the transport was withdrawn in good order. Too high praise cannot be bestowed on the spirit of men who had fought for three days, who had fought over some fifteen miles of country, and yet who were still ready, indeed anxious, to dispute every inch of ground. The speed with which the enemy came up towards Les Bœufs prevented our infantry forming a line of resistance near Le Transloy, and orders were sent from divisional headquarters that the retirement must be by Gueudecourt to High Wood, thence in the direction of Albert. The officers commanding brigades had, however, realised the urgency of such a movement, and were already taking their troops in that direction. Meanwhile, the enemy pressed on towards Flers, and urgent orders were sent out that the infantry must make a still wider detour to Eaucourt l'Abbaye, thence to Bazentin. These orders were, unfortunately, delayed owing to the Germans being in possession of the only road eastwards. Brave efforts were made by despatch-riders, now the only means of communication, to get through. Major W. F. Bruce, D.S.O., M.C., commanding the Signal Company, went out himself to take the messages, and the 140th and 141st Brigades received the orders. Major Bruce, however, had the bad luck to be taken prisoner in his efforts to reach the 142nd Brigade. The G.O.C.'s 140th and 141st Brigades had conferred, and previous to the arrival of the divisional orders had decided that the retirement must be by way of Martinpuich. The 142nd Brigade made for High Wood, where remnants of the battalions arrived at dusk after a trying march. Brigadier-General V. T. Bailey and some of his staff were captured in the vicinity of Flers. The general himself was wounded, and the brigade-major, Captain H. Peel, D.S.O., 8th London Regiment, was killed.

N

When night fell the tired troops of Brigadier-Generals Kennedy and Mildren arrived at the woods above Bazentin-le-Petit. Lieut.-Colonel Maxwell assembled the remaining men of the 22nd, 23rd, and 24th Battalions in High Wood. Here also were the R.E.'s and Pioneers who had done such brilliant work in the afternoon. Major-General Gorringe and his staff were at Contal-maison, and everyone set to work to reorganise, to get food and ammunition to the troops, and to prepare one more check to the enemy's advance.

High Wood! The words will bring poignant memories to many in the 47th Division. An ironic joke of Fate, surely, to send us back through High Wood. Our troops passed the cross erected there to those brave fellows of the 47th who had succeeded in 1916 where others had failed, and many vowed that we would have no peace till High Wood had been wrested again from the hands of the Germans.

The desolation of the Somme country was in keeping with our feelings. Feet were sore with marching over rough country; stomachs were yearning for nourishment; mouths parched; bodies tired with a heavy, numbing fatigue; these things produced a desolate feeling akin to the quiet sorrow of the surrounding country. It was a sharp, cold night. A brilliant moon shone overhead, and one shivered after the heat and toil of the day. German aeroplanes had been flying low all the afternoon, firing machine-guns on the retreating infantry, and bombing the transport and areas where men assembled. A convoy of ration carts loaded with hot drink, food, and ammunition was organised at the Contalmaison crossroads, and, escorted by the Motor Machine-gun Battery, it moved forward towards Bazentin. The rumble of wheels was the only sound to be heard. Occasional Vérey lights reminded us that the enemy was very near; where, exactly, no one knew—nor did one worry, for what was uppermost in the mind then was food and sleep. Food there was—for the convoy got through safely—but very little sleep.

The Germans remained quiet all night. The troops in High Wood were withdrawn to the west of Bazentin-le-Petit, and there the whole remaining force of the Division was organised, and took up a strong position to meet the further attacks of the enemy. This force was placed later under the command of Brigadier-General Kennedy.

During the morning of the 25th a determined attack by the enemy was repulsed with rifle, Lewis-gun and machine-gun fire. After this, the Germans did not press home their attacks, and General Kennedy's force held the position all day. In the afternoon many Germans were seen in and about Bazentin Wood, and we were able to inflict many casualties. On our right the 17th Division had taken up a position covering Mametz Wood and Montauban, and successfully resisted the enemy's attempts to move forward. There was—the first time since March 21st—no need for us to fear a big outflanking movement from the right; we were at last able to face east, and we knew whence to expect the attack. This fact alone caused a great feeling of relief to all commanders, for all had had sharp experience during the last few days of being attacked from all directions.

During the day, Major-General Gorringe had collected many stragglers from all units and divisions and formed them up along the railway west of Contalmaison. This force was given over to Brigadier-General Mildren, who organised it, and occupied a strong position east of La Boisselle. This was to be the next line of defence if the enemy forced us from the Bazentin position.

Our left flank now became exposed. Touch was lost with the 63rd Division, who were already retiring across the River Ancre, and to cover the flank, the R.E. Companies and Pioneers, with No. 11 Motor Machine-gun Battery, were posted to prevent an advance from the north-east. The good news now reached us that the 12th Division was coming up in support, and in the late afternoon these fresh, strong troops came swinging up the La Boisselle Road. The 37th Brigade was the first to arrive, and immediately went out to extend our left flank towards Pozières. But here things had not gone well.

At 6 p.m. the enemy entered Pozières, but not before the ammunition dumps there had been set on fire by the 37th Brigade, and during the evening ammunition exploded all over the area where the village had once been, and a great fire lit up the surrounding country. The retention of Pozières was necessary if we hoped to hold on to our Bazentin position, and on General Gorringe's orders the 37th Brigade prepared to counter-attack, and so clear our left flank. These preparations were in progress when word arrived that the 63rd Division had decided to retire west of the Ancre, and their troops were already on the move. The operation was, therefore, cancelled, and orders were given to the 47th Division to retire during the night (March 25th-26th) to the other side of the Ancre. General Mildren's force was to go first and take up a position below Bouzincourt, covering the crossings of the river. The 37th Brigade was to hold the La Boisselle position until General Kennedy's force had passed ; then it was to fall back and relieve General Mildren. This operation was successfully carried out, and at dawn the forces of Brigadier-Generals Kennedy and Mildren were relieved and entered Senlis and Bouzincourt.

An officer, writing afterwards, thus describes that last march back :

"We came out at 3 a.m. leaving a small rearguard to hang on till 4 a.m. We collected together and marched under the moon *via* Aveluy to Bouzincourt. It was an extraordinary experience. With want of food and sleep, everyone was dog-tired. Still we kept on slowly moving. We passed outposts of another division forming a protective screen. A great fire of an ammunition dump was burning on Pozières Hill, and four more fires further back flickered in incandescent streaks. It was glorious to cross the Ancre River, and get once more among trees and unshattered houses. Slowly we crept on, and the cold, grey morning revealed us, unshaven and weary, marching on . ."

Indeed, this was no ordinary relief. It embraced something more than the mere handing over of the battle-front to another division. It meant that at last the anxiety of having to protect the flank of the great Third Army was over. It meant rest, food, shelter, and—sleep.

The troops were now exhausted. Everywhere men slept— in stables, barns, beds, wagons, and even by the roadside. Wherever a man could find a quiet place, he slept, not caring where the other man was, or what was happening. There was, for the moment, no longer need to care. Many had not slept for six days. After the day's hard fight was over there had been no rest. Night after night the troops had had to march back to the new position assigned them for the morrow's fighting.

The casualty list was a heavy one. The total losses of the Division had been :

	Officers.	Other ranks.
Killed	16	166
Wounded	75	985
Missing	70	1,079
Total	161	2,230

A more strenuous six days had never been endured by the Division. Against the will of everybody, the Division had been forced to retire. Every position taken up had been hotly contested. Had the operation been on a divisional scale, we could have held the Highland Ridge, the Metz Switch, the Lechelle position, Rocquigny and Le Mesnil, the Bazentin Ridge, the La Boisselle heights. But the German break-through north of St. Quentin made all our forward defensive lines impossible, and the wedge which the enemy was able to drive in behind us at Combles forced our further retreat.

The conditions under which the retirement was carried out, especially on the fourth day, prevented the collecting of all the wounded, and although the medical service did wonderful work under most difficult conditions, it was inevitable that many brave fellows were left. But no man who was admitted to an ambulance fell into the hands of the enemy.

The scarcity of roads and the impossible country of the Somme " prairie " made the retirement of artillery and transport especially difficult. The guns and firing battery wagons had to be taken on the roads, where quick movement was hampered by the transport of all other units. But the batteries missed no opportunity of coming into action. There were even times—at Morval, Bazentin, and Pozières, for example—when the fire became concentrated or evenly distributed along the front at will.

The 47th Division may well be proud of the part it took in the retreat, one of the most difficult and nerve-racking operations it was called upon to carry out in the whole war. The task on the right of the Third Army was not an easy one, for the way in which, time after time, the troops had to change front and beat off flank attacks made it doubly difficult.

After the operation, Major-General Sir George Gorringe, the Divisional Commander, who all through set a splendid example of coolness and determination to resist, wrote an inspiring message to the troops. After briefly reviewing the operations, he said :

"No words of mine can adequately express to you my admiration for the gallantry, determination, and endurance of all ranks during the above trying ordeal. We have lost many gallant comrades, but the magnificent spirit of the Division remains, and those of us still left must fight on with determination and now hold on at all costs to the Sector allotted to us, from which, please God, there will be no withdrawal. I thank you one and all for your loyal and untiring energy, with which you have carried out all the above difficult operations ; it has been a trying ordeal, but you have come through it with enhanced credit and honour, and have done your duty to your King and Country in a manner beyond all praise."

    *   *   *   *   *   *

The Division's respite was a brief one. It was destined to be tried in the fire once more before being given a chance to recuperate and make good its losses. From Senlis the Division moved, on March 26th, to the Louvencourt area, the 140th Brigade, Pioneers, Machine-gunners and Engineers being in Louvencourt itself, and the other two infantry brigades in the neighbouring village of Vauchelles-les-Authie.

In order to ensure that the enemy should not penetrate the Vth Corps front, General Fanshawe decided that the 47th Division should take up a line in rear, running through Vadencourt, Harponville, Lealvillers, and Louvencourt, through which the troops then holding the front line could retire in case of necessity. This line was to be held in depth, the bulk of the 47th Division being disposed in the southern half, since the 2nd Division, holding the northern sector of the Corps front line, was not expected to be heavily engaged.

This defence line was occupied on the morning of March 27th, but in the evening it was considered safe to withdraw the troops to billets at Toutencourt and Warloy. That night each unit received a copy of Sir Douglas Haig's famous order, and learnt that at last the withdrawal was to cease. The present line was to be held at all costs. Our backs were to the wall.

On March 28th the 141st Brigade moved up to Senlis. The other two brigades, with the Machine-gun Battalion and the 11th Motor Machine-gun Battery (which left us a few days later) were concentrated in the deserted, but still almost intact, village of Warloy. Advanced Divisional Headquarters were also in Warloy and the rear echelon at Rubempré. Hopes of a longer rest, however, were dashed by the receipt in the evening of orders to relieve the 36th and 37th Infantry Brigades of the 12th Division in the sector in front of Bouzincourt and Martinsart on the following night.

The reliefs were completed by the 142nd and 140th Brigades by 2.15 a.m. on Saturday, March 30th. The Pioneers and Engineers also moved up from Harponville, where they had been working on rear line of defence to Senlis, with a view to consolidating the support line in rear of the 140th Brigade front.

Sir George Gorringe assumed command at 6 a.m. on March 30th of the front held by the 140th and 142nd Brigades. The enemy had succeeded in crossing the River Ancre and our line ran through Aveluy Wood, where it joined that of the 63rd (R.N.) Division, and up the slopes to the high ground east of Bouzincourt.

A few days of comparative quiet on the divisional front followed, but the shelling of the forward area, and especially of Martinsart and Bouzincourt, became more heavy as the German artillery settled down on the other side of the Ancre.

During the night of March 31st the 140th Infantry Brigade took over an additional piece of the front line from the 17th Division (Robertson) on our right. On the night of April 3rd a patrol of the 142nd Brigade blew up Black Horse Bridge over the Ancre.

The battalions were very much reduced in strength and the men weary. The 141st Brigade, however, had had a few days in which to reorganize, and on April 1st a composite battalion formed from the remnants of the 19th and 20th relieved the 15th Battalion of the 140th Brigade, as well as the left company of the 21st, in the line. The 15th moved back to Senlis for a few days' rest before again returning to the line.

The artillery supporting the Division, under the command of our own C.R.A., consisted at this time of two Army Field Artillery Brigades, the 77th and the 48th. The latter, in the valley behind Bouzincourt, had many casualties from mustard gas.

Brigadier-General R. McDouall, who had returned to the Division to replace Brigadier-General Bailey, took over command of the 142nd Infantry Brigade on April 3rd.

The 12th Division had now taken over the line on our right. After a bombardment on April 4th the Germans attacked them in two waves, but were repulsed with heavy losses. Information was received from the Vth Corps at midnight that an attack on the 47th Divisional front was expected to follow next day, and the brigades were warned accordingly.

On the morning of April 5th the infantry of the Division was disposed as follows :

RIGHT BRIGADE   ..   ..   140th Infantry Brigade.

Left Battalion—20th London Regt. (with one company, 19th London Regt. attached) | Right Battalion—15th London Regt.

Support Battalion ..   ..   .. 18th London Regt.

LEFT BRIGADE   ..   ..   142nd Infantry Brigade.

Left Battalion—24th London Regt. | Right Battalion—23rd London Regt.

Support Battalion ..   ..   .. 22nd London Regt.

RESERVE BRIGADE ..   ..   141st Infantry Brigade, consisting of the 17th, 21st, and 19th Battalions, London Regt., all concentrated in Senlis.

From this it will be seen that in several cases battalions were not under the command of their normal brigade.

The storm broke soon after dawn. At 6.30 a.m. the enemy placed a heavy barrage on the left of the divisional front and this shelling quickly spread southwards. Soon the whole of the divisional front and the back areas were being shelled at intervals, special attention being paid to Senlis, Bouzincourt, and Martinsart. There was also some shelling of Warloy.

By 8 o'clock the bombardment was intense, and the enemy had launched an attack with three divisions through the clouds of gas and smoke on the IVth Corps front. The attack came from a south-easterly direction. It was ascertained from prisoners taken during the operations that its objectives were Bouzincourt and Mesnil, thus including the fronts held by the 12th, 47th, and 63rd Divisions.

AVELUY. FROM AVELUY WOOD.

The attack fell first on the 142nd Brigade, whose left battalion (the 24th) was attacked at 7.20 a.m., and the other shortly after. Here the enemy met with some little success, forcing back the left flank of the 23rd Battalion, and contriving to get in behind some of our posts in Aveluy Wood, but his advancing masses were met with sustained rifle, Lewis-gun, and artillery fire which caused tremendous losses.

At 9.48 a.m. the 20th Battalion, on the left of the 140th Brigade, were also attacked, but held their ground. Owing to his success in the S.W. corner of Aveluy Wood the enemy was able to enfilade their position, and as the right of the 142nd Brigade had been driven in somewhat, it became necessary for the 20th Battalion to form a defensive flank northwards towards Northumberland Avenue. Though every one of its Lewis guns was put out of action, the 20th held firm.

The whole line of the Division was now engaged, although no attack had yet been delivered against the 15th Battalion on the extreme right. About 10.30 a.m. the enemy, by a sudden rush, succeeded in breaking the line of the 142nd Brigade in Aveluy Wood between the two battalions, the left company of the 23rd being surrounded and almost annihilated after a desperate resistance.

Orders were given by the Brigadier to the 22nd Battalion, which had been in reserve, to counter-attack and to try to re-establish the line. The counter-attack was delivered by A and D Companies at 4 p.m., but failed to get back to the original line, for the battalion, which had suffered heavy losses, including eight officers, had no longer sufficient weight. Some ground, however, was regained and a continuous line established along the slope above the western edge of Aveluy Wood. A threatened gap between the 24th Battalion and the right battalions of the 63rd Division, which was also exhausted and holding its line with difficulty, was closed by reinforcements from the 22nd Battalion and two companies of Marines. By six o'clock the shelling, which had been incessant since early morning, died down.

General Gorringe decided that a further effort to restore the original line must be made on the following morning, and for this purpose he placed at the disposal of the 142nd Infantry Brigade the only battalion which remained in reserve—the 4th Royal Welsh Fusiliers. The latter were to be used in support of the remaining troops of the 22nd Battalion, who were to attack in a southerly direction as soon after dawn as observation permitted.

Orders to this effect, in confirmation of verbal orders by telephone, were sent to the 142nd Infantry Brigade at 9.30 p.m., but did not reach the brigade until 12.40 a.m. In the meantime, Brigadier-General McDouall had already discussed the proposed counter-attack with the commanders of the left artillery group, the Machine-gun Battalion, and the 4th R.W.F., and had decided to carry out the attack forming up along our own front line in front of the railway. This frontal attack was decided on as affording the simplest forming-up position for the Pioneer Battalion, who had no previous knowledge of the country. Orders to this effect were issued to the 4th R.W.F. by the Brigade.

A copy of these orders reached Divisional Headquarters at 4.15 a.m., and although they were not in accordance with the divisional orders mentioned above, General Gorringe decided that it was then too late to make any alteration, and that the attack should be carried out as arranged by the 142nd Brigade. Owing to the whole of the 22nd Battalion having been used, it was found necessary to carry out the counter-attack with the 4th R.W.F. only.

The Pioneers had been moved forward during the afternoon of April 5th from Senlis to a temporary position along the Bouzincourt-Martinsart road, where they were in support to the left brigade. Here they received at 10 p.m. a warning order from the brigade that they were to be prepared to attack at dawn. A hasty move forward was then made, and by 4 a.m. A and B Companies were assembled for the attack along the bank to the west of Aveluy Wood.

At 5.55 a.m. this desperate attack was launched by the Welshmen. As the official narrative states : " No troops could have deployed better or advanced more steadily under such intense fire, and the leadership of the officers could not have been excelled." But the hostile machine-gun fire made progress impossible for even the most gallant troops.

Two platoons of A Company were able to hold on to one corner of the wood and to silence one enemy machine-gun by bombing and killing the crew, but no further advance could be made in face of the withering fire which came from the wood.

The casualties among the two attacking companies had been heavy, including 9 officers and 65 other ranks killed and 2 officers

and 81 other ranks wounded. Lieut. N. I. Wilson, M.C., who led
B Company, was hit twice in the first few seconds, but staggered
on at the head of his men to the fringe of the wood, where he fell
riddled with bullets.*

During the same morning (about 10 a.m. on April 6th) the enemy
renewed his attack on the junction between the 47th and 63rd
Divisions. Here he not only made no progress, but lost heavily
from our machine-gun fire. The left company of the 24th Battalion
took advantage of his discomfiture to make a sudden local advance,
and captured two machine-guns and 21 prisoners of the 227th
R.I.R., 107th Division. During this operation Lance-Corporal
March, one of a patrol sent out by the centre company, went
forward and personally entered into an engagement with a hostile
patrol. He shot the officer commanding it and brought back his
maps and papers containing information of importance.

In the evening the enemy attacked on the right front of the
142nd Brigade, but were completely repulsed, and the line, as it
then stood, was the high-water mark of the German advance
north of Albert.

The 142nd Brigade, with the 4th R.W.F. and 20th London
Regiment attached, were relieved that night by the 106th Brigade,
35th Division, and withdrew to Warloy and Senlis. The 140th
Brigade remained in the line, without further incident of importance,
until the night of April 8-9th, when they were relieved in the right
sector by the 105th Infantry Brigade, and withdrew to Hedauville,
marching thence to Acheux, where they " embussed " for Beauval
—the first stage on the journey back to the rest area round Canchy,
Le Titre, and the Forest of Crécy. Here the infantry was left to
reorganise, refit, and train until the end of April.

By the appointment of Major J. C. D. Carlisle, D.S.O., M.C.,
to be G.S.O.2, Intelligence, at VIIIth Corps, the Division lost, on
April 10th, an officer who had done distinguished service with it
since its first arrival in France. As regimental officer, as adjutant of
the Civil Service Rifles, as G.S.O.3, as Brigade Major of the 142nd
Brigade, and finally as G.S.O.2 through the trying times of the
last winter he had become known to most of the Division. In

---

* Subsequent attacks were made on Aveluy Wood in much greater force by other
divisions but with unvarying failure   The enemy continued to hold it till forced to
withdraw before our general advance in the following August.

him we lost not only an imperturbably cheerful and efficient Staff officer, but one of the last remaining members of the Divisional Staff who was entirely one of ourselves, a Territorial and an original member of the Division.   No division, however, could have been more fortunate in the Regular officers on its Staff, or have found men who adapted themselves more readily to the strange ways of the Territorial soldier.

Chapter XIV.

THE ARTILLERY IN THE WITHDRAWAL.

NO account of the work of the 47th Division during the German offensive of March, 1918, would be complete without some record of the part played by its gunners, who were separated from the remainder of the Division on the first day of the attack, and spent the next few weeks fighting with the IVth Corps, further north. Their wanderings may well form the subject of a separate chapter.

For the following brief account of the adventures of the Divisional Artillery between March 21st and May 22nd, when they rejoined the Division, we are indebted to the full narrative compiled by Brigadier-General Whitley from reports supplied by the two brigades.

On the morning of March 21st the 235th and 236th Brigades, R.F.A., were at Bus, where they had enjoyed a fortnight out of the line, spent chiefly in training in mobile warfare. Nos. 1 and 2 Sections of the Divisional Ammunition Column were at Pont Noyelles, between Albert and Amiens, where they had lately acquired from Marseilles 150 Indian native drivers. These proved to be quite untrained. Riding and driving had to be taught, and the men's strength built up before they could possibly take the place of British drivers.

In view of the probability of attack the two brigades had worked out a number of schemes and reconstructed many positions to support counter-attacks both on the north and south sides of the Flesquières salient, and A/235 Battery, R.F.A., had been detailed to find sections ready to move up at fifteen minutes' notice for the purpose of dealing with any hostile Tanks which might be used.

It will be remembered that the Vth Corps was holding the Cambrai salient, with the IVth Corps on its left, and the VIIth Corps of the Fifth Army on its right. The whole of the 19th Division and the infantry of the 2nd Division, with the 235th and 236th Brigades, R.F.A., were in the Vth Corps reserve.

From this point the story of the two brigades must be taken separately.

On March 21st the 235th Brigade was to have relieved the 41st Brigade of the 2nd Division about Beaucamp. Guns were to be handed over in position and the relief completed by noon. At 6 a.m., however, this relief was cancelled, and the 235th Brigade was ordered to " stand by."

At noon, its commander, Lieut-Colonel S. W. L. Aschwanden, D.S.O., received orders from the Vth Corps to report to the C.R.A., 19th Division, and for the batteries to rendezvous near Haplincourt. On arrival, he found that the orders had been cancelled, but that his brigade, with the 236th Brigade under Lieut.-Colonel Bowring, was to come under the command of the C.R.A., 17th Division, then at Bertincourt. Here, Lieut.-Colonel Aschwanden was informed that the 235th Brigade would not be required, and the batteries were ordered back to Bus.

At 5 p.m., after another conference at 17th Divisional Artillery Headquarters, the brigade was ordered to occupy a position of readiness in Vélu Wood, and the batteries moved into it about six o'clock. No further instructions were received, and two hours later, in response to a telephone message, the brigade commander was informed that he no longer came under the orders of the 17th Division.

During the night orders were received from the 51st (Highland) Divisional Artillery (IVth Corps) at Frémicourt, to whom the brigade had been attached, instructing it to move northwards, where it came into action early on March 22nd in positions indicated by guides about Beugny.

Lieut.-Colonel Aschwanden was ordered to report to Lieut.-Colonel F. Fleming, D.S.O., who would command a group consisting of the 235th Brigade, and the remnants of his own brigade, which had been roughly handled on the 21st.

Accompanied by his adjutant, the brigade commander went to the map location of group headquarters given to him by the 51st Divisional Artillery, but found that by now it was in front of our front line and that the group commander had left some hours previously. It was now 6 a.m. on the 22nd, and no information could be gleaned as to where the group had gone. After a long search, however, they were located at the old sapper camp near Lebucquière, with no signals, no batteries, and no communications of any kind. The 235th Brigade lent them telephones, and Lieut.-Colonel Aschwanden established his headquarters in close proximity, laying out lines to his batteries which were covering the front of one of the infantry brigades 51st Division, which was being heavily attacked on the front about Beugny.

During the afternoon of March 22nd, as the enemy were advancing in great strength on the line Beaumetz-Morchies, it was decided to withdraw the batteries one at a time to a position of assembly about Haplincourt. The withdrawal was effected before dark with the loss of one gun of B/235 Battery, of which the teams were killed. After two vain attempts to get it away the gun was destroyed.

Each battery remained in action until the last moment and did good work in covering the infantry withdrawal. Lieutenant W. E. Brown, A/235th Battery, gained an M.C. for specially gallant work with his section, which remained in action firing at the advancing Germans over open sights and eventually got clear.

During this phase large numbers of hostile aircraft came over and attacked our infantry positions and the gun teams. The infantry on the right were now coming back fast, and our guns had to drive through them. Owing to large belts of wire few tracks were available for wheeled traffic, and the brigade consequently got badly mixed up with transport and cookers, and it was nearly midnight before the brigade was finally assembled near Haplincourt Wood, C/235 Battery being near Bancourt.

Early on March 23rd the batteries again went into action, covering the line Beugny-Lebucquière, to which the 51st Divisional Infantry had withdrawn. Heavy attacks on both villages were driven off during the day. Late in the afternoon Lieut.-Colonel Aschwanden, after consultation with the group commander, decided to withdraw the batteries, which—especially A/235 and C/235—were now in very forward positions near Riencourt. All the guns were got away with very few casualties during the night, which was comparatively quiet, except for desultory shelling of back areas.

At dawn on March 24th heavy shelling began again, especially on the battery positions and headquarters. Most of the headquarters transport horses were killed and several men wounded. Reports were insistent that Le Transloy, on the right, was in enemy hands, and during the afternoon the batteries were withdrawn to a position of assembly at Ligny-Thilloy. Here Colonel Aschwanden learnt from Brigadier-General T. A. Cubitt, the commander of the 57th Infantry Brigade, 19th Division, that the 19th Division had taken over almost the whole front of the 51st Division, which had lost very heavily in its gallant resistance of the past three days. He was also able at last to obtain a general outline of the situation, and was told that it was intended to withdraw west of Bapaume during the night and to occupy a prepared line.

At about 8.30 p.m. the brigade received orders to move to Loupart Wood and get into action by dawn, covering the line Grévillers-Thilloy. Orders were issued to the batteries, and the brigade commander went in advance to meet battery commanders and reconnoitre positions. On arrival at Loupart Wood he received instructions that all previous orders were cancelled, and that he was to take the brigade to Achiet-le-Petit and to report there to the 51st Divisional Artillery. The batteries were stopped just before it was too late to divert them, and moved by way of Pys, Irles, and Miraumont. From Miraumont, which was reached about midnight, the disorganisation of all traffic control made it impossible to move.

At 10 a.m. on March 25th the traffic was still at a standstill, and it was impossible therefore to carry out orders which had been received from the 51st Divisional Artillery to be in action by dawn covering the line Biefvillers-Loupart Wood. An hour later, however, a move was made and the brigade was brought into action.

Soon after noon Bihucourt and Grévillers were captured and the brigade was ordered to withdraw to Puisieux through Bucquoy. While going through the village of Achiet-le-Petit the batteries came under very heavy and accurate fire, evidently directed by observation, from 8-in. howitzers. The brigade suffered many casualties, but the behaviour of all ranks was excellent and the batteries were collected near Bucquoy.

In accordance with orders received from the 51st Divisional Artillery the brigade came into action just north of Puisieux, but touch could not be established with the infantry and no information could be obtained. At 6 p.m. the brigade commander reported at 51st Divisional Artillery Headquarters, in response to an urgent message. Here he met the C.R.A., 19th Division, who instructed

Photo by]   *[Mendoza Galleries.*

BRIG.-GENERAL SIR EDWARD N. WHITLEY, K.C.B., C.M.G., D.S.O.
C. R. A., 1917-1919.

him to take the 235th Brigade at once to Fonquevillers, and told him that the enemy had taken advantage of a gap between the IVth and Vth Corps and were pushing forward towards Serre and Puisieux.

At Fonquevillers, which was reached about 11 p.m., the brigade bivouacked for the night—the first on which they had been out of action since March 21st.   This was also the first time the harness had been taken off the horses since the beginning of the withdrawal.

On the morning of March 26th the brigade took up positions covering the line Hebuterne-Gommecourt, to which the infantry of the 19th Division had retired.   Officers' mounted patrols were organised and brought back much useful information of enemy movement.   Five attacks were made on Hebuterne during the day. All were repulsed with heavy losses, our guns doing enormous damage.

During the morning it was reported that the enemy had occupied Colincamps and were attacking from there in a north-westerly direction, and for a time the situation was critical.   All transport, including the 47th D.A.C., which was in the vicinity of Sailly-Fonquevillers-Souastre, moved back, with or without orders, and for a time complete chaos existed.   It was said that orders had been given to different units by spies dressed as British staff officers, and that the execution of these orders had become infectious.   Two cases, which were fairly authenticated, of orders given by alleged staff officers came to the notice of the O.C. 235th Brigade, R.F.A.

It was afterwards learned that only small parties of the enemy had entered Colincamps and had been quickly driven out.

In the afternoon a flight of seven German aeroplanes attacked the gunners and teams of 235th Brigade for about a quarter of an hour, and were heavily engaged with Lewis-gun and rifle fire.   Our losses, however, were only two horses killed.

At dusk the line was still held and normal communications were established.   During the night the 19th Division were relieved by the 4th Australian Infantry Brigade, in the sector covered by our guns.

The Australians had only just arrived from the north, fresh and full of vigour, and at once adopted offensive tactics, as did the New Zealand Division on their right.

On March 27th an artillery group was formed, consisting of the 235th Brigade and our old friends of Messines days, the 104th Army

Field Artillery Brigade, now commanded by Lieut.-Colonel Ward, who took command of the group with the 235th Brigade as a sub-group. A regular defence scheme was prepared, observation posts were permanently established, telephonic communication improved, and the situation began to stabilise.

The batteries remained for the next few days in fairly comfortable positions in old gun-pits built in 1916 for the first battle of the Somme. Gun-limbers and teams were kept near the guns, but the remainder of the transport was sent back to waggon lines and billets in Hénu. Here they were joined on March 29th by No. 1 Company of the Divisional Train, and the normal system of supply was restored. For more than a week, owing to the continual movement and frequent changes of orders the brigades, like most other artillery units, had been living more or less " from hand to mouth."

About the end of the month the 104th Army Brigade was withdrawn and replaced by the 93rd Army F.A. Brigade, command of the group passing to Lieut.-Colonel Aschwanden. Fresh positions for the batteries were selected and occupied, and headquarters moved to Château-de-la-Haie, the 93rd Brigade as a sub-group also being located there.

On April 5th the enemy's attack, which fell so heavily on the 47th Division near Aveluy Wood, extended also as far north as Hebuterne. His plans on this part of the front, however, were completely disorganised by a minor operation by the 37th Division, to which the 4th Australian Brigade and the 235th Brigade, R.F.A., were now attached. This operation against enemy positions about Rossignol Wood and Bucquoy was timed for 5.30 a.m. Though it was not entirely successful, as far as objectives were concerned, it resulted in the failure of the German attack and the definite relaxation of all pressure for the time being.

The 235th Brigade experienced five hours of the heaviest hostile shelling. The adjutant and clerks on headquarters staff were all wounded; Lieutenant Green, A/235 Battery, was severely wounded, three men were killed, and a number wounded, and the advanced horse lines suffered severely.

On April 10th the 93rd Brigade was relieved by the 236th Brigade, R.F.A., and the two brigades of the 47th Divisional Artillery were combined in one group, covering first the 37th and later the New Zealand Division. On May 6th the 235th Brigade was relieved by a brigade of the 41st Divisional Artillery and went back to rest at Erondelle, near Abbeville.

* * * * * *

The adventures of the 236th Brigade, R.F.A., under Lieut.-Colonel A. H. Bowring, must now be briefly recorded.

By midday on March 21st this brigade was on the road to Haplin-court with orders to report to the C.R.A. of the 19th Division, IVth Corps. But after it had passed Barastre later orders diverted it to Bertincourt, where the C.R.A., 17th Division, allotted positions near Vélu Wood. By 5 p.m. the batteries were shelling the Germans in Doignies. From six o'clock an hour's barrage was fired to cover a counter-attack by the 17th Division on Doignies, in spite of enemy counter-battery fire.

Towards midnight the batteries were moved back through Bertincourt to Bus, where the transport was picked up, and the whole brigade marched on through Bapaume to reinforce the 6th Division, hard pressed on the north side of the Cambrai road. At Bapaume, A/236 Battery (Captain A. F. R. D. Ryder, M.C.) and B/236 (Major W. J. Barnard, M.C.) were sent north to positions east of Sapignies, while C/236 (Major H. Carey-Morgan) and D/236 (Captain S. Taylor) with Brigade Headquarters took up positions at dawn east of Frémicourt, where barrages had to be carried out at once, as the enemy was approaching Beugny.

Throughout March 22nd the Germans pressed, and during the night on orders from the group commander, Lieut.-Colonel Weber, of the 6th Division, " C " and " D " batteries were moved back into positions west of Frémicourt.

The brigade now came under the 41st Division and the next day (March 23rd) was an anxious one, as the enemy under cover of smoke screens continually forced the infantry to retire. In spite of the ceaseless barrage fire from our guns he was, towards midday on March 24th, established in Vaulx-Vraucourt to the north, from which our batteries were in full view. Under heavy shell-fire the guns were withdrawn to positions nearer Bapaume.

A further retirement was carried out during the night to positions under the shelter of the railway embankment east of Achiet-le-Petit. Major Barnard, of B/236 Battery, had been wounded, and several men killed and wounded during the afternoon. Lieutenant C. H. de Wael, of "D" Battery, was mortally wounded in Achiet-le-Grand during the night.

Morning of the 25th saw the infantry streaming back over the Bihucourt Ridge in front, and the group commander, from a position of observation forward, ordered the brigade again to retire. The teams arrived at the gallop from Achiet-le-Petit, and covered by Tanks and a battery of the 235th Brigade, R.F.A., the guns were pulled out through Achiet and new positions on the eastern outskirts of Bucquoy were taken up, after masses of retiring infantry transport had been cleared away. The enemy was by this time on the positions just vacated, and as the night drew on, by his Verey lights he could be seen to be pushing forward up the Puisieux Valley through the gap which it was now very apparent existed on the immediate right. The teams were shelled out of their lines, and following on this outflanking, by midnight, orders had been received from the C.R.A., 41st Division, who was also in Bucquoy, for a further retirement to the west of Essarts, three miles away.

As dawn broke on March 26th the batteries were coming into action in· the original No Man's Land north of Gommecourt Wood, with teams near by in case of a further retirement. But reinforcing infantry of the 4th Australian Brigade came up and filled the gap on the right and the Bucquoy-Rossignol Wood line held firm, protected by frequent barrages, and a determined attack by the enemy at 5 p.m. failed.

The enemy now appeared to be held up and the teams were sent back to the lines in Bienvillers, where some of them were able to get the first rest they had had from the constant marching and extraordinarily difficult ammunition supply of the last six days and nights.

During these last days of March, although the main retreat was over, continued attacks on Rossignol Wood were held, but there was much shelling, and Lieut.-Colonel Bowring, who was now commanding the group, consisting of his own brigade and two of the 41st Division, was forced to move his headquarters back to the old front line at Gommecourt from a temporary lodgement at the Hannescamps cross-roads; while "D" Battery, with Major H. S. Duncan, M.C., returned to it, moved to better positions under the western trees of Fonquevillers.

On April 5th the 236th Brigade was, like the 235th Brigade, under the orders of the C.R.A., 37th Division, and was supporting the 63rd Infantry Brigade in its counter-attack on Rossignol Wood. On this part of the front the enemy's strong attack which was delivered the same morning was completely foiled, and many prisoners were taken.

From this time the line became stable and trench warfare conditions set in again. The 236th Brigade remained in action with the 42nd and later the New Zealand Divisions until it was finally relieved by the 104th Brigade, R.F.A., pulled out its guns, and marched back by easy stages to the Fourth Army rest area, reaching Liercourt, near Abbeville, on May 9th. Here it enjoyed a well-earned fortnight's rest and made good its losses of men and material.

Mont St Eloi Arras, • October 1917.

Chapter XV.

SUMMER, 1918, AND THE HUNDRED DAYS.

THE success of the German offensive at the end of March shocked the Government and the nation at home into seeing the urgency of the need for more men, and large reinforcements were hastily sent across the Channel.

During the first week in April over 3,000 new troops, mostly boys of eighteen, joined the Division, and had a very uncomfortable first taste of active service in improvised camps in the muddy orchards of Rubempré.

They were absorbed by the brigades on April 9th, when the Division began to move back by way of Beauval and Domart to a pleasant rest near the forest of Crécy. Here for nearly three weeks there was refitting and training, on a green and pastoral countryside untouched by war, such as we had last seen nine months before after the battle of Messines. Time was found for a successful sports meeting at Canchy on April 21st, and on the next day the Train beat the 17th Battalion in the final for the Divisional Football Cup.

At the end of the month the Division was transferred to the Fourth Army, and got ready to take over a section of the Australian Corps front. It was a very different Division from that which had come out of the line a few weeks earlier. All the battalions were full of new officers and men, many of whom had not seen the trenches before, and there had been several changes in command and staff.

On May 2nd the relief of the Australians was complete, and we held a line that ran about 800 yards west of Albert in front of Laviéville, Millencourt, Henencourt, Senlis, and Bouzincourt, well known to us as the area of our rest billets during the Somme fighting of 1916, and again as our Christmas billets in 1917.

The River Ancre flows southwards past Aveluy and through the centre of Albert. Some two miles south of Albert it turns westward and flows through Dernancourt, Buire, Ribemont, and Heilly, to join the Somme at Corbie. The land enclosed by the angle of the river rises in a number of spurs to the ridge upon which stand Senlis, Henencourt and Baisieux.   Between the spurs lie valleys, from Albert towards Bouzincourt and towards Millencourt and Laviéville, and from Ribemont towards Bresle. The whole ridge was strategically important, as the northern bastion of the defences of the Somme valley and Amiens, and the spurs and valleys running up from the Ancre provided an interesting ground for local defence schemes and great scope for defensive works, which were the special care of the higher commands, of whose anxiety the brigades and battalions in the line were daily reminded by personal visits and written orders.

Soon after the beginning of May the Australian Corps "sideslipped" to a position south of the Ancre, and we came under command of the IIIrd Corps, together with the 18th and 58th (London) Divisions, which were our neighbours until we finally left the Somme four months later.   A regular routine was set up, under which two out of the three divisions, brigades and battalions were up and the third back ;   for brigades this meant sixteen days up and eight back. But it was not long before arrangements for further operations began to interrupt the regularity.

May, June and July were in fact very quiet months, but there were many alarms.   At first it was confidently expected that the Germans would make another attempt to capture Amiens and to force their way down the Somme.   An actual day fixed for the attack was several times mentioned in May.   Suspicious sounds were heard a few nights after our arrival, and a subsequent aeroplane reconnaissance reported objects like tanks visible near Fricourt.   A few nights later our engineers blew a line of craters across the Albert-Millencourt road to act as a tank trap.

An alarm nearer home occurred on the night 8-9th May, when a strong party of the enemy attacked an uncomfortable salient at the north end of our trench-line, known by the ill-omened name of " The Hairpin."   The 23rd Battalion garrison of this piece of trench was overpowered, and an immediate counter-attack did not succeed in recapturing the position.   But a further operation by the reserve company, on the following evening, won back the Hairpin with several prisoners.   In this struggle fell Lieutenant J. D. Reid, known to many as bombing-instructor at the Divisional School.

Work of all kinds was plentiful in the sector. It included several new trenches, notably a new communication trench in the left section, the drainage of which was a matter of much discussion, and a support line across the Millencourt valley. The grounds of Henencourt Château were tremendously fortified with concrete machine-gun emplacements, and all over the corps front a number of tunnelled dugouts were made. All these forward works and the enlargement of headquarters farther back kept all the field companies and the pioneers busily occupied, and the infantry did not forget what a working party is. The work was not interrupted by the enemy, and in the back area night bombing was very slight. The occasional attention of a long-range gun to Beaucourt Château did nothing more than interrupt one of several conferences held about this time.

The summer months of 1918, quite apart from the course of operations, were remarkable for two new arrivals. The first was an epidemic of influenza, which during the following winter spread with alarming results to the United Kingdom. The type of fever was fortunately not severe, but it had the effect, especially upon the younger men, of making them unfit for hard work for some weeks after the attack. The effective strength of the Division was thus seriously impaired, and it was only by the efforts of the A.D.M.S. (Colonel Gibbard) and his assistants, who organised field ambulances into convalescent depôts to avoid the wholesale evacuation of sick men, that our man-power was kept up to a practicable working strength. Probably the artillery suffered most severely, since they were engaged in strenuous operations at the beginning of July, and could even less afford than other troops to have their personnel reduced.

The second arrival was as fortunate as the former was unlucky. It was the American Army. Parties of American Intelligence personnel had first visited us at the end of May, and later machine-gun detachments were sent up. On our return to the line, after rest in the Cavillon area, in the middle of July, the whole 33rd American Division was concentrated in the corps area, and the 66th Brigade of this was attached to us during the following weeks, first by companies and later in complete regiments.

The appearance of these new troops, with their fine physique and frank inexperience, had a valuable moral effect on us all, and gave us a wholesome sense of being old soldiers.   The writer had the good fortune to be sent for liaison to the 132nd American Regiment when they first took over a brigade sector of the Divisional front.   Their keenness and their hospitality, and the absence of any ill-founded " cocksureness," are a very pleasant memory.   It was in the allocation of Staff duties and in supply arrangements that they seemed to have most to learn, but whether the difficulties in these respects were due to any inherent weakness, or rather to the precise incompatibility of their organizations with ours, a more competent judge must decide.   It was no surprise to hear how gallantly and well these regiments acquitted themselves in subsequent operations.

We were lucky enough to be supported by our own Divisional Artillery since the end of May, and they moved back with the rest of the Division into corps reserve towards the end of June.   It was a pleasant rest for all and a valuable opportunity for training, for the young troops were not fully broken in to active service conditions, and, although the sector was a quiet one, the strain told quickly on them.   The rest area was a good one, especially for the 141st Brigade, who were at Picquigny, and were there able to bathe and have water sports in the Somme.

The gunners were settled north of the river at Argoeuvres on June 23rd.   Five days later their brigades were on the move forward again, to take part in operations by the Australian corps.   The capture of Hamel and Vaire Wood has since become classical. Strictest secrecy was observed in all preparations, and with the aid of massed guns and many tanks a completely successful and overwhelming attack was launched at dawn on July 4th.   The barrage fire of the guns was especially praised, since they had had little opportunity, in the interest of secrecy, to register upon their barrage lines.   Our 236th Brigade had the satisfaction of turning against the Germans a field gun which was captured in the operations. Both brigades returned to the rest area, but after only two days of rest they were on the move again to relieve the 18th Division on the left sector of the Albert front.   The rest of the Division followed them.

Several personal changes must be noted here.   Early in July, Lieut.-Colonel A. Maxwell left the 23rd Battalion to take command of a brigade ; Lieut.-Colonel Segrave had left the 15th not long before to command a brigade in the 51st Division.   About the same

PATROL OF THE LONDON IRISH ENTERING ALBERT, 1918.

ALBERT CATHEDRAL, 1918.

Facing page 186

time Lieut.-Colonel C. M. Davies (G.S.O.1.) left us, and his place was taken by Lieut.-Colonel B. L. Montgomery: Major J. T. Duffin replaced Major Alexander as D.A.A.G., and Major M. Lewis came to us as G.S.O.2. All these newcomers were with us till the end.

Marshal Foch's great offensive in the Champagne began on July 19th, and from that time onward it became clear that we must all move on soon. We simply had to wait our time. Meanwhile, raids (notably by the 22nd Battalion, on July 24th), patrols, discharges of gas-drums, and constant harassing fire elicited little retaliation.

On August 2nd there were indications that the Germans were withdrawing—explosions were heard in Albert, and they began to shell their own line. We soon established an outpost line along the railway, west of the town, and patrolled freely as far as the Ancre and the western outskirts of Albert. There are photographs in the Imperial War Museum of the 18th Battalion daylight patrols in Albert.

The British offensive began on August 8th, when very successful operations by the Australians and Canadian Corps, south of the Somme, started the Fourth Army's " battle of 100 days." On the following day at 5.30 p.m. the IIIrd Corps began to attack, and the 58th and 12th Divisions made a rapid advance on our right in the angle between the Ancre and the Somme, astride the Corbie-Bray road. By August 13th we had relieved the 58th Division in the line which they had won, just east of Tailles Wood, and our brigades succeeded one another in this uncomfortable position until the next advance was made on August 22nd.

On this date the IIIrd Corps, together with the 3rd Australian Division on their right, planned an advance of about 3,000 yards from a line which ran roughly from the Somme 1,000 yards west of Bray to Albert. From right to left the attacking divisions were the 3rd Australian, the 47th, the 12th, and the 18th.

The 47th Division started from the line of the old Amiens defences, east of Tailles Wood, about 2,000 yards long, and aimed at a final objective, called the Green Line, on the high ground east of Happy Valley, about 3,000 yards long. The south and north boundaries of the Division were therefore divergent straight lines, running roughly east-north-east and north-east respectively. A preliminary objective or Brown Line, roughly on the line of the Bray-Albert road, was first to be seized by the 141st Brigade, and the 142nd Brigade was to advance through them on to the Green Line.

The 140th Brigade was ready further to exploit the advance. Tanks were available to assist the two attacks, and two squadrons of cavalry (1st Northumberland Hussars), together with a fleet of six whippet tanks, were waiting to break through when the Green Line was secured. To give free passage to these the centre portion of the Green Line was left to be captured without a barrage. This part of the front ran in a salient towards the enemy and, moreover, on the reserve slope under his observation. The Corps scheme of attack was based on the general idea that the enemy's resistance would not be severe, that his reserves were dissipated, and that no time would be lost in exploiting further such success as we might achieve. This assumption proved to be wrong.

The 141st Brigade began their advance at 4.45 a.m. and gained their objective without any serious opposition. But in the morning mist and the smoke of battle it was not easy to identify the ground, and most of the Brigade, especially the 20th Battalion on the right, began to consolidate somewhat short of the Brown Line. When the mist cleared away all movement was heavily and accurately shelled.

The 142nd Brigade, also advancing on a three-battalion front (22nd., 23rd., 24th., from right to left), passed through the 141st Brigade up to time. Their further advance met with strong opposition, especially in the centre and on the left, from machine-gun nests. The 24th Battalion suffered many casualties from an exposed left flank ; the 23rd reached the Green Line across Happy Valley, but suffered severely, partly from lack of barrage protection, and were unable, as the event showed, to hold so long a line against a strong counter-attack. The 22nd Battalion made a junction in the chalk-pit on the extreme right of their objective with the Australians, and Lieut.-Colonel Pargiter succeeded in maintaining this position throughout the operation—a most valuable check on enemy counter-attacks and a pivot for our subsequent advance.

Before 9 o'clock the Northumberland Hussars crossed the line, but they met with heavy fire and were compelled to retire at the cost of many casualties. None of the whippet tanks crossed the Green Line. It seems that this scheme of exploitation rested on a miscalculation of the enemy's strength, and the 23rd Battalion could ill afford the barrage protection of which it deprived them.

The day was intensely hot—the hottest, it seems in retrospect, of all the war—and the forward brigades, meeting with unexpectedly severe opposition on this wide front and unable to move without attracting heavy fire, had a most uncomfortable time. The shelling in the forward area also made communication exceedingly difficult and defeated efforts to bring up reserves of ammunition. A supply Tank sent up to Lieut.-Colonel Tolerton, of the 23rd Battalion, was spotted, and became for the time a death-trap to unloading parties, and the Brigade Headquarters in Tailles Wood was continuously bombarded throughout the day.

It was afterwards discovered that the Germans had anticipated our attack, and that their troops were redistributed in depth in order to meet it. A systematic counter-attack had been ordered to start as soon as this redistribution was complete. Soon after 2 o'clock this counter-attack developed, and finally it dislodged our troops from the centre and left of the Green Line. Fortunately the 22nd Battalion, under Lieut.-Colonel L. L. Pargiter, held on to the chalk-pit, from which they threw back a defensive flank connecting up with the rest of the brigade, which rallied on the Brown Line. In this fighting Captain C. H. Oakley specially distinguished himself.

Our operation on August 22nd did not meet with all the success for which we had hoped ; but still less did the counter-operations of the enemy, whose orders had closed with an assertion that " by the end of the day's fighting the outpost zone will again be in our hands." And another captured document referring to the same day's action indicates, if indication were needed, that it was not the quality of our men which baulked us of a full measure of success. " The examination of the captured prisoners," it reads, " presented great difficulty. Those especially of the 23rd London Regiment were apparently excellently schooled in the way they should behave if captured, and they gave very clever evasive answers. The captured sergeant refused absolutely any information."

When the situation after the counter-attack was fully known the 142nd Brigade was withdrawn, and Brigadier-General Kennedy was put in charge of the Brown Line, reinforcing it where necessary with his own troops from the 140th Brigade.

A second attack on the Green Line was made at 1 a.m. on August 24th by the 140th Brigade and the 175th Brigade of the 58th Division, lent to us for the purpose. The assembly was carried out by moonlight, assisted by the capture by the 141st Brigade of some offensive enemy machine-gun posts.* This night attack surprised the enemy and was a complete success. A little difficulty occurred on the extreme left, where the 12th Division was hindered by machine-guns, but General Kennedy sent a tank to deal with these, and the 15th Battalion filled the gap which threatened between the two Divisions.

After this operation the front was handed over to the 58th Division, under whom the 140th Brigade took part in a further advance of 2,000 yards on August 25th, and captured many prisoners.

Then followed three days of rest, refitting, and reinforcement from the Divisional camp, and on August 29th we moved forward to relieve the 12th Division in the line west of Maurepas, and to continue the advance.

We now took our place in a constantly moving battle. Ordered reliefs were impossible, and the 142nd Brigade, which was to lead our advance, simply passed through the 12th Division at 6 a.m. on August 30th, and moved forward as an advance guard, a brigade group complete with R.F.A. and cavalry attached. The line of the advance was due east, and on the right the 24th Battalion went well ahead, but had to wait for the further advance of the 58th Division before they could get over the high ground south-east of Hospital Wood.

The 22nd Battalion on the left met with stronger opposition, especially from Priez Farm and Rancourt, as did the 18th Division farther north. At the end of the day all three battalions were in a line tilted towards south-east and north-west to conform with the position of the Divisions on our flanks. There had been some hard fighting owing to the presence of a newly-arrived German Division, the 232nd. Its quality was not remarkably good, however, and the moral of prisoners taken in large numbers later on fell distinctly low.

But the presence of a fresh Division of the enemy, and his clear intention of fighting for the high ground west of the Canal du Nord,

---

* This feat was cleverly performed by the 18th Battalion. under command of Lieut.-Colonel G. H. Neely. Silently working their way behind the German line of posts, they surrounded, captured, and occupied them, without the enemy being aware of what had happened.

HAPPY VALLEY, BRAY-SUR-SOMME.

put an end for the time to the idea of pursuing with an advance guard. A methodical advance under barrage was planned instead.

On August 31st the 47th Division had merely to swing forward on the right flank to conform with an advance of the 58th Division and Australian Corps. The 142nd Brigade closed in to the left, and the 141st Brigade on the right formed the lower end of the pendulum. The former gained most of their objective during the night by peaceful penetration, and the 141st Brigade moved forward successfully at 5.30 a.m. under a creeping barrage, and gained all the ground required, together with 184 prisoners. The morning was diversified by a determined counter-attack made by a battalion of the German 13th Reserve Division from Rancourt towards Le Forêt and Priez Farm. A part of this attack reached our 18th Battalion and a company of the 19th which had been hastily moved up, and it was completely repulsed after brisk hand to hand fighting ; the rest was caught by artillery barrage and direct machine-gun fire and did not reach our line.

The advance went ahead next day, turned slightly north-east to prepare for a wide encircling movement from the south intended by the IIIrd Corps. The objective was the west edge of St. Pierre Vaast Wood. The 141st Brigade on the right, and the 140th on the left, successfully took this line with many prisoners, and a motor ambulance complete with driver and two doctors, which fell into the hands of the 140th Brigade at Rancourt.

During the morning it was found that the enemy still held Priez Farm, which was on the left of our line, at its junction with that of the 18th Division. The 142nd Trench-mortar Battery and two platoons of the 23rd Battalion were ordered to deal with them. A hurricane bombardment by Stokes mortars was directed on the point, after which the garrison was captured. Eighty of them were taken by Captain Blofeld and one man of his battery.

The operations of September 2nd were designed on a more elaborate plan, in which the rôle of the 47th Division was subsidiary to an extensive attack by the 74th (Dismounted Yeomanry) Division, with Nurlu as its objective. The 142nd Brigade was to secure the south-west edge of Vaux Wood and Monastir Trench, which ran south-east from its lowest point, while the 140th Brigade was to form a defensive flank to the 74th Division, running east-north-east from the southern end of the 142nd Brigade's objective across the canal towards Nurlu. The Divisional southern boundary thus ran clear north of the village of Moislains, but the occupation of their objective by the 140th Brigade obviously presupposed the capture of that place.

The preparations of the Division for this operation were unusual, but very successful. Brigadier-General Mildren was made responsible for holding the existing front and, as his brigade was weak and busy with consolidation, he employed four companies of machine-guns which were placed at his disposal to hold this line. The 140th Brigade moved back west of the Peronne-Bapaume road, where they had time for food and a short rest before starting to move forward at dawn. Meanwhile, the 142nd Brigade came up from rest near Le Forêt and assembled in the line of their advance. A very dark night made these moves difficult, but they were accomplished without mistake.

The 142nd Brigade started at 5.30 a.m. under barrage, and in spite of considerable opposition made good a line of trench (Sorrowitz Trench), which continued northwards Moislains Trench, running west of the village. They captured many prisoners on their way, and a complete battery of 77-mm. guns. Here Captain C. H. Oakley, of the 22nd, was killed—a very gallant young officer who had won his way up until he was second-in-command of his battalion.

It was in this advance that Pte. Jack Harvey of the 22nd Battalion won the Victoria Cross. His company was checked soon after the start by machine-gun fire, whereupon Pte. Harvey ran forward through our own barrage and in face of heavy fire rushed a machine-gun post, shooting two of the team and bayoneting a third. He put the gun out of action, and then made his way along the trench until he came to a dugout, into which he dashed and compelled the surrender of its thirty-seven occupants. These he relieved of much useful property as they filed out of the dugout. In the course of his action Pte. Harvey had dropped a bag of rations which it was his duty as company cook to carry, but he managed to find another, which he duly delivered to his officer some hours later.

The 142nd Brigade could not make good the last 500 yards of their intended advance on the right in face of the opposition from Moislains on the flank; and the fact that Moislains and its vicinity were not clear of the enemy prevented the 140th Brigade from

Sergeant J. HARVEY, V.C.,
22nd Battn. London Regt. (The Queen's).

carrying out the task allotted to them, which was to follow the leading brigade of the 74th Division and to make a defensive flank across the canal covering their further advance from attack from the north.

As it turned out all three battalions of the 140th Brigade were engaged heavily as they moved down the slope towards Moislains, and it was with great difficulty that they established themselves in Moislains Trench, west of the village. This was indeed some of the hardest fighting during the whole advance of the Division, and it was all the more difficult owing to the fact that the brigade was officially not fighting, but following up a successful attack over ground outside the Divisional boundary.

In the centre Lieut.-Colonel Fielding's 15th Battalion lost half its strength in casualties, and was at one time being attacked from the left rear and right front, and by a bombing party in Moislains Trench itself. Similarly Lieut.-Colonel Dawes, on the right, had to meet opposition on both his flanks and from the village at once. But the line of Moislains Trench was consolidated, and the exposed right flank protected by a battery of machine-guns.

Further progress north of the Division released the 141st Brigade, and the Pioneer Battalion cleared St. Pierre Vaast Wood and assisted the 142nd Brigade in their consolidation. The 140th Brigade were relieved as soon as possible by the 142nd Brigade and by troops of the 74th Division, and withdrew to rest near Maurepas.

The IIIrd Corps now waited upon developments on the right, where the Australians were attacking Mont St. Quentin, and there was little activity on September 3rd and 4th beyond active patrolling in the neighbourhood of the Canal du Nord—or rather, the canal cutting, for it contained no water below the lock north-east of Moislains, but seemed rather to be a repository for dead horses and other refuse. On the night 3rd-4th the enemy finally left the village.

On September 5th the 142nd Brigade was holding the line of the Canal due east of Moislains.

At 5.30 a.m. the 141st Brigade, with gunners, cavalry and cyclists attached, started advancing through this line towards the Nurlu ridge. A check occurred on the right, and a factory and some quarries straight ahead were inconvenient obstacles. It was decided to attack again under barrage in the evening, and at 7 p.m.

P

in a violent thunderstorm the 140th and 141st Brigades pushed on without difficulty to the top of the ridge. An enterprising battery of the 112th Brigade R.F.A. had crossed the canal in the afternoon and gave the infantry useful support at that range.

The same two brigades moved on at dawn on September 6th. Little opposition was met, and by the end of the day a line was established east of Liéramont. Forward sections of guns had good targets as the enemy withdrew before our advance.

That same evening the 58th Division came up by 'bus to relieve us, and on the following day the 140th and 141st Brigade were carried back to Heilly and Corbie, while the 142nd Brigade marched to Cléry and thence by 'bus to Méricourt L'Abbaye. Three days later the whole Division was settled in the Fifth Army area.

The work of the pioneers during these operations was mainly conducted under the C.R.E., and consisted in following hard on the heels of the advancing infantry and hastily making tracks fit for artillery and wheeled transport across the devastated area of the old Somme battlefield.

There were occasional diversions, however—for example, that already mentioned, when, on September 2nd, the battle line became comparatively stationary owing to the presence of enemy machine-guns in the depths of St. Pierre Vaast Wood, and the 4th R.W.F. were suddenly ordered to desist from their normal activities and " mop up " the wood.

This minor operation was conducted successfully, and by 8 p.m. the wood was reported clear. Three snipers were rounded up and the advance continued.

With the construction of crossings over the Canal du Nord, and of artillery tracks thence forward towards Liéramont and Nurlu, there came an end to a period of three weeks' strenuous and highly successful work by the engineers and pioneers. Owing to the hastiness of the advance their achievements often passed unnoticed, but they were no mean contribution to the final victory.

By this time the ranks of the Division were much reduced in numbers and further reinforcements were not forthcoming. The operations in which it was to take part afterwards, consisting of a holding attack on the Lille front, were of secondary importance and out of the area of the decisive battle.

NURLU VILLAGE.

LONGUEVAL CROSS ROADS.
(Delville Wood in background.)

It was appropriate enough that the Somme should be our last battlefield, still more so that it should be the scene of our most obvious success, by the crude measurement of ground won from the enemy. For we owed the Germans a double debt on that field, of six months' and of two years' standing. And it was appropriate that it fell to the gunners to fight again over the very ground of our old battles, for a greater proportion of them than of the infantry knew the ground of old, and their weapons were perhaps the best able to pay back with interest what the Germans had given us before. There was frequent opportunity for this repayment, and it was not neglected.

From August 13th to September 4th the brigades of the Divisional Artillery were supporting the 18th Division in the north sector of of the Corps' front. Lieut.-Colonel Aschwanden was commanding the 235th Brigade, and Major Cooper had temporary command of the 236th Brigade. Brig.-General Whitley and his staff remained with the 47th Division throughout. The very successful advance of the 18th Division took them approximately due east through Albert, and our gunners renewed their acquaintance with La Boisselle, Contalmaison, Longueval, Combles and many other such desolate spots known by the names of villages. Several officers of the 236th Brigade inhabited the same dugouts in Caterpillar Valley that they had lived in in 1916, and were there greeted by the same kind of barrage that they had met before.

The battery commanders of the same brigade had a narrow escape from capture at Longueval crossroads, when the " village " was temporarily retaken by the enemy—an incident strangely reminiscent of March, 1918. The tables were very completely turned when the Germans were driven in retreat down the Sailly Saillisel valley and Captain Ryder was able to turn his guns on their transport massed on the very roads along which ours had retreated six months earlier.

It is difficult to do justice to the great enterprise and energy of the gunners during this advance. They never failed to do all and more than the infantry asked, and they did this in the face of peculiar difficulties. Water was scarce, for the Somme was far from the north sector, and the pumping plants supplied only enough to water the animals twice a day. At the same time the demand kept all available transport working at the highest pressure. In spite of the rapid advance, creeping barrages were asked for almost daily, and it is most creditable to all concerned that the ammunition did not fail. Not less creditable was the arrangement of barrage lines at short notice which often deprived battery officers of their small chances of sleep.

Meanwhile, the enemy had abundance of ammunition of all kinds, since he was constantly retiring upon his dumps, and a large share of this fell on the battery positions during the first few days of the advance. On the night of August 21st-22nd, for instance, D/236th Battery had their commander and thirty-five men out of action from gas shell poured upon the position from which they were bound to support the infantry attack; two days later the 235th Brigade needed much skill and some luck to cross the Ancre successfully in Albert; and later on a collection of batteries which had converged at Government Farm was drenched with mustard gas.

There were many smaller instances in which the enemy's harassing fire with shell of various weight and type tested the determination of the gunners very severely. Among a good many casualties mention must be made of the serious loss to the Division in the death of Major P. J. Clifton, D.S.O., commanding A/235 Battery, who was mortally wounded early on August 26th, before the attack on Montauban. Major Clifton had served with us throughout the war, and was well known for his energy and his daring leadership.

The continued fine weather was greatly in our favour, and heightened the contrast between this battle and the muddy fighting of 1916. Roads and tracks could be used which rain would have turned to quagmires, and the dry ground and shelters offered comfortable sleep whenever the chance came. But things moved so fast that every man and beast was used to the utmost. The habit of fixed warfare was still an impediment to many, and a large part of the infantry, now engaged in active fighting for the first time, had not in their minds the peculiarly encouraging contrast of present conditions with less hopeful times. Yet it was everything to know that things were really moving at last. And it was no mere " walk-over." The Germans were there in plenty, and they were being beaten, and no one dreamed now of settling down again to old manners of trench war. A steady flow of prisoners came in, and many machine-guns and larger weapons were captured by the Division.*

---

*Prisoners captured August 22nd—September 6th :—Officers, 23 ; other ranks, 1,442. Material captured August 22nd-31st :—Machine guns, 158 ; minenwerfer, 7 ; field guns, 11 ; trench mortars, 31 ; anti-tank guns, 3 ; 5.9in. howitzers, 2.

Perhaps the change in our warfare is best indicated by the fact that Divisional Headquarters, generally supposed to be an immobile unit, moved forward about every other day during the last ten days of the advance, and the Camp Commandant, faced with the problem of almost nightly pitching his moving tent, was not the least anxious man in the Division.

Communications were simplified by the daily establishment of an advanced Divisional Headquarters near the commander of the leading brigade, and there was a suggestion of other more normal campaigns when, from the high ground west of Moislains, the Divisional Commander was able to watch the progress of the advance up the further side of the valley. If there has been little or no personal reference to General Gorringe in this narrative, it is for the simple reason that he throughout so identified himself with all the interests of his Division, and was so constantly and personally in touch with its operations, that any of us who were lucky enough to serve under him associate him inevitably with every mention of the 47th Division.

[illegible] Année N° [illegible] DEUX PAGES 10 CENTIMES Lundi [illegible] Octobre 1918

LE PROGRÈS DU NORD

ET DU PAS-DE-CALAIS

HONOUR FOR ENGLISH ARMY!

The « Progrès du Nord » first news paper appearing in Lille, after the Hun's departure is very happy to present the grateful hommage of the population, to brave english army, in deliberating Lille.

LE JOUR de la Reconnaissance

A l'heure où paraissent ces lignes, les troupes anglaises et leur chef éminent le général Birdwood font leur entrée officielle dans la ville de Lille au milieu d'une foule qui — il est aisé de le deviner — sera à la fois immense et enthousiaste. C'est la journée de la Reconnaissance

Les Anglais ! Mots évocatoires pour tous ceux qui ont vécu les quatre années terribles. Mots qui signifient pour eux plus que pour d'autres, mots qui sont faits de tant d'illusions, de tant d'impatiences, de tant d'espoirs !

Les Anglais ! Mots que nous avons entendus si souvent sur les lèvres de nos bourreaux, mots dont le Boche, alors sûr de la victoire, nous flagellait à chaque instant.

J'en appelle à tous nos frères de douleur et de misère. Ils n'ont pas oublié, ils n'oublieront jamais ces réponses insolentes par lesquelles nos bourreaux croyaient libérer leur conscience.

L'autorité allemande voulait-elle enlever nos femmes et nos filles en avril 1916 ? Sans vergogne elle déclarait sur ses affiches que les Anglais empêchant le ravitaillement de la population, elle se voyait obligée, *dans notre intérêt*, de vider les foyers et de faire pleurer les mères.

Manquait-on de vivres ? Les nécessités de la guerre obligeaient-elles nos avions à inquiéter l'ennemi ? La paix n'était-elle pas signée malgré le désir des boches, doux agneaux comme chacun sait ? C'était la faute aux anglais, toujours ! Et ainsi les allemands avaient la prétention d'excuser leurs vols, leurs destructions, leurs crimes, sans s'apercevoir qu'ils réussissaient seulement à aggraver leur cas en se montrant à la fois imbéciles et criminels.

Un jour, ces Anglais, qu'on essayait de salir après avoir essayé de les railler cette « méprisable petite armée anglaise », comme l'avait appelée naguère le Kaiser ou un de ses valets officiels, déboucha sous les murs de Lille. Ce que firent les Boches en ce jour mémorable, tout le monde le sait. Empilant en hâte le butin mal acquis dans ses camions et ses chariots, il s'enfuit courageusement vers des régions plus sûres !

Que nos libérateurs le sachent bien. Ils trouvent ici une population qui, malgré les tentatives allemandes, n'a jamais voulu se laisser tromper et qui a toujours opposé aux mensonges de la presse allemande une arme bien française : le sourire, ce sourire que les Boches ne pouvaient comprendre et qui était pour nous un soulagement et une vengeance.

Nous savions ce qu'avait fait, au début de la guerre, l'admirable armée anglaise, petite par le nombre mais grande par la vaillance. Nous savions l'effort prodigieux accompli par l'Angleterre pour forger, en si peu de temps, l'arme efficace qu'elle manie aujourd'hui. Ceci suffisait pour espérer et pour croire et à présent que les temps sont venus, les Lillois sont heureux d'offrir l'hommage reconnaissant des opprimés d'hier à ceux qui ont brisé leurs chaînes.

MARTIN-MAMY.

LES BELLES AVENTURES

Une Lilloise au front

Nous étions quelques-uns, à la Mairie, qui causions de la grande guerre et des dévouements qu'elle a suscités. L'un des causeurs, notre concitoyen Arthur Collin, à qui M. Delesalle adressait l'autre jour des félicitations pour les services qu'il a rendus à la ville de Lille, pendant l'occupation, me prit à part et me dit : « J'ai reçu la visite d'une jeune Lilloise qui vient du front, où elle fait de grandes choses. Voulez-vous la voir ? »

Et, tout de suite, je répond « oui ».

Notre héroïne s'appelle Suzanne Rhein. Elle est la fille d'un ingénieur de notre ville. En mai 1915, bloquée à Lille, elle voulut revoir son père qui combattait sur l'Yser. Déguisées en mendiantes, sa mère et elle traversèrent la Belgique et passèrent en Hollande, après avoir essuyé le feu d'une patrouille allemande. De Belgique, les deux femmes se rendirent en Angleterre, puis en France. Elles s'établirent à Paris. Au mois de mai 1916, elles apprirent la mort de M. Rhein, tombé face à l'ennemi, devant Verdun. Les deux femmes s'enfermèrent dans le silence qui convient aux grandes douleurs.

Et Mlle Suzanne Rhein continua ses études au Lycée Fénelon. Des idées hardies la hantaient et elle se disait que le jour finirait bien par venir où elle pourrait se rendre utile. Il y a six mois, en parcourant un journal, elle y lut qu'une infirmière venait d'être tuée sur le champ de bataille. Sa résolution fut aussitôt prise. Elle erra de bureau en bureau, se heurtant partout à des sourires de gratitude attendrie : « C'est très bien, Mademoiselle, ce que vous nous proposez. Vous êtes malheureusement trop jeune ».

Un Comité anglais, pourtant, l'accueillit, et on la dirigea, sur sa demande vers le front, en qualité d'infirmière du corps expéditionnaire britannique. Elle sert, depuis son engagement, aux premières lignes, portant des boissons chaudes aux combattants qu'elle réconforte de la voix et du sourire.

La présence d'une femme à proximité de la ligne de feu a toujours agi avec une tendre force sur le moral des hommes. Rappelez-vous la scène du siège d'Arras dans le « Cyrano » de M. Rostand et l'arrivée de Roxane parmi les cadets qui n'en peuvent plus. Seulement ce ne sont plus d'innocentes mousquetaires que doit braver notre petite compatriote. Elle mène la dure vie des soldats dont elle partage les périls. Et l'insigne des blessés qu'elle porte épinglé sur sa poitrine atteste que plus d'une fois le vent de la mort a passé sur son visage. Les nuits où la mitraille fait rage, elle descend dans ces abris de fortune où les obus parfois, creusent des brèches. On m'a montré des cartes de visite qui fixent le souvenir de ces heures pathétiques. Uniques titres de noblesse ! Les officiers britanniques y disent leur admiration émue, leur respect charmé.

« — Les bombardements, mademoiselle, doivent être terribles au début ?

— Au début, oui ; mais on s'y fait. Et puis nous avons de belles compensations. Figurez-vous qu'un jour la musique d'une division italienne s'est mise à jouer la *Marseillaise*. Il y avait beaucoup de Français aux environs. Cette *Marseillaise*, à quelques centaines de mètres de l'ennemi, c'était immense, nos hommes en étaient bouleversés.

Une autre fois, je passais près d'un cortège de prisonniers allemands. Un avion boche nous lance des bombes. Les allemands se sauvent avec des cris sauvages. Et les nôtres de rire, de rire... »

Elle rit aussi, d'un rire d'enfant très doux.

Puis son visage reprend son expression sérieuse. Elle n'est plus qu'une jeune fille en visite.

Mais je l'évoque coiffée du casque de guerre sous lequel disparaissent ses lourds cheveux, au milieu de ceux qui vont mourir dans le tonnerre de la bataille.

PAUL-T. PELLEAU

LUDENDORFF DEMISSIONNE

Bâle, 26 octobre. — On mande de Berlin :

Officiel. — Sa Majesté l'empereur et roi, acceptant la demande de retraite du général d'infanterie Ludendorf premier quartier-maître général, commandant en temps de paix la 25e brigade d'infanterie, l'a mis à la disposition.

Sa Majesté, par ordre au général, a décidé en même temps que le régiment d'infanterie du Bas-Rhin n° 39 dont le général était le chef depuis assez longtemps, porterait désormais le nom de Ludendorf.

Bâle 26 octobre. — Le communiqué allemand de cet après-midi, au lieu de la signature habituelle du premier-quartier-maître général Ludendorf porte déjà comme signature : « Le sous chef d'état-major des armées en campagne. »

Les Elus de Douai

vont se rendre dans la ville reconquise

Les Conseillers municipaux de la ville de Douai, actuellement à Paris, se sont réunis hier après midi, dans une salle du Palais Bourbon, sous la présidence de M. Francis Godin, adjoint, faisant fonctions de Maire. MM. Goniaux, député ; Maurice Monier président du Conseil d'arrondissement ; Léon Escoffier, conseillers municipaux de la ville reconquise, assistaient à cette réunion. Ils ont décidé de se rendre à Douai dans le plus bref délai afin d'aviser aux mesures d'urgence qui s'imposent et à la reprise de la vie administrative et économique de la cité.

M. Paul Hayez sénateur du Nord, les accompagnera.

La résurrection du Nord

Ce que dit M. Gustave Dubar

« Nous voulons travailler le plus tôt possible »

Tous les hommes de notre Région, à quelque classe sociale et à quelque fraction de l'opinion politique qu'ils appartiennent, sont absolument d'accord sur ce point que l'on doit tout faire pour assurer dans le plus bref délai la reprise de la vie économique.

Nous nous proposons de publier bientôt à ce sujet, l'opinion de diverses notabilités du monde industriel et politique.

Nous reproduisons aujourd'hui les déclarations que M. Gustave Dubar, Directeur de l'Echo du Nord, a publié dans Excelsior

« Nous sommes tous pressés de reprendre le travail interrompu. Toute la population du Nord veut travailler, et le *plus tôt possible*. Et la meilleure façon, pour le gouvernement français, d'accorder une compensation à ces populations qui subirent quatre années de martyre, c'est de les mettre immédiatement en état de travailler et de réaliser leur activité ; c'est de distribuer rapidement le premier et l'essentiel agent de résurrection et de vie laborieuse : l'argent ; c'est de rembourser sans retard, les dommages créés par la guerre, et d'en finir avec la loi des dommages, votée une première fois par la Chambre, il y a plus d'un an et demi, votée, depuis bien des mois, par le Sénat, et qui attend d'être mise à l'ordre du jour de la Chambre. Que cette loi soit votée immédiatement, que les premiers acomptes soient versés et l'on verra le Nord renaître rapidement de ses cendres, tant il y a, chez les vaillantes populations de cette région, de volonté et d'amour du travail. »

Les déclarations de perte

Avis aux propriétaires de rentes au porteur dépossédés par suite d'événements de guerre

Il est rappelé que le ministre des finances a décidé que les propriétaires de rentes au porteur sur l'Etat, dépossédés par suite de faits de guerre, pourraient, moyennant une simple déclaration de perte adressée à la direction de la Dette inscrite au ministère des finances, faire obstacle aux opérations concernant leurs titres qui seraient demandées au Trésor.

Des formules de déclaration de perte seront envoyées aux intéressés, sur leur demande, par la direction de la Dette inscrite.

FACSIMILE OF THE FIRST NEWSPAPER PUBLISHED IN LILLE AFTER ITS EVACUATION BY THE GERMANS.

Chapter XVI.

LILLE AND THE FINAL ADVANCE.

A TRAIN journey was quite a remarkable occurrence. The Divisional Artillery had not travelled by train since their first journey up the line in 1915, and now they were being carried back to the same area. The Infantry Brigades had made one short journey by train (from Albert to Ytres in the snow) during the last year.

We found our old quarters—Chocques, Auchel, Calonne-Ricouart —much changed. Hutted camps had sprung up everywhere, and the inhabitants had naturally long since tired of entertaining the British Army. During the last spring the war had come inconveniently near ; Chocques was badly knocked about and Béthune was a desolation. Still, it was a very pleasant change after so long a stay by the Somme, and, if the artistic eye of a few missed the rich colour and soft contours of the southern battlefield, the homely sense of most of us preferred the somewhat squalid urbanity of a mining district to the desolate rusticity which we had left. And in war-time the pleasure of revisiting old haunts is more than usually keen.

It was soon known that the Division was to go to Italy by the end of the month to relieve the 7th Division. A small advance party was sent off, and arrangements seemed to be complete. Days were spent in mild training and lively anticipation. The prospect was delightful—a long and interesting journey, a picturesque country, and, from all accounts, a good kind of war. Apart from the distance from home and possible difficulty of leave, the only serious drawback was that our horses must be left behind, to be exchanged for those of the 7th Division, and the thought of this parting was a real grief to many artillery and transport drivers. The entrainment was several times postponed, but when, on September 27th, the Division moved to the neighbourhood of St. Pol, the move seemed quite certain. The 140th Brigade were supplied by an enterprising Brigade Headquarters with maps of the route and a list of useful phrases in Italian. Rations for the journey were actually being loaded on the first train, and we hoped in a few hours' time to say good-bye to France.

But plans were changed again. The great success of the Allies in France culminating in the capture of the Hindenburg Line by the Fourth Army, the capture of Damascus in the East, and the capitulation of Bulgaria showed that the end of the war was near. It was a race against time to settle the issue on the Western Front before winter set in, and neither the time nor the rolling-stock could immediately be spared for our expected move.

Orders came on October 1st, and on the next day the Division began to concentrate in the XI Corps area at Lestrem and La Gorgue, with a view to relieving the 59th Division on the following night. But the Germans were already retreating fast, and the 141st Brigade was hurried forward to take the place of two pursuing brigades.

The operation in which we now took part was not of a really urgent nature, but it was intended to keep in touch with the enemy, to maintain constant pressure, so as to prevent his thinning out his line, and to inflict as much damage upon him as possible during his retreat. At the same time our own troops were to be kept from engagement in heavy fighting. By the end of the day the 141st Brigade had advanced across the Aubers Ridge to a position just east of Radinghem.

There was little fighting except on the right, where the 18th Battalion had come up against machine-guns, with which the enemy, as so often, skilfully embarrassed our pursuit, but the brigade had a difficult job moving forward about four miles on a frontage of well over two miles in new and featureless country. All battalions were very weak, and two out of the three had a trench strength of hardly more than 300. The casualties suffered by the brigade on October 3rd and 4th—120 all ranks—show that the enemy's fire was a considerable obstacle. The result of this advance was to cause the Germans to hurry up reinforcements which were badly needed elsewhere.

The ground of the advance was full of interest. The Aubers Ridge, which now fell so easily into our hands, had been the object of repeated costly attacks since the British Army had been driven from it in October, 1914. It commands a fine view of the plain that stretches far away to the west and north—a very close and watery countryside, intersected with dykes and dotted with farmsteads, singularly ill-suited to the trench warfare of four years.

We could examine at leisure the German defences, the great belts of barbed-wire covering breastworks and trenches, and immensely strong concrete pill-boxes disposed along their trench systems or built into ruined farmhouses. Some of these were demolished, but the majority were intact, although often filled with explosive charges ready to blow the unwary occupant sky high. The sappers made them safe for us, and we were able to enjoy the peculiar stuffy security which German dugouts and blockhouses afford.

Apart from this work, the Royal Engineers and Pioneers were now and onwards mainly busied with repairing roads and bridges to allow transport of all kinds to keep pace with the advance. Large craters had been blown at most crossroads, and bridges and culverts were generally destroyed. It was only by the untiring efforts of sappers and pioneers that supporting artillery and first-line transport were always able to keep up with the leading units.

On October 4th the 142nd Brigade took over the right half of the Divisional front, and pushed on with the 141st Brigade. Opposition was considerably more severe and the strong wire defences of the evacuated trenches were an obstacle. The 22nd Battalion succeeded at some cost in forcing the enemy to leave the village of Beaucamp on our right, and on the left the 19th Battalion secured a footing on the Armentières-Wavrin railway, which was held in some strength, apparently as an outpost position in front of the main Lille defences about a mile farther east.

This was a strong position; a railway embankment, protected by means of wire, gave good advantage to machine-gun posts and snipers, and admirable cover for lateral communication along the front. A determined attack with adequate artillery support could have captured it, but the policy of the Fifth Army was not to make a deliberate attack upon the defences of Lille, but merely to follow closely when pressure north and south compelled the enemy to withdraw.

For the next ten days, therefore, while the line of the railway was still held, no operations were attempted beyond patrolling and raids, to test the resistance of the enemy and to obtain identification of the troops opposing us.

The most considerable raid was made by Captain R. W. Turner's D Company, of the 24th Battalion, on the morning of October 14th against the railway embankment opposite Erquinghem. Artillery co-operation was arranged, including the support of 6-in. trench-mortars. In reconnoitring for their position the Divisional Trench Mortar Officer, Captain J. G. Brown, M.C., unluckily missed our outpost line and cycled past Radinghem into the enemy's country. An able and gallant young officer was thus lost to the Division. The raiders reached the railway and sent patrols into the village, but they were counter-attacked in unexpected strength and withdrew with considerable casualties.

The enemy, however, had fired his usual Parthian shot, and during the next day our line was able to move forward 1,000 yards, so that the centre of the 142nd Brigade held the farmstead of Fin de la Guerre, a very suitable objective. Early on the 16th the advance continued. On the extreme left opposite the 141st Brigade was high ground and the tremendous earthwork of Fort d'Englos, one of the biggest of the forts that girdle Lille. It was intended not to attack this, but to surround it by a forward movement of the 142nd Brigade on the right. As it turned out, however, the strongest resistance came from the right, where the western edge of the suburbs of Lille gave shelter for machine-guns. The direction of the advance was, therefore, turned somewhat northwards, and by the end of the day we held the village of Hallennes and Englos.

Meanwhile, orders for relief had come, and on October 17th brigades of the 57th Division passed through our line, and were able to march straight on to Lille. We thus just missed the satisfaction of being the first British troops to reach the city, and the duty of carrying out elaborate orders for sealing the exits which we had been studying for some days past. Instead, the 47th Division moved back by easy stages to the Norrent-Fontes-St. Hilaire district, and the Artillery to St. Venant, all ready once again to entrain for Italy. But within a few days the journey to

Italy was finally cancelled, and the Division was warned to be ready to accompany the Army Commander on his official entry into Lille on Monday, October 28th.

The week-end was spent in Lomme and Loos, suburbs to the west of Lille, where the magnificence of some of our billets was a striking contrast to the hunger and destitution of many of the victims of the German occupation.

There was great pleasure in feeling that we were in quarters which the enemy had lived in so long and so securely, and a deeper satisfaction in realising to some extent from the appearance and narratives of the French the measure of relief that our advance had brought them. It needed now no imagination to know that it was something more than a few miles of desert that we were fighting for, and that we were up against something worse than a nation of home-loving conscripts driven unwillingly to war. For the sufferings of Lille were among the worst consequences of a systematic militarism, and many who may have found little satisfaction in contemplating wretched groups of tired and dirty prisoners on the Somme felt that the joy of a liberated town was well worth years of discomfort and danger.

The procession started on October 28th at ten o'clock from the Porte Canteleu. The Army Commander (General Birdwood) was preceded by a company of the 22nd Battalion. Behind the Army Staff followed the XIth Corps Commander (Lieut.-General Sir R. Haking) and his Staff.

Then came the 47th Division. The General led the way, followed by some of his Staff, and the three Brigade Groups marched in the order which they had taken in the last operations—142nd, 141st, and 140th. Between the 142nd and 141st Brigades came the C.R.A. (Brig.-General Whitley) and Divisional Artillery Head-quarters, followed by the 235th Brigade R.F.A. and a detachment of the Divisional Ammunition Column. The 236th Brigade R.F.A. and the Machine-Gun Battalion marched between the 141st and 140th Brigades. In rear of the 140th Brigade came the 4th Battalion R.W.F. and detachments, mounted and dismounted, of the Divisional Train and the Mobile Veterinary Section. Within each Brigade Group the affiliated Field Company R.E. followed the Brigade Headquarters ; after them the three battalions and Trench Mortar Battery, and then the affiliated Field Ambulance. A company each from the 140th and 141st Brigades had gone on ahead to form a cordon in the Grande Place.

It was "roses, roses all the way." The tricolour was flying everywhere (one heard pathetic stories of the careful concealment of flags all through the war against the day of victory), with a sprinkling of extemporised (and rather inaccurate) versions of the Union Jack, and American and Belgian flags. Several hundred small flags adorned the rifles and equipment of our units, and flowers were on the guns. Brass bands played, and great crowds along the road and at every window cheered and sang as the troops marched by. A special ovation was given to the Indian drivers in the D.A.C. An enterprising printer had produced posters in red, white, and blue, some with the inscription "Honneur et gloire à la 47me Division, nos Liberateurs," and others with the same message in English.

There was a halt when the head of the procession reached the Grande Place. There the Army Commander presented his fanion (the small red flag with a black cross which is carried behind an army commander in the field) to the Mayor of Lille, M. Delesalle, and received a flag from the city. Then the Mayor and Corporation and the Army, Corps, and Divisional Commanders took their place upon the grand-stand, where a large gathering of officers and civilians—among them the British Secretary of State for War, Mr. Winston Churchill—was assembled. No compliments were paid as the Division marched past. Its smart appearance won general approbation, and a message of congratulation from the Army Commander, with a special word of praise for the Divisional Artillery.

After a few days' rest in the eastern suburbs of Lille the Division moved up to relieve the 57th Division on the west bank of the Scheldt just north of Tournai. The 140th and 141st Brigades took their place in the line on October 31st. Two Portuguese battalions and a Portuguese brigade of field artillery were here attached to us, and the provision for their needs caused no little anxiety to the administrative staff and services, in the absence of interpreters or of any certainty as to their movements. The difficulty was not lessened by the fact that during their attachment to us the distinguishing numbers of the two battalions were changed.

THE ENTRY INTO LILLE, OCTOBER 28TH, 1918.

The Germans had destroyed all bridges across the river, which was swollen with the recent rain, and could not be crossed without a carefully planned operation beyond the scope of our waiting tactics. The villages of Froyennes, Pont-à-Chin, and Ramegnies Chin lay on our line. Froyennes is only a mile from Tournai, and round it stand comfortable châteaux, the houses of local magnates. One of these, a stuccoed building of pseudo-Moorish style, had long been the residence of Prince Rupprecht of Bavaria, against whose army we had often fought. In the villages were neat villas, hastily evacuated and very little damaged, and the country generally had a trim and prosperous appearance, very different from the impoverished French country we had left, as Tournai was different from Lille. A good many civilians stayed on in Froyennes.

For a week nothing was done beyond the usual patrolling and reconnaissance of possible approaches to the river when the time should arrive to cross it. One day a small patrol of the 18th Battalion crossed the river and captured an enemy post. One night a party of Germans attacked a post of the 17th Battalion, but were driven on the following night from the house they occupied.

Meanwhile, the enemy harassed us somewhat with field-guns and machine-guns. He had excellent observation from the railway just east of the Scheldt, and especially from Mont St. Aubert, a steep hill which rose 150 metres high less than two miles north-east of us, and commanded a wonderful view for miles round. We later found a most complete observation-station established here.

Early in the morning of November 8th civilians entered the 74th Division line on our right with the news that the enemy had withdrawn, and later the part of Tournai west of the Scheldt was occupied. Our patrols found the line of the river still strongly held, and shelling in the forward area was unusually vigorous. Everything pointed to an imminent evacuation, and orders were given to arrange for the building of a trestle bridge early next morning at Pont-à-Chin, and a footbridge was successfully placed there during the night.

At dawn on November 9th the 22nd Battalion started crossing the river and pushed straight ahead without opposition. By eleven o'clock the 142nd Brigade reported that Mont St. Aubert was in our hands, and at the same hour the 140th Brigade, whose advance had been delayed by the difficulty of building a footbridge

in their sector, were in La Tombe. Both brigades moved rapidly
forward during the afternoon, and at nightfall we were in the
village of Melles and Morcourt, about five miles east of the river.

The engineers had some difficulty in constructing heavier bridges
across the Scheldt. The Pont-à-Chin trestle bridge was not finished
on the 9th, but by 2.30 p.m. a pontoon bridge was ready near
Froyennes. Forward sections of artillery and infantry first-line
transport started crossing this at once. The approach to the
bridge was by a narrow, muddy road with a dyke on either side,
and in spite of stringent traffic regulations there was a scramble
to get across. It somehow happened that General Kennedy's
mess-cart was the first vehicle to cross the river.

The last casualties of the Division were suffered by the 17th
Battalion, which lost five men on the night of November 8th.
On the next day the five bodies lay wrapped in blankets in the
hall of Prince Rupprecht's château, amid rich furniture and gaudy
decoration. In some such way much that was blatant and insincere
in the world at war served only to throw into deeper relief the
simple realities of loyal service and unselfish death.

The chase was continued on the 10th. In front were the 19th
Hussars with a battery of Royal Horse Artillery, and the 142nd
Brigade followed as the advance guard of the Division. The cavalry
met slight opposition from some machine-gun posts which the
Germans had left behind, but these were soon put to flight by
the R.H.A. One wounded prisoner was sent back. By the end
of the day the 142nd Brigade held an outpost line beyond Frasnes-
lez-Buissenal and Moustier—a day's advance of between six and
seven miles. On November 11th the 140th Brigade was to lead
the way, but orders came early to say that the XIth Corps was
to be "squeezed out" of the line, and that the Division would
concentrate near La Tombe. A little later we heard that hostilities
were to cease at eleven o'clock.

There was nothing dramatic about the end of the war for the
47th Division. News of the Armistice reached the troops on their
march westwards, and it hardly raised a cheer. The 141st Brigade
took charge of Tournai, and Brig.-General Mildren was for a
time military governor there; the rest of the Division kept
Armistice night as best they could in billets in the northern
outskirts of the town.

Chapter XVII.

DEMOBILIZATION.

THE period which began with the Armistice and ended with the return of the " cadres " of units to England may be passed over very briefly, although the five months dragged wearily enough for those who were left till the end. " Nothing of interest to record " is a phrase that recurs often in the war diaries of this time.

On the day following the Armistice Sir George Gorringe held a conference of all commanding officers at La Tombe when plans for " educational and recreational training " and for making the best of things generally for the troops were discussed. The formation of Old Comrades' Associations, which should, in after years, provide an opportunity of renewing war-time friendships and keeping alive the spirit of the Division, was at once put in hand.

For a week or so the 140th and 141st Infantry Brigades were kept busy working under the direction of railway construction companies on the Tournai-Ath railway, to which the Boche had done an almost incredible amount of damage on his retirement. The 142nd Infantry Brigade and the Artillery moved to Cysoing and Bourghelles, on the frontier of France, on November 15th, and Divisional Headquarters to Chereng on the next day. The Portuguese attached infantry and artillery returned to their own division, and everybody settled down to enjoy himself as best he might in an area where at least accommodation for men and horses was fairly comfortable and the British soldier was still welcome after the long German occupation. For it was soon known that the 47th Division was not among the fortunate few which were to go forward to Cologne.

A fortnight after the Armistice, however, the Division was moved back by road through the devastated country behind Lille to billets in the familiar area behind Béthune. We were to finish the war in the same area in which we had first entered it.

Divisional Headquarters were established at Lozinghem. The Artillery, to which the 189th (Army) Brigade R.F.A. was attached, settled in Marles-les-Mines, Lapugnoy, Labeuvrière, Fouquières, and Chocques; the Engineers at Raimbert and Burbure; the Pioneers in Labeuvrière; the 140th Infantry Brigade Group in Auchel, Ferfay, and Cauchy-à-la-Tour; the 141st Infantry Brigade group in Pernes and Lières; the 142nd Infantry Brigade group in Allouagne and Burbure, and the Divisional Train in Lillers, moving later to Camblain Chatelain as the railhead changed from Lillers to Pernes.

In these none too cheerful little mining and agricultural villages, with Christmas festivities and an occasional move into new huts or billets to relieve the monotony, the Division settled down to discuss the great topic of demobilization. For some time matters did not seem to be getting beyond the stage of discussion and the rendering of many returns, except as concerned the so-called "pivotal" men. The most unlikely individuals suddenly discovered that the wheels of British industry could not begin to revolve again until they were returned to civilian life. As these same individuals—no doubt by reason of their "pivotality"— were also in many cases those who had most recently become soldiers, discussion of the matter among the troops sometimes assumed a somewhat acrid tone.

Early in 1919, however, demobilization began in real earnest and the Division grew smaller day by day. There was much inspecting and classifying of horses and mules—some for sale in England, some for disposal in France, and a few for retention in the Regular Army. There were many touching farewells said as men were parted from animals that they had driven and cared for, perhaps, for years, or officers from chargers which had served with them on many battle fronts.

The education scheme, on which a beginning had been made in the Army even before the Armistice, developed to imposing proportions—on paper. Each unit had its classes, and although little useful work could be done in those arms and services which had horses to look after or departmental duties to carry on, a certain amount of progress was made among the infantry, and at least

"THE FOLLIES" DIVISIONAL CONCERT PARTY.

BACK ROW: Rfn. W. V. Tidmarsh, Rfn. C. F. Cherry, Rfn. F. C. Mott, Lieut. E. A. Boughton, Cpl. L. E. Amand, Rfn. H. Collins, Sgt. R. H. Wyatt, Sgt. L. C. Ward, L.-Cpl. S. Dignum, Rfn. J. Cottham, Rfn. A. Hughes, Sgt. R. H. Cobley. MIDDLE ROW: L.-Cpl. G. A. A. Emms (Box Office), Rfn. C. R. Stanton (Scene Painter), Rfn. A. Weddall (Electrician), Sgt. J. W. Nevill (Producer), Rfn. E. Martin (Stage Carpenter), Rfn. F. Perrin (Property Master), Rfn. E. Sawyer (at piano). FRONT ROW: Cpl. J. A. T. Langton, Pte. D. Stewart, Pte. F. Pain (Divisional Cinema Orchestra).

opportunities were given to those who wished to take advantage of them for serious study or technical training with a view to civil life. Lecturers visited the Division and held forth on a multitude of subjects, from " Exploration in Central Asia " to " World Problems after the War."

Athletics naturally occupied much of the time, although it was not always easy to find playing fields. Divisional football cup ties were played during December and January, and D/236 Battery, R.F.A., defeated the Machine-gun Battalion in the final at Auchel.

Concert parties and theatricals—sometimes sadly disorganised by the demobilization at a critical stage of the leading lady— helped to pass away the long evenings. The 15th Battalion produced an admirable pantomime with the topical title, " Pack Up," at Ferfay, and besides the Divisional Follies, who worked hard, as they had done throughout the war, for the amusement of the troops, there were a number of " touring companies " who exchanged visits.

By the end of March, 1919, the units were reduced almost to cadre strength, and Major-General Gorringe left us to return to England. Shortly afterwards he was appointed to command the 10th Division in Egypt, where so many years of his career as a soldier had been spent. He handed over the command of the cadres to Brigadier-General Mildren.

On the eve of his departure Sir George Gorringe issued the following farewell order :

SPECIAL ORDER OF THE DAY.
By Major-General Sir G. F. Gorringe, K.C.B., K.C.M.G., D.S.O.

Friday, March 28th, 1919.

The day has arrived for the 47th (London) Division to cease to exist in France as a Division and for the remnant to be formed into Brigade Groups of Cadres.

The occasion is one on which we who have served in the Division cannot but feel a mutual sense of regret, severing as it does ties which have closely united us for so long. Most of our comrades have already left us to restart their vocations in civil life, others to join the Army of Occupation, and those who remain—the Cadres— will shortly be returning to England, there to be demobilized. Many, also, we shall never meet again ; their lives have been given for the cause for which we, as the 47th Division, were formed and have fought together at Festubert, Loos, Vimy, High Wood, Eaucourt L'Abbaye, Messines, Menin Road, Bourlon Wood, Welsh Ridge, Highland Ridge, Dessart Ridge, Rocquigny to Bouzincourt and Aveluy Wood, Bray, Albert Ridge, Le Forêt, Rancourt, Moislains, Nurlu Ridge, Lieramont, in the advance on Lille and the crossing of the Scheldt, on many a battlefield, in minor operations, and in trench warfare.

Looking back on these past years, we cannot but feel proud and thankful that we have been enabled to take such a prominent part in these operations and in building up the fine record which the Division has achieved. In fact, no less than 97 D.S.O.'s

R

cr bars, 472 M.C.'s or bars, 321 D.C.M.'s or bars, and 1909 M.M.'s or bars have been awarded to the Division. But it is not so much this splendid record of rewards of which we should be most grateful; it is what we have been able to do during the war and our share in winning victory that we may feel so justly proud of.*

On relinquishing command of the 47th Division I desire to place on record my very high appreciation of your devotion to duty, discipline, gallantry and loyalty at all times. No Commander could have been better or more loyally served than I have been by you.

Where all have done so well it is difficult to particularise units or individuals; all have worked together so unselfishly. I wish, however, to specially thank Brig.-General E. N. Whitley, C.B., C.M.G., D.S.O., T.D.; my Brigade Commanders: Brig.-General T. W. Viscount Hampden, C.B., C.M.G.; Brig.-General H. B. P. L. Kennedy, C.M.G., D.S.O.; Brig.-General R. McDouall, C.B., C.M.G., D.S.O.; Brig.-General V. T. Bailey, C.M.G., D.S.O.; Brig.-General W. F. Mildren, C.B., C.M.G., D.S.O., and their Staffs; and the senior members of my Staff, by whose devoted service all duties entrusted to them have been carried out so efficiently, especially Lieut.-Colonel A. J. Turner, C.M.G., D.S.O., R.A.; Lieut.-Colonel B. L. Montgomery, D.S.O.; Lieut.-Colonel S. H. J. Thunder, C.M.G., D.S.O., M.C.; Lieut.-Colonel A. B. Carey, C.M.G., D.S.O., R.E.; Colonel J. D. Ferguson, C.M.G., D.S.O., R.A.M.C.; Colonel T. W. Gibbard, C.B., M.B., K.H.S.; Lieut.-Colonel W. C. Galbraith, C.M.G.; Lieut.-Colonel A. H. Maude, C.M.G., D.S.O.; Captain A. Paterson; Major J. C. D. Carlisle, D.S.O., M.C.; and the Rev. A. E. Wilkinson, M.C.; also the following battalion commanders: Lieut.-Colonel A. Maxwell, C.M.G., D.S.O., T.D.; Lieut.-Colonel G. Dawes, D.S.O., M.C.; Lieut.-Colonel W. H. E. Segrave, D.S.O.; Lieut.-Colonel F. W. Parish, D.S.O., M.C.; Lieut.-Colonel C. J. S. Green, D.S.O., M.C.; Lieut.-Colonel C. F. H. Greenwood, D.S.O., T.D.; and Lieut.-Colonel W. R. Portal, D.S.O., M.V.O.; who in their various capacities have given me the greatest possible support and have been untiring in carrying out so successfully the many operations entrusted to them.

We do not yet know what has been decided as to the future—whether the Division will be re-formed on lines similar to those which existed prior to 1914, or otherwise—but whatever that decision may be, let the spirit of the Division remain and be maintained and fostered by various Old Comrades' Associations which have been and are being formed, and by which, I trust, we shall have opportunities to meet together during many years to come, to remember our happy relations in the past —the splendid co-operation between all branches of the Service in the Division.

My parting request is that you will all do your utmost to maintain the spirit of our comradeship at all times and that it will continue to unite us in future, so that we may be a very powerful factor and tower of strength for good in our country, that our victories in war may be consolidated in peace by that happy bond of true comradeship which is called co-operation, that discipline in civil life, that best of disciplines which we have attained in this war—the subordination of selfishness to the benefit of the community.

G. F. GORRINGE, Major-General.

The debt of the Division to General Gorringe himself it would be hard to estimate too highly. His skill as a commander had been proved in many difficult operations, his coolness in action and his courage were an inspiration to all who served under him, and his unceasing thought for the comfort and welfare of the junior officers and men of the Division, who probably never realised how much they owed to it, was an example, as well as an occasional cause of some anxiety, to the subordinate commanders and staff.

The 47th Division was fortunate in not suffering from the frequent changes in command which were the lot of some divisions. Each

---

* The figures quoted above do not include honours announced in the "Peace Despatch," 1919. A full list of honours awarded to the Division will be found in Appendix G.

of its two commanders remained with it long enough to know the Division well and to earn its confidence. The achievements and the spirit of the Division under their command are the measure of their success and their reward.

Not only in its chief commanders was the 47th Division fortunate. It was allowed to remain to the end what it was from the beginning —a division of London Territorials, and as such it had a homogeneity and a civic patriotism such as few other divisions possessed. The only one of its units which was not recruited in London—the 4th Battalion, Royal Welsh Fusiliers—was composed of Territorials like the Londoners, and quickly assimilated itself. So, too, did the occasional drafts for London battalions which were received from other regiments.

Among the brigade and battalion commanders and the senior Staff officers were many, like Brigadier-Generals Lewis, Mildren, Whitley, and Lord Hampden, who were Territorial officers themselves; and many others, like Brigadier-Generals Cuthbert, Thwaites, Wray, and Kennedy, or Lieut.-Colonels Foot and Thunder, who, though Regular officers themselves, had served long enough before the war as commanders, Staff officers, or adjutants in the Territorial Force to understand the Territorial soldier thoroughly.

To the junior officers, the warrant officers, and the N.C.O.'s, the backbone of the Division, and to the men themselves, it is impossible to pay tribute high enough. The dogged courage and endurance of the Londoner, his unfailing cheerfulness and humour in adversity, have been the subject of so many panegyrics in official despatches, in the Press, and elsewhere, that there is no need to dwell upon them here. If in the pages of this history too little mention has been made of individual acts of heroism or of the personalities of many born leaders of men of whom death or wounds robbed the Division before they had attained high rank, it is due chiefly to the difficulty of selecting from among such numbers.

There were a few, but very few, among the cadres which returned to England in May, 1919, who had served with the 47th Division during all its four years in France and Flanders. The last trainload left Pernes on May 10. The Artillery and divisional troops were finally demobilized at Shoreham a month or so later, and the Infantry brigades at Felixstowe.

But the Division was not doomed to die. On February 16th, 1920, it was reconstituted as part of the new Territorial Army, under the command of Major-General Sir Nevill Smyth, V.C., K.C.B., and the 47th (2nd London) Division lives to carry on the traditions of the men who fought at Loos and Vimy, at High Wood, Messines, and Bourlon.

A POSTER

Exhibited in Lille, on October 28th, 1918, when General Sir W. Birdwood, at the head of the 47th Division, entered the city after its evacuation by the Germans.

Appendix A.

THE ADMINISTRATIVE SERVICES.

ROYAL ARMY SERVICE CORPS.

The 2nd London Divisional Transport and Supply Column, A.S.C., of which the original first line unit afterwards became the 47th Divisional Train, came into being with the Territorial Force in April, 1908. Its first commanding officer was Colonel P. H. Dalbiac, C.B., T.D. He was succeeded in 1912 by Lieut.-Colonel C. F. T. Blyth, C.M.G., T.D., who was commanding the column on mobilisation, the Senior Supply Officer being Major W. Campbell Galbraith. The latter was promoted to command the Train in July, 1916, and on his return to England, in February, 1918, to take up work under the Admiralty, he was in turn succeeded by his S.S.O., Major A. H. Maude, and Captain G. Farr became S.S.O.

In August, 1914, the Territorial T. and S. Columns had not yet been organised on the new basis as Divisional Trains, and still consisted of a Headquarters company and three Brigade companies, from which the 2nd Line Regimental Horse Transport was detached to units on mobilisation, and which each included a section of Mechanical Transport. The latter became the nucleus of the Divisional Supply Column on its formation at the end of 1914, first under the O.C. A.S.C. and later as a separate unit. On arrival in France the mechanical transport unit ceased to form part of the Division and became "Corps Troops."

The early days of mobilisation naturally threw a great strain on the Divisional A.S.C. In addition to the mobilising of the unit itself, arrangements had to be made for clearing up the hurriedly evacuated camps on Salisbury Plain and for feeding a Division at war strength from local resources in the St. Albans area. The derelict rubber works and a part of the adjoining golf-links at St. Albans were taken over and a Supply Depot was formed, which in a very short time was feeding nearly 20,000 men and some hundreds of horses. Supplies were delivered to the more distant units by locally hired mechanical transport, and to those at St. Albans and Hatfield by horse transport, in impressed vehicles of every conceivable type. There was little opportunity for training of any kind, and as soon as a driver could drive a pair of horses—sometimes before—he had to take his share in the never-ending work of the companies.

In March, 1915, the companies entrained with their respective Brigade groups for overseas, and the St. Albans depot was handed over to the 2/2nd London Divisional T. and S. Column (afterwards the 60th Divisional Train), which had been formed under the command of Colonel Dalbiac.

The problem of feeding the Division during its concentration in the First Army area, complicated as it was by the changes of destination and the inexperience of all concerned of conditions in France, was a severe test of the Train and Supply Column. This was the first war trial of the Army Service Corps as reorganised in accordance with the 1911 War Establishments, and things were not yet "cut and dried" and running as smoothly as the later Divisions found them. All fuel, vegetables, straw, bran, and various other commodities had to be provided by local purchase, and Requisitioning Officers were kept busy.

Other periods during which the work of the Train was carried on with the greatest difficulty were during the battles of Loos and of the Somme, 1916, when the condition of the " German road " and the congestion and shelling of Albert railhead rendered the supply situation at times quite interesting ; the preparations for Messines, when large quantities of reserve rations and R.E. material had to be got up to the line by night, and when the railhead at Ouderdom was frequently shelled—on one occasion with heavy casualties ; during the march from Arras to Cambrai and the operations of November 30th, 1917, when refilling point was at one time within 1,000 yards of the front-line.

The withdrawal in March, 1918, and the final advance in October, 1918, across the barrier of the Scheldt and the mined roads round Tournai were the two periods when the greatest strain was put upon all ranks responsible for the supply and transport of the Division, but in spite of many difficulties rations were delivered throughout both these trying periods without any serious hitch.

The troubles resulting from the stretching out of the line of communications, however, did not cease with the Armistice. Delayed pack trains, a wide Divisional area, the necessity for consuming supplies long stored in reserve dumps, and various other causes often rendered the satisfactory feeding of the troops more difficult during the six months following the cessation of hostilities than when the Division was actually in the line.

In August, 1916, shortly before the Division moved up to High Wood, it was decided that Divisional Supply Columns should no longer move with their Divisions from one Army area to another. This resulted in the 47th Divisional Supply Column, of which the Divisional Train had been the parent unit, being separated from the Division and attached to the 17th Division (whose Senior Supply Officer, Major J. H. B. Wigginton, M.C., happened to be an old member of the 47th Train and well known to many in the Division). It was replaced by the 19th Divisional Supply Column, which did excellent work for us until we moved up to the Salient.

Between August, 1916, and the end of 1917 the Division was served by four different Supply Columns :

19th Divisional Supply Column.

5th Australian Divisional Supply Column (British personnel).

5th Australian Divisional Supply Column (Australian personnel).

5th Divisional Supply Column.

This constant changing of columns proved most unsatisfactory from many points of view, and this fact was at last recognised by the higher authorities, so that in December, 1917, the 47th Divisional Supply Column (which afterwards became the 47th Divisional M.T. Company on the reorganisation and amalgamation of supply columns and ammunition sub-parks) rejoined the Division and remained with it until demobilization.

Various " side-lines " in which the Train was engaged at different times included agricultural operations, forestry, charcoal-burning, and the running of the soda-water factory (subsequently handed over, with great relief, to the Divisional Canteen). The articles bought by the Requisitioning Officers included most things from a dogcart to a lamp-wick.

Special mention should be made of the work of the Transport personnel of the Field Ambulances, who were transferred early in the war to the Army Service Corps, and reinforced by H.T. drivers from the Divisional Train and motor-ambulance drivers from the Divisional M.T. Company. They did most gallant and devoted service often under very trying conditions.

SUPPLY CONVOY AT TWO WATERS, HEMEL HEMPSTEAD, 1914.

A REFILLING POINT GROUP, 1918.
Some Quartermasters and Supply Officers.

ROYAL ARMY MEDICAL CORPS.

The part played by the Royal Army Medical Corps in the principal battles in which the 47th Division was engaged has already been briefly described in the story of the operations. The work of the R.A.M.C., however, contributed so largely to the fighting efficiency of the Division at all times, and was performed with such unselfish devotion to duty, that some fuller account of its record must be given here.

When the three field ambulances accompanied their respective brigades to the St. Albans area in August, 1914, each included eight medical officers besides the C.O., and one medical officer was attached to each of the twelve infantry battalions, one to each artillery brigade, and one each to the Divisional Train and Royal Engineers. Besides these there were the A.D.M.S. (then Colonel Harrison) and the D.A.D.M.S. at headquarters and a divisional sanitary officer. Later in the war, owing to the scarcity of medical men, this number was very much curtailed. Units such as the Engineers and Train, which were at times scattered over a wide area, were deprived of their medical officers, and those of other units had to perform this work in addition to their own. Corps and army troops in the divisional area also came under the medical care of the A.D.M.S. Deficiencies due to casualties, leave, and other causes had to be made good within the Division, and this threw a considerable strain on the resources of the field ambulances, so that at times the C.O. was the only officer left at the headquarters of his unit.

The divisional R.A.M.C., too, were the pioneers in arranging for the bathing of the men and the issuing of clean underclothing. This continued from the earliest days in France, when the baths at pitheads in the mining district round Béthune were available for the troops, till about the end of 1916, when the Division was in the Ypres Salient, and for the first time an officer other than a qualified medical man was placed in charge of the laundry and baths.

In short, it will be seen that the duties of the R.A.M.C. were many and varied, and that the demands from all sides for medical officers and other ranks were a source of continual anxiety both to the A.D.M.S. and to field ambulance commanders.

Owing to the decreasing numbers of available medical officers from home, American M.O.'s were attached to the Division for the first time in July, 1917. From the first they proved themselves thoroughly good and efficient officers, and very popular with all ranks. Their help proved invaluable, and their work, under the most trying conditions, was beyond all praise.

The field ambulances went to France in March, 1915, with their respective brigades, having undergone, in the preceding November, considerable changes in personnel. One ambulance, indeed, had an entirely new set of officers, only three of whom had previous experience in the Territorial Force, and great credit is due to the N.C.O.'s for the way in which they helped to train not only the men but the newly-joined officers. Colonel Harrison and his D.A.D.M.S., Colonel Butt, remained in England to take over the medical administration of the second line division. Major C. J. Martin, medical officer of the 23rd Battalion, was appointed D.A.D.M.S., but no A.D.M.S. was appointed till the arrival of the Division in France, when Colonel Nicol joined the Staff. He remained with the Division only some two months, as did each of his successors, Colonel E. L. R. McLeod and Colonel McLaughlin. In August, 1915, Colonel J. D. Ferguson, D.S.O., was appointed A.D.M.S. His administrative ability, keenness, and personality had a striking and lasting effect on the efficiency of the medical services of the Division, which he directed for nearly two years.

From the beginning his chief aim was to ensure the rapid evacuation of the wounded from the line. His strong point was the construction of shell-proof shelters along the line of evacuation both for wounded and R.A.M.C., personnel. Better work could be done in dressing wounded where comparative safety could be ensured, a larger supply of dressings and comforts could be stored, and more aseptic conditions could be maintained.

The evacuation from the line in the early days was an extremely arduous proposition, but the use later of wheeled stretchers and light railways made the journey down from the line to the car-loading post quicker and much more comfortable for all concerned. In the use of these Colonel Ferguson was one of the early pioneers. The construction of the dugouts and shelters was carried out by R.A.M.C. labour, sometimes under R.E. supervision, and sometimes under a medical officer advised by an N.C.O. skilled in some trade pertaining to this class of work.

The R.A.M.C. were exceptionally fortunate in having many skilled N.C.O.'s and men of this type. Latterly the R.A.M.C. had also to construct battalion aid posts.

At Loos much was learned in clearing the wounded, and the experience gained there and in the succeeding period up to the time of the German attack at Vimy, in May, 1916, was very useful in making a record evacuation in the latter battle. The D.D.M.S., IVth Corps, on many occasions afterwards described it to other field ambulances as a model evacuation of wounded.

In the First Battle of the Somme the line was taken over from the outgoing division forty-eight hours before zero. No arrangements in the immediate forward area had been made by the out-going R.A.M.C. for the construction of dressing and collecting posts. By working in relays night and day, and with the ever useful and ever ready help of the R.E.'s, three were hastily constructed. The necessary stores and comforts were hurried up just as the attack was launched.

The Somme fighting of 1916 offered the most severe test to which the divisional R.A.M.C. was put during the whole time the Division was in France. Owing to the assistance given to divisions holding the line for a fortnight before our taking over, and the amount of work done on collecting posts, etc., the men were physically tired before the attack on High Wood took place. The difficulties of transport, owing to the condition of the one road leading up to Bazentin, were enormous. A system of bearer reliefs, as was customary, was at first organised, but the number of casualties among the troops was so heavy that the men had to carry on till they dropped from exhaustion.

On the second day the " carry " from the Cough Drop to Bazentin-le-Grand took a squad of six men four to six hours to accomplish owing to the mud and shell holes. After the first twenty-four hours or so evacuation of wounded became increasingly difficult on account of direct enemy observation. The wounded had therefore to be carried out at night.

The intense darkness of the Somme nights, and the circumventing of shell holes and batteries in the quest for the Cough Drop were, and still are, a nightmare to the R.A.M.C. of the 47th Division. Later the evacuation from the left half of the divisional front (Butte de Warlencourt) became easier, for a light railway line was run up. On the right, owing to the hilly condition of the ground, this was impossible.

The move north to the Ypres salient was warmly welcomed, and here, under Colonel Ferguson, the R.A.M.C. spent the entire winter constructing posts for the June (1917) offensive. The " other ranks " had a very arduous time on these working parties, some of the indispensable N.C.O.'s and men remaining up for six to eight weeks at a time.

Two of these posts deserve special mention—Woodcote Farm on the Ypres-Lille road, and Burridge Post at Kruisstraat. The former was entirely concreted inside under R.E. supervision, and it is certain that by the devising of this scheme Colonel Ferguson was responsible for saving many lives, both of wounded and of R.A.M.C. personnel. Many direct hits by 5.9's were sustained, and without this stronghold the evacuation of wounded of the Division would have been seriously hampered, if not an entire failure.

Burridge Post, so-named by the N.C.O. who was responsible for its supervision, consisted of the " shells " of a small row of cottages with sand-bagged cupolas inside. This formed a car relay post, a walking wounded collecting post, and an aid post for any casualties in the neighbourhood. On the western side, facing the enemy, a large red cross was painted, and it must be put to the credit of the Boche that while all buildings and batteries around were shelled, he left Burridge Post alone. In the salient full use was made of light railways, and, indeed, after this in all the other sectors held by the Division.

Shortly after the Battle of Messines Colonel Ferguson received another appointment, but during the time he was with us he had left his mark for good on the R.A.M.C. of the Division. Colonel T. H. Gibbard, C.B., was a very capable successor. His organising powers were shown especially in field ambulance hospital work, and the Division owed much to him for the way in which, with the help of C.O.'s of field ambulances, he organised the work of combating the influenza epidemic among the troops in the spring of 1918. In July, 1917, Captain H. M. Calder, who had won the D.S.O. for gallantry while serving as a medical officer of the 5th London Field Ambulance, succeeded Major Martin as D.A.D.M.S.

The autumn of 1917 in the Arras sector was to the R.A.M.C. probably the most restful period since the days before Loos. It was well that it was so, for very heavy work was thrown at short notice on the R.A.M.C., as on other units of the Division, at the Battle of Bourlon Wood. The work of the R.A.M.C. in this battle has been described in the foregoing narrative. A special tribute, however, may be paid here to the gallantry of the mechanical transport and horse transport drivers of the Army Service Corps attached to the field ambulances in bringing up their ambulances under heavy shell fire on the morning of the German counter attack.

During the withdrawal of March, 1918, from La Vacquerie to Albert, the R.A.M.C. worked under a very great handicap. They had naturally to retire in advance of the combatant troops, and, consequently, many of the lying wounded fell into enemy hands. The roads, too, were so congested with transport that it was impossible to move at any speed. It was not until Albert was reached that the evacuation of wounded could proceed on normal lines. The plan adopted in most cases, and apparently the only feasible one, was to convey the wounded to the main roads and deposit them there. Some were removed by passing vehicles, and those who could not be taken up were at least found by the enemy and not allowed to die from exposure.

In July 1918, Colonel Gibbard was promoted D.D.M.S., IVth Corps, and Colonel Thomas Fraser, C.B.E., D.S.O., a Scottish Territorial officer who had had considerable experience of divisional R.A.M.C. work as a field ambulance commander in the 29th Division, joined us as A.D.M.S. He worthily carried on the work of his predecessors, and soon became a general favourite with all ranks. He was responsible for the divisional medical arrangements in the Battles of the Somme, 1918, where the actual removal of the wounded to the rear was most successful, being greatly facilitated by the German retreat. Before Lille, too, the work was comparatively easy compared with previous periods. Perhaps the greatest difficulty was the selection of abandoned German posts which could be deemed free from mines.

After the Armistice the main work of the R.A.M.C. consisted in carrying out demobilisation and giving the necessary medical attention to troops scattered throughout an immense area. The ambulance cadres, commanded respectively by Major A. E. Ironside, Major J. H. Jordan, and Major H. M. Calder, were demobilised at Felixstowe in July, 1919.

ROYAL ARMY ORDNANCE CORPS.

Little has been said in the foregoing chapters of the work of the Army Ordnance Department, but its contribution to the fighting efficiency of the Division whose material needs it supplied in trench warfare and in battle was a very considerable one.

Before the war the Territorial Force had no Ordnance personnel of its own. On mobilisation Major G. de S. Dudley was appointed to the 2nd London Division as Deputy Assistant Director of Ordnance Services—or D.A.D.O.S., to give his office the familiar title by which its holder was known in every division. He and the small staff of warrant officers and other ranks of the Army Ordnance Corps who joined him at St. Albans had a difficult task in fitting out the Division for active service. Arms and equipment, boots and clothing were hard to obtain in those early days of the war, and local purchase had often to be resorted to in order to meet demands. The troops already in France had always a prior claim, and sometimes D.A.D.O.S. had the mortification of having to deliver up again stores which he had at last procured. This happened, for example, with " Fuses, T. and P., No. 56," of which there was a shortage. These had to be withdrawn from our Divisional Artillery at Hemel Hempstead at express speed and despatched to catch a night-boat to France for the use of some other divisional artillery going into action.

When the Division was ordered to France the locally purchased transport had to be exchanged for Service pattern vehicles, a big undertaking for the Ordnance and transport personnel. Many trainloads of wagons had to be checked, unloaded, and parked on the golf-links at St. Albans for distribution to units by the Divisional Train.

Major Dudley left the Division, on promotion, not long after its arrival in France. He was succeeded for a few months by Major F. H. Buckland, and in September, 1915, Captain A. T. Shead, who had previously been with the Indian Cavalry Division, was appointed D.A.D.O.S. He remained with the 47th Division until its demobilization, when the disposal of surplus equipment kept the Ordnance Staff busy up till the last moment.

The D.A.D.O.S., who was attached to Divisional Headquarters, was responsible to the G.O.C. for the supply of all war material as authorised. All the units of the Division notified their requirements to him, and he in turn obtained his supplies from bases, gun-parks, and other mysterious sources. Every article had its own peculiar nomenclature, a spade being by no means necessarily a spade, but perhaps " implement, agricultural, diggers, for the use of. G.S., 1." The authority for all demands was laid down in mobilisation store tables and " G.R.O.'s " (General Routine Orders), but anything not there authorised was procurable by special authority. In all there were over 200,000 different items in the ordnance " vocabulary," ranging from a toothbrush to a gun.

Normally between five and fifteen tons of equipment and clothing, costing probably thousands of pounds, were handled every day by the Ordnance Staff of four warrant officers, two sergeants, and eight other ranks, and men attached for duty from other units. After heavy fighting they were called upon to re-equip the Division immediately, which meant about a month's work compressed into twenty-four hours.

The last two years of war found Captain Shead (now Major Shead, M.C.) and his staff very familiar with the probable requirements, and before a battle they would anticipate the needs for refitting, so that replacements would be on the way from the various bases before the battle was over. The time saved was invaluable.

Mobile workshops for armourers, bootmakers, tailors, carpenters, and other craftsmen enabled an immense proportion of the necessary repairs to be done within the Division. At one period our own tailors converted 14,000 ground sheets into mackintosh capes, when there was a shortage of the latter. They also made white suits for patrols when snow was on the ground. The armourers made anti-aircraft and machine-gun mountings in addition to the ordinary work of keeping the Division's weapons in repair. The increase of the Lewis guns from two to sixteen per battalion, and the keeping up of the necessary spare parts for replacements, threw much extra work on this department.

Other periods when special demands were made on and met by the Ordnance personnel were when the 15-pounders of the Artillery were exchanged for 18-pounders at Béthune in 1915 ; when muslin and cotton waste had to be procured and converted into respirators after the first gas attack ; when old motor-car tyres had to be obtained from the back areas to deaden the sound of the wheels of horse transport vehicles at Loos.

During the fighting on Vimy Ridge, in May, 1916, many of our machine-guns were put out of action. These were replaced by others and taken by Ordnance personnel to units the same night. At Bruay, in 1916, new pattern smoke-helmets were issued to 18,000 officers and other ranks. Altogether there were five different issues of gas-masks.

After the withdrawal in 1918 the losses of guns, equipment, and transport were replaced within forty-eight hours, thanks largely to the wonderful work at the bases at Havre and Calais and the gun-parks.

Four motor-lorries from the Divisional Supply Column (or later the M.T. Company) were detached for Ordnance work, and at times of stress the drivers often worked cheerfully night and day without a break.

In short, the Ordnance Service in the Division not only never failed it in emergency, but often achieved the apparently impossible, and C.O.'s and quartermasters will readily acknowledge their debt to Major Shead, to Conductor E. W. Buffee, R.A.O.C., who served with the Division throughout the campaign, to the Brigade Warrant Officers and other Ordnance personnel.

ROYAL ARMY VETERINARY CORPS.

The 2nd London Mobile Veterinary Section, which formed part of the Division throughout the war, did service for the sick and wounded horses and mules as devoted as that of the R.A.M.C. for the personnel. During the greater part of the time it was under the command of Captain J. Southall, who left the Division in March, 1918. The work of the Veterinary officers grew heavier and heavier as their numbers decreased and the number of mounted units in the charge of each grew larger. Lieut.-Colonel W. R. Walker, A.V.C., who had been Assistant-Director of Veterinary Services to the Division since 1912, was responsible for the heavy work entailed for the Veterinary Service on mobilization, when horses, suitable and unsuitable, were collected from all kinds of sources, and when the horsemastership in mounted units was not what it afterwards became. He was succeeded shortly after the Division arrived in France, by Major J. Abson, a Territorial officer from Sheffield, who did valuable work in re-organizing the Veterinary Services in the Division and maintaining them at a high level with the aid of a band of very capable Veterinary officers. None who was privileged to hear them will forget his lectures, and many junior officers and farriers in mounted units owed much to his tuition. Major Abson was succeeded as A.D.V.S. early in 1917 by Major T. Hibbard, who came from the 56th (London) Division, and who directed the Veterinary Services of the Division till demobilization.

ROYAL ARMY CHAPLAINS' DEPARTMENT.

The work of the " Padres " in the Great War might form the theme of a most interesting volume in itself. Many of those who served with the 47th Division had been chaplains to units of it before mobilization, and started with the friendship and confidence of officers and men alike.

The senior chaplain of the Division when it went to France, in March, 1915, was the Rev. H. C. Bell, who was invalided to England in the following August. His successor was the Rev. H. J. Fleming, C.M.G., a Regular Army chaplain of considerable seniority and experience as chaplain to the Royal Military Academy, Woolwich. Mr. Fleming did much towards placing the organisation of the Chaplains' Department in the Division on a thoroughly sound basis before he was promoted, in May, 1916, to be Deputy Assistant

Chaplain-General at IVth Corps. The Rev. C. T. T. Wood, who followed him as senior chaplain, had served since the beginning of the war with the 141st Infantry Brigade, and remained with the Division till August, 1917, when he was transferred to the First Army School at the Base. From August, 1917, till demobilization in 1919 the senior chaplain was the Rev. A. E. Wilkinson, M.C., now Vicar of St. James, Croydon, who had been chaplain before the war of the 6th Battalion, London Regiment, and had served with the 6th, and later with the Divisional Artillery since mobilization.

All these, of course, represented the Church of England, but other denominations were equally fortunate in their representatives. Among the Roman Catholic chaplains an especially well-known figure was the Rev. R. J. Lane-Fox, who was attached to the 141st Infantry Brigade, and displayed great gallantry at the Battle of Loos. He was transferred to the Guards Division in 1916, and while with them won the Military Cross. He made a welcome return to the 47th Division for a few months before the end of the war.

The very great and helpful interest taken at all times in the padres' work by Major-General Gorringe enabled the Chaplains' Department to hold a position in the life of the Division which was probably seldom equalled and certainly never surpassed in any other division in France or elsewhere. It is not always realised how much a chaplain's work can be helped by the goodwill of commanding officers, or impeded by the lack of it.

Certainly the brigade and battalion commanders and the staff of the Division wholeheartedly followed the lead given them by the Divisional Commander in this respect, and a notable example of this was the A.A. and Q.M.G., Lieut.-Colonel Thunder, to whom no chaplain ever appealed in vain for anything he needed for his work, and from whom the S.C.F., in the latter days of the war, gained a reputation for being able to extract motor-cars on all and every occasion.

The allocation of chaplains within the Division was normally as follows :

Divisional Headquarters	..	Senior chaplain.
Divisional Artillery ..	..	One chaplain (C. of E.).
R.E. and Divisional Troops ..		One chaplain (C. of E.).
		One „ (Free Church).
Each Infantry Brigade	..	One chaplain (C. of E.).
		One „ (Roman Catholic).
		One „ (Free Church).

Church of England chaplains usually lived with battalions and others with field ambulances.

The acts of gallantry quietly performed by the padres in battle and in the course of their duty with troops in the line were many. The names of at least seven of them will be found in the list of Military Crosses won while serving with the Division—the Revs. C. T. T. Wood, A. E. Wilkinson, C. G. Woodward, H. Beattie, A. R. Browne-Wilkinson, D. Railton, and B. P. Plumtree; while the Rev. M. Davidson and the Rev. — Williamson and the Rev. R. Bickford were mentioned in despatches.

The loss of the Rev. Basil Plumtree, M.C., who was killed in action, in July, 1917, while attached to the 142nd Infantry Brigade, was deeply felt by his many friends in the Division. Other padres who became casualties were the Rev. R. E. Monro (attached 141st Brigade), who was gassed in Bourlon Wood, the Rev. C. S. Woodward (attached 142nd Brigade), who was wounded on the Somme in October, 1916, and the Rev. G. E. Browne, who was taken prisoner while tending wounded during the German advance in March, 1918. On his return to England from Germany Mr. Browne went out with the Relief Force to North Russia, where he gained the M.C.

THE MILITARY MOUNTED POLICE.

There can have been few divisions in France in which the relations between the Provost-Marshal's branch and the rest of the division were so happy as they were in the Forty-Seventh. The military policeman's lot on active service is not an entirely pleasant one. He has many masters and many thankless tasks to perform. The general popularity of our successive A.P.M.'s and of the corps of M.M.P., coupled with the extremely low record of " crime " of the Division, is sufficient tribute to the efficiency of their work.

Captain the Hon. H. E. Fitzclarence, M.C., who joined the Division at Hooggraaf in October, 1916, and remained with it for two years and a half, will be remembered with affection by all who served with him. His cheery personality and tact, the way in which he could administer a severe " choking-off " with a twinkle in his eye, and his experience as a prison governor and as a soldier, made him an ideal A.P.M., while his inexhaustible fund of anecdote and his keen sense of humour made him welcome in every mess. Squadron-Sergeant-Major E. Lane, the senior warrant officer of the M.M.P., who was with the Division during most of its mobilized service, was another well-known figure and a master of traffic-control. A former A.P.M. writes of him : " He was a remarkable-looking man and rode over nineteen stone. When things went smoothly on the road you might have taken him for a minister of the Gospel, but if things went badly and delays or blocks occurred his vocabulary was a masterpiece, both as regards volubility and changes of expression."

Before the Battle of Messines in 1917 the traffic control work in the salient involved heavy responsibility for the A.P.M. and his traffic officer, Captain R. R. Smart, but their excellent organisation enabled the vast stores of ammunition, supplies, and material to be got up through Ypres to the line as smoothly as possible. Other occasions when the police and traffic work was specially difficult, but was carried out in a way which earned much praise, were the Battle of Cambrai (Nov.-Dec., 1917), and the withdrawal in March, 1918.

DIVISIONAL EMPLOYMENT COMPANY.

In May, 1916, a draft of men from the Middlesex Regiment (Labour Corps) was sent out from England to the 47th Division for non-combatant duties. These, together with fifty men from units of the Division, were formed into the 47th Divisional Employment Company, nearly two hundred strong, which was soon put under command of Captain W. S. Batten-Pooll, North Somerset Yeomanry, and organised for various administrative work in the Division. Detachments from the company managed the divisional baths and laundry, the " delousing " plant (Foden disinfector), and salvage ; and a party of the fittest men was attached to the divisional train for unloading duties at the different dumps. The appointment of permanent staffs to the baths and laundry, which rapidly became expert, ensured the continued efficiency of a department which had been admirably organised by Captain A. F. Robinson (19th Battalion), and contributed greatly to the comfort of the Division. The activities of the salvage party, under Major W. C. B. Williams, M.C. (4th R.W.F.) were varied and ubiquitous, and not only gave peculiar satisfaction to the " Q " Staff of the Division, but rendered real service in the cause of economy.

In 1917 the Company was renamed 241st Divisional Employment Company, and its establishment was increased to 320 by the addition of many headquarters details—Divisional and Brigade staffs, batmen, the " Follies " troupe, and others. Periodic " combing out " removed many of the fitter men, and there was frequent exchange of personnel with unfit men from units in the Division.

Captain Batten-Pooll left the Company in August, 1918, and it came under the command of successive camp commandants. Under this arrangement the responsibility for maintaining the efficiency of the work devolved upon the N.C.O's in charge of the various detachments.

During the retreat in March, 1918, the Baths staff did notably good work at Metz, where the Foden disinfector was kept working, until it was shelled out, and a supply of clean clothing was kept up for men who came back gassed from the line. Sergeant Thirtle was awarded the M.S.M. in recognition of this work.

After the armistice a number of men from the Employment Company were sent to the Rhine; others, including Sergeant P. Hill, remained behind at area headquarters after the last cadres of the Division had left.

Appendix B.

THE DIVISIONAL "FOLLIES."

During the last three years of the Division's service in France the 47th Divisional "Follies" played an important part in the amusement of the troops when out of the line. Formed originally in February, 1916, owing to the initiative of Lieut.-Colonel Thunder, the troupe gave its first performance in March in a hut at Gouy Servins that had been converted into a theatre. The original name chosen for the party was "The Quarante Se(p)t," but this was soon allowed to die a merciful death, and it was simply as "The Follies" that the talented little band of performers achieved a fame which extended to other divisions besides its own.

The original members of the party were Lieutenant E. A. Boughton, Sergeant R. H. Cobley, Rifleman E. Sawyer, Rifleman C. F. Cherry, Rifleman F. C. Mott, Rifleman S. Dignum, and Rifleman W. V. Tidmarsh, all of the 21st Battalion, Corporal L. E. Amand, of the 24th Battalion, and Corporal L. C. Ward, of the 18th Battalion. These were joined later at intervals by Sergeant R. H. Wyatt (5th London Field Ambulance), Rifleman H. Collins, Rifleman A. Hughes, and Rifleman J. Cottham (21st Battalion), Lance-Corporal W. Every (15th Battalion), and Pte. J. Leggett (22nd Battalion). In September, 1917, the party was joined by an orchestra led by an able musician in Sergeant F. H. Stamper, and including Corporal Garnet, Privates Robson, Taylor, Barnes, and Dolder, and later Private Harris (22nd Battalion).

Among the more ambitious productions of the "Follies" were the revue "—— and Halifax," written by Sergeant J. W. Nevill (21st Battalion), and produced in December, 1916, at Halifax Camp, in the Ypres Salient, where it ran for four months and a half; "Ca-y-est," produced at Bertincourt, in December, 1917, the book being by Sergeant Nevill and the music by Sergeant Stamper, and "Alfred Barber and the Forty Winks," a pantomime by Sergeant Wyatt, with music by Lance-Corporal Every, played at Auchel and Lillers at Christmas, 1918.

Some of the most popular numbers, which will call up memories of the brighter moments of the war to thousands of London soldiers, were "Four-and-Nine," the trench scene from the Halifax revue, "That Dear Old Home of Mine," "Wonderful Girl—Wonderful Boy," and the dancing of Hughes and Cottham, better known on the London stage as "Rich and Galvin." Not only were the words and music of many of the songs written by members of the troupe, but they also designed their own posters and painted their own scenery.

Among those for whom special performances were given by "The Follies" were the Queen of the Belgians, General Plumer, General Horne, and some of the American divisions. They also appeared in the Opera House at Amiens for the Croix Rouge Française, in the theatre at Bruay, and for four weeks at IVth Corps Headquarters, and, in the words of a leading member of the troupe, in "sundry corps schools, barns, huts, aeroplane-hangars, farmyards, hospitals, concentration-camps, fields, middens, and other rubbish heaps, by electric light, gaslight, candle light, acetylene, daylight, and in the dark."

The theatre at Halifax Camp was partly burnt down during the winter of 1916-17 owing to a fire which started in some adjoining huts, but performances were continued as usual. This camp was shelled repeatedly through the summer of 1917, and although the theatre was never actually hit, shells landed within a few yards on several occasions. The Bertincourt area was bombed on numerous occasions while shows were in progress, the roof of the theatre being pierced, but the performances were continued.

On three separate occasions in 1918 the whole of the party was attached to Field Ambulances for duty in the line. The strength of " The Follies " was reduced in March, 1918. Among those who returned to their units was Corporal (now Sergeant) Ward, the " leading lady," who was shortly afterwards wounded and lost his left hand.

In March, 1919, demobilization began to break the party up, but new recruits were brought in, and the Division could still provide a concert-party up to the time when it ceased to exist as a division, though there were few of the original Follies among the wearers of the familiar green-and-black costumes.

THE FOLLIES: "THAT DEAR OLD HOME OF MINE."

THE DIVISIONAL FOLLIES, 1917.

Appendix C.
ORDER OF BATTLE.
ARTILLERY.

The original order of battle was as follows, all batteries being four-gun batteries :

5TH (LONDON) BRIGADE (15-pdr.) R.F.A.
 12th County of London Battery, R.F.A.
 13th   do.
 14th   do.
 5th London Brigade Ammunition Column.
6TH (LONDON) BRIGADE (15-pdr.) R.F.A.
 15th County of London Battery, R.F.A.
 16th   do.
 17th   do.
 6th London Brigade Ammunition Column.
7TH (LONDON) BRIGADE (15-pdr.), R.F.A.
 18th County of London Battery, R.F.A.
 19th   do.
 20th   do.
 7th London Brigade Ammunition Column.
8TH LONDON (HOWITZER) BRIGADE (5-in.), R.F.A.
 21st County of London Battery, R.F.A.
 22nd   do.
 8th London Brigade Ammunition Column.
2ND LONDON HEAVY (4.7-in.) BATTERY, R.G.A.
2ND LONDON DIVISIONAL AMMUNITION COLUMN.

SUBSEQUENT CHANGES.

Mar., 1915. The Divisional Artillery proceeded to France as above, and almost immediately the 2nd London Heavy Battery, R.G.A., was taken away.

Nov., 1915. The Divisional Artillery was re-armed, the Field Batteries with 18-pounders, and the Howitzer Batteries with 4.5-in.

May, 1916. Three new four-gun 18-pounder Batteries were posted to the Divisional Artillery, two made up from 34th Battery, R.F.A., and one from 93rd Battery, R.F.A., also D/176th 4.5-in. Howitzer Battery, and the nomenclature and organisation of Brigades was changed as follows :

235TH BRIGADE, R.F.A. (late 5th London Brigade, R.F.A.)
 A/235 Battery (late 12th Coy. of Lon.), R.F.A.
 B/235   ,, 13th ,,
 C/235   ,, 14th ,,
 D/235   ,, D/176 Battery, R.F.A.
236TH BRIGADE, R.F.A. (late 6th London Brigade, R.F.A.)
 A/236 Battery (late 15th Coy. of Lon.), R.F.A.
 B/236   ,, ,, 16th ,,
 C/236   ,, ,, 17th ,,
 D/236   ,, ,, 22nd ,,

May, 1916.　237TH BRIGADE, R.F.A. (late 7th London Brigade, R.F.A.)
　　　　　　　A/237 Battery (late 18th Coy. of Lon.), R.F.A.
　　　　　　　B/237　　　,,　　　,, 19th　　　,,
　　　　　　　C/237　　　,,　　　,, 20th　　　,,
　　　　238TH BRIGADE, R.F.A. (late 8th Lon. (How.) Bde., R.F.A.)
　　　　　　　34th Battery, R.F.A.
　　　　　　　B/238　　　,,　　(late 34th Battery, R.F.A.)
　　　　　　　C/238　　　,,　　(late 93rd Battery), R.F.A.
　　　　　　　D/238　　　,,　　(late 21st Coy. of Lon.), R.F.A.
　　　　All Brigade Ammunition Columns were abolished and merged
　　　in the 47th Divisional Ammunition Column.

Dec., 1916.　All Batteries were made six-gun Batteries, and the final
　　　reorganisation took place as follows :
　　　235TH BRIGADE, R.F.A.
　　　　　　　B/235 Battery, R.F.A. (late B/235 and half A/235)
　　　　　　　B/235　　　,,　　　　　　　,, C/235　　　,, A/235)
　　　　　　　C/235　　　,,　　　　　　　,, C/237　　　,, A/237)
　　　　　　　D/235　　　,,　　　　　　　,, D/238　　　,, D/235)
　　　236TH BRIGADE, R.F.A.
　　　　　　　A/236 Battery, R.F.A. (late A/236 and half C/236)
　　　　　　　B/236　　　,,　　　　　　　,, B/236　　　,, C/236)
　　　　　　　C/236　　　,,　　　　　　　,, B/237　　　,, A/237)
　　　　　　　D/236　　　,,　　　　　　　,, D/236　　　,, D/235)
　　　Headquarters 237th and 238th Brigades, R.F.A., were
　　　abolished, and A/238 and half B/238 Batteries, R.F.A., were
　　　combined into 34th Battery, R.F.A., again, and posted to
　　　189th (Army) Brigade, R.F.A., while C/238 Battery, R.F.A.,
　　　with the remaining half of B/238 Battery, was posted to 104th
　　　(Army) Brigade, R.F.A.

TRENCH MORTARS.

June, 1916.　X/47 T.M. Battery (four 2-in. mortars) formed within Division.
　　　　　　　Y/47　　　　　do.　　　　　　　　　　do.
　　　　　　　Z/47　　　　　do.　　　　　　　　　　do.
Nov., 1916.　V/47 (Heavy) T.M. Battery (two 9.45 in. mortars) formed.
Feb., 1918.　V/47 (Heavy) T.M. Battery withdrawn from Division, becoming
　　　　　　　V Corps H.T.M. Battery.
Feb., 1918.　All 2-in. mortars withdrawn, and replaced by twelve 6-in.
　　　Newton mortars. These were constituted into two Batteries
　　　called " X " and " Y," and formed of personnel of the former
　　　" X," " Y," and " Z " Batteries.
　　　The Trench Mortar Organisation of the Divisional Artillery
　　　from this date until February, 1919, was therefore :
　　　X/47 T.M. Battery ;
　　　Y/47 T.M. Battery.

ENGINEERS.

Aug. 4th, 1914.　3rd London Field Company, R.E.
　　　　　　　4th London Field Company, R.E.
　　　　　　　2nd London Divisional Signal Company, R.E.
Oct., 1914.　2/3rd London Field Company, R.E., raised in Division.
Jan., 1915.　3rd London Field Company, R.E., left Division for 28th
　　　　　　　Division, B.E.F.
　　　　　　　2/3rd London Field Company, R.E., left Division for
　　　　　　　2/2nd London Division.
Mar. 15th, 1915.　4th London Field Coy., R.E. ..　}　to B.E.F. with Division.
　　　　　　　2nd Lon. Div. Signal Coy., R.E.　}
April 11th, 1915.　3rd London Field Company, R.E., rejoined Division.

June 20th, 1915. 2/3rd London Field Company, R.E., joined Division from England.

Feb. 1st, 1917. Field Companies re-numbered as follows :

    3rd London Field Coy.—517th Field Coy., R.E.
    4th   do.   —518th   do.
    2/3rd   do.   —520th   do.

To Mar., 1919. 517th Field Company, R.E.
    518th Field Company, R.E.
    520th Field Company, R.E.
    47th Divisional Signal Company, R.E.

PIONEER BATTALION.

Sep., 1915, to ⎱ 1/4th Battalion, Royal Welsh Fusiliers.
Mar., 1919 ⎰

INFANTRY.

4TH LONDON INFANTRY BRIGADE.

Aug. 4th, 1914. 1/13th Batt. London Regt. (Kensington).
    1/14th Batt. London Regt. (London Scottish).
    1/15th Batt. London Regt. (Civil Service Rifles).
    1/16th Batt. London Regt. (Queen's Westminster Rifles).

SUBSEQUENT CHANGES.

Sep. 15th, 1914. 1/14th Batt. London Regt. entrained for France.
Oct. 17th, 1914. 1/28th Batt. London Regt. (Artists Rifles) joined the Brigade.
Oct. 26th, 1914. 1/28th Batt. London Regt. entrained for France.
Nov. 1st, 1914. 1/16th Batt. London Regt. entrained for France.
Nov. 3rd, 1914. 1/13th Batt. London Regt. entrained for France.
Nov. 5th, 1914. 1/6th Batt. London Regt. joined Brigade.
Nov. 5th, 1914. 1/7th Batt. London Regt. joined Brigade.
Nov. 6th, 1914. 1/8th Batt. London Regt. joined Brigade, the Order of Battle on this date then being :
    1/6th Batt. London Regt.
    1/7th Batt. London Regt.
    1/8th Batt. London Regt. (Post Office Rifles).
    1/15th Batt. London Regt. (Civil Service Rifles).
Mar. 17th, 1915. Brigade entrained for France.
May 12th, 1915. Brigade renamed 140TH INFANTRY BRIGADE.
June, 1915. 140th Light Trench Mortar Battery formed.
Nov. 16th, 1915. 1/4th Battalion London Regt. joined Brigade.
Dec., 1915. 140th Machine Gun Company formed.
Feb. 1st, 1918. 1/17th Battalion London Regt. (Poplar and Stepney Rifles) joined the Brigade from 141st Infantry Brigade.
Feb. 1st, 1918. 1/21st Battalion London Regt. (First Surrey Rifles) joined the Brigade from 142nd Infantry Brigade.
Feb. 2nd, 1918. Nucleus of 1/6th, 1/7th, and 1/8th Battalions London Regt. proceeded to join 58th (London) Division.
Feb., 1918. 140th Machine Gun Company absorbed by 47th M.G. Batt. the Order of Battle then being :
    1/15th Batt. London Regt. (Civil Service Rifles).
    1/17th Batt. London Regt. (Poplar and Stepney Rifles).
    1/21st Battalion London Regt. (First Surrey Rifles).
    140th Light Trench Mortar Battery.

5TH LONDON INFANTRY BRIGADE.

Aug. 4th, 1914. 1/17th Battalion London Regt.
    1/18th Battalion London Regt.
    1/19th Battalion London Regt.
    1/20th Battalion London Regt.

SUBSEQUENT CHANGES.

Mar. 9th, 1915.	Brigade entrained for France.
May 12th, 1915.	Brigade renamed 141ST INFANTRY BRIGADE.
June, 1915.	141st Light Trench Mortar Battery formed.
Dec., 1915.	141st Machine Gun Company formed.
Feb. 1st, 1918.	1/17th Battalion London Regt. transferred to 140th Infantry Brigade.
Feb. 1918.	141st Machine Gun Company merged in 47th M.G. Batt., the Order of Battle then being :

        1/18th Battalion London Regt.
        1/19th Battalion London Regt.
        1/20th Battalion London Regt.
        141st Light Trench Mortar Battery.

6TH LONDON INFANTRY BRIGADE.

Aug. 4th, 1914.	1/21st Battalion London Regt.
	1/22nd Battalion London Regt.
	1/23rd Battalion London Regt.
	1/24th Battalion London Regt.

SUBSEQUENT CHANGES.

Mar. 1915.	Brigade entrained for France.
May 12th, 1915.	Brigade renamed 142nd INFANTRY BRIGADE.
June, 1915.	142nd Light Trench Mortar Battery formed.
Nov. 16th, 1915.	1/3rd Battalion London Regt. joined Brigade.
Dec., 1915.	142nd Machine Gun Company formed.
Feb. 7th, 1916.	1/3rd Battalion London Regt. left Brigade.
Feb., 1918.	142nd Machine Gun Company absorbed by 47th M.G. Batt.
Feb., 1918	1/21st Battalion London Regt. transferred to 140th Infantry Brigade, the Order of Battle then being :

        1/22nd Battalion London Regt.
        1/23rd Battalion London Regt.
        1/24th Battalion London Regt.
        142nd Light Trench Mortar Battery.

MACHINE GUN CORPS.

Feb. 28th, 1918.	47th Machine Gun Battalion formed.

ARMY SERVICE CORPS.*

Aug. 4th, 1914.	2ND LONDON DIVISIONAL TRAIN.
	Headquarters and Headquarters Company.
	No. 2 (4th London Brigade) Company.
	No. 3 (5th London Brigade) Company.
	No. 4 (6th London Brigade) Company.
Aug., 1914.	2nd London Divisional Supply Column formed.
Aug., 1915.	Train Companies renumbered as under :

        455th (H.T.) Company, A.S.C.
        456th (H.T.) Company, A.S.C.
        457th (H.T.) Company, A.S.C.
        458th (H.T.) Company, A.S.C.

ROYAL ARMY MEDICAL CORPS.

Aug. 4th, 1914.	4th London Field Ambulance.
	5th London Field Ambulance.
	6th London Field Ambulance.
Mar. 14th, 1915.	47th Divisional Sanitary Section formed.
April, 1917.	47th Divisional Sanitary Section withdrawn, and posted to Second Army as an Army unit.

ARMY VETERINARY CORPS.*

Aug., 1914, to } 2nd London Mobile Veterinary Section.
Mar., 1919. }

LABOUR CORPS.

May, 1917. 241st Divisional Employment Company formed, absorbing 47th Divisional Salvage Company and other details.

---

* These corps became the Royal Army Service Corps and the Royal Army Veterinary Corps respectively on November 25th, 1918.

Appendix D.

The following list shows:

I.—Commanders and Staff of the 47th (London) Division during the period of its mobilization, 1914-1919, with the dates of appointment.

II.—Commanders of (A) Infantry Battalions; (B) Artillery Brigades and Batteries; (C) Field Companies and Signal Company, R.E.; (D) Divisional Train; (E) Field Ambulances.

NOTE.—In List I. the original date of appointment is given. In List II. the date given is that of relinquishing the appointment; the first name in each case is that of the officer commanding the unit on mobilization, or in the case of units formed during the war, of the first commanding officer.

Names of officers killed in action while in command are marked †.

Rank and decorations given are those held or won during tenure of the appointment.

I.—COMMANDERS AND STAFF.

DIVISIONAL COMMANDERS.

Date of
Appointment.

Mar. 31, 1912.	Major-General C. C. Monro, C.B.
Aug. 5, 1914.	Major-General T. L. N. Morland, C.B, D.S.O.
Aug., 1914.	Major-General Sir C. St. L. Barter, K.C.B., C.V.O.
Sept. 29, 1916.	Major-General Sir G. F. Gorringe, K.C.B., K.C.M.G., D.S.O.

GENERAL STAFF OFFICER, GRADE I.

Aug. 5, 1914.	Lt.-Col. W. Thwaites, C.B., R.A.
June 2, 1915.	Lt.-Col. Hon. W. P. Hore-Ruthven, D.S.O., Scots Guards.
Aug. 20, 1915.	Lt.-Col. B. Burnett Hitchcock, D.S.O., Notts and Derby Regt.
June 15, 1916.	Lt.-Col. J. T. Weatherby, Oxford and Bucks L.I.
Nov. 17, 1916.	Lt.-Col. A. J. Turner, D.S.O., R.A.
Feb. 21, 1918.	Lt.-Col. C. M. Davies, D.S.O., Rifle Brigade.
July 14, 1918.	Lt.-Col. B. L. Montgomery, D.S.O., R. Warwickshire Regt.

GENERAL STAFF OFFICER, GRADE II.

Feb. 17, 1912.	Lt.-Col. W. Thwaites, R.A.
Aug. 5, 1914.	Major E. H. Collen, D.S.O., R.G.A.
Mar. 23, 1915.	Major B. Burnett Hitchcock, D.S.O., Notts and Derby Regt.
June 5, 1915.	Major N. W. Webber, D.S.O., R.E.
May 24, 1916.	Major R. S. McClintock, D.S.O., R.E.
Feb. 17, 1917.	Major H. C. B. Kirkpatrick, D.S.O., M.C., K.O.S.B.
Nov. 24, 1917.	Major J. C. D. Carlisle, D.S.O., M.C., Civil Service Rifles.
April 9, 1918.	Major W. Carden Ree, M.C., Royal Irish Fusiliers.
July 6, 1918.	Major Max Lewis, M.C., General List.

GENERAL STAFF OFFICER, GRADE III.

Aug. 4, 1914.	Capt. H. R. A. Hunt, 25th Punjabis.
Mar. 25, 1916.	Capt. J. D. Carlisle, M.C., Civil Service Rifles.
Jan. 2, 1917.	Capt. R. de B. Cazalet, General List.
April 9, 1917.	Capt. J. I. Piggott, M.C., Special List.
April 5, 1918.	Capt. T. W. Nelson, M.C., General List.
May 13, 1918.	Capt. G. C. Turner, M.C., 23rd Batt., London Regt.

INTELLIGENCE OFFICER.

Feb. 22, 1917.	Lieut. R. H. Unwin, R.F.A. (T.)

A. A. & Q.M.G.

Aug., 1914.	Lt.-Col. A. N. Lysaght.
1914.	Lt.-Col. R. M. Foot, C.M.G., R. Inniskilling Fusiliers (R. of O.).
Feb. 5, 1916.	Lt.-Col. S. H. J. Thunder, C.M.G., D.S.O., M.C., Northamp. Regt.

D.A.A.G. (D.A.A. & Q.M.G.)

Oct. 2, 1911.	Major H. V. M. de la Fontaine, East Surrey Regt.
July, 1915.	Major P. Hudson, The King's (Liverpool Regt.).
Feb. 16, 1916.	Major H. I. Nicholl, Bedfordshire Regt. (R. of O.).
June 17, 1916.	Capt. G. E. Hope, Grenadier Guards.
July 3, 1916.	Major M. Alexander, M.C., Rifle Brigade.
July 7, 1918.	Major J. T. Duffin, M.C., General List.

D.A.Q.M.G.

Aug., 1914.	Lt.-Col. G. E. Pereira, C.M.G., D.S.O., Grenadier Guards (R. of O.).
July, 1915.	Major E. Craig-Brown, Cameron Highlanders.
Mar., 1916.	Major R. O. Schwarz, M.C., Special Reserve.
Mar. 8, 1917.	Major A. J. Stephenson-Fetherstonhaugh, D.S.O., M.C., Worcestershire Regt. (S.R.)

C.R.A.

April 1, 1912.	Brig.-Gen. J. C. Wray, C.M.G., M.V.O., R.A.
Feb., 1916.	Brig.-Gen. E. W. Spedding, C.M.G., R.A.
Mar. 31, 1917.	Brig.-Gen. E. N. Whitley, C.B., C.M.G., D.S.O., R.F.A. (T.).

C.R.E.

April 15, 1910.	Lt.-Col. H. H. Taylor, T.D.
Aug. 15, 1914.	Col. A. H. Kenney, C.M.G., D.S.O., R.E.
July 27, 1915.	Lt.-Col. S. D'a. Crookshank, D.S.O., C.I.E., M.V.O., R.E.
Nov., 1916.	Lt.-Col. W. S. Traill, D.S.O., R.E.
May, 1917.	Lt.-Col. H. S. Christie, D.S.O., R.E.
Nov. 25, 1917.	Lt.-Col. A. B. Carey, C.M.G., D.S.O., R.E.
Nov. 1, 1918.	Lt.-Col. H. J. Couchman, D.S.O., M.C., R.E.

A.D.M.S.

Aug., 1914.	Col. C. E. Harrison, C.V.O.
Mar., 1915.	Col. C. E. Nicol, D.S.O.
May, 1915.	Col. R. L. R. MacLeod.
July, 1915.	Col. A. M. McLaughlin.
Aug. 18, 1915.	Col. J. D. Ferguson, C.M.G., D.S.O.
June 1, 1917.	Col. T. W. Gibbard, K.H.S., C.B.
July 23, 1918.	Col. T. Fraser, D.S.O., R.A.M.C. (T.).

D.A.D.M.S.

Aug., 1914.	Col. E. Butt.
Mar., 1915.	Major C. J. Martin, R.A.M.C. (T.).
July 22, 1917.	Capt. H. M. Calder, D.S.O., R.A.M.C. (T.).

A.P.M.

Aug., 1914.	Capt. L. C. D. Jenner, K.R.R.C. (R. of O.).
Sept., 1914.	Lt.-Col. C. B. Wood, Royal Scots (R. of O.).
Feb., 1916.	Major E. R. A. Hall, The King's (Liverpool Regt.).
Dec., 1916.	Capt. the Hon. H. E. FitzClarence, Special List.
Oct. 20, 1918.	Capt. E. J. Rendall.
Feb. 14, 1919.	Lieut. F. R. Goodland, R. Lancaster Regt. (S.R.).

D.A.D.O.S.

Aug. 16, 1914. Major G. de S. Dudley, A.O.D.
May 15, 1915. Major H. Buckland, A.O.D.
Dec. 15, 1915. Major A. T. Shead, M.C.. A.O.C.

A.D.V.S.

June 8, 1912. Lt.-Col. W. R. Walker, A.V.C. (R. of O.).
May 31, 1915. Major J. Abson, D.S.O., A.V.C. (T.).
Jan. 20, 1917. Major T. Hibbard, T.D., A.V.C. (T.).

INFANTRY BRIGADE COMMANDERS.
140th (4th London) Infantry Brigade.

Oct., 1913. Brig.-Gen. F. J. Heyworth, Scots Guards.
Nov. 26, 1914. Brig.-Gen. G. J. Cuthbert, C.B., C.M.G., Scots Guards.
July 11, 1916. Brig.-Gen. Viscount Hampden, C.B., C.M.G., 10th Hussars and Herts Regt.
May 17, 1917. Brig.-Gen. H. B. P. L. Kennedy, C.M.G., D.S.O., K.R.R.C.

141st (5th London) Infantry Brigade.

Sept. 9, 1911. Brig.-Gen. C. FitzClarence, V.C., Irish Guards.
Sept., 1914. Brig.-Gen. G. C. Nugent, Irish Guards.†
June 2, 1915. Brig.-Gen. W. Thwaites, C.B., R.A.
July 8, 1916. Brig.-Gen. R. J. Bridgford, C.B., C.M.G., D.S.O., K.S.L.I.
Aug. 19, 1916. Brig.-Gen. R. McDouall, C.B., C.M.G., D.S.O., The Buffs.
Oct., 1917. Brig.-Gen. J. F. Erskine, C.B., C.M.G., D.S.O., M.V.O.
Jan. 2, 1918. Brig.-Gen. W. F. Mildren, C.B., C.M.G., D.S.O., 6th Batt., Lon. Regt.

142nd (6th London) Infantry Brigade.

April 11, 1912. Brig.-Gen. the Hon. C. S. Heathcote Drummond Willoughby, C.M.G.
Aug. 14, 1915. Brig.-Gen. F. G. Lewis, C.B., C.M.G., T.D., 13th Batt. Lon. Reg.
Feb. 5. 1917. Brig.-Gen. V T. Bailey, C.M.G., D.S.O., The King's (Liverpool Regt.)
April 1, 1918. Brig-Gen. R. McDouall, C.B., C.M.G., D.S.O., The Buffs.
Dec. 11, 1918. Brig.-Gen. L. F. Ashburner, D.S.O., M.V.O., Royal Fusiliers.

II.—COMMANDING OFFICERS.

(A) Infantry Battalions.

1/6th Battalion, London Regiment.

Lt.-Col. G. D. M. Moore . .	To June 6, 1915.
Col. T. W. Simpson, V.D. . .	„ Aug. 10, 1915.
Lt.-Col. W. F. Mildren, C.B., C.M.G., D.S.O., T.D. . .	„ Jan. 2, 1918.

1/7th Battalion, London Regiment.

Lt.-Col. G. A. A., Viscount Hood. .	„ Sept., 1914.
Col. E. Faux, C.M.G., V.D. . .	„ May 31, 1915.
Lt.-Col. C. J. Salkeld Green, M.C. . .	„ Aug. 8, 1915.
Col. E. Faux, C.M.G., V.D., T.D. . .	„ Sept. 24, 1916.
Lt.-Col. C. J. Salkeld Green, D.S.O., M.C., T.D. . .	„ Feb. 6, 1918.

1/8th Battalion, London Regiment, (Post Office Rifles).

Lt.-Col. J. Harvey, D.S.O. . .	„ Oct., 1915.
Lt.-Col. A. Maxwell, D.S.O.	„ May, 1916.
Lt.-Col. W. J. Whitehead, D.S.O. . .	„ Nov., 1916.
Major H. Peel, D.S.O., M.C.	„ Jan., 1917.
Lt.-Col. W. B. Vince, D.S O., M.C.	„ Mar., 1917.
Lt.-Col. A. Maxwell, C.M.G., D.S.O., T.D.	„ July, 1917.
Lt.-Col. R. E. de Vesian . .	„ Aug., 1917.
Lt.-Col. W. B. Vince, D.S.O., M.C.	„ Feb., 6, 1918.

1/15th Battalion, London Regiment (P.W.O. Civil Service Rifles).

Lt.-Col. A. J. C. G., Earl of Arran, K.P.	..	..	To Nov., 1914.
Lt.-Col. (Bt.-Col.) A. M. Renny	..	..	..	,, July, 1915.
Lt.-Col. H. V. Warrender, D.S.O.	..	..	..	,, Nov., 1916.
Lt.-Col. W. F. K. Newson	..	..	..	..	,, Jan., 1917.
Lt.-Col. H. Marshall, M.C.	..	..	..	..	,, July, 1917.
Lt.-Col. F. W. Parish, D.S.O., M.C.	..	..	..	,, Sept. 1, 1917.
Lt.-Col. W. H. E. Segrave, D.S.O.	..	..	..	,, Aug. 22, 1918.
Lt.-Col. R. C. Fielding, D.S.O.	..	..	..	,, Demobilization.

1/17th Battalion, London Regiment (Poplar and Stepney Rifles).

Lt.-Col. J. Godding	..	..	..	..	,, Oct., 1915.
Lt.-Col. E. H. Norman, D.S.O.	..	..	..	,, Feb., 1917.
Major F. R. Grimwood, D.S.O.	..	..	..	,, May, 1917
Lt.-Col. W. H. Hughes, M.C.	..	..	..	., Feb., 1918.
Lt.-Col. F. W. Parish, D.S.O., M.C.	..	..	..	,, July, 1918.
Lt.-Col. H. S. Kaye, D.S.O., M.C.	..	..	..	,, Demobilization.

1/18th Battalion, London Regiment (London Irish Rifles).

Lt.-Col. E. G. Concanon, D.S.O., T.D.	..	..	..	,, May, 1915.
Lt.-Col. J. P. Tredennick, D.S.O.	..	..	..	,, June, 1916.
Major W. Parker	..	..	..	..	,, July, 1916.
Lt.-Col. J. P. Tredennick, D.S.O.	..	..	..	,, Aug., 1916.
Major J. H. Trinder, M.C.	..	..	..	..	,, Sept. 15, 1916.†
Lt.-Col. B. McM. Mahon, D.S.O., M.C.	..	..	,, Feb., 1917.
Lt.-Col. D. B. Parry, D.S.O.	..	..	..	,, Dec., 1917.
Lt.-Col. G. H. Neely, D.S.O., M.C.	..	..	..	,, March, 1918.
Lt.-Col. G. H. Neely, D.S.O., M.C.	..	..	..	,, Demobilization.

1/19th Battalion, London Regiment (Poplar and Stepney Rifles).

Lt.-Col. P. T. Westmorland, C.M.G., D.S.O.	..	..	,, June 2, 1915.
Lt.-Col. H. Collison-Morley	..	..	..	,, Sept. 25,1915.†
Lt.-Col. A. P. Hamilton, M.C.	..	..	..	,, Sept. 15, 1916.†
Major C. H. Fair, D.S.O.	..	..	..	..	,,
Lt.-Col. J. G. Stokes, D.S.O., M.C.	..	..	..	,,
Lt.-Col. E. J. Collett	..	..	..	..	,,
Lt.-Col. R. S. I. Friend, D.S.O.	..	..	..	,,
Major J. J. Sheppard, D.S.O., M.C.	..	..	..	,, May, 1918.
Lt.-Col. H. de L. Ferguson, D.S.O.	..	..	..	,, Aug., 1918.
Major J. J. Sheppard, D.S.O., M.C.	..	..	..	., Sept., 1918.
Lt.-Col. Hutchisson	..	..	..	..	,, Dec., 1918.
Major C. J. Bantick	..	..	..	..	,, Demobilization.

1/20th Battalion, London Regiment (Blackheath and Woolwich).

Lt.-Col. H. A. Christmas	..	..	..	..	,, Sept., 1914.
Col. E. J. Moore, C.B., V.D.	..	..	..	..	,, Feb., 1915.
Lt.-Col. A. B. Hubback, C.M.G.	..	..	..	,, March, 1916.
Lt.-Col. G. A. B. Carr	..	..	..	..	,, May, 1916.
Lt.-Col. W. H. Matthews, D.S.O.	..	..	..	,, Aug., 1916.
Lt.-Col. W. Parker, D.S.O.	..	..	..	..	,, April, 1917.
Lt.-Col. W. H. Matthews, D.S.O.	..	..	..	., July, 1917.
Lt.-Col. B. McM. Mahon, D.S.O., M.C.	..	..	..	,, Nov., 1917.
Major R. Groves-Raines, D.S.O.	..	..	..	,, Dec., 1917.
Major E. R. Collett, D.S.O.	..	..	..	..	,, Feb., 1918.
Lt.-Col. F. R. Grimwood, D.S.O.	..	..	..	,, March, 1918.
Major H. S. Read, M.C.	..	..	..	..	,, May, 1918.
Lt.-Col. W. B. Vince, D.S.O., M.C.	..	..	..	,, Demobilization.

1/21st Battalion, London Regiment (First Surrey Rifles).

Lt.-Col. M. J. B. Tomlin	..	..	..	..	,, May 1, 1915.
Lt.-Col. W. F. Morris	..	..	..	..	,, Aug. 31, 1915.
Lt.-Col. H. B. P. L. Kennedy, D.S.O.	..	..	..	,, May 17, 1917.
Lt.-Col. A. Hutchence, M.C.	..	..	..	,, Sept. 30, 1917
Major C. W. B. Heslop	..	..	..	..	,, Oct., 1917.
Lt.-Col. G. Dawes, D.S.O., M.C.	..	..	..	,, Nov., 1918.
Lt.-Col. W. G. Newton, M.C.	..	..	..	,, Demobilization.

1/22nd Battalion, London Regiment (The Queen's).

Lt.-Col. E. J. Previté, V.D.	..	..	To Dec. 1, 1915.
Lt.-Col. V. A. Flower, D.S.O.	..	..	„ Jan. 26, 1917.
Lt.-Col. C. F. H. Greenwood, D.S.O., T.D.	..	..	„ Mar. 4, 1917.
Lt.-Col. C. J. Salkeld Green, D.S.O., M.C.	..	..	„ July 9, 1918.
Lt.-Col. L. L. Pargiter, D.S.O.	..	..	„ Sept. 7, 1918.
Lt.-Col. C. F. H. Greenwood, D.S.O., T.D.	..	..	„ Demobilization.

1/23rd Battalion, London Regiment.

Lt.-Col. Lord H. Montagu-Douglas-Scott, C.M.G., D.S.O.		„	May 18, 1915.
Lt.-Col. H. S. J. Streatfeild, D.S.O.	..	„	Sept. 15, 1915.
Lt.-Col. T. G. W. Newman, D.S.O.	..	„	April 10, 1916.
Lt.-Col. H. H. Kemble, D.S.O., M.C.	..	„	June 7, 1917.†
Major T. C. Hargreaves, D.S.O.	..	„	June 28, 1917.
Lt.-Col. A. Maxwell, C.M.G., D.S.O., T.D.	..	„	June 30, 1918.
Lt.-Col. R. H. Tolerton, D.S.O., M.C.	..	„	July 31, 1918.
Major A. Totton, M.C.	..	„	Aug. 13, 1918.
Lt.-Col. R. H. Tolerton, D.S.O., M.C.	..	„	Demobilization.

1/24th Battalion London Regiment (The Queen's).

Lt.-Col. W. G. Simpson, C.M.G.	..	„	March, 1916.
Lt.-Col. W. Parker	..	„	May, 1916.
Lt.-Col. G. A. Buxton-Carr, D.S.O., T.D.	..	„	May, 1917.
Lt.-Col. G. E. Millner, D.S.O., M.C.	..	„	Mar., 1918.
Major T. O. Bury, T.D.	..	„	March, 1918.
Major A. T. Fearon, M.C.	..	„	May, 1918.
Lt.-Col. R. S. I. Friend, D.S.O.	..	„	Aug., 1918.
Major F. Gordon Gill, D.S.O.	..	„	Sept., 1918.
Capt. S. Hamilton-Walker, M.C.	..	„	Sept., 1918.
Lt.-Col. L. L. Pargiter, D.S.O.	..	„	Dec., 1918.
Lt.-Col. S. C. Marriott, T.D.	..	„	Demobilization.

1/4th Battalion, Royal Welsh Fusiliers.

Lt.-Col. F. C. France-Hayhurst	..	„	May, 9, 1915.†
Lt.-Col. G. E. Pereira, C.M.G., D.S.O.	..	„	Feb., 1916.
Lt.-Col. W. C. W. Hawkes, D.S.O.	..	„	Mar. 27, 1917.
Lt.-Col. C. E. Fitch	..	„	June 26, 1917.
Lt.-Col. W. H. Matthews, D.S.O.	..	„	Jan. 24, 1918.
Lt.-Col. H. Marshall, M.C.	..	„	Aug., 1918.
Lt.-Col. J. H. Langton, D.S.O.	..	„	Demobilization.

The two Battalions from the 1st London Brigade which formed part of the 47th Division from November, 1915, to February, 1916, and the three Battalions of the 4th London Brigade which left the Division before the end of 1914 to join the British Expeditionary Force, were commanded during their service with the 47th Division as follows :

1/3rd Battalion, London Regiment (Royal Fusiliers) :
Lt.-Col. A. A. Howell.

1/4th Battalion, London Regiment (Royal Fusiliers) :
Lt.-Col. L. T. Burnett.
Major W. G. Clark, D.S.O.

1/13th Battalion, London Regiment (Kensington) :
Lt.-Col. F. G. Lewis, T.D.

1/14th Battalion, London Regiment (London Scottish) :
Lt.-Col. G. A. Malcolm.

1/16th Battalion, London Regiment (Queen's Westminster Rifles) :
Lt.-Col. R. Shoolbred, T.D.

(B) Artillery Brigades.

NOTE.—Details of the reorganization of the Divisional Artillery in May, 1916, and of the subsequent reorganization from four-gun to six-gun Batteries in December, 1916, will be found in Appendix C.

5th London Brigade, R.F.A.

Lt.-Col. E. C. Massy, C.B., C.M.G., D.S.O.	.. ..	To May, 1916.

12th County of London Battery.

Major W. P. Mylrea	..	„ Jan., 1915.
Major D. Cookes, D.S.O.	..	„ May, 1916.

13th County of London Battery.

Major A. G. Scammell, D.S.O.	..	„ May, 1916.

14th County of London Battery.

Major R. L. York, D.S.O.	..	„ May, 1916.

5th London Brigade Ammunition Column.

Capt. N. C. M. MacMahon	..	„ Sept., 1915.
Capt. H. H. Pollock, M.C.	..	„ May, 1916.

6th London Brigade, R.F.A.

Lt.-Col. R. J. MacHugh, T.D.	..	„ April, 1915.
Lt.-Col. A. C. Lowe, D.S.O.	..	„ May, 1916.

15th County of London Battery.

Major H. Bayley, D.S.O.		
Major W. Cooper, M.C.	..	„ May, 1916.

16th County of London Battery.

Major A. C. Gordon, D.S.O.	..	„ May, 1916.

17th County of London Battery.

Major F. G. Ensor		
Major P. J. Clifton, D.S.O.	..	„ May, 1916.

6th London Brigade Ammunition Column.

Capt. W. D. Austin	..	„ Feb., 1915.
Capt. R. R. Wansbrough	..	„ April, 1915.
Major P. A. Love	..	„ May, 1916.

7th London Brigade, R.F.A.

Col. C. E. Chambers, V.D.	..	„ Nov., 1915.
Lt.-Col. W. E. Peal, D.S.O.	..	„ May, 1916.

18th County of London Battery.

Major H. J. Mead	..	„ Aug., 1915
Major E. H. Marshall, D.S.O.	..	„ May, 1916

19th County of London Battery.

Major H. G., Lord Gorell	..	„ May, 1916.

20th County of London Battery.

Major W. E. Peal	..	„ Nov., 1915.
Major N. E. Wood	..	„ May, 1916.

7th London Brigade Ammunition Column.

Capt. E. F. Callaghan	..	„ Jan., 1915.
Capt. M. T. G. Clegg	..	„ 1915.
Capt. C. W. Egerton-Warburton	..	„ May, 1916.

8th London Brigade, R.F.A.

Lt.-Col. W. B. Emery, C.B., C.M.G. ..	..	„ Nov., 1914.
Lt.-Col. E. H. Eley, C.M.G., D.S.O. ..	..	„ May, 1916.

21st County of London Battery.

Major E. Eton, D.S.O.	..	„ March, 1916.
Major A. J. Cowan, D.S.O.	..	„ May, 1916.

22nd County of London Battery.

Major E. H. Eley	..	„ Nov., 1914.
Major C. A. Pollard, D.S.O.	..	„ May, 1916.

8th London Brigade Ammunition Column.

Capt. C. A. Pollard	..	„ Nov., 1914.
Capt. E. C. White	..	„ May, 1916.

235th Brigade, R.F.A.

Lt.-Col. E. C. Massy, C.B., C.M.G., D.S.O.	To March, 1917.
Lt.-Col. A. C. Gordon, D.S.O.	„ April, 1917.
Lt.-Col. W. B. Grandage	„ May, 1917.†
Lt.-Col. A. C. Gordon, D.S.O.	„ Dec., 1917.†
Lt.-Col. S. W. L. Aschwanden, D.S.O.	„ Demobilization.

A/235 Battery.

Capt. G. B. Winch	„ Dec., 1916.
Major P. J. Clifton, D.S.O.	„ Aug., 1917.
Major R. G. Tomlinson	„ Sept., 1917.
Major F. G. Stapley	„ Dec., 1917.
Major P. J. Clifton, D.S.O.	„ Aug., 1918.†
Major P. H. Pilditch	„ Demobilization.

B/235 Battery.

Capt. A. E. Shuter	„ Dec., 1916.
Major E. R. Hatfield, D.S.O.	„ Dec., 1917.
Major F. G. Stapley	„ July, 1918.
Major S. L. Keymer	„ Demobilization.

C/235 Battery.

Major E. R. Hatfield, D.S.O.	„ Dec., 1916.
Major E. H. Marshall, D.S.O.	„ Oct., 1917.
Major T. H. Flynn	„ Demobilization.

D/235 Battery.

Capt. F. de Witt	
Capt. H. J. McVeagh	„ Dec., 1916.
Major A. J. Cowan, D.S.O.	„ Sept., 1918.
Major M. J. K. O'Malley Keyes	„ Feb., 1919.
Major A. J. Cowan, D.S.O.	„ Demobilization.

236th Brigade, R.F.A.

Lt.-Col. A. C. Lowe, D.S.O.	„ Sept., 1917.
Lt.-Col. A. H. Bowring	„ Nov., 1918.
Lt.-Col. the Hon. H. G. O. Bridgeman, D.S.O.	„ Demobilization.

A/236 Battery.

Major W. Cooper, M.C.	„ Oct., 1918.
Major N. Christopherson, M.C.	„ Demobilization.

B/236 Battery.

Major A. C. Gordon, D.S.O.	„ Mar., 1917.
Major H. C. Morgan	„ Sept., 1917.
Major W. J. Barnard, M.C.	„ Demobilization.

C/236 Battery.

Major P. J. Clifton, D.S.O.	„ Dec., 1916.
Major N. E. Wood	„ Sept., 1917.
Major H. Carey-Morgan	„ May, 1918.
Major A. F. Yencken	„ Demobilization.

D/236 Battery.

Major C. A. Pollard, D.S.O.	„ Sept., 1917.
Major H. S. Duncan, M.C.	„ Aug., 1918.
Major S. Taylor, M.C.	„ Nov., 1918.
Major H. S. Duncan, M.C.	„ Demobilization.

237th Brigade, R.F.A.

Lt.-Col. W. E. Peal, D.S.O.	„ Dec., 1916.

A/237 Battery.

Major E. H. Marshall, D.S.O.	„ Dec., 1916.

B/237 Battery.

Major H. G., Lord Gorell	„ Dec., 1916.†

C/237 Battery.

Major N. E. Wood	„ Dec., 1916.

238th Brigade, R.F.A.

Lt.-Col. E. H. Eley, C.M.G., D.S.O.	„ Dec., 1916.

34th *Battery, R.F.A.*
  Major C. W. Massy, D.S.O., M.C... .. .. .. To Dec., 1916.
B/238 *Battery.*
  Capt. W. Swinton .. .. ,, Dec., 1916.
C/238 *Battery.*
  Capt. Cutter .. .. ,, Dec., 1916.
D/238 *Battery.*
  Major A. J. Cowan .. .. ,, Dec., 1916.

47th Divisional Ammunition Column.

  Lt.-Col. A. C. Lowe, D.S.O. .. .. ,, April, 1915.
  Major R. R. Wansbrough .. .. ,, Aug., 1915.
  Lt.-Col. H. G. Mead .. .. ,, Jan., 1916.
  Lt.-Col. H. Hale .. .. ,, Jan., 1917.
  Lt.-Col. H. B. Allen .. .. ,, May, 1918.
  Major H. H. Pollock, M.C. .. .. ,, Demobilization.

Divisional Trench Mortar Officer.

  Major Webber .. .. To March, 1916
  Capt. J. G. Brown, M.C. .. .. ,, Oct. 5, 1918.†
  Capt. J. G. Blaver .. .. ,, Demobilization.

(C) Royal Engineers.

517th (3rd London) *Field Company.*
  Major H. S. Sewell, T.D. .. .. To Jan. 17, 1915.†
  Major W. S. Mulvey .. .. ,, Mar., 1915.
  Capt. D. M. T. Morland, M.C. .. .. .. ,, April, 1915.
  Capt. W. H. Hillyer, M.C. .. .. ,, April, 1915.
  Major H. H. Stephens .. .. ,, June, 1915.
  Major A. G. Birch, D.S.O. .. .. ,, Sept. 15, 1916.
  Capt. J. B. Faber, M.C. .. .. ,, Sept., 1916.†
  Capt. D. M. T. Morland, M.C. .. .. .. ,, Dec., 1916.
  Major A. O. Laird, M.C. .. .. ,, 1918.
  Major W. Walker, M.C. .. .. ,, Demobilization.
518th (4th London) *Field Company.*
  Major S. Marsh .. .. ,, Mar., 1915.†
  Major E. B. Blogg, D.S.O. .. .. ,, Mar. 21, 1916.†
  Capt. W. H. Hillyer, M.C. .. .. ,, May, 1916.†
  Capt. D. M. T. Morland, M.C. .. .. .. ,, Sept. 21, 1916.
  Capt. S. H. Fisher, M.C. .. .. ,, Mar. 9, 1917.
  Major P. J. Mackesy, M.C. .. .. ,, June 1, 1917.
  Major F. P. Bray, M.C. .. .. ,, Mar., 22, 1918.
  Major J. H. Richards, M.C. .. .. ,, Oct., 1918.
  Major J. W. Douglas, D.S.O. .. .. ,, Mar., 1919
520th (2/3rd London) *Field Company.*
  Major H. E. T. Agar .. .. ,, Dec., 1915.
  Major S. G. Love, D.S.O., M.C. .. .. .. ,, Jan., 1919.
47th (2nd London) *Divisional Signal Company.*
  Major Sir L. C. W. Alexander, Bt., D.S.O. .. ,, Dec., 1915.
  Major W. F. Bruce, D.S.O., M.C. .. .. .. ,, Mar. 24, 1918.
  Major N. Porteous, M.C. .. .. ,, Demobilization.

(D) Divisional Train.

47th (*London*) *Divisional Train.*
  Lt.-Col. C. F. T. Blyth, C.M.G., T.D. .. .. To July 29, 1916.
  Lt.-Col. W. Campbell Galbraith, C.M.G. .. .. ,, Feb. 2, 1918.
  Lt.-Col. A. H. Maude, C.M.G., D.S.O. .. .. ,, Demobilization.
Senior Supply Officers.
  Major W. Campbell Galbraith, C.M.G. .. .. ,, July 29, 1916.
  Major A. H. Maude, D.S.O. .. .. ,, Feb. 2, 1918.
  Capt. G. Farr .. .. ,, Demobilization.

(E) Field Ambulances.

1/4th London Field Ambulance.
Lt.-Col. A. E. Jerman	.. ..	.. To Dec. 16, 1916.
Lt.-Col. A. J. Williamson, D.S.O.	.. .. ..	„ 1919.
Major A. E. Ironside	.. ..	.. „ Demobilization.

1/5th London Field Ambulance.
Lt.-Col. E. B. Dowsett, D.S.O.	.. ..	„ Dec., 1914.
Lt.-Col. E. Lloyd-Williams, T.D.	.. ..	„ Sept., 1916.
Capt. S. Clark	.. ..	„ Oct., 1916.†
Lt.-Col. N. C. Rutherford, D.S.O.	.. .. ..	„ Oct., 1917.
Lt.-Col. J. MacMillan, D.S.O., M.C.	.. .. ..	„ Feb., 1919.
Major J. H. Jordan, M.C.	.. ..	„ Demobilization.

1/6th London Field Ambulance.
Lt.-Col. W. M. O'Connor	.. ..	,. „ 1916.
Lt.-Col. H. K. Dawson	.. ..	.. „ 1917.
Lt.-Col. F. Coleman ..	.. ..	.. „ 1917.
Lt.-Col. H. K. Dawson	.. ..	..
Major H. M. Calder ..	.. ..	.. „ Demobilization.

Appendix E.

BATTLE HONOURS OF THE 47th DIVISION.

The following table gives the official names of the battles and other engagements in which the 47th (London) Division took part, as they appear in the Report of the Battles Nomenclature Committee. This report, as approved by the Army Council, was published in 1921. In it the principal engagements are classified as " battles," " actions," or " affairs " under general headings as given below. The relative importance of the " battles " is indicated in the report by two different sizes of type, and chronological and geographical limits (of which only the former are given below) are fixed for each engagement.

TRENCH WARFARE, 1914-16.

Summer Operations, 1915.

BATTLE OF FESTUBERT	May 15–25
THE BATTLE OF LOOS	Sept. 25–Oct. 8
and subsequent	
Actions of the Hohenzollern Redoubt ..	Oct. 13–19

Local operations, 1916.

German attack on Vimy Ridge	May 21

THE ALLIED OFFENSIVE, 1916.

Operations on the Somme.

THE BATTLES OF THE SOMME, 1916 ..	July 1–Nov. 18
BATTLE OF FLERS-COURCELETTE	Sept. 15–22
BATTLE OF THE TRANSLOY RIDGES	Oct. 1–18
including the	
Capture of Eaucourt l'Abbaye and attacks on the Butte de Warlencourt.	

THE ALLIED OFFENSIVES, 1917.

The Flanders Offensive.

THE BATTLE OF MESSINES, 1917 .. .. June 7–14
THE BATTLES OF YPRES, 1917* .. .. July 31–Nov. 10

The Cambrai Operations.

BATTLE OF CAMBRAI, 1917 .. .. Nov. 20–Dec. 3
　　The German counter-attacks .. .. Nov. 30–Dec. 3

THE GERMAN OFFENSIVES, 1918.

The Offensive in Picardy.

THE FIRST BATTLES OF THE SOMME, 1918 .. Mar. 21–April 5
BATTLE OF ST. QUENTIN .. .. Mar. 21–23
FIRST BATTLE OF BAPAUME .. .. .. Mar. 24–25
FIRST BATTLE OF ARRAS, 1918 .. .. .. Mar. 28
　　(Artillery Brigades only)
BATTLE OF THE ANCRE, 1918 .. .. .. April 5

THE ADVANCE TO VICTORY, 1918.

The Advance in Picardy.

THE SECOND BATTLES OF THE SOMME, 1918 Aug. 21–Sept. 3
BATTLE OF ALBERT, 1918 .. .. Aug. 21–23
SECOND BATTLE OF BAPAUME .. .. .. Aug. 31–Sept 3
The Final Advance in Artois.

---

* Although the 47th Division was in the line for some three weeks within the limits, both geographical and chronological, fixed for this group of battles, the Infantry did not take part in any of the major operations included. It was in Xth Corps Reserve at the Battle of Pilckem Ridge (July 31–Aug. 2) and its two tours of duty in the line, which were among the most unpleasant in its experience, fell between the Battle of Langemarck, 1917 (Aug. 16–18) and the Battle of the Menin Road Ridge (Sept. 20–25). The Artillery Brigades, however, were engaged in the Battles of Pilckem Ridge, Langemarck, 1917, and Polygon Wood (Sept. 26–Oct. 3).

TRENCH NEAR MAROC, JUNE, 1915.

GENERAL DE BRIGADE GOUGET DE LANDRES, commanding 184th French
Brigade, with men of the 141st Infantry Brigade, at the junction of the
French and British front lines.

Facing page 240

Appendix F.

Some historical notes concerning units which served with the 47th (London) Division during the war will be found below. The list shows:

(a) Regimental titles born since the formation of the Territorial Force in April, 1908.

(b) Honorary colonels on mobilization or appointed during the war.

(c) Headquarters at the time of mobilization.

(d) Titles of the old Volunteer Corps from which the units are directly descended, with the date of formation in brackets.

(e) Honours won by previous active service.

(f) Regimental badge.

(g) Full-dress uniform. (In the case of artillery, engineers, and departmental corps the badge and uniform are the same as those of the Regular branches of the respective corps.)

5th London Brigade, R.F.A.—*Headquarters*, 76, Lower Kennington Lane, S.E. ; *Former Volunteer unit*, 3rd Middlesex R.G.A. (1861).

6th London Brigade, R.F.A.—*Hon. Colonel*, Viscount Esher, G.C.B., G.C.V.O. *Former Volunteer units*, 1st Surrey Artillery Volunteers, 1st City of London, R.G.A. (1883) ; *Headquarters*, 105, Holland Road, Brixton, S.W.

7th London Brigade, R.F.A.—*Headquarters*, High Street, Fulham, S.W. ; *Former Volunteer unit*, 1st City of London, R.G.A.

8th London (Howitzer) Brigade, R.F.A.—*Hon. Colonel*, Col. F. Griffith ; *Headquarters*, Oaklands, St. Margaret's Road, Plumstead, S.E. ; *Former Volunteer unit*, 2nd Kent, R.G.A.

47th (2nd London) Divisional Royal Engineers.—*Hon. Colonel*, Col. E. T. Clifford, C.B.E., T.D., D.L. ; *Headquarters*, Duke of York's Headquarters, Chelsea. ; *Former Volunteer unit*, 1st Middlesex Volunteer Engineers (1860). The 1st Middlesex Volunteers, R.E., is the oldest Volunteer Corps, R.E. The first member, Col. McLeod of McLeod, was enrolled on February 6th, 1860. The headquarters was at Whiteheads Grove and Kensington Museum. In December, 1865, a new headquarters was opened at College Street, Fulham Road, Chelsea. In December, 1910, the headquarters was moved to the present site—the Duke of York's Headquarters, Chelsea. During the South African War two sections of the corps served in South Africa. The total number of the rank and file who lost their lives in the war of 1914-1919 was 177. The 2nd London Divisional Signal Company, R.E., came into being in 1913, when the 2nd London Divisional Telegraph Company, formed in 1908, under the command of Captain H. H. S. Marsh, absorbed the Infantry Brigade Signallers.

6th (City of London) Battn., The London Regiment (Rifles).—*Hon. Colonel*, Field-Marshal Earl Roberts, V.C., K.G., K.P., O.M., V.D. ; *Headquarters*, 57a, Farringdon Road, London, E.C. ; *Former Volunteer unit*, 2nd London Rifle Volunteers (1861), with whom the 48th Middlesex were amalgamated in 1872. " South Africa, 1900-1902 " ; *Badge*, Maltese Cross ; *Uniform*, Green, facings scarlet.

7th (City of London) Battn., The London Regiment.—*Hon. Colonel*, Col. E. C. Stevenson, V.D. *Headquarters*, 24, Sun Street, Finsbury Square, E.C. ; *Former Volunteer unit*, 3rd (City of) London, R.V.C. (1859) ; " South Africa, 1900-1902 " ; *Badge*, St. Paul's Cathedral on Regimental Colour ; on cap and buttons, grenade with " 7 " on bomb ; *Uniform*, Scarlet, facings buff.

T

8th (City of London) Battn., The London Regiment (Post Office Rifles).—*Hon. Colonel*, Col. the Marquess of Cambridge, G.C.B., G.C.V.O., C.M.G., A.D.C. ; *Headquarters*, 130, Bunhill Row, E.C. ; *Former Volunteer units*, 49th Middlesex R.V. (1868), 24th Middlesex (Post Office) V.R.C. ; " Egypt, 1882," " South Africa, 1899-1902 " ; *Badge*, as Rifle Brigade ; *Uniform*, Green, facings black ; Detachments served in Egypt in 1882 and 1885, and over 1,100 men in the South African War. The Army Post Office Corps and the Royal Engineer Special Telegraph Reserve were originally raised by this corps.

13th (County of London) Battn., The London Regiment (Kensington).—*Hon. Colonel*, Major-General Sir A. E. Turner, K.C.B. ; *Headquarters*, Iverna Gardens, Kensington, W. ; *Former Volunteer units*, 2nd (South) Middlesex R.V., 4th Middlesex (West London Rifles) (1859) ; " South Africa (1900-1902) " ; *Badge*, The arms of the Royal Borough of Kensington ; motto, *Quid nobis ardui* ; *Uniform*, Grey, facings scarlet.

14th (County of London) Battn., The London Regiment (London Scottish).—*Hon. Colonel*, the Duke of Argyll, K.G., K.T., V.D. ; *Headquarters*, 59, Buckingham Gate, Westminster, S.W. ; *Former Volunteer units*, 15th Middlesex R.V., 7th Middlesex R.V. ; " South Africa, 1900-1902 " ; *Badge*, In front of a circle inscribed with the motto " Strike Sure," St. Andrew's cross surmounted by a lion rampant ; *Uniform*, Grey, facings blue.

15th (County of London) Battn., The London Regiment (Prince of Wales' Own Civil Service Rifles).—*Hon. Colonel*, H.R.H. the Prince of Wales ; *Headquarters*, Somerset House, Strand, W.C. 2 ; *Former Volunteer units*, Somerset House Volunteers (1798), Excise Corps and Customs Corps (1804), Civil Service Volunteers (1859), known then as the Civil Service Rifle Brigade, 21st Middlesex Volunteers, P.W.O. Civil Service Rifle Volunteers, 12th Middlesex (1880) ; " South Africa, 1900-1902 " ; *Badge*, Prince of Wales' feathers ; *Uniform*, Light grey, facings dark blue and silver.

16th (County of London) Battn., The London Regiment (Queen's Westminster Rifles).—*Headquarters*, Queen's Hall, 58, Buckingham Gate, Westminster, S.W. ; *Former Volunteer unit*, The Queen's Westminsters ; " South Africa, 1900-1902 " ; *Badge*, A portcullis surmounted by a crown ; *Uniform*, Grey, facings scarlet.

17th (County of London) Battn., The London Regiment (Poplar and Stepney Rifles).—*Hon. Colonel*, Col. W. B. Bryan, V.D. ; *Headquarters*, 66, Tredegar Road, Bow, E. ; *Former Volunteer units*, 15th Middlesex (Customs and Docks) V.R.C. (1860), the 2nd Tower Hamlets V.R.C. ; " South Africa, 1900-1902 " ; *Uniform*, Green, facings black.

18th (County of London) Battn., The London Regiment (London Irish Rifles).—*Hon. Colonel*, Field-Marshal H.R.H. the Duke of Connaught, K.G., K.T., K.P., V.D. ; *Headquarters*, Duke of York's Headquarters, Chelsea ; *Former Volunteer units*, London Irish Volunteers (1860), 16th Middlesex V.R.C. ; " South Africa, 1900-1902 " ; *Badge*, Within a wreath of shamrock leaves the harp and crown ; *Uniform*, Green, facings light green.

19th (County of London) Battn., The London Regiment (St. Pancras).—*Hon. Colonels*, Col. Sir W. J. Brown, K.C.B., V.D. (1899), Major-General Sir William Thwaites, K.C.M.G., C.B., D.S.O. (1918) ; *Headquarters*, 76, High Street, Camden Town, N.W. 1 ; *Former Volunteer unit*, 17th North Middlesex Volunteers R.C. ; " South Africa, 1900-1902 " ; *Badge*, Maltese Cross surrounded with laurel and surmounted with a crown ; *Uniform*, Scarlet, facings green.

20th (County of London) Battn., The London Regiment (Blackheath and Woolwich), —*Hon. Colonel*, I. H. Benn, M.P. ; *Headquarters*, Holly Hedge House, Blackheath, S.E. ; *Former Volunteer units*, 2nd V.B. Royal West Kent Regiment (1859), 3rd V.B. Royal West Kent Regiment (1860) (formerly the Woolwich Arsenal Corps, the 26th Kent) ; " South Africa, 1900-1902 " ; *Badge*, White horse ; *Uniform*, Scarlet, facings black.

21st (County of London) Battn., The London Regiment (First Surrey Rifles).— *Hon Colonel,* Col. Ernest Villiers, V.D., A.D.C.; *Headquarters,* 4, Flodden Road, Camberwell, S.E.; *Former Volunteer units,* The Bermondsey Volunteers and the Armed Associations of Bermondsey, Southwark, Newington, Rotherhithe, and Camberwell (1794), 1st Regiment of Surrey Volunteers (1803), East Surrey, or Hanover Park Rifle Club (1852), 1st Surrey (South London) Rifle Volunteers (1859); " South Africa, 1900-1902 "; *Badge,* Maltese Cross, surmounted by Imperial Crown on a scroll bearing the motto " Concordia Victrix." Centre of cross contains a rifle bugle surrounded by " 1st Surrey Rifles "; *Uniform,* Green, facings scarlet.

22nd (County of London) Battn., The London Regiment (The Queen's).— *Hon. Colonel,* Col. B. K. Bevington, V.D.; *Headquarters,* 2, Jamaica Road, Bermondsey, S.E. 16; *Former Volunteer units,* Bermondsey Volunteers (1793) and Bermondsey Loyal Volunteers (1798), afterwards disbanded, 10th Surrey (1859) and 23rd Surrey Volunteers (1861), amalgamated later as the 4th Surrey Administrative Battn. (1863), 6th Surrey Rifle Volunteers (1881), 3rd V.B. the Queens Royal West Surrey Regiment (1883); " South Africa, 1900-1902 "; *Badge,* The Paschal Lamb; *Uniform,* Scarlet, facings blue.

23rd (County of London) Battn., The London Regiment.— *Hon. Colonel,* Col. B. T. L. Thomson, V.D.; *Headquarters,* 27, St. John's Hill, Clapham Junction; *Former Volunteer Units,* Newington Surrey Rifles (1799-1814), 7th Surrey Rifles (1859), 26th Surrey Rifle Corps (1874), 4th Vol. Battn. East Surrey Regiment (1880); " South Africa, 1900-1902 "; *Badge,* An eight-pointed star surmounted by a crown and circle with the words " South Africa, 1900-02 " and in the centre the arms of Guildford (Guildford Castle). Underneath a scroll with the words " 23rd Battn. the London Regiment "; *Crest,* An annulet ensigned with a cross patée and interlaced with a saltire conjoined in base " Loyalty unites us "; *Uniform,* Scarlet, facings white.

24th (County of London) Battn., The London Regiment (The Queen's).— *Hon. Colonel,* Col. Alured Faunce de Laune; *Headquarters,* 71, New Street, Kennington, S.E.; *Former Volunteer units,* 8th Surrey, 4th V.B. the Queen's, Royal West Surrey Regiment; " South Africa, 1900-1902 "; *Badge,* The Paschal Lamb; *Uniform,* Scarlet, facings blue.

4th (Denbighshire) Battn., The Royal Welsh Fusiliers.— *Hon. Colonel,* Col. W. C. Cornwallis-West, V.D.; *Headquarters,* Drill Hall, Poyser Street, Wrexham; *Former Volunteer units,* 1st Denbighshire Rifle Volunteers (1859), 1st Vol. Battn. Royal Welsh Fusiliers (1881); " South Africa, 1900-1902 "; *Badge,* Grenade, with Prince of Wales' feathers in a circle inscribed " Royal Welsh Fusiliers "; *Uniform,* Scarlet, facings blue. 1st Battn. embarked for service overseas November 5th, 1914, served in 3rd Brigade, 1st Division, from December, 1914, to September, 1915, engaged at Givenchy (January, 1915), Neuve Chapelle (March, 1915), and Festubert (May, 1915); served with 47th Division from September, 1915, to end of war.

4th London Field Ambulance.— *Headquarters,* School of Ambulance, Brookhill Road, Woolwich.

5th London Field Ambulance.— *Hon. Colonel,* Col. C. H. Hartt, T.D., *Headquarters,* 159, Greenwich Road; *Former Volunteer unit,* No. 2 (Greenwich) Company, R.A.M.C. Volunteers.

6th London Field Ambulance, R.A.M.C.— *Headquarters,* Duke of York's Headquarters, Chelsea, S.W.

47th (2nd London) Divisional Train, R.A.S.C.— *Hon. Colonel,* Col. Sir E. W. D. Ward, Bt., G.B.E., K.C.B., K.C.V.O.; *Headquarters,* Duke of York's Headquarters, Chelsea, S.W.; *Former unit,* Formed as 2nd London Divisional Transport and Supply Column in April, 1908, absorbing the A.S.C. Company of the 2nd London Volunteer Brigade.

HONOURS LIST.

The following is the list of honours awarded for services with the 47th (London) Division during the war. It is compiled from the record kept at Divisional Headquarters on active service, when details were often hard to obtain and the means of ascertaining the result of recommendations sent in were not always available. There may be, therefore, a few errors and omissions, but the list is as complete as it is possible to make it.

During the withdrawal in March, 1918, the record came very near destruction at Combles, where surplus kit and documents were dumped and set on fire only just before the Germans entered the place. Fortunately, however, this record, which could not have been replaced, was saved, and eventually it was brought to England with the cadre of the Division.

The dates given, where possible, are those of the **London Gazette,** or of its publication in **The Times**. In many cases, however— especially in the case of immediate awards—the date is that of the authority for the award received at Divisional Headquarters, and corresponds more nearly with that of the act of gallantry recognised.

An asterisk denotes that the name appears elsewhere in the list of decorations. The rank given is that held at the time of recommendation.

In cases where the award of bars only to the D.S.O., M.C., and M.M. are recorded, the decoration itself was won before the holder joined the 47th Division.

Owing to the length of the list it has been found impossible to include the names of those mentioned in dispatches, of which the approximate numbers were :—Officers, 570 ; other ranks, 300.

VICTORIA CROSS.

HARVEY, J., Pte.	..	..	22nd Battn.	13/11/18
*KEYWORTH, L. J., L.-Cpl.	..	..	24th Battn.	24/7/15

ORDER OF THE BATH.
KNIGHT COMMANDER.

BARTER, C. ST. L., Major-Gen. .. Divl. Commander .. -/-/16

COMPANIONS.

GIBBARD, T. W., Col.	A.D.M.S.	..	17/6/18
HAMPDEN, T. W., Viscount, Brig.-Gen.	140th Inf. Bde. ..	..	4/6/17
LEWIS, F. G., Brig.-Gen.	142nd Inf. Bde. ..	..	1/1/17
*McDOUALL, R., Brig.-Gen. ..	142nd Inf. Bde. ..	..	1/1/19
*MILDREN, W. F., Brig.-Gen. ..	141st Inf. Bde. ..	..	1/1/19
*WHITLEY, E. N., Brig.-Gen. ..	C.R.A.	..	1/1/19

ORDER OF ST. MICHAEL & ST. GEORGE.
KNIGHT COMMANDER.

GORRINGE, SIR G. F., Major-Gen. .. Divl. Commander .. 1/1/18

COMPANIONS.

BAILEY, V. T. (Liverpool Regt.), Brig.-Gen.	142nd Inf. Bde.		3/6/18
BLYTH, C. F. T., Lt.-Col. ..	47th Div. Train, A.S.C.		14/1/16
COLLETT, E. J. (M'sex Regt.), Lt.-Col.	19th Battn.		3/6/19
CUTHBERT, G. J. (Scots Guards), Brig.-Gen.	140th Inf. Bde.		14/1/16
ELEY, E. H., Lt.-Col.	8th London Bde., R.F.A.		3/6/16
FAUX, E., Lt.-Col.	7th Battn.		14/1/16
FERGUSON, J. D., Lt.-Col. ..	A.D.M.S.		1/1/17
FOOT, R. M., Lt.-Col.	A.A. & Q.M.G. ..		14/1/16
GALBRAITH, W. C., Major ..	47th Div. Train, A.S.C.		14/1/16
HEATHCOTE-DRUMMOND-WILLOUGHBY, Hon. C. S., Brig.-Gen.	142nd Inf. Bde.		14/1/16
HUBBACK, A. B., Lt.-Col. ..	20th Battn.		3/6/16
KENNEDY, H. P. B. L. (K.R.R.C.), Brig.-Gen.	140th Inf. Bde.		3/6/18
*McDOUALL, R. (The Buffs) Brig.-Gen.	141st Inf. Bde.		4/6/17
*MAUDE, A. H., Lt.-Col. ..	47th Div. Train, R.A.S.C.		1/1/19
*MILDREN, W. F., Lt.-Col. ..	6th Battn.		14/1/16
SIMPSON, W. G., Lt.-Col. ..	24th Battn.		14/1/16
*THUNDER, S. H. J., Lt.-Col. (Northamptonshire Regt.)	A.A. & Q.M.G. ..		1/1/19
TURNER, A. J., Lt.-Col. ..	G.S.O.1		1/1/18
WESTMORLAND, P. T., Lt.-Col. ..	19th Battn.		14/1/16
WRAY, J. C., Brig.-Gen. ..	C.R.A.		14/1/16

DISTINGUISHED SERVICE ORDER.
D.S.O. AND TWO BARS.

DAWES, G., M.C. (S. Staffs. Regt.), Lt.-Col.
21st Bn., Lon. Regt. ; D.S.O., 7/1/18; 1st bar, 3/5/18 ; 2nd bar, 30/9/18

TWO BARS TO D.S.O.

SEGRAVE, W. H. E. (H.L.I.), Lt.-Col.
15th Battn. ; 1st bar, 18/1/18 ; 2nd bar, 3/5/18

D.S.O. AND ONE BAR.

BIRCH, A. G., Major .. .. .. 47th Div. R.E. ; D.S.O., 14/1/16 ; bar, 4/10/16
LOVE, S. G., Major .. .. .. 47th Div. R.E. ; D.S.O., 2/1/18 ; bar, 6/5/18
MAXWELL, A., Lt.-Col. .. .. 8th Bn. ; D.S.O., 2/6/16 ; bar, 2/1/18

D.S.O.

ABSON, J., Major	Army Veterinary Corps	14/1/16
ALEXANDER, Sir L. C. W., Bt., Major	47th Div. Signal Coy. ..	14/1/16
BATTYE, B, C., Major, R.E. ..	Brig.-Major, 141st Inf. Bde.	16/6/16
BAWDEN, V. C., Capt. ..	17th Battn.	1/1/17
BAYLEY, H., Major	6th Lon. Bde., R.F.A. ...	12/10/15
BIRD, J. W., Major	6th Lon. Field Ambce...	21/10/15
BLOGG, E. B., Major	47th Div. R.E.	21/10/15
BRIDGEMAN, The Hon. H. G. O., Maj.	Brig.-Major, R.A. ..	7/11/17
*BRUCE, W. F., Major	47th Div. Signal Co. ..	2/1/18
BUXTON-CARR, G. A., Lt.-Col. ..	24th Battn.	1/1/17
*CALDER, H. M., Major	D.A.D.M.S.	1/1/17
*CARLISLE, J. C. D., Major	15th Battn., G.S.O.2 ..	2/1/18
CHRISTIE, H. R. S., Lt.-Col. ..	C.R.E.	2/1/18
CLIFTON, P. J., Major	6th Lon. Bde., R.F.A. ...	1/1/17
COWAN, A. J., Major	235th Bde., R.F.A. ..	2/1/18
COWAN-DOUGLAS, J. R., M.C., Capt...	H.L.I., Bde.-Maj., 141st Inf. Bde.	3/6/19
CROOKSHANK, S. D'A., Lt.-Col. ..	C.R.E.	3/6/16
DAWSON, H. K., Lt.-Col.	6th Lon. Fd. Ambce. ..	4/6/17
DOLPHIN, E. J., Major	20th Battn.	4/6/17
DURRANT, A. W., Capt.	23rd Battn.	1/1/18
ESCOMBE, W. M. L., Capt.	20th Battn.	24/7/15
EVANS, F. E., Major	17th Battn.	14/1/16
FAIR, C. H., Major	19th Battn.	1/1/17
*FIGG, D. W., Capt.	24th Battn.	24/7/15
*FLOWER, V. A., Lt.-Col.	13th Bn., com. 22nd Bn...	1/1/17
FOSTER, R. T., Major	Bde-Maj., 140th Inf. Bde.	1/1/17
FRIEND, R. S. I., Lt.-Col.	The Buffs, com. 19th Bn.	11/7/17
GAIN, R. S., Capt.	11th, att. 20th Battn. ..	8/11/18
*GIBBS, L. M., Capt. Coldstream Gds.	Bde.-Maj. 140th Inf. Bde.	3/6/19
GILL, F. G., Major	24th Battn.	13/10/18
*GLASCODINE, R. K., Capt.	20th Bn., O.C. Div. Obs'rs.	17/6/18
GORDON, A. C., Major	235th Bde., R.F.A. ..	29/10/15
GORELL, Lord, Major..	237th Bde., R.F.A. ..	16/10/16
GRAHAM, C. J., Capt.	4th Battn., Bde.-Major, 142nd Inf. Bde. ..	30/9/18
*GREEN, C. J. S., Lt.-Col.	7th Battn.	4/6/17
GREENWOOD, C. F. H., Lt.-Col. ..	22nd Battn.	2/1/18
GRIMWOOD, F. R., Major	17th Battn.	4/6/17
GUILD, A. M., Major	Highland Cyc. Battn., att. 19th Battn.	3/6/19
HARGREAVES, T. C., Major	23rd Battn.	3/10/16
HARVEY, J., Lt.-Col.	8th Battn.	12/10/15
HATFIELD, E. R., Capt.	5th Lon. Bde., R.F.A. ...	10/10/16
*HAWKES, W. C. W., Lt.-Col. (106th Pioneers)	4th R.W.F.	1/1/17
*HUGHES, E. W., Major	6th Bn., att. 140th Bde. H.Q.	2/1/18

*Hughes, W., Lt.-Col.	6th Bn., com. 17th Bn.	2/1/18
*Hunt, H. R. A., Capt., 25th Punjabis	G.S.O.3	15/6/16
*Kemble, H. H., Lt.-Col.	15th Bn., com. 23rd Bn.	1/1/17
*Kennedy, H. P. B. L., Lt.-Col.	21st Battn.	3/6/16
Kirkpatrick, H. C. B., Capt., K.O.S.B.	G.S.O.2	4/6/17
*Langton, J. H., Major	4th R.W.F.	2/1/18
Lowe, S. J., Major, Royal Fus.	Bde.-Maj., 141st Inf. Bde.	21/10/15
*Macmillan, J., Lt.-Col.	5th Lon. Field Ambce.	1/1/19
*Mahon, B. MacM., Capt.	18th Battn.	4/6/17
*Mann, H. U., Capt.	18th Battn.	11/7/17
Marshall, E. H., Major	235th Bde., R.F.A.	4/6/17
Massy, E. C., Lt.-Col.	5th Lon. Bde., R.F.A.	1/1/17
Matthews, W. H., Major	20th Battn.	3/6/16
*Maude, A. H., Major	47th Div. Train, A.S.C.	1/1/17
*Mildren, W. F., Lt.-Col.	6th Battn.	10/3/17
*Millner, G. E., Lt.-Col.	24th Battn.	2/1/18
Murphy, W. H., Major	18th Bn., com. 23rd Bn.	7/1/18
*Neely, G. H., Lt.-Col.	6th Bn., att. 18th Bn.	13/10/18
Newman, T. G. W., Major	23rd Battn.	14/1/16
Norman, E. H., Lt.-Col.	R. W. Kent Regt., com. 20th Battn.	3/6/16
*Pargiter, L. L., Lt.-Col.	M'sex Regt., com. 22nd Bn.	19/9/18
Parish, F. W., Lt.-Col.	K.R.R.C., com. 17th Bn.	3/5/18
Parker, W., Lt.-Col.	24th Battn.	1/1/17
Parry, D. B., Lt.-Col.	18th Battn.	28/9/17
*Peel, H., Capt.	8th Battn., Staff Capt., 141st Bde.	2/1/18
Pollard, C. A., Major	8th Lon. Bde., R.F.A.	14/1/16
Pope, S. B., Capt.	58th Vaughan's Rifles, att. 142nd Bde. H.Q.	3/6/16
Porteous, N., Major	47th Div. Signal Co.	3/6/19
Pusch, F., Lieut.	19th Battn.	1/1/16
*Read, H. S., Major	20th Battn.	3/6/19
Rutherford, N. C., Lt.-Col.	5th Lon. Field Ambce.	9/7/17
*Sanders, H. J., Capt.	24th Battn.	17/10/18
Scammell, A. G., Major	5th Lon. Bde., R.F.A.	3/6/16
*Sheppard, J. J., Major	19th Battn.	3/6/19
Stephenson-Fetherstonhaugh, A. J., Major	D.A.Q.M.G.	1/1/19
*Stokes, J. G., Capt.	19th Battn.	2/7/17
Thornhill, J. E., Capt.	Seaforth Highl'rs., att. 23rd Battn.	14/1/16
*Thunder, S. H. J., Lt.-Col.	(Northamptonshire Regt.), A.A. & Q.M.G.	15/2/17
*Tolerton, R. H., Lt.-Col.	23rd Battn.	3/6/19
Tredennick, J. P., Lt.-Col.	(R. Dublin Fus.), 18th Bn.	14/1/16
*Vince, W. B., Lt.-Col.	8th Battn.	7/1/18
Warrender, H. V., Lt.-Col.	15th Battn.	3/6/16
Webber, N. W., Major	G.S.O.2	3/6/16
Westley, J. H. S., Capt.	(P.W.O. Yorkshire Regt.), Bde.-Maj. 140th Inf. B.	3/6/16
Whitehead, W. J., Lt.-Col.	6th Bn., att. 8th Bn.	1/1/17
*Whitley, E. N., Brig.-Gen.	C.R.A.	2/1/18
Williamson, A. J., Lt.-Col.	4th Lon. Field Ambce.	3/6/18

BREVET PROMOTIONS.

*ALEXANDER, M., Capt., Rifle Brigade — D.A.A.G., Bt.-Major .. 17/6/18
BURNETT-HITCHCOCK, B. F., Lt.-Col. — G.S.O.1, Bt.-Lt.-Col. .. 3/6/16
CLEMENS, L. A., Capt., S. Lancs. Regt. — Bde.-Major, 141st Bde., Bt.-Major 4/6/17
*COOPER, W., Major .. .. .. — 236th Bde., R.F.A., Bt.-Major 1/1/19
*DEVERELL, F., Capt. .. .. — 8th Bn., Staff Capt., 140th Inf. Bde., Bt.-Major 3/6/19
DUBS, G. R., Capt., K.R.R.C. .. — Bde.-Maj., 140th Inf. Bde., Bt.-Major 3/6/18
*FLOWER, V. A., Major .. .. — 13th Bn., att. 22nd Bn., Bt.-Major 3/6/16
*HAMILTON, A. P., Capt. .. .. — 18th Battn., Bt.-Major .. 3/6/16
*HOUSE, A. J., Capt. .. .. .. — 22nd Bn., Staff Capt. 141st Inf. Bde., Bt.-Major .. 3/6/19
*HUNT, H. R. A., Capt., 25th Punjabis — Div. H.Q., Bt.-Major .. 14/1/16
*KENNEDY, H. P. B. L., Lt.-Col. .. — 21st Bn., Bt.-Lt.-Col. .. 4/6/17
*KENNEDY, H. P. B. L., Brig.-Gen. — Com. 140th Inf. Bd., B.-Col. 1/1/19
*LANGTON, J. H., Lt.-Col. .. .. — 4th R.W.F., Bt.-Lt.-Col. 3/6/19
LEWIS, F. E. C., Maj., E. Lancs. Regt. — Att. 47th Battn., M.G.C., Bt.-Major 3/6/19
MAUDE, C. G., Capt., Royal Fusiliers — Adjt., 24th Bn., Bt.-Major 3/6/16
*MAXWELL, A., Lt.-Col. .. .. — 8th Battn., Bt.-Major .. 3/6/16
NICHOLL, H. I., Major .. .. — Div. H.Q., Bt.-Major .. 3/6/16
*PARGITER, L. L., Lt.-Col., M'sex. Regt. — Com. 22nd Bn., Bt.-Major 3/6/19
PEREIRA, G. E., Lt.-Col., Gren. Guards, R. of O. .. .. .. — Com. 4th R.W.F., Bt.-Col. 3/6/16
*THUNDER, S. H. J., Lt.-Col. Northamptonshire Regt. .. .. .. — Div. H.Q., Bt.-Lt.-Col. .. 1/1/18
THWAITES. W., Brig.-Gen. .. .. — 141st Inf. Bde., Bt.-Col. 14/1/16

MILITARY CROSS AND THREE BARS.

GILKES, H. A., Lieut. .. .. — 21st Bn.; M.C., 11/7/17; 1st bar, 20/1/18; 2nd bar, 13/4/18; 3rd bar, 13/10/18

MILITARY CROSS AND TWO BARS.

*ANDERSON, W. Capt. .. .. — 235th Bde., R.F.A.; M.C., 7/7/17; 1st bar, 24/9/17; 2nd bar, 19/10/17
SMITHER, S. T., Capt. .. .. — 10th Bn., att. 15th Bn.; M.C., 2/7/17; 1st bar, 11/5/18; 2nd bar, 17/10/18

MILITARY CROSS AND ONE BAR.

ASHBY, C. E., Lieut. .. .. — 18th Bn.; M.C., 29/4/17; bar, 31/12/17
BAYLIS, R. V., Lieut. .. .. — 47th M.G. Bn.; M.C., 6/5/18; bar, 28/9/18
BLOFELD, R. M., Capt. .. .. — 22nd Bn., att. 142nd T.M.B.; M.C., 5/6/17; bar, 26/10/18
BOWLER, L. W. H., Capt. .. .. — 22nd Bn.; M.C., 11/3/18; bar, 30/9/18
BROPHY, C. M., Lieut. .. .. — R.A.M.C., att. 18th Bn.; M.C., 11/6/16; bar, 6/10/16
BURNAY, C. F., Capt. .. .. — 18th Bn.; M.C., 7/7/17; bar, 13/10/18

GRANDE PLACE, BETHUNE, 1915.

BETHUNE : THE BELFRY TOWER, 1918.

Facing page 248

DAVIES, E. B., Sec.-Lieut. ..	8th Bn. ; M.C., 3/10/16 ; bar, 3/5/18
DIXON, H. B. F., Lieut. ..	6th Lon. Fd. Ambce. ; M.C., 6/10/16 ; bar, 1/5/18
FOTHERINGHAM, W., Capt. ..	R.A.M.C., att. 19th Bn. ; M.C., 2/7/17 ; bar, 31/12/17
GOODES, G. L., Sec.-Lieut. ..	4th Lon. Bn., att. 140th T.M.B. ; M.C., 3/6/16 ; bar, 3/10/16
GOZNEY, C. M., Capt. ..	R.A.M.C., att. 15th Bn. ; M.C., 2/7/17 ; bar, 17/10/18
HEATHCOTE, G. C., Lieut. ..	24th Bn. ; M.C., 26/4/18 ; bar, 22/11/18
IRONSIDE, A. E., Capt. ..	4th Lon. Fd. Ambce. ; M.C., 11/6/16 ; bar, 3/6/18
JACKMAN, I. H., Lieut. ..	21st Bn. ; M.C., 11/7/17 ; bar, 17/10/18
JOHNSON, H. A., Lieut. ..	24th Bn., att. 142nd T.M.B. ; M.C., 26/4/18 ; bar, 6/7/18
LAWS, J., Sec.-Lieut. ..	21st Bn., att. 142nd T.M.B. ; M.C., 29/5/18 ; bar, 13/10/18
McKAY, G. M., Sec.-Lieut. ..	21st Bn. ; M.C., 8/6/16 ; bar, 6/10/16
MADDOX, L. G., Sec.-Lieut. ..	22nd Bn. ; M.C., 23/8/18 ; bar, 30/9/18
MAGINN, P. A., Lieut. ..	18th Bn. ; M.C., 3/6/16 ; bar, 27/6/16
MARTIN, G. B., Capt. ..	10th, att. 15th Bn. ; M.C., 11/5/18 ; bar, 29/8/18
*NEELY, G. H., Capt. ..	6th Bn. ; M.C., 10/3/17 ; bar, 3/1/18
OAKEY, C. H., Capt. ..	22nd Bn. ; M.C., 3/7/18 ; bar, 30/9/18
PEPPIATT, L. E., Capt. ..	19th Bn. ; M.C., 9/5/18 ; bar, 17/10/18
*READ, H. S., Major	20th Bn. ; M.C., 3/10/16 ; bar, 9/15/18
ROBINSON, H. H., Capt. ..	R.A.M.C., att. 21st Bn. ; M.C., 6/10/16 ; bar, 3/6/18
RUNDELL, L. E., Capt. ..	7th Bn. ; M.C., 24/2/16 ; bar, 8/6/16
RYDER, A. F. R. D., Capt. ..	236th Bde., R.F.A. ; M.C., 15/6/16 ; bar, 13/10/18
TAYLOR, H. A., Sec.-Lieut. ..	21st Bn. ; M.C., 8/6/16 ; bar, 6/11/16
TOWNSEND, T. A., Capt. ..	R.A.M.C., att. 24th Bn. ; M.C., 6/11/16 ; bar, 7/1/18
WARDLEY, D. J., Lieut. ..	R. Fus., att. 23rd Bn. ; M.C., 21/6/17 ; bar, 26/4/18
WATSON, C. P., Capt. ..	18th Bn. ; M.C., 27/9/16 ; bar, 29/4/17
WILLIAMS, G., Capt. ..	20th Bn. ; M.C., 3/6/16 ; bar, 16/6/16

BAR TO M.C.

*GIBBS, L. M., Capt., Coldstream Gds.	Bde.-Maj., 140th Inf. Bde. (Sec. from 7th Bn. Lon.R.)	28/9/18
HODGSON, F., Sec.-Lt., 50th M.G. Bn.		3/10/18
LE ROUGETEL, J. H., Lieut., Northamptonshire Regt.	Att. 47th Bn., M.G.C. ..	30/9/18
PALMER, C. R., Sec.-Lieut.	7th Battn.	1/1/18

MILITARY CROSS.

AGIUS, A. J. J. P., Capt.	3rd Battn.	14/1/16
ALEXANDER, A. C., Sec.-Lieut. ..	8th Battn.	1/1/18
*ALEXANDER, M., Capt. ..	R.B., D.A.A. & Q.M.G.	5/6/17
ALLISON, H. W., Sec.-Lieut. ..	24th Battn. ..	21/6/17
ALLSOP, B. G. K., Capt. ..	47th Div. Train, A.S.C.	3/6/18
ARNSBY, W. S., Sec.-Lieut.	20th Battn.	9/5/18
AYERS, P. S., Lieut.	236th Bde., R.F.A. ..	26/8/18

*BAILEY, F. F., Lieut. & Q.M.	6th Bn., att. 17th Bn.	1/1/19
BALFOUR, F. D., Capt.	1/1st Northern Cyclists Bn., att. 15th Lon. Regt.	11/3/18
BANNIGAN, C., Capt.	R.A.M.C., att. 24th Bn.	21/6/17
BARCLAY, W. J., Sec.-Lieut.	19th Battn.	3/1/18
BARKER, F. C., Sec.-Lieut.	21st Battn.	11/7/17
BARKWORTH, R. C., Sec.-Lieut.	R. Fus., att. 23rd Bn.	14/1/16
BARNARD, W. J., Capt.	236th Bde., R.F.A.	9/7/17
BARNES, A. D., Sec.-Lieut.	23rd Battn.	7/1/18
BARNES, B., Capt.	15th Bn., att. 140th M.G.C.	2/6/16
BARNETT, C. E., Sec.-Lieut.	15th Battn.	28/9/18
BARROW, T. H., Lieut.	22nd Battn.	29/11/18
BARTLETT, H. W., Sec.-Lieut.	19th Battn.	27/10/16
BASEDEN, L., Sec.-Lieut.	24th Battn.	8/6/16
BASWITZ, A., Lieut.	22nd Battn.	14/1/16
BATES, G. G., Capt.	15th Battn.	27/10/16
BAXTER, J., C.S.M.	24th Battn.	26/6/17
BEATTIE, E. H., Rev.	Army Chaplains Dept.	11/5/18
BENWELL, H. A., Sec.-Lieut.	22nd Battn.	3/7/18
BIRD, E. T., Sec.-Lieut.	21st Battn.	8/6/16
BISHOP, L. E., Capt.	7th Battn.	1/10/17
BLACKHURST, S., Sec.-Lieut.	7th Battn.	2/7/17
BLACKWELL, A. F., Lieut.	236th Bde., R.F.A.	13/9/16
BLOFELD, D., Sec.-Lieut.	22nd Battn.	20/7 16
BOOTH, A., Sec.-Lieut.	17th Battn.	6/10/16
BOOTH, T. J., Sec.-Lieut.	6th, att. 15th Battn.	17/10/18
BORRADAILE, L. D., Sec.-Lieut.	20th Battn.	3/8/16
BOSS, T. H., Capt.	Northern Cyc. Bn., att. 8th Battn.	2/7/17
BOUCHER, C. W. L., Sec.-Lieut.	20th Battn.	13/10/18
BOWN, A. M., Lieut.	235th Bde., R.F.A.	17/5/17
BOYD, D. F., Lieut.	235th Bde., R.F.A.	28/5/18
BRACHI, M., Lieut.	2/3rd Lon. Field Co., R.E.	11/6/16
BRADLEY, R. L., Lieut.	22nd Battn.	3/10/16
BRAY, F. P., Major	518th Field Co., R.E.	3/6/18
BRETT, G. A., Capt.	23rd Battn.	21/11/17
BRETT, T. P., C.S.M.	15th Battn.	3/10/16
BREWER, E. B., Capt.	7th Bn., att. 140th T.M.B.	12/3/17
BRIGGS, F. A., Sec.-Lieut.	24th Battn.	13/10/18
BROOKS, T. W., Capt.	6th Battn.	3/10/16
BROWN, J. G., Lieut.	Y/47 T.M. Battery	14/7/16
BROWNE-WILKINSON, A. R., Rev.	Att. 17th Battn.	17/10/18
*BRUCE, W. F., Capt.	47th Div. Signal Co.	14/1/16
BUDENBERG, C. F., Sec.-Lieut.	520th Lon. Fd. Co., R.E.	7/7/16
BURGIS, H. L., Lieut.	236th Bde., R.F.A.	19/10/17
BURROUGHS, P. W., Capt.	24th Battn.	26/4/18
BURT-SMITH, B., Sec.-Lieut.	6th Battn.	19/5/16
*CALDER, H. M., Major	D.A.D.M.S.	17/10/18
CARLESS, T. F. G., Capt.	5th M'sex., att. 18th Bn.	13/10/18
*CARLISLE, J. C. D., Lieut.	15th Battn.	1/1/17
CARLTON, C. H., Capt.	6th Lon. Fd. Ambce.	20/5/18
CARR, E. N., Lieut.	24th Battn.	21/10/15
CARR, J. W., Sec.-Lieut.	24th Battn.	21/11/17
CARTER, R. H., Capt.	8th Bn., att. 17th Bn.	19/9/18
CATTELL, A. G., Capt.	24th Battn.	22/11/18
CATTON, E. G., Sec.-Lieut.	21st Battn.	28/9/18
CHAMBERS, P. E. H., Lieut.	21st Battn.	28/9/18
CHANDLER, J., Sec.-Lieut.	19th Battn.	27/9/16
CHAPPELL, H. J., Sec.-Lieut.	17th Battn.	5/10/17
*CHARMAN, A. E., C.S.M.	21st Battn.	28/9/18

CHATTERTON, J., Sec.-Lieut...	7th Battn.	24/2/16
CHIVERS, S. G., C.S.M.	8th Battn.	15/7/16
CHRISTIAN, E., Lieut.	5th Lon. Bde., R.F.A.	15/6/16
CHRISTOPHERSON, C. B., Capt.	Welsh Rt., att. 4th R.W.F.	3/6/19
CHRISTOPHERSON, N., Lieut.	235th Bde., R.F.A.	3/6/18
CLARKE, L. J., Capt. ..	22nd Bn., att. Div. Sig. Co.	11/7/17
CLARKE, R. S., Sec.-Lieut.	47th M.G. Bn.	28/9/18
CLARKE, W. A., Capt.	17th Battn.	13/1/18
CLINTON, L. S., Lieut.	23rd Battn.	24/7/15
COLEMAN, F., Major ..	6th Lon. Fd. Ambce.	30/9/18
COLLINS, J. E., Sec.-Lieut.	24th Battn.	26/4/18
COOK, H., Capt.	22nd Battn.	21/6/17
COOK, R. J., Sec.-Lieut.	7th Battn.	2/7/17
COOMBE, G. A., Lieut.	24th Battn.	21/6/17
•COOPER, W., Major ..	236th Bde., R.F.A.	3/1/18
COPE, J. V., Capt.	5th Lon. Fd. Ambce.	31/12/17
CORBY, S. F., Capt.	21st Battn.	14/1/16
CORSAN, J. C., Sec.-Lieut.	236th Bde., R.F.A.	1/1/17
CORSAN, R. A., Capt.	236th Bde., R.F.A.	26/11/16
COURT, A. C., Capt. ..	R.A.M.C., att. 23rd Bn.	21/6/17
COX, T., R.S.M.	23rd Battn.	15/7/16
CRISP, G. W., Lieut.	23rd Battn.	30/9/18
CROFTS, F. W., Lieut.	17th Battn.	16/6/16
CROOK, G. T., Sec.-Lieut.	235th Bde., R.F.A.	22/8/17
CROSSLAND, M. E., Capt.	20th Battn.	3/1/18
CROWTER, C., Sec.-Lieut.	21st Battn.	29/12/17
CRUMP, J., Sec.-Lieut.	19th Battn.	3/10/16
CULLIFORD, L. A. O., Sec.-Lieut.	2/3rd Lon. Fd. Co., R.E.	19/5/16
CURRAN, E. J., Sec.-Lieut.	16th, att. 20th Battn.	13/10/18
DANBY, L. J., Capt. ..	19th Bn., Staff Capt., 141st Bde. ..	14/1/16
DARLOT, O. H., Lieut.	22nd Battn.	30/9/18
DAVENPORT, P., Capt.	15th Battn.	2/7/17
DAVEY, W. H., C.S.M.	20th Battn.	16/6/16
DAVIES, C. G., Sec.-Lieut.	24th Battn.	24/7/15
DAVIES, H. V., Lieut.	4th R.W.F.	11/3/18
DAVIES, P., Capt.	6th Lon. Fd. Ambce.	30/9/18
DAVIS, T. S., Capt. ..	235th Bde., R.F.A.	3/6/19
•DEVERELL, F., Capt. ..	8th Battn.	2/7/17
DODGSON, P. H., Lieut.	237th Bde., R.F.A.	1/1/17
DRUITT, C. E. H., Capt.	140th M.G. Co.	1/1/18
DUNNE, J. Capt. & Q.M.	20th Battn.	3/6/19
DYER, W. F., Lieut. ..	20th Battn.	14/1/16
EAMES, S. H. W., Capt.	19th Bn., att. 141st T.M.B.	29/4/17
EASTWOOD, C. S., Capt.	21st Battn.	3/6/18
EDMUNDS, J., Lieut. ..	21st Battn.	29/12/17
EDWARDS, O., Sec.-Lieut.	235th Bde., R.F.A.	7/7/17
ELKINGTON, H. G., Lieut.	21st Battn.	3/5/18
ENTWISTLE, F., Lieut.	23rd Battn.	14/1/16
ERSKINE, A. D., Sec.-Lieut...	47th Battn., M.G.C.	3/11/18
EVE, H. U., Capt. ..	6th Battn.	10/3/17
EVE, R. N., Lieut.	7th Battn.	2/7/17
EWEN, H. S., Sec.-Lieut	23rd Battn.	7/1/18
FABER, J. B., Lieut. ..	47th Div., R.E. ..	3/6/16
FAIRLEY, R., Lieut. & Q.M.	8th Battn.	3/1/18
FALLON, P., Capt.	15th Battn.	11/3/18
FARRINGTON, C. H., Sec.-Lieut.	R. Lancs, att. 6th Bn.	10/3/17
FEA, C. A., Sec.-Lieut.	17th Bn., att. 18th Bn. ..	13/10/18
FEARON, A. T., Capt.	23rd Battn.	14/1/16
FERGUSON, H. G., Capt.	520th Field Co., R.E. ..	13/10/18

FISHER, J. W., R.S.M.	22nd Battn.	21/6/17
FISHER, S. H., Capt.	4th Lon. Fd. Co., R.E.	5/6/17
FITZCLARENCE, The Hon. H. E., Capt.	A.P.M.	1/1/19
FLEMING, J. E., Capt.	22nd Battn.	7/8/18
FOULKES-ROBERTS, P. R., Capt.	4th R.W.F.	8/6/16
Fox, H., Capt.	19th Battn.	3/1/18
FURLEY, A., Capt., Gloucester Regt.	Staff Capt., 142nd Bde.	20/12/18
GAMAGE, L. C., Lieut.	24th Battn.	1/1/17
GAULD, J., Sec.-Lieut.	19th Battn.	17/10/18
GIBBON, C. H., Sec.-Lieut.	16th Bn. att. 18th Bn.	13/10/18
GIBSON, C. L., Lieut.	17th Battn.	17/10/18
GIBSON, P. M., M.M., Sec.-Lieut.	5th M'sex., att. 17th Bn.	28/9/18
GILKES, M. H., Sec.-Lieut.	21st Battn.	1/10/15
GILKS, H. L., Capt.	28th Bn., att. 6th Bn.	1/1/17
*GLASCODINE, R. K., Capt.	20th Bn., att. 141st T.M.B.	3/10/16
GOLDSBURY, C. M., Sec.-Lieut.	7th Battn.	26/7/17
GOOSEY, F., Lieut.	24th Battn.	26/4/18
GRAY, F., M.M., Sec.-Lieut.	15th Battn.	17/10/18
GRAY, S. A., Lieut.	23rd Battn.	30/9/18
*GREEN, C. J. S., Capt.	7th Battn.	3/6/16
GROSE, H. J., Sec.-Lieut.	24th Battn.	23/8/18
HALL, C. A., Lieut.	8th Battn.	1/1/18
HALLETT, H. I. P., Lieut.	24th Battn.	14/1/16
*HAMILTON, A. P., Capt.	18th Battn.	21/10/15
HAMILTON, J. D., Capt.	22nd Battn.	21/6/17
HARDS, P. A., Sec.-Lieut.	17th Battn.	2/7/17
HARMAN, A. J., Lieut.	23rd Battn.	7/1/18
HARMAN, H. H., Sec.-Lieut.	7th Battn.	3/6/18
HARRIS, R. H., C.S.M.	15th Battn.	6/6/16
HASKINS, S. C., Capt.	19th Bn., att. 141st M.G.Co.	14/1/16
HEARD, G. T., Sec.-Lieut.	17th Battn.	17/10/18
HEBBLETHWAITE, A. S., Capt.	6th Lon. Fd. Ambce.	29/4/17
HEMSLEY, H. N., Sec.-Lieut.	R. Fus., att. 21st Bn.	6/11/16
HEWITT, A., Sec.-Lieut.	20th Battn.	6/11/16
HEWITT, A. E., Sec.-Lieut.	22nd Bn., att. 142nd T.M.B.	21/6/17
HITCH, J. O. B., Sec.-Lieut.	21st Battn.	11/3/18
HOLDSWORTH, S., Sec.-Lieut.	23rd Battn.	26/4/18
HOLLAND, V. J., Sec.-Lieut.	235th Bde., R.F.A.	5/6/17
HOLLIDAY, R. J., Capt.	24th Bn., Staff Capt. 142nd Inf. Bde.	14/1/16
HONE, H. R., Lieut.	18th Battn.	9/5/18
HOOK, E. T., Capt.	Welsh Rt., att. 4th R.W.F.	3/6/18
HOSTE, W. E., Sec.-Lieut.	15th Battn.	11/3/18
*HOUSE, A. I., Capt.	22nd Battn.	8/6/16
HOWES, A., R.S.M.	24th Battn.	1/1/17
HUDSON, R. G., Sec.-Lieut.	19th Battn.	11/7/16
HUGHES, A. M., Major	4th Lon. Fd. Ambce.	3/6/19
*HUGHES, E. W., Capt.	6th Bn., Staff Capt. 140th Inf. Bde.	3/6/16
HUGHES, P. C., Lieut.	City of Lon. Yeo., att. 23rd Battn.	3/6/19
*HUGHES, W., Capt.	6th Battn.	14/1/16
HULSE, J. H., Sec.-Lieut.	5th, att. 19th Battn.	17/10/18
HUTCHENCE, A., Capt.	21st Battn.	14/1/16
HUTCHISON, F. D., Capt.	20th Battn.	3/10/16
HYAMS, H. D., Sec.-Lieut.	23rd Battn.	3/1/18
ILLINGWORTH, G. F., Lieut.	235th Bde., R.F.A.	19/10/17
IMISON, J. A., Sec.-Lieut.	E. Surrey Rt., att. 23rd Bn.	21/6/17
IND, W. E., Lieut.	15th Battn.	1/1/17
IVEY, W. L., Sec.-Lieut.	15th Battn.	11/5/18

JAMES, W. T., Lieut.	8th, att. 17th Battn.	17/10/18
JONES, C. A., Lieut. & Q.M.	23rd Battn.	1/1/19
JONES, D. W., Lieut.	47th Div. Signal Co.	3/11/18
JONES, S., C.S.M.	6th Battn.	8/6/16
JORDAN, J. H., Capt.	R.A.M.C.	6/10/16
JULIAN, F. B., Capt.	4th Lon. Fd. Ambce.	31/12/17
JURISS, M., Sec.-Lieut.	7th Battn.	19/5/16
KEANE, P. F. F., Lieut.	18th Battn.	1/1/19
KEEBLE, C. V., Sec.-Lieut.	24th Battn.	21/6/17
KELLY, T. A., Capt.	24th Battn.	3/6/16
*KEMBLE, H. H., Capt.	15th Battn.	14/1/16
KENT-JONES, L. J., Sec.-Lieut.	23rd Battn.	1/1/18
KINDELL, F. P., Lieut.	8th Lon. Bde., R.F.A.	14/1/16
KNOWLES, A., Sec.-Lieut.	R.E., att. 142nd Inf. Bde.	17/10/18
*LAING, J. O. C., C.S.M.	21st Battn.	8/6/16
LAIRD, A. M. C., Capt.	17th Battn.	28/9/18
LARN, C. F., Lieut.	47th Battn., M.G.C.	28/9/18
LASCELLES, Hon. E. C., Capt.	R.B., Staff Capt., 140th Inf. Bde.	14/1/16
LEDGERTON, C. B. C. N., Sec.-Lieut.	17th, att. 23rd Battn.	30/9/18
LE POER-POWER, A. A. R. D., Lieut.	R.A.S.C., att. 23rd Bn.	19/11/18
LEWIS, J. C. M., Sec.-Lieut.	4th R.W.F., att. 8th Bn.	2/7/17
LEWIS, W., Lieut.	23rd Battn.	19/6/17
LOCK, A. H. J., Lieut. & Q.M.	4th R.W.F.	5/6/17
LONGLEY, R. C., Sec.-Lieut.	24th Battn.	24/11/17
*LOVE, S. G., Capt.	Div. Engineers	14/1/16
LOWMAN, P. R., Lieut.	140th Machine Gun Co.	3/6/18
LOYD, W. E., Lieut.	520th Field Co., R.E.	7/7/17
McDONALD, M. J., Capt.	6th Battn.	3/10/16
MacDOUGALL, T. M., Lieut.	18th Battn.	11/7/17
MACKENZIE, F. S., Sec.-Lieut.	18th Battn.	29/4/17
MACLAGAN, W. C., Lieut.	19th Battn.	11/3/18
*MACMILLAN, J., Lieut.	R.A.M.C., att. 23rd Bn.	14/1/16
McNICOL, W., Lieut.	18th Battn.	31/12/17
*MAHON, B. MacM., Capt.	18th Battn.	25/5/16
MALLETT, R. E. A., Lieut.	18th Battn.	9/9/17
MALONEY, T., Sec.-Lieut.	47th Battn., M.G.C.	6/5/18
*MANN, H. U., Capt.	18th Battn.	14/1/16
MANSON, E. P., Sec.-Lieut.	M'sex. Regt., att. 22nd Bn.	8/6/16
MARRIOTT, N. F., Lieut.	140th Machine Gun Co.	3/10/16
MARSHALL, H., Major	7th Hants, att. 15th Bn.	4/1/18
MARTIN, R., Lieut. & Q.M.	21st Battn.	3/6/19
MASTERS, E. A., Capt.	47th Div. Train, R.A.S.C.	4/1/18
MATTHEWS, P. T., Sec.-Lieut.	24th Battn.	4/1/18
MAXTED, C. B., Sec.-Lieut.	6th Battn.	2/7/17
MAYES, R. C., Sec.-Lieut.	22nd Battn.	30/9/18
MAYHEW, E. W., Capt.	22nd Battn.	20/7/16
MAYNARD, J. E., Major	6th Battn.	4/1/18
MEREDITH, E. C., Sec.-Lieut.	20th, att. 24th Battn.	13/10/18
MIDDLETON, R., Capt.	15th Battn.	3/1/18
MILEMAN, V. W., Sec.-Lieut.	7th Battn.	27/10/16
*MILLNER, G. E., Capt.	24th Battn.	14/1/16
MITCHELL, A. McK., Sec.-Lieut.	23rd Battn.	21/6/17
MITCHELL, J. B., Sec.-Lieut.	8th Battn.	3/6/16
MOBBERLEY, L. W., Sec.-Lieut.	24th Battn.	8/6/16
MORETON, H. A. V., Sec.-Lieut.	23rd Battn.	29/5/18
MORLAND, D. M. T., Lieut.	3rd Lon. Fd. Co., R.E.	24/7/15
MORRIS, L. C., Sec.-Lieut.	15th Battn.	2/7/17
MUNRO, R. G., Sec.-Lieut.	18th Battn.	11/1/16
NEEDHAM, L. W., Lieut.	20th Battn.	27/10/16

NEWTON, W. G., Lieut.	28th, att. 23rd Battn.	3/10/16
NORRISH, F., Sec.-Lieut.	20th Battn.	7/7/17
NOTTINGHAM, B. D., Sec.-Lieut.	20th Battn.	27/7/17
O'BRIEN, K. R., Major	17th, att. 22nd Battn.	30/10/18
O'CONNELL, C., Sec.-Lieut.	21st Battn.	8/6/16
ORDISH, H. T., Capt.	6th Battn.	2/7/17
OSBORNE, F., Sec.-Lieut.	15th Battn.	2/6/16
OWEN, J. P., Sec.-Lieut.	3rd, att. 4th R.W.F.	14/1/16
OWERS, F. T., Sec.-Lieut.	13th, att. 22nd Battn.	7/1/18
OXLEY, P. F., Sec.-Lieut.	Z/47 T.M.B.	9/7/17
PAKENHAM, T. C., Lieut.	(Coldstream Gds.), 142nd M.G. Co.	4/7/17
PALMER, G. E., Capt.	23rd Battn.	21/11/17
PARSONS, T. C., Lieut.	(E. Lancs Regt.), 140th M.G. Co.	4/1/18
PAYNE, E. M., Capt.	23rd Battn.	26/4/18
PATERSON, A., Capt.	22nd Battn.	3/6/19
PEACOCK, F. C., Sec.-Lieut.	R.F.A., V/47 T.M.B.	7/7/17
PEATE, E. W., Lieut.	7th, att. 4th R.W.F.	3/6/19
*PEEL, H., Sec.-Lieut.	8th Battn.	14/1/16
PERRETT, R. E., Sec.-Lieut.	20th Battn.	4/1/18
PHILLIPS, F. E., R.S.M.	6th Battn.	3/6/18
PHILLIPS, W. E., Sec.-Lieut.	23rd Battn.	21/11/17
PLUMPTREE, B. P., Rev.	Army Chaplains Dept.	11/6/16
PLUNKETT, H. J., Sec.-Lieut.	9th, att. 6th Battn.	3/1/18
POLL, D. E., Lieut.	24th Battn.	3/11/18
POLLOCK, H. H., Capt.	47th Div. Amm. Col.	5/6/17
POTTER, J., Capt.	R.A.M.C., att. 24th Bn.	26/4/18
PRESTON, J. F., Sec.-Lieut.	7th Battn.	2/7/17
PRICE, L. H. B., Sec.-Lieut.	4th R.W.F.	9/5/18
RABY, V. H., Capt.	7th, att. 22nd Battn.	3/6/19
RAILTON, D., Rev.	Army Chaplains Dept.	6/11/16
*RATHBONE, W. L. C., Sec.-Lieut.	15th Battn.	3/10/16
REAH, H. W., Sec.-Lieut.	517th Field Co., R.E.	3/6/19
RICHARDS, F. R., Lieut.	22nd Battn.	7/8/18
ROBERTS, C. H. H., Lieut.	21st Battn.	21/10/15
ROBERTS, H. O. C., Lieut.	7th Battn.	21/10/15
ROBERTSON, O. J., Capt.	23rd Bn., att. Div. Sig. Co.	3/6/16
ROBINSON, C. R., Sec.-Lieut.	47th Battn., M.G.C.	28/9/18
ROSS, R. S., Sec.-Lieut.	11th, att. 24th Battn.	15/11/18
ROWLEY, F. F., C.S.M.	24th Battn.	8/6/16
RUTHVEN, H., Capt.	21st Battn.	8/6/16
SALE, H. A., Sec.-Lieut.	141st Machine Gun Co.	1/1/17
SAMPSON, A. C., Sec.-Lieut.	22nd, att. 6th Battn.	9/8/17
*SAMUEL, T. A. S., Sec.-Lieut.	15th Battn.	3/1/18
*SANDERS, H. J., Sec.-Lieut.	24th Battn.	3/10/16
SANDILANDS, J. E., Capt.	5th Lon. Fd. Ambce.	2/7/17
SAUMAREZ, R. S., Capt.	22nd Battn.	1/1/17
*SAUNDERS, C. J., Capt.	24th Battn., Staff Capt., 142nd Bde.	5/6/17
SAVILL, M., Capt.	24th Battn.	31/12/17
SCHWARZ, R. O., Capt.	D.A.Q.M.G.	1/1/17
SCOTT, G., Capt.	5th Lon. Fd. Ambce.	1/1/17
SEGAR, S. M., Sec.-Lieut.	20th Battn.	9/5/18
SELLAR, T. McC., Capt.	R.A.M.C., att. 18th Bn.	3/11/18
SHEAD, A. T., Capt.	Army Ordnance Corps	1/1/17
SHELLEY, H., C.S.M.	20th Battn.	16/6/16
SHENNAN, W. D., Sec.-Lieut.	47th Div. Signal Co.	21/10/15
*SHEPPARD, J. J., Sec.-Lieut.	19th Battn.	5/6/17
SHIELDS, C. R. C., Sec.-Lieut.	24th Battn.	8/6/16

SHINGLER, J. S. M., Lieut. ..	.. 4th R.W.F.	3/7/17
SIEVERS, R. F., Sec.-Lieut. ..	.. 24th Battn.	6/9/17
SIMEONS, L. T., Sec.-Lieut. ..	.. 47th Div. Signal Co. ..	18/5/18
SIMMONS, W. J., Lieut.	.. 17th Battn.	28/9/18
SKAER, W., C.S.M.	.. 23rd Battn.	30/9/18
SMITH, C. H., C.S.M. ..	.. 20th Battn.	3/6/18
SMITH, C. L. E., Sec.-Lieut.	.. 20th Bn., att. Z/47 T.M.B.	7/7/17
SMITH, H. T., Capt.	.. 21st Battn.	6/11/16
SMITH, I. W., Sec.-Lieut. ..	.. 518th Field Co., R.E. ..	7/7/17
SNELL, J., C.S.M.	.. 21st Battn.	8/8/16
SOUTHON, J. E., Sec.-Lieut.	.. 17th Battn.	6/11/17
SPENCER, J. W., Sec.-Lieut.	.. 14th, att. 6th Battn. ..	10/3/17
STANCOURT, G. H. R., Sec.-Lieut. ..	.. 6th, att. 18th Battn. ..	13/10/18
STAPLES H. A., Sec.-Lieut...	.. 18th Battn.	27/10/16
STEELE, E. G., Sec.-Lieut. ..	.. 20th Battn.	27/10/16
STEVENS, A. H., Lieut. ..	.. 235th Bde., R.F.A. ..	10/10/16
*STEWART, C. H. J., Sec.-Lieut.	.. 18th Battn.	29/4/17
STICKLAND, A. L., Capt. ..	.. 21st Battn.	3/5/18
*STOKES, J. G., Capt. ..	.. 19th Battn.	19/5/16
STONE, F. N., Sec.-Lieut. ..	.. 21st Battn.	11/3/18
STUBBING, H., Sec.-Lieut. ..	.. 18th Battn.	3/6/18
SUTTON, D., Capt.	.. 7th Battn.	1/1/17
TANSLEY, L. B., Capt.	.. 236th Bde., R.F.A. ..	3/6/18
TAYLOR, F. E., Sec.-Lieut. ..	.. 18th Battn.	13/10/18
TAYLOR, G. F., Sec.-Lieut. ..	.. 11th, att. 23rd Battn. ...	13/10/18
TAYLOR, R. E., Sec.-Lieut. ..	.. 7th Battn.	6/10/16
TAYLOR, S., Capt.	.. 236th Bde., R.F.A. ..	3/6/19
TEMPLEMAN, F. D. R., Sec.-Lieut.	.. 22nd, att. 17th Battn. ...	17/10/18
THOMAS, A., Lieut.	.. 8th Battn.	21/10/15
THOMAS, M. E., Sec.-Lieut. ..	.. 517th Field Co., R.E. ..	29/4/17
THOMAS, R. W., Lieut. ..	.. 7th Battn.	1/1/18
THOMPSON, C., Sec.-Lieut. ..	.. 22nd Battn.	3/10/16
TIDD, R. R., Capt.	.. 2/11th, att. 21st Battn...	28/9/18
*TOLERTON, R. H., Capt. ..	.. 23rd Battn.	21/6/17
TOMLIN, R. A., Sec.-Lieut. ..	.. 22nd, att. 23rd Battn. ...	30/9/18
TOSH, J. C. P., Lieut. ..	.. Div. Engineers	5/6/17
*TOTTON, A., Capt. ..	.. 18th Battn.	4/1/18
TOWNEND, R. D. G., Capt. ..	.. 47th Div. Train, R.A.S.C.	3/6/16
TRAFFORD, S., Sec.-Lieut. ..	.. 20th Battn.	13/10/18
TREGURTHA, M. J., Sec.-Lieut.	.. 142nd M.G. Co.	4/1/18
TREZONA, F. J., C.S.M. ..	.. 20th Battn.	15/7/16
TRIM, E. J., Capt.	.. 19th Battn.	2/10/16
TRUSCOTT, F. G., Sec.-Lieut. ..	.. (Suffolk R.) Div. Cyc. Co.	14/1/16
TURNER, G. C., Capt. ..	.. 23rd, att. 21st Battn. ..	3/6/18
TURNER, H. M., C.S.M. ..	.. 8th Battn.	4/1/18
TURNER, R. W., Lieut. ..	.. R.W. Kent, att. 24th Bn.	13/10/18
TYLER, G. E., Sec.-Lieut. ..	.. 19th Battn.	3/10/16
ULLMAN, R. B., Lieut. ..	.. 236th Bde., R.F.A. ..	27/7/17
UNWIN, R. H., Lieut. ..	.. Divisional H.Q. .. · ..	3/6/19
*VINCE, W. B., Major.. ..	.. 8th Battn.	1/1/17
VINCENT, C. R. C., Sec.-Lieut.	.. 18th Battn.	31/12/17
WALEY, S. D., Sec.-Lieut. ..	.. 22nd Battn.	23/8/18
WALKER, S. H., Capt. ..	.. 24th Battn.	3/11/18
WALKER, W. F., Lieut. ..	.. 520th Field Co., R.E. ..	11/1/18
WARD, R. P., Capt.	.. 4th R.W.F.	1/1/17
WARE, H. E. B., Lieut. & Q.M.	.. 5th Lon. Fd. Ambce. ..	4/1/18
WATSON, G. H., Lieut. ..	.. 47th Battn., M.G.C. ..	17/10/18
WEAVER, F., Capt.	.. 22nd Battn.	11/3/18
WEBB, P. L., Capt.	.. 18th Battn.	1/1/17
WELCH, C. W., Lieut. ..	.. 19th Battn.	31/12/17

WESTON, G. P., Sec.-Lieut. ..	.. 20th Battn.	16/6/18
*WHEELER, W. R., Capt. ..	.. 22nd Battn.	17/10/16
WHELAN, L. T., Capt. ..	.. R.A.M.C., att. 8th Battn.	6/6/17
WHIDBORNE, B. S., Lieut. ..	.. 235th Bde. R.F.A., att.	
	X/47 T.M.B.	1/1/17
WHITE, C. G., Capt.	.. V/47 T.M.B.	7/7/17
WHITE, J. B., Sec.-Lieut. ..	.. 7th, att. 19th Battn. ..	17/10/18
WIGGINTON, J. H. B., Major	.. 47th Div. Train, A.S.C...	4/1/18
WIGNEY, C. R. D'A., Sec.-Lieut. ..	7th Battn.	3/10/16
WILKINSON, A. E., Rev. ..	.. Army Chaplains Dept. ...	16/10/16
WILKINSON, C., Sec.-Lieut. ..	.. 236th Bde., R.F.A. ..	9/7/17
WILL, W. B., Sec.-Lieut. ..	.. 14th, att. 8th Battn. ..	2/7/17
WILLIAMS, D. J., Lieut. ..	.. 4th R.W.F.	9/5/18
WILLIAMS, T. R., Capt. ..	.. 4th R.W.F.	7/1/18
WILLIAMS, W. C. B., Capt. ..	.. 4th R.W.F.	3/10/16
WILLIAMS, W. J., Capt. ..	.. 16th R. Fus., att. 24th Bn.	21/6/17
WILLS, T. E., Capt.	.. 47th Div. Train, A.S.C.	5/6/17
WILSON, A., Sec.-Lieut. ..	.. 15th Battn.	11/3/18
WILSON, G. R., Sec.-Lieut. ..	.. 19th Battn.	27/7/17
WILSON, N. I., Lieut. ..	.. 3rd, att. 4th R.W.F. ..	11/3/18
WILSON, R. G. M., Capt. ..	.. 47th Div. Signal Co. ..	3/6/18
WINTERFLOOD, L. W., Sec.-Lieut. ..	7th, att. 19th Battn. ..	17/10/18
WOOD, C. T., Rev. ..	.. Army Chaplains Dept. ..	3/6/16
WOODWARD, C. S., Rev. Canon	.. Army Chaplains Dept. ..	6/10/16
WOOLLEY, E. J., Capt. ..	.. 22nd Battn.	14/1/16
WRAIGHT, G. F. H., Capt. ..	.. 18th Battn.	13/10/18
WRAY, C. R., Sec.-Lieut. ..	.. 23rd, att. 21st Battn. ..	28/9/18
WRAY, W. B., Lieut. & Q.M.	.. 22nd Battn.	1/1/19
WRIGHT, H. C., Lieut. ..	.. 17th Battn.	14/1/16
WRIGHT, H. J., R.S.M. ..	.. Scots Gds., att. 7th Bn...	4/1/18

ORDER OF THE BRITISH EMPIRE.
COMMANDER.

FRASER, T., Colonel	.. A.D.M.S.	3/6/19

OFFICERS.

ANDERSON, N. G., Capt. ..	.. 47th Div. Train, R.A.S.C.	3/6/19
CRAIG, T., Capt.	.. Mobile Vet. Sec., R.A.V.C.	3/6/19
HIBBARD, T., Major ..	.. D.A.D.V.S.	3/6/19

MEMBERS.

BEER, A. J., Lt. & Q.M. ..	.. 24th Battn.	3/6/19
BEVANS, M., Staff S.M. ..	.. Div. Train, att. 5th Lon.	
	Fd. Ambce.	3/6/19
SMALL, G. J., R.S.M. ..	.. 23rd Battn.	3/6/19
*WHITBOURN, E., Staff Q.M.S.	.. Div. Train, att. Div. H.Q.	3/6/19

MEDAL.

*HINTON, H., Staff S.M. ..	.. Div. Train, att. Div. H.Q.	23/1/20

D.C.M. AND BAR.

DRURY, S. C., C.S.M. ..	.. 520th Fd. Co., R.E.	
	D.C.M., 14/1/16; bar, 6/5/18	
MATTOCK, C. A., Cpl. ..	.. 8th Bn. D.C.M., 25/2/16; bar, 3/6/16	
*SHONK, E. G., Sgt.	.. 22nd Bn. D.C.M., 8/6/16; bar,2/7/17	
SUGARS, R. C., Cpl.	.. 15th Bn., att. 140th M.G.C.	
	D.C.M., 3/6/16; bar, 19/6/16	

BRIG.-GENERAL R. McDOUALL, C.B., C.M.G., C.B.E., D.S.O.
Commanding 141st Infantry Brigade, 1916-1917, and 142nd Infantry Brigade, 1918.

DISTINGUISHED CONDUCT MEDAL.

ALLAN, F. M., Pte., 7 Bn. .. 14/1/16
ALLEN, H. J. O., L.-Cpl., 6 Bn. 14/1/16
ALLEN, H. J. W., Pte., 24 Bn. 24/7/15
ALLEN, J., Sgt., 6 Bn. .. 10/3/17
AMSDEN, C. S., L.-Cpl., 15 Bn. 15/5/18
AVEY, P. H., R.S.M., 23 Bn... 3/6/18
*AVRAMACHIS, V., Sgt., 24 Bn. 26/6/17
AYLWARD, W. P., Gnr., 236
  Bde., R.F.A. 28/5/18
*BACON, C. W. C., Sgt., 7 Bn... 2/7/17
*BAILEY, F. F., C.S.M., 6 Bn... 3/6/16
BAILEY, W. J., L.-Cpl., 6 Bn. 10/3/17
BAKER, A., Sgt., 7 Bn. .. 1/10/17
BAKER, F., Spr., Sig. Co. .. 14/1/16
*BARKHAM, G. H., Sgt., 18 Bn. 3/10/16
BARRETT, A. E., Sgt., 235
  Bde., R.F.A. 9/7/17
BARTLETT, R. W., Cpl., 238
  Bde., R.F.A. 22/10/16
BAXTER, G., Sgt., 24 Bn. .. 21/11/17
*BAYLEY, G. J., C.S.M., 19 Bn. 1/10/17
BEALE, J. R., L.-Cpl., Sig. Co. 24/7/15
BEER, R. H., Sgt., 22 Bn. .. 3/10/16
*BELLISS, T., Sgt., 520 Fd. Co.,
  R.E. 1/1/19
*BELTRAM, J., Sgt., 517 Fd.
  Co., R.E. 1/5/18
BENNETT, F. K., Sgt., 20 Bn. 6/10/16
BERRY, A. B., Pte., 22 Bn... 24/7/15
BETTS, L. B., L.-Cpl., 141
  M.G. Co. 3/10/16
BEVANS, H. E., S.S.M., 5 Lon.
  Fd. Amb. 3/6/18
BIGGS, S. H., Sgt., 21 Bn. .. 3/6/19
BOND, A. C., Sgt., 20 Bn. .. 6/10/16
BOTLANDER, G. A., Pte., 22 Bn. 19/5/16
*BOWERS, C. C., Sgt., 7 Bn. .. 2/7/17
*BOWMAN, H. E., Sgt., 15 Bn. 17/10/18
BRANTOM, W. H., Pte., 15 Bn. 24/7/15
BRAZIER, J. W., Sgt., 235 Bde.,
  R.F.A. 3/6/18
*BRETTELL, C. W., B.S.M., 236
  Bde., R.F.A. 3/11/18
BRIAN, A. J., Sgt., 23 Bn. .. 24/7/15
BROOKLAND, W. C., Sgt., 20 B. 1/1/19
*BROOKS, F. G., Cpl., 7 Bn. .. 11/3/18
BULL, H. L., Pte., 22 Bn. .. 16/10/18
BUNCE, A., Sgt., 19 Bn. .. 27/10/16
BUNCE, J., Sgt., 19 Bn. .. 3/10/16
BURDEN, R. H., C.S.M., 15 Bn. 11/7/17
*BURGESS, H. J., Cpl., 19 Bn... 2/12/16
BURKE, F. J., Rfn., 6 Bn. .. 24/7/15
*BURLEY, W. G., Sgt., 21 Bn... 30/9/19
BUSH, H. A., R.S.M., 22 Bn... 30/9/18
BUSS, J., Cpl., 21 Bn. .. 28/9/18
BUTLER, A., Cpl., 6 Bn. .. 3/10/16
*BUTLER, A., Sgt., 19 Bn. .. 9/5/18
BUTLER, J., Sgt., 22 Bn. .. 30/9/18

BYE, E. A., Sgt., 20 Bn. .. 6/11/16
CANEY, C., Cpl., 22 Bn. .. 2/7/17
CAREY, R. A. F., Pte., 20 Bn. 24/7/15
CARR, E., Pte., 24 Bn. .. 24/7/15
CARTER, T. H., Cpl., 23 Bn... 31/5/18
CASE, E. J., Sgt., 17 Bn. .. 1/1/19
CHALLONER, F. G., Rfn., 6 Bn. 1/12/15
*CHARMAN, A. E., Sgt., 21 Bn. 21/12/17
*CHESNEY, H., R.S.M. 20 Bn... 1/1/19
CHRISTEY, F., Sgt., 15 Bn. .. 1/12/15
*CHURCHMAN, W. B., Sgt., 2/3
  Lon. Fd. Co. 5/1/18
CLARK. E. L., Pte., 22 Bn. .. 17/10/18
CLARKE, P., Spr., 1/3 Lon. Fd.
  Co. 3/10/16
*COGGER, O., Sgt., 24 Bn. .. 3/11/18
COLE, A., Rfn., 21 Bn. .. 16/2/16
COLE, G. H., Sgt., 20 Bn. .. 16/6/16
*COLLINS, H., C.S.M., 7 Bn... 1/1/17
*CONWAY, H. F., B.S.M., 237
  Bde., R.F.A. 5/1/18
COOKE, E., Sgt., 15 Bn. .. 3/1/18
COOKE, F. A., Sgt.-Maj. (Gren.
  Gds.), att. 23 Bn... .. 24/7/15
CORRALL, C. R., Pte., 22 Bn. 19/1/16
COUSINS, C., Pte., 23 Bn. .. 21/11/17
COUSINS, W. B., C.S.M., 22 Bn. 11/7/17
COX, C. W., Sgt., 22 Bn. .. 20/7/16
COX, J. A., C.S.M., 6 Bn., att.
  140 M.G. Co. 3/6/16
CRISFORD, J. R., L.-Cpl., 7 Bn. 24/2/16
CUNNINGHAM, A. J., Sgt., 18 B. 14/1/16
CUSS, F. S., Rfn., 6 Bn. .. 14/1/16
DACHTLER, W. F., C.S.M., 23 B. 5/1/18
*DAVIES, T., Sgt., 4 R.W.F... 3/6/18
DAY, A. E., Pte., 7 Bn. .. 24/7/15
DEATH, E., Rfn., 6 Bn. .. 14/1/16
*DENCHFIELD, S. J., B.S.M.,
  D.A.C. 1/1/17
DICKENSON, J. A., L.-Cpl. 24 B. 3/10/16
DILLINGHAM, J., C.S.M., 19 Bn. 14/1/16
DINNAGE, A., L.-Cpl., Sig. Co. 24/7/15
DOUGLAS, W. M., L.-Cpl., 15 B. 17/10/18
DOWLING, P., L.-Cpl., 19 Bn. 24/7/15
DOWN, —, Spr., Sig. Co. .. 14/1/16
DOWNER, J. C., R.Q.M.S., 21 B. 3/6/19
*DUNN, W. J., L.-Cpl., 23 Bn. 3/10,16
EASTLAKE, F. W., Rfn., 21 Bn. 14/1/16
EDWARDS, G., Pte., 23 Bn. .. 14/1/16
EDWARDS, S. A., Bdr., 8 Lon.
  Bde., R.F.A. 1/12/15
*ELLIS, W., L.-Cpl., 4 R.W.F. 16/2/16
ETCHES, W., Spr., Div. Engrs. 1/12/15
EUSTACE, D. J., Cpl., 22 Bn. 17/10/18
EVERARD, J., Dvr., Div. Train 14/1/16
EVERETT, P. W., Sgt., 17 Bn. 3/10/16
FAIRLEIGH, P. E., C.S.M., 18 B. 3/6/16
*FAVELL, H., C.S.M., 22 Bn... 30/9/18

U

*NOTTINGHAM, E. B., Sgt., 15 Bn., att. 140 T.M.B. .. 11/5/16
OMER, C., Pte., 23 Bn. .. 21/6/17
*OWENS, G., C.S.M., 4 R.W.F. 5/1/18
OWENS, J. D., Cpl., 20 Bn... 16/6/16
*OXMAN, R. H., Sgt., 23 Bn... 24/7/15
PARKER, W., Sgt., Div. Cy. Co. 14/1/16
PARKINSON, B. L., C.S.M., 21 Bn. 11/1/18
PARRY, D., Pte., 4 R.W.F... 3/10/16
PARSONS, J. W., L.-Cpl., 4 R.W.F. 14/1/16
PARTRIDGE, J. J. L., B.S.M., 235 Bde., R.F.A. .. 3/6/19
*PAYNE, H., Sgt., 8 Bn. .. 1/1/18
PEACHY, B., L.-Cpl., 21 Bn... 3/10/16
PEAKE, F., Sgt., 18 Bn. .. 25/5/16
PEAT, R. J., C.S.M., 8 Bn. .. 24/7/15
PERKS, J., S.S.M., A.S.C. .. 5/1/18
POOLE, J. E. S., L.-Cpl., 15 Bn. 28/9/18
PORTER, W. S., Sgt., 22 Bn. 14/1/16
PRICE, W. J., B.S.M., 5 Lon. Bde., R.F.A. 14/1/16
PRIOR, S. T., Bdr., 235 Bde., R.F.A. 11/7/16
PROUND, F. M., C.S.M., 24 Bn. 31/12/17
PUGSLEY, B. J., Rfn., 17 Bn. 14/1/16
PULLEN, G., Pte., 4 R.W.F... 1/12/15
QUICK, E. J., Cpl., 4 Lon. Fd. Co. 3/6/16
RADALL, E., Spr., 3 Lon. Fd. Co. 14/1/16
RANDALL, E. L., Rfn., 8 Bn. 2/7/17
REDDING, E. J., L.-Cpl., 6 Bn., att. 140 T.M.B. 15/5/16
RICHARDS, H. E. M., Bdr., 7 Lon. Bde., R.F.A... .. 24/7/15
*RIDDLE, H. B., Sgt., 15 Bn... 3/10/16
*RIDDY, A. E., Cpl., 22 Bn., att. 142 T.M.B. .. 17/7/17
ROBERTS, F., Sgt., 6 Bn. .. 2/7/17
ROBERTS, J. E., Drmr., 23 Bn. 3/6/16
*ROBERTS, W., C.S.M., 4 R.W.F. 9/5/18
ROBERTSON, T. C., C.S.M., 15 Bn. 11/7/17
ROBINSON, R. D., Cpl., 19 Bn. 3/6/19
ROLPH, R. D., Sgt., 17 Bn... 2,7/17
ROWE, R. A., L.-Cpl., 21 Bn. 3/6/19
RUDHALL, H., Pte., 24 Bn... 21/11/17
RUSHFORTH, C. H., Rfn., 8 Bn. 3/6/16
RUSHFORTH, S., Cpl., 8 Bn... 14/1/16
SAGAR, H. H., Rfn., 18 Bn... 24/7/15
SALMON, H., C.S.M., 15 Bn... 3/6/19
SAUNDERS, F. B., Sgt., 23 Bn. 3/6/16
SCHERMULY, C. D., R.S.M., 17 Bn. 31/12/17
SHADWELL, A., Sgt., 7 Bn. .. 6/6/17
SHELLARD, R. H., Rfn., 21 Bn. 24/7/15
*SILVESTER, H. A., Sgt., 21 Bn. 30/9/18
*SIMKINS, B., L.-Cpl., 520 Fd. Co. 11/5/18

SIMPSON, W., Sgt., 8 Bn. .. 2/7/17
SMITH, A., Pte., 22 Bn. .. 20/7/16
SMITH, G. B., Sgt., 15 Bn. .. 11/5/18
SMITH, S. W., Pte., 20 Bn. .. 24/7/15
SOUTHAM, A., Sgt., 19 Bn. .. 14/1/16
STANTON, W. A., Sgt., 8 Bn. 3/10/16
STEELE, G. W., Cpl., 7 Bn... 8/6/16
STEPHENS, D., Sgt., Div. Eng. 14/1/16
*STEPHENS, S. G., Sgt., 24 Bn. 31/12/17
STEVENS, W. O., Sgt., 18 Bn. 14/1/16
*STEWART, C. H. J., Pte., 20 Bn. 1/12/15
SUCKLING, C. W., L.-Cpl., 24 B. 8/6/16
SULLIVAN, E., C.S.M., 22 Bn. 1/5/18
SULLIVAN, E. A., Pte., 22 Bn. 8/6/16
TANNER, C. W., Sgt., 19 Bn. 6/5/16
*TARR, J., Sgt., 17 Bn. .. 3/6/19
*TAYLOR, A. J., Sgt., 7 Bn. .. 1/12/15
THEIS, C., L.-Cpl., 24 Bn. .. 21/11/17
*THELWELL, J., Cpl., 4 R.W.F. 3/6/16
THOMAS, K. D., Sgt., 15 Bn... 3/6/19
THOMPSON, A. B., Pte., 24 Bn. 14/1/16
*TIDMARSH, S., Sgt., 21 Bn... 28/9/18
TILBY, J. A., C.S.M., 18 Bn. 13/10/18
TILLEY, J., Rfn., 18 Bn. .. 11/1/16
TINDAL, G., L.-Cpl., 20 Bn... 16/6/16
TREW, W. A., Sgt., 24 Bn. .. 3/6/19
TURNEY, W. E., Sgt., 23 Bn. 21/11/17
TYERS, H., R.S.M., 18 Bn. .. 9/5/18
TYRRELL, F. G., Rfn., 8 Bn. 2/7/17
VINCENT, G. E., Rfn., 18 Bn. 24,7/15
VOISEY, J. T., Pte., 22 Bn... 1/12/15
WAGHORN, D. L., Pte., 20 Bn. 14/1/16
WALTERS, W. H., Pte., 24 Bn. 24/7/15
WARK, J. A., Sgt., M.G. Bn. 28/9/18
WARNER, S., L.-Cpl., 7 Bn... 24/2/16
WATSON, M. O., Drmr., 23 Bn. 1/12/15
WEBB, J. A., Sgt., 18 Bn., att. 140 Inf. Bde. H.Q... .. 3/6/19
WEIR, G., L.-Cpl., 20 Bn. .. 6/10/16
*WELLS, L. H., Pte., 19 Bn... 31/12/17
*WELLS, R., C.S.M., 4 R.W.F. 9/5/18
WEST, G. W., C.S.M., 24 Bn. 31/12/17
WHITE, C. E., C.Q.M.S., Coldstream Gds., att. 4 R.W.F. 3/6/16
WHITE, J. E. P., C.S.M., M.G. Bn. 1,1/19
WICKES, E. L., C.S.M., 21 Bn. 3/6/18
WIGZELL, H. K., Cpl., 21 Bn. 14/1/16
WILLIAMS, E. O., Pte., 4 R.W.F. 3/10/16
WILLS, H. J., Q.M.S., 19 Bn. 14/1/16
WILSON, G. W., Sgt., 6 Bn... 3/1/18
*WILSON, J. H., Sgt., 235 Bde., R.F.A. 28/5/18
WINDLE, W., Sgt., 8 Bn. .. 3/10/16
WITHERIDGE, P., S.M., 8 Bn. 3/6/16
WOOD, A. E., L.-Cpl., 23 Bn. 21/6/17
*WOOD, J. W., Sgt., 4 Lon. Fd. Amb. 6/10/16
WOOD, P. G., Rfn., 18 Bn... 24/7/15

WOOD, W., Sgt., 17 Bn. .. 12/3/16	WYMAN, A. E., L.-Cpl., 6
WOODLEY, A. G., Rfn., 17 Bn. 14/1/16	Bn. 19/5/16
WOODMAN, W., B.S.M., 5 Lon.	*YELF, A., C.S.M., 6 Bn. .. 1/12/15
Bde., R.F.A. 3/6/16	YOUNG, J. H., S.M., Div. Arty.
WOODWARD, C. F., C.S.M., 20	H.Q. 6/6/17
Bn. 9/9/17	

MILITARY MEDAL AND TWO BARS.

		M.M.	1st bar.	2nd bar.
SHOWELL, J. M., Cpl. .. .. 24th Battn.		3/6/16	1/11/16	11/10/18
TRACEY, P. J., Sgt. .. .. 22nd Battn.		4/4/18	19/9/18	15/10/18

MILITARY MEDAL AND ONE BAR.

			M.M.	Bar.
ALINGTON, G. W. S., Rfn.	.. 17th Battn.	..	16/9/18	7/10/18
ARMFIELD, H. L., Pte. ..	.. 15th Battn.	..	26/9/17	2/5/18
BAKER, W. M., Pte. ..	.. 7th Battn. ..	..	1/10/16	24/6/17
BALL, W. A., Pte.	.. 24th Battn.	..	8/6/16	5/10/18
BARLOW, F., Sgt. ..	.. 4th Lon. Fd. Amb.		15/9/16	7/10/18
BARNEY, G. A. F., Pte.	.. 19th Battn.	..	1/9/17	24/12/17
BARWELL, G. H., L.-Cpl. ..	.. 24th Battn.	..	5/10/18	11/10/18
BELL, J. H., L.-Cpl. ..	.. 22nd Battn.	..	19/9/18	15/10/18
BOND, R. E., Pte. ..	.. 7th Battn. ..	..	27/10/16	26/9/17
BROWETT, A., L.-Cpl. ..	.. 21st Battn.	..	7/10/16	28/12/17
BUCKENHAM, J., Sgt. ..	.. 22nd Battn.	..	22/4/18	7/7/18
BUNCLARK, A. V., L.-Cpl. ..	.. 22nd Battn.	..	8/6/16	10/10/16
BURTON, W., Sgt. ..	.. 18th Battn.	..	22/4/17	26/6/17
BUSWELL, P. E., Sgt. ..	.. 23rd Battn.	..	2/10/16	16/6/17
CANDLER, J. E., L.-Cpl.	.. 6th Battn. ..	..	2/10/16	28/12/17
CHAPLIN, G., Pte. ..	.. 22nd Battn.	..	10/10/16	18/6/17
CHAPMAN, W. J., Sgt. ..	.. 24th Battn.	..	5/10/18	11/10/18
CHURCH, W. C., Sgt. ..	.. 6th Battn. ..	..	15/9/16	2/10/16
CLARK, W. S., Rfn. ..	.. 18th Battn.	..	3/6/16	22/6/16
CONNELLY, G., Pte. ..	.. 24th Battn.	..	29/10/16	11/10/18
COOPER, F. O., Sgt. ..	.. 23rd Battn.	..	3/1/17	29/12/17
COPPS, G. A., Sgt. ..	.. 24th Battn.	..	5/10/18	11/10/18
CROSTHWAITE, W., Sgt. ..	.. 22nd Battn.	..	7/7/18	27/10/18
CROW, A. M., Pte. ..	.. 19th Battn.	..	7/7/16	1/9/17
CUTTING, T. R., Cpl. ..	.. 5th Lon. Fd. Amb.		23/6/17	7/10/18
DOWNWARD, A. J., Sgt.	.. 24th Battn.	..	5/10/18	11/10/18
DUNN, A., Cpl. ..	.. 22nd Battn.	..	20/12/17	7/10/18
EDGINGTON, A., Cpl. ..	.. 22nd Battn.	..	8/6/16	20/12/17
EDWARDS, J. M., Cpl. ..	.. 21st Battn.	..	3/6/16	5/11/16
FOOTE, C., L.-Cpl. ..	.. 22nd Battn.	..	20/12/17	22/4/18
GISBY, V. F., Gnr. ..	.. 235th Bde., R.F.A.		7/10/16	14/10/17
GRIFFITHS, A. C., L.-Cpl.	.. 8th Battn. ..	..	15/9/16	7/10/16
HANBURY, B., Pte. ..	.. 23rd Battn.	..	7/10/16	21/4/18
HARRIS, W. E., Cpl. ..	.. 21 Bn., at 142 T.M.B.		14/11/17	29/5/18
HATLEY, F. J., L.-Cpl. ..	.. Sig. Co. ..	..	8/9/17	23/10/18
HEAD, F. G., Cpl. ..	.. 17th Battn.	..	16/6/16	30/9/17
HEATH, A. T., L.-Cpl. ..	.. 23rd Battn.	..	2/10/16	16/6/17
HIBBARD, C. J., Rfn. ..	.. 17th Battn.	..	16/9/18	16/11/18
HILLS, F. H., L.-Cpl. ..	.. 24th Battn.	..	29/10/16	21/4/18
HORNSBY, G., Spr. ..	.. Sig. Co. ..	..	15/6/16	13/10/16
HUGHES, D., Pte. ..	.. 4th R.W.F.	..	24/10/16	6/5/18

HUGHES, E. F., Sgt.	15 Bn. at 140 B. Obs.	7/4/18	19/9/18
HUNTLEY, J. C., Pte.	7th Battn.	24/6/17	28/12/17
HYATT, E., Pte.	24th Battn.	7/10/16	19/4/18
JACKSON, C., Pte.	24th Battn.	29/10/16	19/4/18
JARMAN, H. L., Pte.	24th Battn.	8/6/16	7/10/16
JENNINGS, A., Pte.	19th Battn.	15/9/16	20/7/17
JOHNSON, W. J., L.-Cpl.	23rd Battn.	20/5/18	9/10/18
JONES, H. T., L.-Cpl.	23rd Battn.	2/10/16	14/11/17
KAILL, A. W., L.-Cpl.	19th Battn.	15/9/16	23/6/17
KELSEY, H. J. R., Pte.	15th Battn.	24/10/16	18/1/17
KNIGHT, N. G., Cpl.	15th Battn.	28/12/17	2/5/18
LEE, H. S., Rfn.	18th Battn.	5/10/18	13/11/18
LOVELESS, L. C., Sgt.	18th Battn.	25/5/16	14/10/17
MANNERING, R. H., Pte.	22nd Battn.	10/10/16	7/10/18
MAYNARD, S., Pte.	23rd Battn.	16/6/17	21/4/18
MILLS, J. F., L.-Cpl.	6th Battn.	17/5/16	2/10/16
MISSEN, E. H., Rfn.	17th Battn.	16/9/18	22/10/18
MOORE, A. W., L.-Cpl.	22nd Battn.	18/6/17	3/6/18
MOORE, W. F., Pioneer..	Sig. Co.	15/6/16	23/6/17
NEWMAN, H. J., Sgt.	21st Battn.	3/6/16	3/6/16
NUNN, J. T., Rfn.	8th Battn.	3/6/16	7/10/16
OTTLEY, A. J., Cpl.	Sig. Co.	2/10/16	23/6/17
PENN, F. R., L.-Cpl.	18th Battn.	15/9/16	7/10/16
PORTER, E. A., L.-Cpl.	24th Battn.	14/11/17	11/10/18
REDMAN, R. J., Gnr.	235th Bd., R.F.A.	11/5/17	23/6/17
REYNOLDS, W., Sgt.	Sig. Co.	15/6/16	11/10/18
RIDGEWAY, G., Sgt.	17th Battn.	16/9/18	7/10/18
ROBSON, A. H., Sgt.	4th Lon. Fd. Amb.	3/6/16	23/6/17
RUSSELL, J. H., Cpl.	17th Battn.	16/9/18	7/10/18
*SCUDAMORE, N. R. W., L.-Cpl.	23rd Battn.	7/5/17	16/6/17
SELLICK, J. A., Cpl.	4th Lon. Fd. Amb.	29/10/16	23/4/18
SERMON, C., Sgt.	142nd M.G. Co.	29/10/16	20/6/17
SERFF, B., Sgt.	22nd Battn.	20/12/17	19/9/18
SHIRLEY, R., Pte.	15th Battn.	28/6/17	2/5/18
*SKILTON, J. F., Cpl.	22nd Battn.	20/12/17	19/9/18
SMITH, J., Cpl.	235th Bde., R.F.A.	14/10/17	7/5/18
STAUNTON, E. W., Cpl.	19th Battn.	5/10/18	27/10/18
SULLIVAN, T. A., Sgt.	6th Lon. Fd. Amb.	29/7/16	7/10/18
TAMPLIN, G. F., Cpl.	22nd Battn.	5/5/17	23/8/18
THRESHER, S. W., Pte.	24th Battn.	2/6/17	26/6/17
*TIDMARSH, S., L.-Cpl.	21st Battn.	2/10/16	28/12/17
TOOLEY, F. W., Sgt.	22nd Battn.	22/4/18	6/7/18
WAKEFIELD, E., Cpl.	21st Battn.	20/6/17	30/12/17
WELLER, R. C., Sgt.	20th Battn.	23/6/17	5/10/18
WILLIAMS, F., Cpl.	4th R.W.F.	10/10/16	27/7/17

BAR TO MILITARY MEDAL.

BARNES, R. J., L.-Cpl.	15th Battn.		7/10/18
BROWN, J. J., Pte.	22nd Battn.		18/6/17
PALMER, H., Rfn.	21st Battn.		16/9/18
WEISBERG, T., Rfn.	21st Battn.		16/9/18
WHITTAKER, W., Pte.	24th Battn.		8/11/18

MILITARY MEDALS.

ABLIN, J. G., Cpl., 6 Bn. .. 2/10/16
ABRAHAMS, J., L.-Cpl., 4 Lon.
  Fd. Amb. 15/9/16
ABREY, A. R., L.-Cpl., 23 Bn. 13/11/18
ACKROYD, S., Fitter S.Sgt.,
  238 Bde., R.F.A. 15/9/16
ADDICOTT, E., Rfn., 6 Bn. .. 2/10/16
ADULPHUS, B., Rfn., 17 Bn... 7/10/16
ALDEN, W., Pte., 20 Bn. .. 5/10/18
ALEXANDER, D., L.-Cpl., 21 B. 15/9/16
ALFORD, D. W., L.-Sgt., 19 Bn. 19/10/16
ALLCOCK, H. S., Bdr., 236
  Bde., R.F.A. 19/10/16
ALLEN, G. A., Rfn., 17 Bn... 7/10/18
ALLEN, W. C., Rfn., 17 Bn... 7/10/18
ALLIT, W., Pte., 24 Bn. .. 11/10/18
ALLSWORTH,W.,L.-Cpl., 24 Bn. 14/11/17
AMEY, H. J., Pte., 15 Bn. .. 28/12/17
AMSDEN, R., L.-Cpl., 23 Bn... 20/5/18
ANDREWS, A. E., Cpl., 22 Bn. 18/6/17
ANDREWS, A. E., Pte., 24 Bn. 7/10/16
ANDREWS, G. C., L.-Cpl., 15 B. 15/9/16
ANDREWS, J. L., L.-Cpl., 8 Bn. 7/10/16
ANGEL, R. L., L.-Cpl., 15 Bn. 17/9/18
ANSELL, C. H., Pte., 22 Bn... 10/10/16
ANTRIM, A. E., L.-Sgt., 8 Bn. 24/6/17
APPLEBY, R. G., L.-Cpl., 18 Bn. 26/6/17
APPLEFORD, J. D., Rfn., 21 Bn. 8/6/16
APPLETON, W., H., Sgt., 24 Bn. 20/12/17
ARMSTRONG, A. B., Sgt., 24 Bn. 8/6/16
ARMSTRONG, J. S., Pte., 15 Bn. 16/9/18
ARMSTRONG, L. F., L.-Cpl., 15
  Bn. 28/6/17
ARNEY, G. B. F., Sgt., 23 Bn. 16/6/17
ARNOLD, S., Sgt., 15 Bn. .. 28/6/17
ARTHUR, R. J., Pte., 15 Bn... 25/12/17
ASHBOLT, W. E., Rfn., 17 Bn. 16/6/16
ASHDOWN, P. E., Pte., 15 Bn. 2/5/18
ASHWORTH, J., Sgt., Sig. Co. 11/10/18
ASPDEN, R., L.-Cpl., 6 Bn. .. 2/10/16
ASTINS, F., E., Cpl., 17 Bn. .. 7/10/18
ATTREE, A., C., L.-Cpl., 22 Bn. 15/9/16
ATTWATER, C., Sgt., 17 Bn. .. 15/9/16
AUSTIN, G. A., Pte., 22 Bn. .. 4/8/18
AUSTIN, P. W., Rfn., 21 Bn... 16/9/18
AUSTIN, W. H., Sgt., 236 Bde.,
  R.F.A. 15/9/16
AUTEY, H. A., Pte., 15 Bn. .. 25/12/17
*AVRAMACHIS, V., Cpl., 24 Bn. 7/10/16
AXFORD, E. W., Pte., 15 Bn. ..19/10/16
AYRES, F., Pte., 23 Bn., att.
  142 M.G. Co. 20/6/17
BACHELL, G. T., L.-Cpl., 15 Bn. 19/10/16
*BACON, C. W. C., L.-Cpl., 7 Bn. 7/10/16
BAILEY, C. V., Dvr., 520 Fd.
  Co. 15/9/16
BAILEY, W., Pte., 4 R.W.F... 3/6/19
BAILEY, W. C., Cpl., 8 Bn. .. 24/6/17

BAILY, C. H., L.-Cpl., 24 Bn. 15/9/16
BAINES, R. J., Pte., 15 Bn. .. 28/12/17
BAKER, A., L.-Cpl., 7 Bn. .. 24/6/17
BAKER, A. A., Pte., 24 Bn. .. 29/10/16
BAKER, E., Cpl., 6 Bn. .. 3/10/16
BAKER, E., Sgt., 21 Bn. .. 13/9/16
BAKER, F. L., Rfn., 6 Bn. .. 6/3/17
BAKER, H. A., Cpl., 7 Bn. .. 21/7/17
BAKER, N. L., Pte., 24 Bn. .. 11/10/18
BAKER, S., Cpl., 236 Bde.,
  R.F.A. 15/9/16
BAKER, W. R., Pte., 6 Lon. Fd.
  Amb. 18/12/17
BALDICK, R. N., Sgt., 17 Bn. 15/9/16
BALDREY, W., Sgt., 18 Bn. .. 3/6/16
BALDWIN, W., Sgt., 24 Bn. .. 8/6/16
BALL, C., L.-Cpl., 22 Bn. .. 10/10/16
BALLANTINE,W. E., Rfn., 8 Bn. 3/6/16
BALLARD, F., Gnr., 235 Bde.,
  R.F.A. 20/5/18
BALSTER, A. G., L.-Cpl., 17 Bn. 19/9/18
BAND, H., Pte., 20 Bn. .. 5/10/18
BANKS, E., Pte., R.A.M.C., att.
  4 Lon. Fd. Co. R.E. .. 7/7/16
BANKS, H., Sgt., 18 Bn. .. 15/9/16
BANTING, G. E., Sgt., 24 Bn. 14/11/17
BARBER, H. S., Rfn., 8 Bn. .. 15/9/16
BARCLAY, G., Pte., 7 Bn. .. 15/9/16
BARCLAY, G., Pte., 19 Bn. .. 27/10/18
BARCLAY, J., Pte., M.G. Bn... 30/4/18
BARDEY, R., Dvr., 235 Bde.,
  R.F.A. 10/10/16
BARKER, F. R., Sgt., 21 Bn... 16/9/18
BARKER, H., Rfn., 17 Bn. .. 7/10/18
BARKER, H. W., Pte., 24 Bn... 21/4/18
BARKER, J., Spr., N. Mid. Div.
  R.E., att. 520 Fd. Co. .. 15/12/17
BARKER, J. W., S.-Sgt., 5 Lon.
  Fd. Amb. 15/9/16
BARKER, L., Sgt., 20 Bn. .. 15/9/16
*BARKHAM, G. H., Sgt., 18 Bn. 22/4/17
BARKWORTH, S. T., L.-Cpl.,
  20 Bn. 16/6/16
BARNARD, B., L.-Cpl., 20 Bn. 23/6/17
BARNES, A. J., Sgt., 17 Bn. .. 15/9/16
BARNES, D. S., Rfn., 21 Bn... 20/6/17
BARNES, W., Cpl., 140 M.G.
  Co. 24/6/17
BARRATT, A. A., L.-Cpl., 22 Bn. 21/10/18
BARRELL, R. J., Pte., 20 Bn. 30/12/17
BARRETT, R. W., Sgt., 18 3n. 3/6/16
BARROW, L., L.-Cpl., 23 Bn... 16/6/17
BARTLETT, B. M., Cpl., 23 Bn. 29/12/17
BARTLETT, H., L.-Cpl., 20 Bn. 27/7/16
BARTLETT, W.E., Pte., 20 Bn.,
  att. Div. Obs. 19/9/18
BARTON, A. H., Cpl., 20 Bn... 15/9/16
BATEMAN, F.A., L.-Cpl., 22 Bn. 18/6/17

BATEMAN, T., Pte., 4 R.W.F. 30/4/18
BATES, S., Sgt., 17 Bn. .. 15/9/16
BATHURST, S. E., Sgt., 24 Bn. 28/10/16
BATTY, J., Pte., 20 Bn. .. 2/10/16
BAXTER, A., L.-Cpl., 6 Bn. .. 2/10/16
BAXTER, H. J., L.-Cpl., 142 M.G. Co. 16/4/17
*BAYLEY, G., Sgt., 19 Bn. .. 3/6/16
BAYLIE, F., 2nd Cpl., 47 Div. Sig. Co., R.E. 3/6/19
BAYNTON, A. W., Sgt., 22 Bn. 20/12/17
BAYTON, H. T., Pte., 22 Bn... 20/5/18
BEADLE, C. W., Pte., 15 Bn... 15/9/16
BEANEY, E., Cpl., Y/47 T.M.B. 9/7/16
BEAR, H. D., L.-Cpl., 17 Bn... 7/10/18
BEASLEY, R. J. B., L.-Cpl., 15 Bn. 15/9/16
BEAVINS, S., Pte., 23 Bn. .. 7/10/18
BECKWITH, E., Pte., 24 Bn... 11/10/18
BEDDOES, A. G., Rfn., 17 Bn. 27/10/17
BEER, G. R., L.-Cpl., 518 Lon. Fd. Co., R.E. 23/6/17
BEESELEY, J., Rfn., 17 Bn... 16/6/16
BELCHER, J., L.-Cpl., 19 Bn. 31/5/17
BELCHER, S., Sgt., 237 Bde., R.F.A. 15/9/16
BELL, G., Sgt., 8 Bn... .. 15/9/16
BELLINGER, A. E., Dvr., 22 Bn. 10/10/16
BELLINGHAM, F. S., L.-Cpl., 15 Bn. 28/8/17
*BELLISS, T., Cpl., 520 Fd. Co., R.E... .. .. 19/5/16
*BELTRAM, J., Sgt., 517 Fd. Co., R.E... .. .. 22/4/17
BENN, W., Pte., 22 Bn. .. 8/6/16
BENNETT, P., Pte., 24 Bn. .. 11/10/18
BENNISON, A., Pte., 22 Bn... 7/10/18
BENSTEAD, A. J., Pte., 23 Bn. 6/11/18
BENTLEY, A. E., Rfn., 17 Bn. 13/5/17
BENTLEY, W., Pte., 142 M.G. Co. 20/6/17
BERRY, W. E., L.-Cpl., 517 Fd. Co., R.E. 23/6/17
BEST, C. H., Sgt., 18 Bn. .. 5/10/18
BEST, S., Sgt., 23 Bn... .. 21/11/17
BETHEL, F. E., Gnr., 235 Bde., R.F.A. 16/7/17
BETTS, W. C., Pte., 7 Bn. 19/10/16
BILLINGS, G., Rfn., 21 Bn. .. 27/11/18
BILLINGTON, H., Bdr., 235 Bde., R.F.A. 23/6/17
BINDON, W., Pte., 22 Bn. .. 4/8/18
BINYON, H. C., Rfn., 17 Bn... 7/10/18
BIRD, C., L.-Sgt., 20 Bn. .. 15/9/16
BIRD, J., Pte., 24 Bn... .. 21/4/18
BISHOP, C. H., Cpl., 15 Bn. 7/10/16
BITTON, B., Sgt., 6 Bn. .. 2/10/16
BLACK, J., Sgt., 235 Bde., R.F.A. ,, ,, .. 20/5/18

BLACKSTAFFE, W. P., Sgt., Sig. Co. 11/10/18
BLACKWOOD, A. E., Pte., 24 Bn. 11/10/18
BLAKE, E. W., L.-Cpl., E. Kent R., att. 142 Bde. 7/10/18
BLAKE, H. J., Sgt., A.V.C., att. 235 Bde., R.F.A. 19/11/18
BLANCHFLOWER, V. G., Rfn., 21 Bd. 19/9/18
BLAND, H. R., Sgt., 23 Bn. .. 15/9/16
BLISS, W. C., Sgt., 8 Bn. .. 3/6/16
BLOOD, G. W., Rfn., 21 Bn. .. 25/4/18
BLOWS, C., Rfn., 17 Bn. .. 2/10/16
BLOXAM, L. W., 24 Bn., att. 142 Bde. H.Q. 21/4/18
BOAST, A., Pte., 5 Lon. Fd. Amb. 28/12/17
BODDY, H. L., Rfn., 21 Bn... 3/6/16
BOND, L. E., Rfn., 6 Bn. .. 15/9/16
BOOL, V. C., Pte., 20 Bn. .. 23/6/17
BORDER, A. H., Rfn., 17 Bd. 23/6/17
BORLEY, E. A., Sgt., 24 Bn... 21/6/17
BOSHER, W. H., Pte., 23 Bn. 16/6/17
BOTT, G. A., Pte., 15 Bn. .. 16/9/18
*BOUGHTON, A., Sgt., 21 Bn... 7/10/18
BOULT, A. F., Sgt., 21 Bn. .. 29/10/16
BOUCHER, A. G., Sgt., 24 Bn. 15/9/16
*BOWERS, C. C., Sgt., 7 Bn. .. 10/4/17
BOWLES, W. G., L.-Cpl., 18 Bn. 5/10/18
BOWMAN, C. J., Sgt., 8 Bn. .. 15/9/16
*BOWMAN, H. E., Sgt., 15 Bn. 28/12/17
BOWMAN, W., Pte., 24 Bn. .. 21/6/17
BOWN, H. G., S.S.M., Div. Tr. 12/12/17
BOYCE, E. A., Sgt., 17 Bn. .. 7/10/18
BOYCE, E. T., Bdr., 236 Bde., R.F.A. 11/12/18
BOYDEN, G. T., Dvr., 236 Bde., R.F.A. 2/7/17
BRABNER, J. H., Cpl., D.A.C. 30/3/17
BRACE, J., Spr., Sig. Co. .. 2/10/16
BRADFORD, M. E., Pte., 15 Bn. 19/10/16
BRADLEY, A. F., Pte., 15 Bn. 7/10/18
BRADLEY, W., Sgt., 236 Bde., R.F.A. 2/7/17
BRADSHAW, A., Pte., 5 Lon. Fd. Amb. 15/9/16
BRADSHAW, D. G., L.-Cpl., 15 Bn. 28/12/17
BRAND, E. L., C.Q.M.S., 8 Bn. 3/6/16
BRANDUM, H., Rfn., 17 Bn. .. 23/6/17
BRANNIGAN, W., L.-Cpl., 18 Bn. 22/4/17
BRAYDON, S. R., Pte., 24 Bn. 7/10/16
BRECKON, H. W., Pte., 15 Bn., att. 140 M.G. Co. 24/6/17
BREEN, J. A., Sgt., 22 Bn. .. 8/6/16
BREESE, A. E., L.-Cpl., 18 Bn. 13/11/18
BREEZE, H. R., Pte., 24 Bn... 5/10/18
BRENNAN, F., L.-Cpl., 24 Bn. 28/12/17
BRESSY, S. H., L.-Cpl., 15 Bn. 2/6/16

BRETT, C. H., Gnr., 236 Bde.,
R.F.A. 2/7/17
BRETT, C. J., Pte., 6 Bn.   .. 6/3/17
*BRETTELL, C. W., Sgt., 236
Bde., R.F.A. 12/10/16
*BRIDGEN, H. E., L.-Cpl., Sig.
Co. 23/6/17
BRIDGES, S. C., L.-Cpl., 23 Bn.,
att. 142 T.M.B. 6/3/17
BRIGGS, G. K., Pte., 23 Bn... 28/12/17
BRISTOWE,S.H., L.-Cpl., 22 Bn. 18/6/17
BROCKWELL, A. P., L.-Cpl., 8
Bn. 7/10/16
BROMFIELD, S., Pte., 23 Bn... 6/11/18
BROOKES, F. C., Pte., 19 Bn. 5/10/18
BROOKS, A., Pte., 24 Bn.   .. 21/6/17
BROOKS, A. W., Pte., 23 Bn... 5/10/18
*BROOKS, F. G., Cpl., 7 Bn.   .. 1/10/17
BROOKS, T. R., Sgt., 140 M.G.
Co. 7/10/16
BROOME, H., Pte., 19 Bn.   .. 15/9/16
BROWN, B. R., Cpl., 21 Bn... 29/10/16
BROWN, C. J., Sgt., 6 Bn.   .. 25/12/17
BROWN, E., Dvr., D.A.C.   .. 30/3/17
BROWN, E. W., L.-Cpl., M.G.
Bn. 7/10/18
BROWN, F., Pte., 15 Bn.   .. 28/12/17
BROWN, G. L., Sgt., 15 Bn.   .. 7/10/18
BROWN, W., Sgt., 18 Bn.   .. 26/12/17
BROWN, W. Y., Rfn., 21 Bn... 19/9/18
BROWNING, F. E., Sgt., 15 Bn. 28/12/17
BROWNING, W. G., Pte., 7 Bn. 25/12/17
BROWNSALL, A., Pte., 7 Bn... 19/10/16
BRYANT, A., Sgt., 20 Bn.   .. 27/7/16
BRYCESON, T. G., Sgt., 235
Bde., R.F.A. 20/11/16
BUCK, C. A. S., Rfn., 18 Bn... 2/10/16
BUCKLEY, G. J., Pte., 24 Bn. 7/10/16
BUCKLEY, J. R., Pte., 4 Lon.
Fd. Amb. 7/10/18
BUFFIN, T., Rfn., 6 Bn.   .. 2/10/16
BULCRAIG,F. J., L.-Cpl., 23 Bn. 15/9/16
BULLARD, S. A., Pte., 19 Bn. 20/7/17
BULLOCK, C. F., Pte., 15 Bn... 28/6/17
BULLOCK, F., Rfn., 6 Bn.   .. 8/6/17
BULTER, A., Sgt., 23 Bn.   .. 19/9/18
BUNN, H. C., L.-Cpl., 20 Bn... 2/10/16
BUNN, H. C., Cpl., 21 Bn.   .. 15/9/16
BUNNAGE, E. A., Pte., 22 Bn. 18/6/17
BURDEN, S., Sgt., 7 Bn.   .. 7/10/16
BURGESS, A., Rfn., 21 Bn.   .. 29/10/16
*BURLEY, W. G., Sgt., 21 Bn... 20/2/18
BURNELL, R. H., Cpl., Div.
Train 22/4/18
BURNS, V., L.-Cpl., 20 Bn.   .. 27/10/16
BURROUGHS, J., Cpl., 17 Bn... 16/9/18
BURROWS, F., Gnr., 235 Bde.,
R.F.A. 20/11/16
BURTENSHAW, H. F., Bdr.,
D.A.C., att. X/47 T.M.B. .. 8/3/17

BURVILLE, C., Rfn., 6 Bn.   .. 24/6/17
BUSBY, L. J., Cpl., 6 Bn.   .. 24/6/17
BUSHELL, W., L.-Cpl., 5 Lon.
Fd. Amb. 15/9/16
BUTCHER, H., Cpl., 17 Bn.   .. 7/10/18
*BUTLER, A. L., Sgt., 19 Bn... 21/11/17
BUTLER, R., Cpl., 237 Bde.,
R.F.A. 15/9/16
BUTLER, R., Cpl., 21 Bn., att.
142 M.G. Co. 11/6/16
BUTT, G., Pte., 24 Bn.   .. 11/10/18
BYART, A. G., Pte., 22 Bn.   .. 19/9/18
BYOTT, G. V., Pte., 22 Bn.   .. 7/10/18
CABLE, C., Cpl., 24 Bn.   .. 5/10/18
CADDICK, J. H., L.-Cpl., 6 Bn. 24/6/17
CAMP, G., Pte., 22 Bn.   .. 15/9/16
CAMP, G. F., Sgt., 20 Bn.   .. 5/10/18
CAMPBELL, H. E., Pte., 24 Bn. 29/10/16
CAMPBELL, W. P., L.-Cpl., 21
Bn. 16/9/18
CAMPKIN, D., Pte., 24 Bn.   .. 11/10/18
CANNON, T. G., L.-Cpl., 22 Bn. 4/8/17
CANTLE, J. C., Cpl., 24 Bn.   .. 6/9/17
CAPELL, R., L.-Cpl., 6 Lon. Fd.
Amb. 15/9/16
CAPON, E., Rfn., 6 Bn.   .. 2/10/16
CARD, E., L.-Cpl., 24 Bn.   .. 2/3/18
CARDEN, H., Pte., 24 Bn.   .. 21/6/17
CARE, C., Pte., 23 Bn.   .. 7/10/18
CARPENTER, A., Sgt., 5 Lon.
Bde., R.F.A. 15/9/16
CARPENTER, F. H., Pte., 24 Bn. 21/6/17
CARROLL, R., Cpl., 18 Bn.   .. 27/10/18
CARROLL, W. G., Sgt., 5 Lon.
Fd. Amb. 15/9/16
CARSWELL, H., Bdr., 235 Bde.,
R.F.A. 11/5/17
CARTER, C., Pte., 19 Bn.   .. 19/10/16
CARTER, E., Pte., M.G. Bn. .. 16/9/18
CARTER, J. T., Gnr. 236 Bde.,
R.F.A. 10/10/16
CARTER, R., Sgt., 236 Bde.,
R.F.A. 2/7/17
CARTMAN, A. P., Pte., 22 Bn. 7/7/18
CARTWRIGHT, F. G., Sgt., 4
R.W.F. 29/12/17
CARVER, P., Sgt., 22 Bn.   .. 19/9/18
CASLAW, J. McC., L.-Cpl., 24
Bn. 5/10/18
CATNER, A., L.-Cpl., 23 Bn... 21/4/18
CAUGHLIN, T. L., Sgt., 8 Bn... 28/12/17
CAVE, C., L.-Cpl., Div. Cyc.
Co. 15/9/16
CHALK, F., Pte., 7 Bn.   .. 24/6/17
CHALLIS, F., Rfn., 18 Bn.   .. 29/10/16
CHALMERS, W., Dvr., 235 Bde.,
R.F.A. 6/12/18
CHAMBERS, A. E., Sgt., 4
R.W.F. 28/12/17
CHAMBERS, F., Sgt., 22 Bn.   .. 20/12/17

CROSS, A., Bdr., 236 Bde.,
R.F.A. 14/10/17
CROSS, N. H., Rfn., 17 Bn. .. 16/9/18
CROSSLEY, W. G., Pte., 15 Bn.,
att. 140 T.M.B. 15/5/16
CROW, F. D., Rfn., 8 Bn. .. 31/6/17
CROYDON,W.G., L.-Cpl., 24 Bn. 21/6/17
CRUDGINGTON,G.,L.-Cpl., 7 Bn. 28/12/17
CRYSTAL, H. A., Bdr., 236 Bde.,
R.F.A. 2/7/17
CULLEN, J. W., Sgt., 18 Bn... 20/8/19
CURRIE, J. E. T., Sgt., 1/3 Fd.
Co. 15/9/16
CURWEN, A., Pte., 19 Bn. .. 1/9/17
CUSHING, F., Pte., 23 Bn. .. 21/4/18
CUTLER, S., L.-Cpl., 24 Bn... 14/11/17
CUTTING, R., Pte., 23 Bn. .. 28/6/17
CUTTS, E. T., Pte., 15 Bn. .. 1/1/18
DAGLEAS, J. A., Gnr., 235 Bde.,
R.F.A. 7/5/18
DAINTY, J., L.-Cpl., 22 Bn. .. 22/4/18
DALE, J. W., Bdr., 236 Bde.,
R.F.A. 2/7/17
DALEY, W., Spr., Sig. Co. .. 11/10/18
DANCE, T. W., Rfn., 17 Bn... 7/10/18
DANN, E. C., Sgt., 18 Bn. .. 29/4/17
DANN, E. J., Rfn., 21 Bn. .. 16/9/18
DANN, F., C.Q.M.S., 22 Bn... 15/9/16
DARE, S., Bdr., 236 Bde.,
R.F.A. 2/7/17
D'ARCY, J., Dvr., Div. Train.. 15/9/16
DARMODY,J.F., L.-Cpl., 15 Bn. 7/10/18
DARVELL, G., L.-Cpl., 17 Bn. 24/12/17
DAVEY, J. T., Gnr., D.A.C... 3/7/17
DAVEY, W. H., Cpl., 7 Bn. .. 24/6/17
DAVEY, W. L., Pte., 24 Bn... 16/6/17
DAVIES, C., L.-Cpl., 21 Bn. .. 29/10/16
DAVIES, J., Sgt., 4 R.W.F. .. 10/10/16
DAVIES, J. H., Sgt., 24 Bn. .. 21/6/17
DAVIES, R., Pte., 4 R.W.F... 28/12/17
*DAVIES, S., Sgt., 4 R.W.F. .. 1/1/18
*DAVIES, T., Sgt., 4 R.W.F. .. 30/4/18
DAVIES, T. H., Pte., 4 R.W.F. 30/4/18
DAVIES, W. L., Pte., 23 Bn... 2/10/16
DAVIES, W. R., Sgt., 4 R.W.F. 2/10/16
DAVIES, A. G., Gnr., 237 Bde.,
R.F.A. 7/10/16
DAVIS, A. T., Cpl., 141 M.G.
Co. 2/10/16
DAVIS, F., Pte., 24 Bn. .. 7/10/16
DAVIS, H., Sgt., Div. Train.. 28/7/17
DAVIS, H. W., Sgt., 17 Bn. .. 7/10/16
DAVIS, W. E., L.-Cpl., 15 Bn. 25/12/17
DAWKINS, A. J., L.-Cpl., E.
Surrey Regt., att. 23 Bn. .. 6/11/18
DAWSON, A., Sgt., M.G. Bn... 16/9/18
DAWSON, E. S., L.-Cpl., 21 Bn. 15/9/16
DAWSON, V. L., Pte., 15 Bn... 16/9/18
DAY, J. A., L.-Cpl., 23 Bn. .. 14/11/17
DAY, P., Rfn., 18 Bn... .. 24/12/17

DEAN, A., Pte., 6 Lon. Fd.
Amb. 11/6/16
DEATH, R. A., S-Sgt., A.S.C.,
Div. H.Q. 15/9/16
DEE, T. H., L.-Cpl., 18 Bn., att.
141 T.M.B. 22/4/17
DEERE, H. E., Pte., 5 Lon. Fd.
Amb. 21/12/17
DENNINGS, C., Sgt., 20 Bn. .. 15/9/16
DENNIS, E. F., Pte., 4 Lon. Fd.
Amb. 29/10/16
DENYER, B., Cpl., 17 Bn. .. 24/12/17
DEW, A., Cpl., 17 Bn... .. 7/10/18
DEW, F. G., Sgt., 21 Bn. .. 15/9/16
DEW, G. R., Pte., 23 Bn. .. 19/9/18
DEWAR, W., Sgt., 237 Bde.,
R.F.A. 15/9/16
DICK, J., Pte., E. Surrey Regt.,
att. 23 Bn. 7/10/18
DICKENS, G. R., L.-Cpl., 7 Bn. 7/10/16
DICKER, F., L.-Cpl., 18 Bn... 3/1/18
DICKESON, F. R., Pte., 6 Lon.
Fd. Amb. 2/8/17
DICKS, F. R. J., Pte., 23 Bn... 2/10/16
DICKSON, W. D., Cpl., 17 Bn. 24/12/17
DIFFORD, G. St. J., Pte., 23 B. 16/6/17
DILLEY, W., Pte., 7 Bn. .. 24/6/17
DINGLEY, J., 2nd Cpl., 518 Fd.
Co. 23/6/17
DIPROSE, G., L.-Cpl., 142 M.G.
Co. 26/6/17
DIPROSE, E. F., L.-Cpl., 23 Bn. 16/6/17
DIXON, A. E., C.Q.M.S., 24 Bn. 15/9/16
DIXON, A. W., Rfn., 8 Bn. .. 24/6/17
DIXON, W., Spr., 1/3 Lon. Fd.
Co. 15/9/16
DOCK, J. J., L.-Cpl., 6 Bn. .. 24/6/17
DOHERTY, M., Pte., 22 Bn. .. 22/4/18
DOHERTY, P., Sgt., 17 Bn. .. 25/4/18
DONALD, A. D., Cpl., 15 Bn... 18/11/18
DONOVAN, P., Sgt., 21 Bn. .. 29/10/16
DOONAN, J., Rfn., 18 Bn. .. 22/4/17
DORMAND, E. H., Rfn., 18 Bn. 22/4/17
DOUGLAS, A., Pte., 4 Lon. Fd.
Amb. 28/12/17
DOULT, W. H., L.-Cpl., 22 Bn. 29/10/16
DOVE, J. A., Rfn., 6 Bn. .. 6/8/17
DOWNES, D., Rfn., 17 Bn. .. 7/10/16
DOWNS, G. H., Pte., 7 Bn. .. 28/12/17
DOWNWARD, A., Cpl., M.G. Bn. 7/10/18
DOWSETT, W. J., Sgt., 22 Bn. 20/8/19
DOYLE, F., Pte., 19 Bn. .. 2/10/16
DOYLE-THOMAS, R. S. E., Rfn.,
18 Bn. 24/12/17
DREWE, W. H., C.S.M., 20 Bn. 5/10/18
DREWETT,W.R., C.S.M., 22 Bn. 15/9/16
DRURY, R., L.-Cpl., 142 M.G.
Co. 20/6/17
DUCK, H., Sgt., 7 Bn... .. 8/6/16
DUCKMAN, H. W., Pte., 22 Bn. 10/10/16

DUDGEON, A. P., Pte., 6 Lon.
Fd. Amb. 19/9/18
DUGUID, C. D., Sgt., 17 Bn... 15/9/16
DUNMOW, S. J., L.-Cpl., 17 Bn. 15/9/16
DUNN, L., Sgt., 140 M.G. Co. 25/12/17
*DUNN, W. J., Sgt., 23 Bn. .. 7/10/18
DUNSTER, H., Rfn., 21 Bn. .. 15/9/16
DUNSTER, W., Sgt., 22 Bn. .. 8/6/16
DURBRIDGE, W. E., Cpl., 24 Bn. 11/10/18
DUTHIE, F. W., Pnr., Sig. Co. 26/9/17
DYER, D. M., Pte., 15 Bn., att.
140 Bde. H.Q. 19/9/18
DYER, J. W., Rfn., 21 Bn. .. 19/9/18
EAREY, J. W., Spr., 517 Fd.
Co. 23/4/18
EASTWOOD, W. J., L.-Cpl., 21
Bn., att. 142 T.M.B. .. 6/3/17
EATON, R. C. G., Gnr., 236
Bde., R.F.A. 2/7/17
EDEN, E., Sgt., 21 Bn. .. 7/10/18
EDGLEY, E. E., Pte., 15 Bn... 15/9/16
EDMONDS, B., L.-Cpl., 22 Bn. 29/10/16
EDMONDS, G. W., Rfn., 18 Bn. 7/7/16
EDNEY, H., Pte., E. Surrey
Regt., att. 23 Bn. 19/9/18
EDWARDS, E. W., Cpl., 22 Bn. 19/9/18
EDWARDS, F. J., Sgt., 238 Bde.,
R.F.A. 15/9/16
EDWARDS, G. E., Sgt., 7 Bn... 28/12/17
EDWARDS, H. C., Rfn., 8 Bn. 24/6/17
EDWARDS, J. C., Rfn., 8 Bn... 25/12/17
EDWARDS, L. D., Pte., 15 Bn. 7/10/18
EDWARDS, T. G., Sgt., 4 R.W.F. 12/6/17
EDWARDS, W., Pte., 7 Bn. .. 7/10/16
ELDRIDGE, P., Dvr., 7 Bde.,
R.F.A. 15/9/16
ELLIOTT, J., Gnr., Y/47 T.M.B. 9/7/16
ELLIS, G., Sgt., 4 R.W.F. .. 28/12/17
ELLIS, H. E., Pte., 23 Bn. .. 7/10/18
*ELLIS, W., C.S.M., 4 R.W.F... 16/9/18
ELLWOOD, F., Pte., 5 Lon. Fd.
Amb. 19/9/18
ELMORE, J., Rfn., 18 Bn. .. 30/4/18
ELSEY, W. G., Rfn., 17 Bn. .. 25/4/18
EMERY, W. J., Pte., 24 Bn. .. 5/10/18
EMLER, H. J., L.-Cpl., 15 Bn. 7/10/16
ERRINGTON, T., Pte., 22 Bn... 29/10/16
ESTHILL, C. F., Cpl., 18 Bn... 1/7/17
ETHERIDGE, E. T., Pte., M.G.
Bn. 16/9/18
EVANS, D., Gnr., X/47 T.M.B. 19/5/16
EVANS, E., Rfn., 8 Bn. .. 15/9/16
EVANS, F., Cpl., 5 Lon. Fd.
Amb. 11/6/16
EVANS, F., Rfn., 18 Bn. .. 7/10/16
EVANS, W. O., Sgt., 4 R.W.F. 19/5/16
EVERED, W., Cpl., M.G. Bn... 5/10/18
EVERETT, E. A., Pte., 24 Bn. 8/6/16
EVERETT, G. A., Cpl., 24 Bn. 3/12/18
EYDEN, E., Pte., 24 Bn. .. 7/10/16

FAIRMAN, C. D., Pte., 7 Bn... 28/12/17
FAITHFUL, L., Rfn., 21 Bn. .. 20/6/17
FARMER, R. E., Sgt., 23 Bn... 20/8/19
*FAVELL, H., Sgt., 22 Bn. .. 18/6/17
FAWCETT, H., Gnr., 238 Bde.,
R.F.A. 12/10/16
FAYERS, S., L.-Cpl., 23 Bn. .. 16/6/17
FEARNLEY, L., Pte., 20 Bn. .. 23/6/17
FEESEY, R. W., Sgt., 15 Bn... 28/12/17
FENWICK, A. V., L.-Cpl., 8 Bn. 19/6/16
FERGUSON, D., Pte., 142 M.G.
Co. 16/4/17
FERGUSON, J., Cpl., 24 Bn. .. 11/10/18
FERRIS, B. T., L.-Cpl., 7 Bn.,
att. 140 T.M.B. 15/5/16
FEWSTER, A. L., Pte., 15 Bn. 17/9/18
FIELD, F., Rfn., 17 Bn. .. 30/9/17
FINCH, R. C., Pte., M.T. Co.,
A.S.C. 13/11/18
FINLAYSON, D. A., Sgt., 4 Fd.
Co., R.E. 15/9/16
FINNIS, A. A., Gnr., 238 Bde.,
R.F.A. 15/9/16
FIRMAGER, T., L.-Cpl., 23 Bn. 6/11/18
*FIRNEE, H., Sgt., 8 Bn. .. 7/10/16
FITZGERALD, H. B., L.-Cpl.,
23 Bn. 16/7/17
FIVEASH, H. G., Sgt., 5 Lon.
Fd. Amb. 19/9/18
FLANGAN, L., Pte., 15 Bn. .. 2/6/16
FLANAGHAN, T., Sgt., Y/47
T.M.B. 23/6/17
FLETCHER, F., L.-Cpl., 20 Bn. 23/6/17
FLETCHER, J. R., Pte., 23 Bn. 19/9/18
*FLETCHER, S., L.-Cpl., 15 Bn. 25/12/17
FLIGHT, A. B., Pte., 15 Bn... 7/10/18
FLINN, B. B., Cpl., 20 Bn. .. 27/10/18
FOLDS, C. E., Pte., 15 Bn., att.
140 Bde. H.Q. 19/9/18
FOORD, N., Pte., 4 Lon. Fd.
Amb. 28/12/17
FOREMAN, W., Rfn., 21 Bn... 8/9/18
FORREST, R., Rfn., 17 Bn. .. 7/10/18
FOSTER, C. C., Pte., 7 Bn. .. 26/9/17
FOSTER, H., Pte., 15 Bn. .. 15/9/16
FOUCHEAU, A., Pte., 22 Bn... 19/9/18
FOWLER, G., Gnr., 235 Bde.,
R.F.A. 15/8/17
FOWLER, G. E., Sgt., 15 Bn... 28/6/17
FRANCIS, R. G., Sgt., 18 Bn... 5/10/18
*FRANCIS, W. H., Rfn., 17 Bn. 7/10/18
FRANKS, A. H., Rfn., 17 Bn... 24/12/17
FREEMAN, G. D., Rfn., 17 Bn. 7/10/18
FREEMAN, H. E., L.-Cpl., 6 Bn. 2/10/16
FREEMAN, S., Sgt., 236 Bde.,
R.F.A. 20/8/19
FREY, W. J., Cpl., 18 Bn., att.
141 M.G. Co. 3/6/16
FRIEND, A., Rfn., 21 Bn. .. 7/10/18
FRIEND, H. E., L.-Cpl., 24 Bn. 7/10/16

FROST, W. E., Rfn., 17 Bn... 24/10/16
FRY, T. J., Sgt., 8 Bn.   .. 3/6/16
FRY, T. P., Sgt., 21 Bn.   .. 3/6/16
FULLER, C. E., L.-Cpl., 7 Bn. 27/10/16
FULLER, H. O., Pte., 24 Bn... 5/10/18
FURNIVAL, L. S., Bdr., 235
    Bde., R.F.A. 10/10/16
GADD, C., Pte., 7 Bn...   .. 10/4/17
GADSBY, J., Pte., 142 M.G. Co. 24/5/17
GALEN, J. J., Cpl., 15 Bn. .. 7/10/18
GALLANT, N., Sgt., 15 Bn. .. 25/12/17
GANDELL, W. E., Rfn., 8 Bn. 7/10/16
GARDNER, P. W., L.-Cpl., 5 Lon.
    Fd. Amb. 7/10/18
GARNER, W. J., L.-Cpl., 15 Bn. 19/10/16
GARNHAM, G. T., Sgt., 17 Bn. 15/9/16
GARNHAM, J. W., L.-Cpl., 24
    Bn. 20/12/17
GARRETT, F., Cpl. 17 Bn. .. 16/9/18
GARRETT, J., L.-Cpl., 18 Bn... 19/10/16
GARROD, W. G., Sgt., 6 Bn... 6/3/17
GATER, E., Spr., 520 Fd. Co... 23/6/17
GAY, G., L.-Cpl., 23 Bn. .. 29/12/17
GENTRY, E. Q., Spr., 520 Fd.
    Co. 11/6/16
GEORGE, A., Rfn., 18 Bn. .. 5/10/18
GEORGE, W. R., Pte., 22 Bn. 27/10/18
GIBBONS, J. S., Cpl., Z/47
    T.M.B. 23/6/17
GIBBONS, S., Cpl., 18 Bn. .. 22/4/17
GIBBONS, W. C., Sgt., 20 Bn. 23/6/17
GIBBS, H., Sgt., 4 Lon. Fd.
    Amb. 18/12/17
GIBBS, W. B., L.-Cpl., M.G.
    Bn. 16/9/18
GIBSON, F. W., L.-Cpl., 18 Bn. 3/6/16
GILBERT, J., Sgt., 24 Bn. .. 15/9/16
GILES, A. E., Sgt., 20 Bn. .. 29/10/16
GILES, H., Sgt., 23 Bn. .. 21/4/18
GILL, H. V., Pte., 7 Bn. .. 7/10/16
GIRLING, H. W., Cpl., 6 Bn... 24/6/17
GODFREY, J. A., Cpl., 517 Fd.
    Co. 18/11/18
GOLD, A., Rfn., 6 Bn...   .. 24/6/17
GOLD, F. J., L.-Cpl., 4 Lon. Fd.
    Amb. 6/8/17
GOLDSMITH, B., Sgt., 21 Bn... 2/10/16
GOODE, J. E., Sgt., 6 Bn. .. 6/3/17
GOODHEW, A. H., Pte., 4 Lon.
    Fd. Amb. 29/10/16
GOODING, D., Sgt., 15 Bn. .. 7/10/16
GOODMAN, T. J., Sgt., 520 Fd.
    Co. 23/6/17
GORDON, E. J., Pte., 7 Bn. .. 24/6/17
GORING, F. A., Sgt., 15 Bn. .. 4/5/18
GORMAN, F., Spr., 520 Fd. Co. 6/3/17
*GOSLIN, F. S., Sgt., 235 Bde.,
    R.F.A. 15/8/17
GOUGH, A. F., Gnr., 235 Bde.,
    R.F.A. 19/9/17

GOULD, W. A., Bdr., 235 Bde.,
    R.F.A. 20/5/18
GRANT, F. J., Rfn., 8 Bn. .. 7/10/16
GRANT, H. G., Rfn., 17 Bn... 16/9/18
*GRAY, A. S., R.S.M., Div. Engs.28/10/16
GRAY, W., Rfn., 17 Bn. .. 7/10/18
GRAY, A. S., Cpl., 23 Bn., att.
    142 M.G. Co. 15/9/16
GRAY, F., Sgt., 15 Bn. .. 29/10/16
GRAY, W. H., L.-Cpl., 6 Bn... 6/3/17
GREANEY, J., L.-Cpl., 22 Bn. 18/6/17
GREEN, G., L.-Cpl., 22 Bn. .. 29/10/16
GREEN, H. A., Pte., M.G. Bn. 7/10/18
GREEN, H. R., Sgt., 6 Bn. .. 15/9/16
GREEN, M. E., Sgt., 24 Bn. .. 14/11/17
GREEN, S., Pnr., Sig. Co. .. 24/12/17
GREENFIELD, B., Bdr., 235
    Bde., R.F.A. 20/5/18
GREENSLADE, W. W., Cpl., 6
    Bn. 25/12/17
GREIG, T. P., L.-Cpl., 15 Bn... 28/2/18
GRIBBLE, W. C., Spr., 520 Fd.
    Co. 15/9/16
GRIFFIN, E. T., Pte., 7 Bn. .. 1/10/16
GRIFFITHS, D., Pte., R.W.F... 18/11/18
GRIFFITHS, H. T., L.-Cpl., 24 B. 21/6/17
GRIMSEY, R. F., L.-Cpl., 24 B. 14/11/17
GRIMSHAW, G. E., 2nd Cpl.,
    Sig. Co. 1/5/18
GROHMANN, A., Sgt., 23 Bn... 28/12/17
GULLICK, C. J., L.-Cpl., 6 Bn. 25/12/17
GURRY, A. C., Pte., 4 Lon. Fd.
    Amb. 7/10/18
GUSH, E. E., L.-Cpl., 21 Bn... 8/6/16
HAACKE, E. C., L.-Cpl., 6 Bn. 2/10/16
HAAGMANN, E., Rfn., 8 Bn... 28/12/17
HACKETT, J., L.-Cpl., 21 Bn... 15/9/16
HAGUE, P. S., Sgt., 15 Bn. .. 16/9/18
HAIGH, G., Spr., Elec. Engrs. 15/9/16
HALE, J., C.Q.M.S., 24 Bn. .. 20/12/17
HALES, A. C., Pte., 15 Bn. .. 19/10/16
HALES, C. H., L.-Cpl., 21 Bn. 19/5/16
HALL, F., Sgt., 6 Bn...   .. 15/9/16
HALL, F. G., Sgt., 6 Bn. .. 15/9/16
HALL, F. J., Sh. Smith, 238 Bde.,
    R.F.A. 9/6/16
HALL, M. W., L.-Cpl., 15 Bn. 2/6/16
HALL, V. C., Cpl., 24 Bn. .. 5/10/18
HALLAWAY, M., Pte., 4 Lon.
    Fd. Amb. 28/12/17
HALLETT, P., Rfn., 18 Bn. .. 13/11/18
HALLS, G., Pte., 7 Bn. .. 24/6/17
HALLS, W. J., Pte., 24 Bn. .. 7/10/16
HALLS, T., Bdr., H.Q.R.A. .. 15/9/16
HALTON, T., Cpl., 520 Fd. Co. 5/10/18
HAMMOND, E. C., Dvr., 4 Fd.
    Co. 15/9/16
HANCOCK, C., Sgt., 4 Lon. Fd.
    Amb. 29/10/16
HANCOCK, C. H., L.-Cpl., 22 Bn. 19/9/18

HANDLEY, W. A., Pte., 22 Bn. 7/10/18
HANDS, E., Rfn., 8 Bn. .. 13/7/16
*HANDS, W. C., L.-Cpl., 18 Bn. 3/6/16
HANKINS, E. C., Sgt., 17 Bn. 16/9/18
HANNA, C. H., L.-Cpl., 15 Bn. 25/12/17
HARDEN, J., Sgt., 19 Bn. .. 1/9/17
HARDY, L. J., Rfn., 17 Bn. .. 7/10/18
HARE, A. D. E. W., Sgt., 15 Bn. 15/9/16
HARLING, W. W., Pte.,
R.A.M.C., att. 235 Bde.,
R.F.A. 15/6/16
HARMAN, F., Rfn., 17 Bn. .. 19/10/16
HARMER, E., Sgt., 22 Bn. .. 15/9/16
HARMER, F. G., Sgt., 24 Bn.,
att. 142 T.M.B. 15/9/16
HARPER, E. C., Sgt., 18 Bn... 5/10/18
HARRINGTON, S., Pte., 23 Bn. 20/5/18
HARRINGTON, T. W., Pte., 24
Bn. 28/12/17
HARRIS, D., Rfn., 6 Bn. .. 6/3/17
HARRIS, J., Pte., 7 Bn. .. 24/6/17
HARRIS, R. A., Pte., R.W.F... 20/8/19
HARRIS, S., L.-Cpl., 19 Bn. .. 5/10/18
HARRIS, W. H., Pte., 15 Bn... 3/6/16
HARRISON, H. H., Pte., 19 Bn. 23/6/17
HARRISON, J., Gnr., 237 Bde.,
R.F.A. 7/10/16
HARRISON, M. J. J. C., Rfn., 17
Bn. 7/10/18
HARRISON, W. H., Gnr., 236
Bde., R.F.A. 15/9/16
HARROCKS, C. E., Sgt., 8 Bn... 28/12/17
HART, C. H., Pte., 24 Bn. .. 2/6/16
HART, S., L.-Cpl., 6 Bn. .. 2/10/16
HARTS, V., Pte., 20 Bn. .. 23/6/17
HARVEY, G., Gnr., Y/47
T.M.B. 14/1/16
HARYOTT, J. A. H., Cpl., 3 Lon.
Fd. Co. 2/10/16
HATT, T. E., Sgt., 18 Bn. .. 1/7/17
HAWKES, A. R., L.-Cpl., 17 Bn. 19/10/16
HAWKINS, C., Sgt., 19 Bn. .. 5/10/18
HAWKINS, T. H., Sgt., 6 Bn... 6/3/17
HAWKINS, W., Sgt., 23 Bn. .. 19/9/18
HAY, J. H., Cpl., X/47 T.M.B. 7/3/18
HAYCOCK, S. F., Sgt., 15 Bn. 3/11/16
HAYEMES,W.J., L.-Cpl., 24 Bn. 21/4/18
HAYES, A. E. J., Dvr., 236
Bde., R.F.A. 11/12/18
HAYES, H. J., Rfn., 8 Bn. .. 3/6/16
HAYES, W. A., Sgt., M.G. Bn. 16/9/18
HAYLEY, H., Cpl., X/47 T.M.B.16/10/18
HAYNES, G. E., Rfn., 18 Bn... 15/9/16
HAYSMAN, L., Pte., 22 Bn. .. 10/10/16
HAYWARD, C. R., Sgt., 8 Bn. 16/7/17
HAZELWOOD, A. W., Pte., 24
Bn., att. 142 T.M.B. .. 8/9/18
HAZLETT, F. C., Sgt., 236 Bde.,
R.F.A. 15/9/16
HEARD, H. E., Pte., 22 Bn... 20/12/17

HEARN, S., Pte., 15 Bn. .. 25/12/17
HEATH, G. H., Dvr., 235 Bde.,
R.F.A. 25/2/19
HENDERSON, G., Cpl., 21 Bn.,
att. 142 T.M.B. 15/9/16
HENDRY, H. O., L.-Cpl., 7 Bn. 7/10/16
HENINGTON, S., Spr., 520 Fd.
Co. 23/4/18
*HENRICK, E. A., Cpl., 24 Bn. 7/10/16
HERBERT, S. K., Pte., 5 Lon.
Fd. Amb. 19/9/18
HERLIKY, M., Pte., 24 Bn. .. 21/4/18
HERWIN, E., Pte., M.G. Bn... 21/10/18
HERYET, R., Pte., 20 Bn. .. 2/10/16
HESLEWOOD, A., Rfn., 21 Bn. 25/4/18
HEWITT, S. F., Pte., 22 Bn... 19/9/18
HEWSON, A. E., Rfn., 17 Bn... 16/7/17
HIBBERT, F., L.-Cpl., 19 Bn... 1/9/17
HICKEY, C. T., Sgt., M.G. Bn. 27/4/18
*HICKMAN, E. H., Cpl., Z/47
T.M.B. 15/6/16
HICKS, H. E., L.-Cpl., 15 Bn. 2/5/18
HIGGINS, J. L., Sgt., M.G. Bn. 30/4/18
HIGH, S. B., Sgt., 235 Bde.,
R.F.A. 20/11/16
HILES, J. H. A., Sgt., 22 Bn... 21/10/18
HILL, A. G., Cpl., 18 Bn. .. 26/6/17
HILL, E. J., Pte., 22 Bn. .. 14/8/18
HILL, F. T., Sgt., 24 Bn. .. 11/10/18
HILL, G. W., Cpl., 236 Bde.,
R.F.A. 2/7/17
HILL, H. G., Cpl., 23 Bn. .. 15/9/16
HILL, J., L.-Cpl., 6 Lon. Fd.
Amb. 7/10/18
HILLS, F. W., Gnr., 236 Bde.,
R.F.A. 15/9/16
HILLS, H. W., Spr., 520 Fd.
Co. 19/5/16
HILLS, L. G., L.-Cpl., 21 Bn... 8/6/16
HINDE, W. T., Bdr. Tptr.,
H.Q.R.A. 15/9/16
HIRST, J., Sgt., 20 Bn. .. 15/9/16
HISCOCKS, P. C., Cpl., 15 Bn. 28/12/17
HITCHCOCK, A. V. B., Sgt., 235
Bde., R.F.A. 19/9/17
HITCHCOCK, H. H., Sgt., 18 Bn. 29/4/17
HITCHCOCK, R.W.,Rfn., 18 Bn. 2/10/16
HOARE, H. S., Spr., Sig. Co... 15/9/16
HOBBS, A. E., L.-Cpl., 19 Bn. 23/6/17
HOBDEN, F. C., Pte., 24 Bn... 21/6/17
HOCKING, P. F., Sgt., 21 Bn... 20/6/17
HOCKLEY, H. J., Pte., 15 Bn. 17/9/18
HOGWOOD, H., Drmr., 15 Bn. 2/5/16
HOLDWAY, J. A., Dvr., 236
Bde., R.F.A. 9/5/18
HOLE, J. E., Pte., 24 Bn. .. 5/10/18
HOLLAND, G.A.,L.-Cpl., 23 Bn. 2/10/16
HOLLINGTON, T. W., L.-Cpl.,
17 Bn. 7/10/16
HOLLINGWORTH, F., Rfn., 8 Bn. 7/10/16

HOLLOWAY, H. J., C.Q.M.S.,
22 Bn. 15/9/16
HOLLOWAY, R., Rfn., 21 Bn. 6/6/17
HOLMAN, F. J., 2nd Cpl., 520
Fd. Co. 19/5/16
HOLMES, A., Pte., 15 Bn. .. 28/11/18
HOLNESS, E., Pte., 5 Lon. Fd.
Amb. 11/6/16
HOLT, F., Pte., 15 Bn., att. 140
M.G. Co. 15/9/16
HOMBURG, W. J., Gnr., 235
Bde., R.F.A. 17/7/17
HONEY, J., Rfn., 17 Bn. 24/12/17
HONIG, H., Pte., 7 Bn. .. 24/6/17
HOOD, J. E., L.-Cpl., 19 Bn... 27/10/18
HOOPER, G. W., L.-Cpl., 4 Fd.
Co. 2/10/16
HOPE, F., Rfn., 17 Bn. .. 7/10/18
HOPE, W., L.-Cpl., 24 Bn. .. 13/8/18
HOPKINS, A. W., Pte., 24 Bn. 6/9/17
HOPKINS, P., Bglr., 21 Bn. .. 7/10/16
HORAN, C., Pte., 22 Bn. .. 21/10/18
HORLEY, W. E., Pte., 7 Bn... 19/10/16
HORN, H., C.S.M., 19 Bn. .. 5/10/18
HORWOOD, A. G., L.-Cpl., 140
M.G. Co. 7/10/16
*HOUGHTON, H., Sgt., 6 Bn. .. 3/6/16
HOW, T., Sgt., 23 Bn... .. 14/11/17
HOW, W. G., Pte., 19 Bn. .. 2/10/16
HOWARD, G. B., Sgt., 17 Bn... 7/10/18
HOWARD, W. T., Rfn., 8 Bn... 7/10/16
HOWARTH, G. F. W., Pte., 19
Bn. 15/9/16
HOWELL, F. A., Cpl., 17 Bn... 24/10/16
HUBBARD, G., Cpl., 17 Bn. .. 16/9/18
HUBBARD, O. J., Rfn., 18 Bn. 26/12/17
HUCKSTEPP, A. R., Rfn., 21 Bn. 29/10/16
HUGGINS, P., Pte., 7 Bn. .. 24/6/17
HUGHES, E., Sgt., 19 Bn. .. 24/12/17
HUGHES, F. T., Sgt., 22 Bn... 22/4/18
HULLAND, R. P., L.-Cpl., 6 Bn. 19/10/16
HUMPHREY, H. J., L.-Cpl., 18
Bn., att. 141 T.M.B. .. 19/10/16
HUMPHRIES, G. E., Spr., Sig.
Co. 2/10/16
HUNT, C., L.-Cpl., 23 Bn. .. 6/11/18
HUNT, D. L. A., Pte., 6 Lon.
Fd. Amb. 2/8/17
HUNT, M. R., Rfn., 6 Bn. .. 24/6/17
HURST, R. C., Sgt., 18 Bn. .. 22/4/17
HUSON, A., Rfn., 6 Bn. .. 17/5/16
HUTCHINSON, L., Pte., 15 Bn. 3/11/16
HYDER, H., Pte., 7 Bn. .. 24/6/17
HYNES, J. A., Sgt., 235 Bde.,
R.F.A. 20/5/18
IBBETT, C., C.S.M., 15 Bn. .. 17/9/18
INGLES, J. H., Pte., 22 Bn. .. 19/9/18
INGRAM, O. W., Gnr., 236 Bde.,
R.F.A. 26/8/16
IRVING, W. J., Sgt., 15 Bn. .. 7/10/16

IRWIN, W. L., Pte., 15 Bn. .. 25/12/17
IVES, E. I., Cpl., 17 Bn. .. 7/10/18
IVES, W. E., Rfn., 18 Bn. .. 26/6/17
JACOBS, A., Rfn., 17 Bn. .. 19/10/16
JAGO, P. J., Sgt., 8 Bn. .. 28/12/17
JANAWAY, W. H., Rfn., 21 Bn. 27/11/18
JANES, H., Pte., 4 Lon. Fd.
Amb. 28/12/17
JEANS, C., Gnr., 235 Bde.,
R.F.A. 20/11/16
JEATER, H. W., L.-Cpl., 518
Fd. Co. 23/6/17
JEFFERIES, W., Cpl., 18 Bn... 22/4/17
JEFFERY, J. P., L.-Cpl., 8 Bn.,
att. 140 T.M.B. 14/3/17
JEFFREYS, H. A., Sgt., 17 Bn. 16/9/18
JENKIN, A., Pte., 24 Bn. .. 8/6/16
JENNER, J. H., Rfn., 8 Bn. .. 15/9/16
JEPHCOTT, H. B., Rfn., 8 Bn. 28/12/17
JOHNS, A., L.-Cpl., 23 Bn. .. 20/8/19
*JOHNS, J., L.-Cpl., 22 Bn. .. 10/10/16
JOHNS, T. H., Cpl., Y/47 T.M.B. 14/7/16
JOHNSON, F., Rfn., 6 Bn. .. 2/10/16
JOHNSON, H. R., By.-S.M., 21
Bn., att. 142 T.M.B. .. 19/9/18
JOHNSON, J., Pte., 23 Bn. .. 2/10/16
JOHNSON, F. A., L.-Cpl., 23 Bn. 19/9/18
JOHNSON, S. E., Rfn., 8 Bn... 7/10/16
JOHNSON, T., Pte., 4 Lon. Fd.
Amb. 27/10/16
JOHNSON, W., Rfn., 6 Bn. .. 25/12/17
JONES, A., Pte., 22 Bn. .. 19/9/18
JONES, A., Sgt., 4 R.W.F. .. 28/12/17
JONES, A., Cpl., 4 R.W.F. .. 28/6/17
JONES, A. J., L.-Cpl., 21 Bn... 7/10/16
JONES, A. R., Pte., 4 R.W.F. 28/12/16
JONES, D., Pte., 22 Bn. .. 10/10/17
JONES, F. J., L.-Cpl., 21 Bn... 15/9/16
JONES, G., Pte., 4 R.W.F. .. 8/6/16
JONES, J., Sgt., 4 R.W.F. .. 28/12/17
JONES, L. A., Pte., 4 R.W.F... 8/6/16
JONES, O. M., Pte., 4 R.W.F. 28/6/17
JONES, P., Pte., 7 Bn. .. 1/10/17
JONES, R., Sgt., 4 R.W.F. .. 19/5/16
JONES, R., L.-Cpl., 4 R.W.F. 30/4/18
JONES, W., Pte., 4 R.W.F. .. 28/12/17
*JORDAN, C., Cpl., 18 Bn. .. 29/10/16
JORDAN, F., Pte., 22 Bn. .. 3/6/16
JORDAN, T., Pte., 20 Bn. .. 5/10/18
JOY, H. G., Sgt., 22 Bn. .. 15/9/16
JUDSON, E. F., Pte., 15 Bn... 7/10/18
KAMPFE, H. G., Rfn., 18 Bn. 24/12/17
KAVANAGH, J., Dvr., 235 Bde.,
R.F.A. 15/9/16
KAYE, A., Cpl., 18 Bn. .. 5/10/18
KEARNEY, W., Rfn., 17 Bn. .. 23/6/17
KEEP, A., Cpl., 23 Bn. .. 7/10/18
KELLY, F., Rfn., 21 Bn. .. 15/9/16
KELSEY, F. G., Rfn., 18 Bn... 24/12/17
KEMP, C., L.-Cpl., 21 Bn. .. 29/10/16

KEMP, W., Rfn., 17 Bn. .. 30/7/18
KENNINGS, R., Pte., 22 Bn... 22/4/18
KENT, J. A., Sgt., 24 Bn. .. 15/9/16
KERRY, A. J., L.-Cpl., 24 Bn. 11/10/18
KEYSER, E. F., L.-Cpl., 20 Bn. 15/9/16
KILBURN, F. C., Sgt., 237 Bde.,
R.F.A. 15/6/16
KIMBER, E. H., Rfn., 6 Bn... 6/8/17
KINDELL, R., Pte., 15 Bn. .. 8/9/18
KING, A. J., Sgt., 19 Bn. .. 11/7/16
KING, A. R., Dvr., 236 Bde.,
R.F.A. 16/10/18
KING, H., Pte., 4 R.W.F. .. 24/10/16
KING, J. E., Pte., 24 Bn. .. 7/10/16
KING, L. E., Sgt., 23 Bn. .. 15/6/16
KING, R. D., Pte., 20 Bn. .. 1/7/17
KING, W. C., Sgt., 21 Bn. .. 15/9/16
KING, W. T., Pte., 20 Bn. .. 23/6/17
KINGHAM, S. G., Sgt., 18 Bn. 26/12/17
KINGSTON, A. R., Cpl., 21 Bn. 16/9/18
KNIBB, W., L.-Cpl., 8 Bn. .. 15/9/16
KNIGHT, A., Pte., 7 Bn. .. 28/12/17
KNIGHT, H., L.-Cpl., 19 Bn... 15/9/16
KNOTT, G. E., Pte., 15 Bn. .. 2/5/18
KNOWLES, E., L.-Cpl., 518 Fd.
Co. 23/4/18
KNOWLES, W. H., Dvr., 235
Bde., R.F.A. 20/5/18
KRAMER, G., Cpl., 8 Bn. .. 13/7/16
KYNASTON, T. V., 2nd Cpl.,
4 Fd. Co. 15/9/16
LAINSBURY, L.W., Rfn., 17 Bn. 7/10/18
LAIT, C. J., Pte., 24 Bn .. 20/12/17
LAMB, R. C., 2nd Cpl., 518 Fd.
Co. 28/2/18
LAMBERT, W., Rfn., 21 Bn... 7/10/16
LAMBERTH, B., L.-Cpl., 21 Bn. 15/9/16
LAMING, A. H., Sgt., 8 Bn. .. 7/10/16
LAMKIN, W., Cpl., 8 Bn., att.
140 T.M.B. 24/6/17
LANCASTER, S. C., Rfn., 21 Bn. 10/9/17
LANE, A. R., Pte., 140 M.G.
Co. 7/10/16
LANE, C. J. V., Pte., 24 Bn... 21/4/18
LANE, C. W., Pte., 23 Bn. .. 19/9/18
LANE, J. H., Rfn., 21 Bn. .. 23/1/18
LANE, M., Sgt., 20 Bn. .. 15/9/16
LANE, W., Rfn., 18 Bn. .. 22/4/17
LANES, F., Rfn., 18 Bn. .. 30/4/18
LARKINS, F. J., L.-Cpl., 23 Bn. 29/12/17
LATTER, S. A., Cpl., 18 Bn. .. 24/12/17
LAWLER, A., Sgt., 8 Bn. .. 15/9/16
LAWRENCE, C. E., Sgt., 19 Bn. 5/10/18
*LAWRENCE, F. J., Gnr., D.A.C. 7/10/16
LAWSON, A. H., L.-Cpl., 22 Bn. 15/9/16
LAY, H. J., Cpl., 21 Bn. .. 29/10/16
LAYFIELD, T. L., Pte., 23 Bn. 2/10/16
LAZARUS, P., Pte., 23 Bn. .. 19/9/18
LEA, C., Sgt., 19 Bn... .. 26/9/17
LEADER, G., Pte., 22 Bn. .. 7/10/18

LEARY, J. H., Sgt., 18 Bn. .. 24/12/17
LEARY, W., Cpl., 7 Bn. .. 1/1/18
LECOMBER, J., Rfn., 17 Bn... 16/9/18
LEE, C., Sgt., 4 R.W.F. .. 10/10/16
LEE, J. M. D., Pte., 20 Bn. .. 30/4/18
LEEK, A. E., L.-Cpl., Div.
Train, att. 5 Lon. Fd. Amb. 15/12/17
LEHAN, W. C., Pte., 15 Bn. .. 19/10/16
LEITCH, A., Pte., 24 Bn. .. 11/10/18
LESLIE, J., Sgt., 23 Bn. .. 28/12/17
LESLIE, R., Rfn., 6 Bn. .. 2/10/16
LEVEY, E., Rfn., 17 Bn. .. 25/4/18
*LEVEY, O. L. H., C.S.M., 15 Bn. 7/10/18
LEVINSKEY, A., Rfn., 17 Bn. 29/8/17
LEWINGTON, C. J., Pte., 15 Bn. 17/9/18
LEWIS, A. E., Pte., 24 Bn. .. 8/6/16
LEWIS, A. M., L.-Cpl., 18 Bn.,
att. 141 T.M.B. 22/4/17
LEWIS, F. A., Sgt., 15 Bn. .. 7/10/16
LEWIS, W. A., Sgt., 4 R.W.F. 28/6/17
LIDDIARD, C. J., Pte., 22 Bn. 7/10/18
LIGHT, H., Gnr., Y/47 T.M.B. 25/2/19
LINCOLN, F. W., Pte., 140
M.G. Co. 8/6/16
LINDLEY, A., L.-Cpl., M.G. Bn. 11/10/18
LINNELL, H. J., Pte., 15 Bn... 15/9/16
LIPPIATT, F. J. O., Sgt., 236
Bde., R.F.A. 2/7/17
*LISHMAN, T. B., Sgt., 18 Bn... 22/4/17
LITCHFIELD, H., Pte., 15 Bn.,
att. 140 M.G. Co. 15/9/16
LITTLE J. T., Pte., 24 Bn. .. 21/4/18
LLOYD, A., L.-Cpl., 22 Bn. .. 10/10/16
LLOYD, E., Sgt., 4 R.W.F. .. 24/10/16
LLOYD, F. W., Rfn., 17 Bn... 16/6/16
LOADER, S. T., L.-Cpl., 23 Bn. 7/5/17
LOCK, A. H., Pte., 24 Bn. .. 7/10/16
LOCKWOOD, P. J., Rfn., 17 Bn. 2/10/16
LOHMANN, B. H., Pte., 20 Bn. 15/9/16
LONGMAN, S., Rfn., 21 Bn. .. 16/9/18
LONGMUIR, H. F., Cpl., 24 Bn. 9/12/16
LOTHIAN, R., Rfn., 6 Bn. .. 6/3/17
LOVE, J. W., Pte., 22 Bn. .. 18/6/17
LOVELOCK,H.W., L.-Cpl., 7 Bn. 8/6/16
LOWE, T. S., Pte., 22 Bn. .. 20/12/17
LOWTHORP, A. T., Pte., 24 Bn. 15/9/16
LUCAS, H. G., Cpl., 22 Bn. .. 19/9/18
LUMSDEN, J., Rfn., 6 Bn. .. 24/6/17
LUPTON, F., Sgt., 236 Bde.,
R.F.A. 9/5/18
LUTON, J., Pte., 7 Bn. .. 26/4/17
LYNE, R., Cpl., Elec. Engrs... 15/9/16
McCABE, H., Pte., 5 Lon. Fd.
Amb. 23/6/17
McCANN, T., Rfn., 17 Bn. .. 23/6/17
McCLEAN, J., Rfn., 18 Bn. .. 13/11/18
McCREA, F., Sgt., 23 Bn. .. 16/6/17
McCULLUM, S., L.-Cpl., 7 Bn. 24/6/17
MACDONALD, J.W., Cpl., 22 Bn. 18/6/17
McEWEN, W. T., Pte., 22 Bn. 22/4/18

MACFARLANE, W. W., Sgt., 18
Bn. 15/9/16
McGREGOR, J. H., Rfn., 6 Bn. 24/6/17
McIVER, E. A., C.Q.M.S., Div.
Train 7/10/16
MACKEY, G. W., L.-Cpl., 8 Bn. 25/12/17
MACKIE, A., Pte., 6 Lon. Fd.
Amb. 19/9/18
McKINLEY, W. R., Sgt., 15 Bn. 2/6/16
*MACKINTOSH, D., Sgt., 142
M.G. Co. 30/4/18
McLEAN, A., L.-Cpl., 520 Fd.
Co. 19/5/16
McLEOD, F. W., Rfn., 18 Bn. 5/10/18
McMILLAN, J., Rfn., 18 Bn... 15/11/17
McMONIES, D., Pte., M.T. Co.,
att. 6 Lon. Fd. Amb. .. 19/9/18
McMULLEN, J., Pte., 142 M.G.
Co. 28/12/17
MACNAMARA, W., Rfn., 18 Bn. 1/7/17
McSWEENEY, D., Pte., 22 Bn. 19/9/18
McTAGGART, C., Pte., 22 Bn. 4/8/18
MADDOCK, F. E., Pte., 23 Bn. 21/4/18
MAEDER, F., Rfn., 17 Bn. .. 9/1/17
MAHONEY, W., L.-Cpl., 19 Bn. 2/10/16
MAIDMENT, F., Cpl., 23 Bn... 14/11/17
MAIDMENT, W., Pte., 20 Bn... 5/10/18
MAKEPEACE,W.G., Pte., 23 Bn. 6/11/18
MALES, W. H., Pte., 6 Bn. .. 8/6/16
MALKINSON, C., Sgt., 19 Bn... 19 10/16
MALONEY, J. L., Pte., 15 Bn. 25/12/17
MANNING, G., Pte., 22 Bn. .. 19/9/18
MANSER, F., L.-Cpl., 20 Bn... 2/10/16
MANSFIELD, W. E., Cpl., 17 Bn. 7/10/18
*MANTHORP, C., Sgt., 15 Bn... 28/12/17
MARCH, G. W. F., Rfn., 21 Bn. 11/6/16
*MARCH, V., L.-Cpl., 24 Bn. .. 2/3/18
MARCHANT, W., Rfn., 6 Bn... 24/6/17
MARGETTS, L. M., Pte., 23 Bn. 20/12/17
MARKHAM, A. W., Pte., 19 Bn. 24/12/17
MARKHAM, C. A., Rfn., 8 Bn. 6/8/17
MARLEY, B. L., Sgt., 142 M.G.
Co. 28/12/17
MARR, G., Sgt., 7 Bn. .. 15/9/16
MARRITT, F. C., Cpl., 6 Bn. .. 6/3/17
MARSHALL, E. A., Cpl., 17 Bn. 11/7/17
MARSON, G., L.-Cpl., 7 Bn. .. 24/6/17
MARTIN, T., Pte., 23 Bn. .. 7/10/16
MARTIN, W., Spr., 520 Fd. Co. 14/7/16
MARTINDALE,A.P., Sgt., 18 Bn. 30/6/17
MASCALL, E. C., Pte., 141 M.G.
Co. 24/7/17
MASON, A. J., L.-Cpl., 15 Bn. 7/10/16
MASON, E., Rfn., 6 Bn. .. 24/6/17
MATHESON, F. E., Pte., 15 Bn. 7/10/18
MATTHEWS, W., Pte., 24 Bn... 7/10/16
MAUL, J., Pte., 22 Bn. .. 4/8/18
MAUNDER, H. F., Pte., 15 Bn. 2/5/18
MAY, L. C., Pte., 22 Bn. .. 15/9/16
MAYES, A. E., Rfn., 8 Bn. .. 28/2/18

*MEAD, A. W., Pte., 24 Bn. .. 3/6/16
MEAD, H. A., Pte., 20 Bn. .. 2/10/16
MEADE, H. W., Pte., 23 Bn... 28/12/17
MEADER, F., Pte., 7 Bn. .. 24/6/17
MEDUS, W., Sgt., Elec. Engrs. 15/9/16
MEERING, E., Gnr., 237 Bde.,
R.F.A. 7/10/16
MELLORS, W., Cpl., 238 Bde.,
R.F.A. 14/6/16
MELVILLE, R., Dvr.,520 Fd.Co. 3/1/18
MENEER, A., Gnr., 235 Bde.,
R.F.A. 15/6/16
MERRILL, E., Pte., 5 Lon. Fd.
Amb. 29/9/16
MERRITT, H. C., L.-Cpl., 1/3
Lon. Fd. Co... .. .. 2/10/16
MESSENGER, H., Pte., 22 Bn. 16/7/16
METCALFE, H., Rfn., 17 Bn... 7/10/18
METHERINGHAM,G.,Cpl., 20 Bn. 1/9/17
MEW, W., Sgt. Drmr., 24 Bn. 18/11/18
MICHAEL, H. W., Cpl., 19 Bn. 1/9/17
MIDDLETON, A. H., Pte., 20 Bn. 30/12/17
*MIDDLETON, R. A., Rfn., 21 Bn. 2/1/18
MILES, G., L.-Cpl., 19 Bn. .. 30/4/18
MILES, W. A., Rfn., 17 Bn. .. 19/10/16
MILLER, C., Rfn., 17 Bn. .. 16/6/16
MILLER, J. E., Rfn., 18 Bn... 5/10/18
*MILLER, W. F., Sgt., 18 Bn... 15/9/16
MILLETT, F., Rfn., 6 Bn. .. 17/5/16
MILLS, C., Sgt., M.G. Bn. .. 16/9/18
MILLS, J. R., L.-Cpl., 21 Bn... 20/6/17
MILLS, T., Pte., 7 Bn... .. 1/1/18
MILLSOM, S. T., Pte., 5 Lon.
Fd. Amb. 23/6/17
MILLSON, C. T., Pte., M.G. Bn. 16/9/18
MILROY, D. H. J., Pte., 15 Bn. 28/12/17
MILTON, J. W., Pte., 5 Lon.
Fd. Amb. 28/12/17
MILNER, M. J., L.-Cpl., 15 Bn. 19/10/16
MISSIONS, A., Cpl., 7 Bn. .. 28/12/17
MISSIONS, A., Cpl., 7 Bn. .. 28/12/1
MITCHELL, G., Sgt., E. Surrey
R., att. 23 Bn... .. .. 6/11/18
MONCHO, A., Spr., Sig. Co. .. 3/6/16
*MONCK, H., Sgt., 7 Bn. .. 25/10/16
MOORE, H., Cpl., Elec. Engrs. 15/9/16
MOORE, S., Rfn., 6 Bn. .. 19/10/16
MOORE, T. F., Pte., 20 Bn. .. 30/4/18
MORGAN,W. W., Pte., M.G. Bn. 17/9/18
MORRILL, A., Pte., 20 Bn. .. 2/10/16
MORRIS, E., Pte., 4 R.W.F... 7/10/16
MORRIS, J., Rfn., 18 Bn. .. 22/4/17
MORRIS, W. A., Rfn., 17 Bn... 16/9/18
MORRIS, W. D., Rfn., 6 Bn... 2/10/16
MOSS, E., Rfn., 21 Bn. .. 20/12/17
MOSS, E. H., Rfn., 18 Bn. .. 5/10/18
MOXEY, S., L.-Cpl., 8 Bn. .. 7/10/16
MOYNE, R., Rfn., 8 Bn. .. 13/7/16
MULLIN, J. C., Sgt., 24 Bn. .. 15/9/16
MULLINS, W. E., Cpl., 21 Bn. 20/6/17

BRIG.-GENERAL F. G. LEWIS, C.B., C.M.G., T.D.
Commanding 142nd Infantry Brigade, 1915-1917.

MUNDAY, F. A., Pte., 20 Bn... 5/10/18
MURDIN, E., Pte., E. Surrey R.,
att. 23 Bn... .. 6/11/18
MURPHY, A., Rfn., 6 Bn. .. 15/9/16
MURPHY, A., Cpl., M.G. Bn... 7/10/18
MURPHY, W. J., Sgt., 18 Bn... 1/9/17
MURRAY, F., Pte., M.T. Co., att.
5 Lon. Fd. Amb. 23/4/18
MURRAY, R., Rfn., 17 Bn. .. 24/10/16
MURRIL, W. H., Rfn., 21 Bn... 19/9/18
MUSSABINI, J., L.-Cpl., 1/4 Fd.
Co. 7/7/16
MYATT, A. F. W., Pte., 15 Bn. 28/6/17
MYERS, J., Rfn., 17 Bn. .. 30/7/17
NEAL, J., Cpl., 24 Bn... .. 11/10/18
NEAL, W. J., Sgt., 24 Bn. .. 20/12/17
NEALE, A. E., Pte., 23 Bn. .. 6/11/18
NEALE, S. C., Pte., 5 Lon. Fd.
Amb. 23/4/18
NEALE, W. R., Pte., 24 Bn... 7/10/16
*NEILL, J. J., Sgt., 15 Bn. .. 28/6/17
NELSON, G. W., L.-Cpl., 15 Bn. 16/9/18
NEVE, E. M., Pte., 24 Bn. .. 29/10/16
NEWMAN, A. M., Sgt., 23 Bn. 20/8/19
NEWMAN, W. J., L.-Cpl., 21
Bn. 29/10/16
NEWTON, C., Pte., 7 Bn. .. 7/10/16
NEWTON, J. W., Sgt., M.G. Bn. 30/4/18
NEWTON, N., Pte., 15 Bn. .. 28/6/17
NEWTON, R. G., L.-Cpl., 7 Bn. 8/6/17
NICHOLAS, R. S., Pte., 15 Bn. 15/9/16
NICHOLLS, C. W., Pte., 22 Bn... 16/7/16
NICHOLLS, T., Sgt., 4 R.W.F. 30/4/18
NIGHTINGALE, J., L.-Cpl., M.G.
Bn. 16/9/18
NOBLE, A., Cpl., 19 Bn. .. 25/9/16
NODDER, J., L.-Cpl., 7 Bn. .. 24/6/17
NOEL, G. W., Pte., 23 Bn. .. 2/10/16
*NOEL, W. P., Cpl., 6 Lon. Bde.,
R.F.A. 3/6/16
NORFORD, W., Cpl., 7 Bn. .. 24/6/17
NORMAN, F. D., Cpl., 23 Bn... 19/9/18
NORMAN, H., Cpl., 23 Bn. .. 20/5/18
NORRIS, H. R., Rfn., 18 Bn... 26/6/17
NOTT, A. H., Sgt., 236 Bde.,
R.F.A. 20/8/19
NUTT, G., Pte., 19 Bn. .. 15/9/16
OAKEY, A., L.-Cpl., 21 Bn. .. 7/10/18
OASTLER, A. C., Dvr., 236 Bde.,
R.F.A. 2/7/17
O'DONNELL, W. J., Sgt., M.G.
Bn. 30/4/18
OLDFIELD, E. J., L.-Cpl., 18 Bn. 19/10/16
OLIVER, J., Staff-Sgt., A.S.C.,
M.T., att. 6 Lon. Fd. Amb. 15/9/16
ONIONS, T. H., Pte., 24 Bn... 21/6/17
ORAM, F. J., Pte., 20 Bn., att.
141 T.M.B. 17/5/17
ORBELL, R., Rfn., 17 Bn. .. 23/6/17
O'REGAN, P., Pte., 24 Bn. .. 25/11/18

ORRISS, C., Bdr., 238 Bde.,
R.F.A. 11/10/16
ORTON, W., Rfn., 17 Bn. .. 16/9/18
OWEN, R. G., L.-Cpl., 21 Bn. .. 25/4/18
OWEN, W. R., Sgt., M.G. Bn. 7/10/18
OWENS, E. T., Pte., 4 R.W.F. 28/6/17
PACE, E., Pte., 19 Bn. .. 1/9/17
PACKMAN, E., Pte., 22 Bn. .. 21/10/18
PAGE, F. G., Rfn., 21 Bn. .. 27/10/18
PAICE, W., Cpl., 23 Bn. .. 28/12/17
PAINE, E., Rfn., 18 Bn. .. 22/4/17
PALMER, F. A., Cpl., 19 Bn... 11/7/16
PARKER, F., Pnr., Sig. Co. .. 2/10/16
PARKER, H., Rfn., 17 Bn. .. 16/9/18
PARKIN, W. R., L.-Cpl., 23 Bn. 29/12/17
PARKINS, A. C., Pte., 24 Bn... 11/10/18
PARKYN, J. R., Sgt., 22 Bn. .. 20/12/17
PARNCUTT, G. L., Pte., 20 Bn. 30/12/17
PARNELL, C. H., L.-Cpl., 6 Bn. 6/3/17
PAROSSIEN, F. E., L.-Cpl., 21
Bn. 29/10/16
PARRISS, H., Pte., 6 Lon. Fd.
Amb. 18/12/17
PARROTT, A., Sgt., 21 Bn. .. 20/6/17
PARRY, B., Rfn., 17 Bn. .. 15/9/16
PARRY, J. B., Pte., 24 Bn. .. 7/10/16
PASSMORE, W., L.-Cpl., 19 Bn. 23/6/17
PATERSON, M., Sgt., 236 Bde.,
R.F.A. 10/10/16
PATRICK, F. W., Sgt., 18 Bn. 5/10/18
PATSTON, H. R., Rfn., 8 Bn... 7/10/16
PATTISON, S., Cpl., 15 Bn. .. 25/12/17
*PATTISON, H., Rfn., 8 Bn. .. 3/6/16
PEAD, R. D., Sgt., 17 Bn. .. 23/6/17
PEARCE, A. A., Cpl., 235 Bde.,
R.F.A. 19/9/17
PEARCE, J., Gnr., 236 Bde.,
R.F.A. 16/10/18
PEARSE, A. E., Pte., 15 Bn... 28/6/17
PEMBERTON, H. W., L.-Cpl.,
8 Bn. 24/6/17
PENFOLD, J., Pte., 22 Bn. .. 7/7/18
PENNELL, C. E., Cpl., 6 Bn... 24/6/17
PENNICARD, C. D., Sgt., 22 Bn. 15/9/16
PEPPERILL, A., L.-Cpl., 8 Bn. 28/12/17
PERCY, H., Sgt., 23 Bn. .. 19/9/18
PERRONS, C. A., Pte., 24 Bn... 7/10/16
PERRY, E. C., Sgt., 520 Fd. Co. 23/6/17
PERRY, T. H., Cpl., 8 Bn. .. 25/12/17
PERRYMAN, W. C., S.-Sgt., 4
Lon. Fd. Amb. 3/6/17
PERT, W. D., Gnr., 237 Bde.,
R.F.A. 7/10/16
PETT, E. J., L.-Cpl., 15 Bn... 28/12/17
PETTITT, G., Pte., 7 Bn. .. 26/9/17
PHELAN, S. F., L.-Cpl., 22 Bn. 14/8/18
PHELPS, W., Sgt., 24 Bn. .. 21/6/17
PHILBY, C., Pte., 22 Bn. .. 15/9/16
PHILLIPS, A., Pte., M.T. Co.,
att. 4 Lon. Fd. Amb. .. 23/4/18

X

PHILLIPS, C. B., Pte., 15 Bn... 2/5/18
PHILLIPS, E., Dvr., 8 Bde.,
   R.F.A. 15/9/16
PHILLIPS, F. G., L.-Cpl., Div.
   Train, att. 5 Lon. Fd. Amb. 15/12/17
PHILLIPS, G. B., Cpl., M.G. Bn. 7/10/18
PHILLIPS, L., Rfn., 18 Bn. .. 24/12/17
PHILPOTTS, W. C., Sgt., 236
   Bde., R.F.A. 2/7/17
PILGRIM, K., Pte., 15 Bn. .. 4/11/16
PILLEY, E. C., Sgt., 7 Bn. .. 28/12/17
PINCHAM, A., Pte., M.T. Co.,
   att. H.Q.R.A. 6/7/18
PINDER, H. F., Sgt., 15 Bn... 7/10/18
PIPE, J. W., Sgt., 21 Bn. .. 25/4/18
PITCHER, H. A., Sgt., 18 Bn... 22/4/17
PLANT, A. E. B., Sgt., 8 Bn... 24/6/17
PLUMLEY, A. W., Rfn., 17 Bn. 24/12/17
PLUMMER, D., Dvr., Div. Train,
   att. 5 Lon. Fd. Amb. .. 16/7/17
PLUMMER, P. G., Rfn., 8 Bn... 15/9/16
PLUMRIDGE, J. S., Dvr., Div.
   Train 15/9/16
PLUNKETT, H., Sgt., 19 Bn... 19/5/16
POLLARD, J. E., Rfn., 8 Bn... 15/9/16
POLLARD, S., Pte., 23 Bn. .. 16/7/17
PONSFORD, E. J., Pte., 22 Bn. 19/9/18
POOLE, A., Rfn., 17 Bn. .. 16/6/16
POOLE, S. G., Pte., 20 Bn. .. 5/10/18
PORTCH, W. T., Cpl., 15 Bn... 28/12/17
PORTWAY, J., Pte., 24 Bn. .. 16/10/18
POTTER, L. S., Pte., M.G. Bn. 30/4/18
POWELL, A., Rfn., 21 Bn. .. 2/10/16
POWELL, W. H., Sgt., Div.
   Train 16/4/18
PRAGNELL, F. J., Pte., 23 Bn. 7/10/16
PRAGNELL, H., Sgt., 1/3 Fd.
   Co. 15/9/16
PRALET, E., Rfn., 17 Bn. .. 16/9/18
PRESSEY, J. H., Cpl., 23 Bn... 11/12/17
PRICE, C., Gnr., 237 Bde.,
   R.F.A. 7/10/16
PRICE, E. C., Sgt., 22 Bn. .. 5/5/17
PRICE, J. H., Rfn., 8 Bn. .. 3/6/16
PRICE, N., Pte., 4 R.W.F. .. 19/5/16
PRICE, R. H., Sgt., 22 Bn. .. 20/12/17
PRICE, R. L., Pte., 15 Bn. .. 28/11/18
PRICE, W. H. L., Sgt., 5 Lon.
   Fd. Amb. 18/12/17
PRIME, J., Pte., 24 Bn. .. 2/6/17
PRISLEY, C., Pte., 20 Bn. .. 15/9/16
PROCKTER, L. A., Pte., 24 Bn. 15/9/16
PROCTOR, A. J., Pte., 19 Bn... 7/7/16
PRUCE, B., Cpl., 21 Bn. .. 2/10/16
PUMMERY, C. W., Sgt., 235
   Bde., R.F.A. 17/9/17
PURCHASE, A. R., Tptr., 237
   Bde., R.F.A. 6/9/16
PURCHASE, J., Pte., 23 Bn. .. 7/10/18
PUTNAM, T. G., Pte., 20 Bn... 5/10/18

QUIRK, H. P., Pte., 15 Bn. .. 7/10/18
RAMSAY, C. V., Rfn., 18 Bn... 24,12/17
RANCE, C. H., Sgt., 24 Bn. .. 25/11/18
RAND, J., Rfn., 17 Bn. .. 16/7/17
RANSON, W., Rfn., 18 Bn. .. 7/10/16
RAPPS, F., L.-Cpl., 15 Bn. .. 8/6/16
RASBERRY, M. C., Cpl., 7 Bn.,
   att. 140 T.M.B. 24/6/17
RATTRAY, G., Pte., 24 Bn. .. 7/10/16
RAY, A., Pte., 23 Bn... .. 28/12/17
RAYNER, J. B., Rfn., 8 Bn. .. 24/6/17
REDDICK, G., Rfn., 21 Bn. .. 8/6/16
REDHEAD, E. H., L.-Cpl., 23
   Bn. 14/11/17
REDMAN, L., Cpl., 22 Bn. .. 3/6/16
REEVES, A. S., Pte., 22 Bn... 29/10/16
REGAN, J., L.-Cpl., 17 Bn. .. 27/10/17
REID, J. B. C., Sgt., 21 Bn... 2/1/18
RENIE, F. A., Pte., 20 Bn. .. 2/10/16
REVELL, B., Rfn., 8 Bn., att.
   140 T.M.B. 14/3/17
REYNER, A., Cpl., M.T. Co.,
   att. 6 Lon. Fd. Amb. .. 20/2/18
RHODES, A., Sgt., 8 Bn. .. 7/10/16
RHODES, E., Pte., 23 Bn. .. 2/10/16
RIBBITS, A. W., Rfn., 21 Bn... 7/10/18
RICE, W., Pte., 20 Bn. .. 16/6/16
RICHARDS, A. E., Cpl., 20 Bn. 3/6/16
RICHARDS, B. J., Cpl., 6 Bn... 7/10/16
RICHARDS, J., Pte., 23 Bn. .. 7/10/18
RICHARDSON, A. E., L.-Cpl.,
   20 Bn. 2/10/16
RICHARDSON, E. E., L.-Cpl.,
   21 Bn. 29/10/16
RICHARDSON, W., Cpl., 24 Bn. 19/5/16
RICHBELL, J., L.-Cpl., 8 Bn.,
   att. 140 T.M.B. 8/3/17
RICKARD, W., Sgt., 5 Lon. Fd.
   Amb. 29/9/16
RICKELLS, W., L.-Cpl., 24 Bn. 11/10/18
RICKER, E., Pte., 6 Lon. Fd.
   Amb. 18/12/17
RICKS, V. B., Pte., E. Surrey
   R., att. 23 Bn. 20/5/18
*RIDDY, A. E., Sgt., 22 Bn. .. 5/10/18
RIDGELEY, S. A., Cpl., 15 Bn. 7/10/18
RIDLEY, A., Pte., 20 Bn. .. 5/10/18
RIDLEY, R. H., Rfn., 21 Bn... 16/9/18
RINGE, W. F., Cpl., Sig. Co... 20/6/17
RITCHINGS, A. A. W., L.-Cpl.,
   15 Bn. 28/6/17
RIVERS, A. J., Pte., 142 M.G.
   Co. 29/10/16
RIX, A. V., Pte., 23 Bn. .. 16/6/17
ROAKE, C. W., L.-Cpl., 22 Bn.,
   att. 142 T.M.B. 14/11/17
ROBERTS, A. W., Pte., 20 Bn. 16/6/16
ROBERTS, G., Pte., 4 R.W.F. 8/6/16
ROBERTS, H., Pte., 19 Bn. .. 26/12/17
ROBERTS, P. T., Cpl., 24 Bn... 8/6/16

ROBERTS, W. E., Sgt., 18 Bn.   23/4/17
ROBERTS, W. L., Pte., 4 R.W.F.   30/4/18
ROBERTSON, J., Sgt., 23 Bn...   3/1/17
ROBINS, G. W., Sgt., 17 Bn...   30/9/17
ROBINSON, A., Pte., 24 Bn...   25/11/18
ROBINSON, A. S. C., Pte., 24
   Bn. 8/6/16
ROBINSON, J., L.-Cpl., 520 Fd.
   Co. 14/11/17
ROBINSON, T., Rfn., 17 Bn...   24/12/17
ROCK, W., Pte., 6 Lon. Fd.
   Amb. 23/6/17
RODWELL, J. A., Sgt., 17 Bn.   25/4/18
ROGERS, J. M., Sgt., 4 R.W.F.   24/10/16
ROGERS, M., Sgt., 4 R.W.F...   28/12/17
ROLFE, A. T., Pte., 23 Bn.   ..   7/10/18
ROOKE, L. H. H., Pte., 24 Bn.   21/6/17
ROSE, G. T., Pte., 4 R.W.F...   30/4/18
ROSE, J., Cpl., 6 Bn...   10/3/17
ROSE, W. T., L.-Cpl., 6 Bn...   24/6/17
ROUSE, W. T., Spr., 1/4 Fd.
   Co. 7/7/16
ROUT, F., Pte., 19 Bn.   5/10/18
ROWE, E., Cpl., 18 Bn.   ..   22/4/17
ROWLANDS, T., Sgt., 4 R.W.F.   28/6/17
ROYLANCE, W. G., Pte., 15 Bn.   19/10/16
RUCKERT, W., Bdr., 236 Bde.,
   R.F.A. 2/7/17
RUFFELL, S. G., Rfn., 6 Bn...   25/12/17
RUMBLE, A., Cpl., 236 Bde.,
   R.F.A. 22/9/17
RUSH, C. M., C.S.M., 6 Bn.   ..   15/9/16
RUSHBROOK, D., Rfn., 21 Bn.   19/9/18
RUSSELL, F., Pte., 24 Bn.   ..   14/11/17
RUSSELL, J., Sgt., 15 Bn.   ..   7/10/16
RYAN, F. C., Rfn., 18 Bn.   ..   19/10/16
RYAN, W., Pte., 24 Bn.   4/7/17
SADLER, B. G., L.-Cpl., 23 Bn.,
   att. 142 T.M.B. 18/6/17
SAGAR, H., Rfn., 21 Bn.   ..   20/6/17
SAGE, H. J., Gnr., 237 Bde.,
   R.F.A. 15/9/16
SAGE, W., Pte., 7 Bn...   ..   19/10/16
SAINSBURY, F. A., Sgt., 21 Bn.   20/12/17
SALISBURY, E., C.Q.M.S., 23
   Bn. 15/9/16
SALISBURY, T., Spr., 4 Fd. Co.   15/9/16
SALT, J. A., Cpl., 8 Bn.   ..   24/6/17
SANDERSON, W. K., Pte., 15
   Bn. 15/9/16
SANDIFORD, W. G., L.-Cpl.,
   Div. Train 16/6/17
SANSOME, E. J. O., Cpl., 235
   Bde., R.F.A. 15/9/16
SARAH, E. J., Dvr., 1/3 Fd. Co.   15/9/16
SARGANT, T., Cpl., 20 Bn.   ..   21/7/17
SAUNDERS, A. H., Cpl., 17 Bn.   7/10/16
SAUNDERS, W. H., Pte., 23 Bn.   28/12/17
SCAIFF, E., Sgt., M.G. Bn.   ..   21/10/18
SCANLON, J. P., L.-Cpl., 19 Bn.   31/5/17

SCARSBROOK, G. F., L.-Cpl., 17
   Bn. 30/9/17
SCHMALZEN, A. P., L.-Cpl., 17
   Bn. 7/10/18
SCHOFIELD, E., Staff-Sgt., 6
   Lon. Fd. Amb. 11/6/16
SCIPIO, G. E., L.-Cpl., 18 Bn.   26/6/17
SCOTT, E. F., Sgt., 24 Bn., att.
   142 Bde. H.Q. 21/4/18
SCOTT, H. E., Rfn., 6 Bn.   ..   24/6/17
SCOTT, J., Pte., 22 Bn.   ..   16/7/16
SEALE, W., L.-Cpl., 21 Bn.   ..   16/9/18
SEARLE, L., Sgt., 6 Bn.   ..   6/8/17
SEDDON, J. H., Sgt., 7 Bn.   ..   24/6/17
SELDON, S. J., Spr., Sig. Co...   11/10/18
SEWELL, G. H., Pte., 24 Bn...   5/10/18
SEXTON, H. J., Cpl., 21 Bn...   29/10/16
SEXTON, W. G., Cpl., 21 Bn...   20/6/17
SHACKEL, G. J., Cpl., 1/4 Fd.
   Co. 7/7/16
SHANLEY, T., Rfn., 18 Bn.   ..   24/12/17
SHARPE, R. H., Sgt., 22 Bn...   18/6/17
SHATTOCK, G., Pte., 23 Bn.   ..   19/9/18
SHAW, A. W., Sgt., 6 Lon. Fd.
   Amb. 18/12/17
SHAW, F. W. R., Pte., E. Surrey
   R., att. 23 Bn. 19/9/18
SHAW, J., Sgt., V/47 T.M.B...   23/6/17
SHAW, R., Pte., 140 M.G. Co...   24/6/17
SHAW, W., Rfn., 6 Bn.   ..   2/10/16
SHELDON, F. R., Rfn., 8 Bn...   25/12/17
SHELLEY, H. H., Spr., Sig. Co.   15/9/16
SHELTON, F. J., L.-Cpl., 18 Bn.   15/9/16
SHEPHERD, G., L.-Cpl., 7 Bn.   24/6/17
SHEPHERD, R. J., Cpl., 6 Lon.
   Fd. Amb., att. Div. Train..   14/6/18
SHEPHERD, W., L.-Cpl., 7 Bn.   15/9/16
SHEPHERD, W. J., Rfn., 17 Bn.   23/6/17
SHERRY, L. R., L.-Cpl., 20
   Bn. 2/10/16
SHEW, G., Pte., 20 Bn.   ..   30/12/17
SHILCOCK, A., Pte., 24 Bn...   21/6/17
SHOEMACK, E., L.-Cpl., 18 Bn.   5/10/18
SHUSTER, R., Staff-Sgt., A.O.C.   28/10/16
SIBSON, A., L.-Cpl., 23 Bn.   ..   26/6/17
*SILVESTER, H. A., Sgt., 21 Bn.   25/4/18
SILLICK, F. S., Pte., 22 Bn.   ..   4/8/18
SIMCOX, J. E., Sgt., M.G. Bn.   7/10/18
*SIMKINS, B., L.-Cpl., 520 Fd.
   Co. 3/1/18
SIMONS, A., Rfn., 21 Bn.   ..   27/11/18
SIMPSON, C., Sgt., 20 Bn.   ..   15/9/16
SIMPSON, J., Bdr., 235 Bde.
   R.F.A. 23/6/17
SIMPSON, W. A., Rfn., 18 Bn.   19/10/16
SIMPSON, W. G., Pte., 22 Bn.   22/4/18
SINGLETON, L. W., Pte., 24 Bn.   21/6/17
SLEIGH, H., L.-Cpl., 17 Bn...   24/10/16
SLOUGH, T. W., Sgt., 6 Lon.
   Fd. Amb. 19/9/18

SMALL, F. G. H., Sgt., 23 Bn.,
  att. 142 M.G. Co. 15/9/16
SMALL, J. A., Cpl., 8 Bn. 24/6/17
SMALLMAN, E., Rfn., 17 Bn... 15/9/16
*SMEED, F. A., Pte., 5 Lon. Fd.
  Amb. 22/4/17
SMEDLEY, H. L., Pte., 15 Bn.,
  att. 140 T.M.B. 15/5/16
SMITH, A. C., L.-Cpl., 5 Lon.
  Fd. Amb. 29/9/16
SMITH, C. B. L., Pte., 24 Bn... 8/6/16
SMITH, E. A., Gnr., 236 Bde.,
  R.F.A. 10/10/16
SMITH, F., Cpl., 4 Lon. Fd.
  Amb. 15/9/16
SMITH, G., Pte., 20 Bn. .. 1/9/17
SMITH, H., Sgt., 17 Bn. ..27/10/17
SMITH, J. T., L.-Cpl., M.G.
  Bn. 27/4/18
SMITH, J. W., Cpl., X/47
  T.M.B. 16/10/18
SMITH, J. W. G., L.-Cpl., 20
  Bn. 21/7/17
SMITH, P. W., Pte., 23 Bn. .. 15/9/16
SMITH, R., Sgt., 21 Bn. .. 7/10/18
SMITH, R. J., Pte., 23 Bn. ..14/11/17
SMITH, S., L.-Cpl., 18 Bn. .. 22/4/17
SMITH, S. A., Pte., 15 Bn., att.
  Div. Obs. 19/9/18
SMITH, W. A., Pte., 23 Bn. .. 21/4/18
SMITH, W. G. A., Pte., 22 Bn. 19/9/18
SMITH, W. J., Sgt., 4 Lon. Fd.
  Amb. 19/9/18
SNOW, H. B., L.-Cpl., 6 Bn... 24/6/17
SNOWDEN, F., Cpl., Y/47
  T.M.B. 13/4/17
SNYDER, J. L., Gnr., 237 Bde.,
  R.F.A. 15/9/16
SOLE, T. J., L.-Cpl., 22 Bn... 16/7/16
SOUSTER, A., Pte., 23 Bn. .. 6/11/18
SOUTH, C., Cpl., 23 Bn. .. 7/10/18
SOUTHWOOD, G. W., Pte., 22
  Bn. 19/9/18
SPARHAM, A., Pte., 15 Bn. ..25/12/17
SPARKS, G., Rfn., 6 Bn. .. 6/3/17
SPARLING, T. W., Rfn., 6 Bn. 6/3/17
SPEAR, A., Sgt., 24 Bn. .. 21/6/17
SPEAR, B. H., Cpl., 17 Bn. .. 25/4/18
SPEARMAN, W., Rfn., 17 Bn... 24/12/17
SPENCE, W., Rfn., 17 Bn. .. 25/4/18
SPOONER, J., L.-Cpl., 21 Bn... 15/9/16
SPRINGETT, L. S., Pte., 23 Bn. 16/6/17
SQUIBB, W. F., Sgt., 23 Bn... 20/5/18
STAIG, A. J., L.-Cpl., 8 Bn. .. 7/10/16
STANTON, J., Cpl., 24 Bn. .. 21/4/18
STANTON, W. S., Pte., 15 Bn. 24/10/16
STARNS, C., Sgt., 22 Bn. .. 20/12/17
STEAD, C., Rfn., 17 Bn. .. 16/9/18
STEELE, A., Pte., 7 Bn. .. 15/9/16
STEELE, H. J., Sgt., 15 Bn... 9/1/17

STENNING, E. C., L.-Cpl., 17
  Bn. 25/4/18
*STEPHENS, S. G., Pte., 24 Bn. 7/10/16
STEPHENSON, A., Sgt., 22 Bn. 7/10/18
STEPHENSON, R. H., L.-Cpl., 22
  Bn. 19/9/18
STEPHENSON, T. G., Sgt., 20
  Bn. 27/2/18
STEVENS, A. H., Sgt., 236
  Bde., R.F.A. 14/10/17
STEVENS, G. H., Dvr., 236
  Bde., R.F.A. 9/5/18
STEVENS, H., L.-Cpl., 6 Bn... 6/3/17
STEVENS, J., Rfn., 17 Bn. .. 7/10/16
STEVENS, P. F., Pte., 5 Lon.
  Fd. Amb. 11/6/16
STEVENS, R., L.-Cpl., 22 Bn. 29/10/16
STEVENS, W. R., Rfn., 18 Bn. 5/10/18
STILLMAN, C. G., Cpl., 1/3 Lon.
  Fd. Co. 29/10/16
STOAKES, E. J., Cpl., 22 Bn... 14/12/18
STOCKER, G., Cpl., 22 Bn. .. 18/6/17
STOCKER, J. H., Pte., 4 R.W.F. 11/10/16
STOCKING, A. A., Sgt., 22 Bn. 3/6/16
STODART, F. A., Pte., 15 Bn... 7/10/16
STOKES, G. H., Sgt., 24 Bn... 15/9/16
STOKES, S. E., Bdr., 235 Bde.,
  R.F.A. 20/11/16
STONER, H., L.-Cpl., 6 Bn. .. 24/6/17
STOREY, T. W., Cpl., 19 Bn... 2/10/16
STOREY, W., Pte., 4 Lon. Fd.
  Amb. 11/6/16
STOREY, W. R., Pte., 19 Bn... 1/9/17
STORIE, J., Sgt., 24 Bn. .. 11/10/18
STORK, L. A., Pte., 5 Lon. Fd.
  Amb. 15/9/16
STOW, H. R., Gnr., 235 Bde.,
  R.F.A. 7/5/18
STRAFFORD, H., Pte., 4 R.W.F. 28/6/17
STRANG, J., Rfn., 8 Bn. .. 28/2/18
STRINGER, A., Pte., 6 Lon. Fd.
  Amb. 30/6/17
STRINGER, E. C., Rfn., 21 Bn. 8/6/16
STRUGNELL, E., Pte., 15 Bn... 2/5/18
STRUGNELL, L. W., Cpl., 23 Bn. 3/1/17
STUART-RICHARDSON, J. C.,
  Cpl., Sig. Co. 15/9/16
SUFFOLK, J. H., Spr., Sig. Co. 28/12/17
SUGGARS, A., Dvr., 235 Bde.,
  R.F.A. 15/9/16
SUGGARS, T. H., Rfn., 8 Bn... 25/12/17
SULLINGS, E. N., Sgt., 17 Bn. 27/10/17
SULLIVAN, E. E., Pte., 20 Bn. 21/7/17
SUMMERFIELD, D. F., Sgt., 24
  Bn. 15/9/16
SUMNER, H. J., Pte., 7 Bn. .. 8/6/16
SUMPTER, T. R., Cpl., 17 Bn. 30/9/17
SURRIDGE, A. J., Pte., 15 Bn. 7/10/18
SUTTLE, A., L.-Cpl., 24 Bn. .. 20/12/17
SUTTON, J., Pte., 19 Bn. .. 26/12/17

Swain, J. H., Cpl., 15 Bn.	14/1/17	Tickle, P. J., Cpl., 15 Bn.	2/5/16
Swait, A., Pte., Div. Cyc. Co.	15/9/16	Tillson, E. F., Rfn., 8 Bn.	3/6/16
Swan, S. S., Pte., 4 R.W.F.	30/4/18	Timmons, J., Spr., Sig. Co.	11/10/18
Swanson, A., Cpl., 6 Bn.	24/6/17	Tingey, A., Cpl., 17 Bn.	30/7/18
Swinscoe, E., Pte., 5 Lon. Fd. Amb.	23/6/17	Titterell, F. A., Cpl., 15 Bn.	28/6/17
Swinson, E. L., Spr., 1/3 Lon. Fd. Co.	2/10/16	Tooke, H. H., Spr., Sig. Co.	8/9/18
Sycamore, H. W., C.Q.M.S., 22 Bn.	20/8/19	Toole, V., Bdr., 236 Bde., R.F.A.	25/2/19
Symons, H., L.-Cpl., 6 Lon. Fd. Amb.	18/12/17	Trafford, E. H., Sgt., 20 Bn.	15/9/16
Symons, S. B., Dvr., 236 Bde., R.F.A.	2/7/17	Treadwell, T. H., Sgt., 6 Lon. Fd. Amb.	18/12/17
Tait, R. A., Rfn., 8 Bn.	3/6/16	Tredwell, W., Gnr., D.A.C.	3/7/17
*Tarr, J., Sgt. 17 Bn.	29/9/18	Treeby, A., Pte., 8 Bn., att. 140 M.G. Co.	25/12/17
Tarr, W. R., Sgt., 21 Bn.	16/9/18	Treves, H. G., Sgt., 15 Bn.	25/12/17
Tatam, A., Sgt., 18 Bn.	26/6/17	Troughton, F. E., Sgt., 20 Bn.	5/10/18
Taverner, W., Rfn., 18 Bn.	5/10/18	Trump, W. H., Pte., 6 Lon. Fd. Amb.	7/10/18
Taylor, A. C., Sgt., 15 Bn.	7/10/16	Trumper, G. J., Pte., 22 Bn.	10/10/16
Taylor, A. L., Rfn., 6 Bn.	2/10/16	Tuhill, H. J., Bdr., 236 Bde., R.F.A.	11/12/18
Taylor, C., Sgt., M.G. Bn.	7/10/18	Turnbull, H., Sgt., 6 Lon. Bde., R.F.A.	15/9/16
Taylor, F. G., Pte., 7 Bn.	28/12/17	Turnbull, T. A., L.-Cpl., 8 Bn.	24/6/17
Taylor, G., Pte., 22 Bn.	10/10/16	Turner, B. L., Sgt., 22 Bn.	7/10/18
Taylor, J., Pte., 22 Bn.	16/7/16	Turner, L. B. M., Cpl., X/47 T.M.B.	23/6/17
Taylor, J. E., Cpl., 8 Bn.	24/6/17	Turner, J., Sgt., 4 R.W.F.	30/4/18
Taylor, J. E., Pte., 15 Bn.	25/12/17	Turner, P. W., Sgt., 17 Bn., att. 141 T.M.B.	15/9/16
Taylor, J. F., Pte., 19 Bn.	2/10/16	Turner, T. E. F., C.S.M., 15 Bn.	7/10/18
Taylor, S. R., Dvr., Div. Train	15/9/16	Twine, R., Spr., Sig. Co.	11/10/18
Taylor, T., Sgt., 23 Bn.	15/9/16	Twitchell, L., Dvr., D.A.C.	7/10/16
Taylor, T. A., Sgt., 21 Bn.	8/6/16	Twitchen, H. O., Pte., 15 Bn.	16/9/18
Taylor, T. H., Rfn., 21 Bn.	15/9/16	Twyman, W., Sgt., 5 Lon. Fd. Amb.	29/9/16
Taylor, W. J., Gnr., Y/47 T.M.B.	16/2/17	Tyrie, C. A., Sgt., 22 Bn.	4/8/16
Tellery, S. J., Pte., 22 Bn.	7/10/18	Tyrell, C. T., L.-Cpl., Div. Train	24,7/17
Terry, R., Pte., 22 Bn.	10/10/16	Tysom, H., Cpl., 20 Bn.	5/10/18
Tetlow, E., L.-Cpl., 22 Bn.	7/10/18	Underwood, A. E., Cpl., 15 Bn.	28/12/17
*Thelwell, J., Cpl., 4 R.W.F.	1/1/18	Underwood, C., Cpl., 520 Fd. Co.	15/12/17
Thomas, C. B., Sgt., 24 Bn.	28/12/17	Underwood, E. G., L.-Cpl., 15 Bn.	7,10,18
Thomas, E., Rfn., 6 Bn.	19/5/16	Usherwood, J. H., Cpl., 24 Bn.	21/4/18
Thomas, F., Dvr., H.Q.R.A.	15/9/16	Valden, J. F., Pte., 4 Lon. Fd. Amb.	29/10/16
Thomas, H., Pte., 24 Bn.	11/10/18	Vandome, H., Gnr., 238 Bde., R.F.A.	12/10/16
Thompson, A. A., L.-Cpl., 24 Bn.	51/0,18	Vanlint, J., L.-Cpl., 17 Bn., att. 141 T.M.B.	19/10/16
Thompson, H. P., Rfn., 6 Bn.	24/6/17	Vernham, H. A., Pte., 15 Bn.	25/12/17
Thompson, J. F., Sgt., 6 Bn.	3/6/16	Vernon, W., Sgt., 23 Bn.	19/4/18
Thompson, W., Pte., 19 Bn.	5/10/18	Vicary, C. T., L.-Cpl., 22 Bn.	7/7/18
Thomson, J. E., Pte., 6 Lon. Fd. Amb.	15/9/16	Vinall, H. F., Rfn., 6 Bn.	6/8/17
Thomson, N., Sgt., 19 Bn.	24/12/17	Vince, W. J., Cpl., 23 Bn.	18/6/17
Thomson, R., Sgt., 520 Fd. Co.	5/10/18		
Thorne, T. C., L.-Cpl., 6 Bn.	28/10/16		
Thornett, C., Sgt., 6 Bn.	24/6/17		
Thornhill, C. W., Cpl., M.G. Bn.	27/4/18		
Thornton, H., Cpl., 517 Fd. Co.	23/4/18		
Thorpe-Tracey, R. J. S., L.-Cpl., 6 Bn.	3/6/16		

WILL, H. N., L.-Cpl., 20 Bn... 28/10/16
WILLIAMS, B. A., S.-Sgt., 6
  Lon. Fd. Amb. 19/9/18
WILLIAMS, E., Pte., 4 R.W.F.   30/4/18
WILLIAMS, H., Cpl., 1/3 Fd.
  Co. 15/9/16
WILLIAMS, J., Rfn., 6 Bn.   ..   2/10/16
WILLIAMS, J. E., Sgt., 4 R.W.F.10/10/16
WILLIAMS, P., Sgt., 4 R.W.F.   28/6/17
WILLIAMS, S., Rfn., 17 Bn...   8/9/18
WILLIAMS, S., L.-Cpl., 21 Bn. 20/12/17
WILLIAMS, S., L.-Cpl., 21 Bn.   25/4/18
WILLIAMSON, J., Rfn., 17 Bn.,
  att. 141 T.M.B. 19/10/16
WILLMER, W. L., Rfn., 18 Bn. 24/12/17
WILLMORE, H. J., Rfn., 17 Bn.   7/10/16
WILLOUGHBY, C. V., Cpl., 23
  Bn. 7/10/18
WILSON, A. J., Bdr., 5 Lon.
  Bde., R.F.A. 15/9/16
WILSON, C. H., Pte., 15 Bn...   28/6/17
WILSON, J. A., L.-Cpl., 7 Bn. 28/12/17
*WILSON, J. H., Cpl., 235 Bde.,
  R.F.A. 19/9/17
WILSON, W., Dvr., 235 Bde.,
  R.F.A. 15/9/16
WINCKLESS, L. F., C.Q.M.S.,
  23 Bn. 15/9/16
WINFIELD, W., Rfn., 17 Bn...   16/9/18
WINGATE, E. J., Sgt., 6 Bn...   2/7/17
WINGROVE, G., Cpl., 17 Bn...   7/10/16
WINSTANLEY, C., Rfn., 18 Bn. 24/12/17
WINTER, E., Cpl., 7 Bn.   ..   28/12/17
WINTER, W., Pte., 7 Bn.   ..   28/12/17

WOLTON, E. F. E., Pte., 23 Bn.   7/10/18
WOLVIN, S., Pte., 15 Bn.   ..   2/5/18
WOOD, C. H., L.-Cpl., Div.
  Train..   ..   ..   ..   23/7/17
WOOD, J., Dvr., 235 Bde.,
  R.F.A. 15/9/16
WOODHOUSE, G., Rfn., 17 Bn.   7/10/16
WOODS, H., Cpl., 24 Bn.   ..   21/4/18
WOODS, W., Rfn., 17 Bn.   .. 24/12/17
WOODWARD, C. W., Cpl., 18
  Bn. 16/6/16
WOOLF, F. de Pte., 24 Bn.   .. 27/10/18
WOOLGAR, G. H., L.-Cpl., 18
  Bn. 13/11/18
WOOLNER, C. H., Cpl., 517 Fd.
  Co. 20/8/19
WORKMAN, W., Gnr., 235 Bde.,
  R.F.A. 23/6/17
WREN, F. C., Cpl., 24 Bn.   ..   7/10/16
WRIGHT, A., Pte., 17 Bn.   ..   7/10/16
WRIGHT, A. J., Pte., M.G. Bn.   30/4/18
WRIGHT, J. E. T., Pte., 24 Bn.   7/10/16
WRIGHT, W., Sgt., 17 Bn.   ..   16/9/18
WRIGHT, W. S., Pte., 15 Bn... 28/12/17
WYATT, C. T., Cpl., 24 Bn.   ..   5/10/18
YELLAND, R. H., L.-Cpl., 8 Bn.   7/10/16
YOUELL, F., Rfn., 21 Bn.   ..   23/1/18
YOUNG, A., Bdr., Z/47 T.M.B.   15/6/16
YOUNG, E. W., Sgt., 8 Bn.   ..   24/6/17
YOUNG, H. A., Gnr., 236 Bde.,
  R.F.A. 15/6/16
YOUNG, J., Pte., 23 Bn.   ..   19/9/18
YOUNGS, L., Pte., 4 Lon. Fd.
  Amb. 11/6/16

MERITORIOUS SERVICE MEDAL.

AYLETT, W., Sub. Condr.,
  A.O.C. 17/6/18
BAGULEY, W. H., C.Q.M.S.,
  Div. Train 18/10/16
BAILEY, S., Cpl., 4 R.W.F.   ..   19/9/18
BALSOM, S. H., R.Q.M.S., 4
  R.W.F. 17/6/18
BARNES, J. A., Pte., R.A.S.C.,
  att. Div. H.Q. 18/1/19
BARRETT, A. F., Sgt., R.G.A.,
  X/47 T.M.B. 17/6/18
*BEER, A. J., C.Q.M.S., 24 Bn.   6/6/17
BENNETT, R. H., Cpl., D.A.C.   3/6/19
BIGGS, S. F., Sgt., 24 Bn.   ..   17/6/18
BLACKETT, R., Whlr. Q.M.S.,
  235 Bde., R.F.A...   ..   3/6/19
BOALER, H., L.-Cpl., 19 Bn...   3/6/19
BOARD, W., Cpl., 20 Bn., att.
  141 T.M.B. 17/6/18
BOURKE, A., Cpl., 520 Fd. Co.   17/6/18
BRETT, G. F., Bdr., 236 Bde.,
  R.F.A. 17/6/18

BRIDLE, S. H., Sgt., Div. Train   18/1/19
BUCKERIDGE, C. F., Cpl., H.Q.
  R.A. 18/10/16
BUFFEE, E. W., Conductor,
  A.O.C. 5/1/18
BURGESS, J. S., Cpl., 18 Bn...   3/6/19
BURKMAR, G., Bde. Q.M.S.,
  142 Inf. Bde. 17/6/18
BURROWS, F. L., Sgt.-Maj.,
  6 Lon. Fd. Amb. 17/6/18
BURTON, W. H., Farr. Sgt.,
  235 Bde., R.F.A. 18/1/19
BUTLER, C., S.S.M., Div. Train   17/6/18
CARR, T., Fitter, 237 Bde.,
  R.F.A. 18/10/16
CARROLL, P. J., Sgt., 15 Bn.,
  att. Div. Obs. 17/6/18
CHANCE, R., Sgt., Sig. Co.   ..   3/6/19
CHARLESWORTH, H., Pte., 19
  Bn. 5/1/18
CHARNOCK, G., S.-Sgt. Sdlr.,
  236 Bde., R.F.A. 3/6/19

CLARIDGE, B., Cpl., 18 Bn. .. 3/6/19
CLARK, W., Bdr., D.A.C. .. 3/6/19
CLOVER, H., C.Q.M.S., 19 Bn. 3/6/19
COBLEY, R., Sgt., 21 Bn. .. 3/6/19
COLE, F. H., C.Q.M.S., 17 Bn. 3/6/19
COLLEY, W. J. F., C.Q.M.S.,
18 Bn. 18/1/19
COLLINGS, T. M., R.S.M., M.G.
Bn. 18/1/19
COLLINS, D., Sgt., 8 Bn. .. 18/10/16
*COLLINS, H., C.S.M., 7 Bn. .. 18/10/16
CONEY, H. R. H., L.-Cpl., 15
Bn. 18/10/16
COOPER, E. E., Sgt., 21 Bn.,
att. 140 Bde. H.Q... .. 3/6/19
CORBY, F. J., Sgt., 6 Lon. Fd.
Amb. 3/6/19
CORKE, E. R., Sgt., 20 Bn. .. 3/6/19
CORNEY, H., Sub. Condr.,
A.O.C. 3/6/19
Cox, F. J., Sgt., A.O.C. .. 18/10/16
Cox, W. C., C.Q.M.S., 22 Bn. 18/1/19
CRICK, E. C., Col.-Sgt., 15 Bn. 18/10/16
CUFF, E., Sgt., 235 Bde., R.F.A. 18/10/16
CURTIS, C. J., L.-Cpl., 517 Fd.
Co. 17/6/18
DAVIES, E., Sgt., 4 R.W.F... 18/1/19
DAVIS, J. F., Sgt., 140 M.G. Co. 17/6/18
*DENCHFIELD, S. J., Sgt.-Maj.,
D.A.C. 18/1/19
DOYLE, F. W., Dvr., 236 Bde.,
R.F.A. 18/10/16
*DREWETT, G. H. A., B.Q.M.S.,
236 Bde., R.F.A. 18/10/16
DROWLEY, E. J., Sgt., 22 Bn. 3/6/19
EAGER, G. L., Sgt., 15 Bn.,
att. Div. Obs. 18/10/16
ELLSEY, H. W., C.S.M., 24 Bn. 3/6/19
FARLEY, A. E., Sgt., M.M.P... 3/6/19
FIELD, R. J., S.M., 7 Bn., att.
140 T.M.B. 17/6/18
FINNEGAN, L. W., Sgt., Div.
Train 18/10/16
FOOTE, G. B., L.-Cpl., 15 Bn. 5/1/18
FORBES, J. G. A., S.M., 4 Lon.
Fd. Amb. 5/1/18
FRANKLIN, A., S.-Sgt., 6 Lon.
Fd. Amb. 18/1/19
FRY, H., Farr. Sgt., D.A.C... 3/6/19
GARNER, W. J., Spr., 518 Fd.
Co. 26/7/18
GARWOOD, J. R., Sgt., 24 Bn.,
att. 142 Bde. H.Q... .. 17/6/18
GELLATLY, S. H., Sgt., M.G.
Bn. 18/1/19
GLOVER, C. H., Pte., M.T. Co.,
R.A.S.C. 18/1/19
*GOSLIN, F. S., Sgt., 235 Bde.,
R.F.A. 18/10/16
*GRAY, A. S., R.S.M., Div. Engrs. 3/6/19

GREEN, J. A., Cpl., 235 Bde.
R.F.A. 3/6/19
*GREEN, L. E., C.S.M., Sig. Co. 3/6/19
GREENSLADE, W., Sgt., 19 Bn. 18/1/19
GRIFFIN, E. P., B.S.M., D.A.C. 17/6/18
GRINT, L. A., S.-Sgt., Div.
Train 18/10/16
GROOMBRIDGE, H. A., C.S.M.,
Div. Train 3/6/19
GUY, W. H, S.S.M., Div.
Train 17/6/18
HALL, D., S.-Sgt., A.O.C., att.
24 Bn. 18/1/19
HALL, R., S.-Sgt., A.O.C., att.
236 Bde., R.F.A. .. 5/1/18
HANCOCK, G., Cpl., 237 Bde.,
R.F.A. 18/10/16
HARRIS, C., C.Q.M.S., 8 Bn... 17/6/18
HART, W. B., R.Q.M.S., 15 Bn. 3/6/19
HAYTER, H. J., C.S.M., Div.
Train 3/6/19
HEAWOOD, P., L.-Cpl., 20 Bn.,
att. Div. Obs. 17/6/18
HEWINS, F. G., Cpl., 19 Bn... 3/6/19
HIBBERT, J. H., C.Q.M.S.,
M.G. Bn. 3/6/19
HINTON, H., S.-Sgt., Div. H.Q. 18/10/16
HOLE, F. J., Q.M.S., 8 Bn., att.
140 Bde. H.Q. 18/1/19
HOPCRAFT, H. E., C.S.M., Div.
Train 17/6/18
HOWLEY, A., Cpl., 238 Bde.,
R.F.A. 18/10/16
HUGHES, H. J., C.Q.M.S., 7 Bn. 18/10/16
HUNT, P., Sgt., A.O.C. .. 18/1/19
HUNTER, M., Sgt., 14 Bn., att.
D.H.Q. 18/10/16
HUTT, F. G., Pte., 15 Bn., att.
D.H.Q. 3/6/19
HYDE, W., Cpl., Y/47 T.M.B. 18/1/19
ILES, F. W., Sgt., Div. Train.. 3/6/19
IRONS, P. J., Sgt., 236 Bde.,
R.F.A. 18/10/16
JAMES, W., S.-Sgt., 4 Lon. Fd.
Amb. 17/6/18
JAMIESON, E., Cpl., 518 Fd.
Co., att. D.H.Q. 5/1/18
JOHNSON, A. W., C.Q.M.S., 6
Bn. 6/6/17
JONES, F. E., S.S.M., Div.
Train, att. 4 Lon. Fd. Amb. 18/1/19
JONES, T. W., Sgt., Div. Train,
att. 6 Lon. Fd. Amb. .. 3/6/19
KING, W. W., C.Q.M.S., 18 Bn. 3/6/19
KINGSLEY, C. H., Cpl., 18 Bn. 3/6/19
LAING, D. J., Sgt., 23 Bn. .. 18/1/19
LANE, E., Sq.-S.M., M.M.P... 17/6/18
LANE, J., R.Q.M.S., 17 Bn... 17/6/18
LANSLEY, G. W., C.Q.M.S., 241
Emp. Co. 18/1/19

*LAWRENCE, F. J., Bdr., D.A.C.   3/6/19
LAWRENCE, J., Sgt., A.V.C...   17/6/18
*LEVEY, O. L. H., C.S.M., 15
  Bn. 3/6/19
LEWIS, R. W. J., Sgt., 22 Bn.   3/6/19
LONG, A. C., Cpl., 517 Fd. Co.   18/1/19
LUKES, A. E., Cpl., A.S.C., att.
  Div. H.Q. 5/1/18
LUKES, J. T., Pte., 19 Bn., att.
  Div. H.Q. 3/6/19
MABE, J. R., Cpl., Div. Train,
  att. Div. H.Q. 6/6/17
MACKAY, J., Sgt., Sig. Co.   ..   5/1/18
MACKENZIE, A. D., Cpl., 15 Bn.   17/6/18
MACKINTOSH, D., Sgt., 142 M.G.
  Co. 17/6/18
MALLETT, J., Farr.-Staff Sgt.,
  Div. Train 18/10/16
*MARTIN, R., R.Q.M.S., 21 Bn.   5/1/18
MASSEY, W., C.S.M., 4 R.W.F.   3/6/19
*MASTERS, R. H., Sgt., 21 Bn.   18/1/19
*MILLER, W. F., R.S.M., 18 Bn.   5/1/18
MILLWARD, P. C., Sgt., 18 Bn.   3/6/19
MOORE, W. H., Sgt., 15 Bn...   17/6/18
MORRIS, W. R., C.Q.M.S., 4
  R.W.F. 5/1/18
MOSS, W. N., Sgt., Sig. Co.   ..   3/6/19
NORTON, A., Sgt., 7 Bn.   ..   18/10/16
OWEN, P. S., S.Q.M.S., Div.
  Train, att. Div. H.Q.   ..   18/10/16
PAICE, R. G., C.Q.M.S., Div.
  Train 18/1/19
PAPWORTH, J. M., C.S.M., M.G.
  Bn. 3/6/19
PARSONS, A., Sgt., Div. Train   18/1/19
PARTRIDGE, A. C., Sgt., 18 Bn.   18/1/19
PATER, S. P., L.-Cpl., 23 Bn.,
  att. Div. Obs. 18/1/19
PATRICK, F. G., Sgt., 24 Bn...   3/6/19
PEACHY, H. O., B.Q.M.S., 237
  Bde., R.F.A. 18/10/16
PEASE, B., C.S.M., Sig. Co.   ..   18/1/19
PERCIVAL, T. W., R.Q.M.S.,
  6 Bn. 5/1/18
PETT, H. F., Sgt., 20 Bn.   ..   3/6/19
POORE, A. J., Sgt., Sig. Co.   ..   3/6/19
PRICE, W., Sgt., 4 R.W.F.   ..   17/6/18
PRITCHARD, W. C., Sgt., 15 Bn.   3/6/19
RANDLES, J. H., Sgt., 4 R.W.F.   18/1/19
RENDLE, C. H. R., Q.M.S., 23
  Bn., att. 142 T.M.B.   ..   3/6/19
REYNOLDS, E., C.Q.M.S., 4
  R.W.F. 18/1/19
RICHARDSON, W. J., B.Q.M.S.,
  235 Bde., R.F.A. 6/6/17
ROBERTS, H., Sgt., M.M.P. ..   18/1/19

ROBERTS, N. G., C.Q.M.S., 20
  Bn. 3/6/19
*ROBERTS, W., C.S.M., 4 R.W.F.   17/6/18
ROBERTSON, R. J., Q.M.S., 6
  Lon. Fd. Amb., att. Div. H.Q.   18/1/19
RODWELL, E., Sgt., 23 Bn.   ..   18/10/16
ROSE, H., R.Q.M.S., 20 Bn...   5/1/18
SAWYER, F. C., C.S.M., Div.
  Train 18/1/19
SHELLEY, D. F., B.S.M., D.A.C.   3/6/19
SHOTBOLT, R., Sgt., 17 Bn.   ..   3/6/19
SIMPSON, E., R.Q.M.S., 19 Bn.   18/1/19
SLOCOMBE, A. V., C.Q.M.S.,
  24 Bn. 3/6/19
SMITH, A., Sgt., 22 Bn.   ..   5/1/18
SMITH. C. A., Farr. Sgt., 236
  Bde., R.F.A. 19/10/16
SMITH, J., Sgt., R.A.V.C.   ..   3/6/19
SOMPER, J., C.Q.M.S., Div.
  Train 18/10/16
SOPER, G. H., Sgt., 24 Bn.   ..   18/10/16
SPANNER, H., Sgt., 19 Bn.   ..   17/6/18
SPARROW, G. A., Cpl., R.A.S.C.,
  att. Div. H.Q. 3/6/19
SPENCER, P. J., Sgt., 22 Bn.,
  att. 142 Bde., H.Q.   ..   18/10/16
STEELE, F. A., B.Q.M.S., 236
  Bde., R.F.A. 18/1/19
STRONG, P. G. L., Sgt., 15 Bn.   18/1/19
SWIFT, E. G., Pte., 20 Bn.   ..   3/6/19
THAIN, A. E., C.Q.M.S., 18 Bn.   3/6/19
THIRTLE, H. G., Sgt., Div. Emp.
  Co. 3/6/19
THORN, F., C.S.M., 520 Fd. Co.   3/6/19
THOMAS, J. F., R.Q.M.S., 18
  Bn. 18/1/19
TOOTHILL, W. T., Rfn., 6 Bn.   6/3/17
TUCK, W. G. M., Cpl., 15 Bn...   18/10/16
TUTT, A. E. H., L.-Cpl., 24 Bn.,
  att. Div. H.Q. 17/6/18
TYRRELL, C. B., Sgt., 23 Bn...   18/1/19
VERE, S. H., Sgt., Sig. Co.   ..   18/1/19
WALDEN, O. A., Sgt., 22 Bn...   18/1/19
WALKER, J., Sgt., M.G. Bn...   3/6/19
WARWICK, F. J., R.Q.M.S.,
  22 Bn. 17/6/18
WEEDON, A. H., Sgt., D.A.C.   3/6/19
WELSH, A. E., Sgt., 23 Bn.   ..   18/1/19
*WHITBOURN, E., Cpl., Div.
  Train, att. Div. H.Q.   ..   18/10/16
WHITE, F. H., Sgt., M.M.P...   3/6/19
WILLIAMS, J., Spr., 518 Fd. Co.   18/1/19
WILSON, E. C., Cpl., Sig. Co...   18/10/16
WORBEY, T., Sgt., R.A.V.C...   3/6/19
WRIGHT, B. S., Sgt., D.A.C...   18/1/19
YATES, H., Pte., 19 Bn.   ..   3/6/19

ALBERT MEDAL.

FELDWICK, A. E., Cpl.	8th Battn.	11/6/17
*RATHBONE, W. L. C., 2nd Lieut. ..	15th Battn.	11/6/17
WILLIAMS, S., L.-Cpl.	6th Battn.	4/1/18

FOREIGN DECORATIONS.

FRENCH.

Chevalier de la Legion d'Honneur.

*ANDERSON, W., Capt.	235th Bde., R.F.A. ..	25/4/18
*FIGG, D. W., Capt.	24th Battn.	5/11/15
*HAWKES, W. C. W., Lt.-Col. ..	(106th Pioneers) 4th R.W.F.	14/2/17
*HUNT, H. R. A., Capt. ..	(25th Punjabis) G.S.O.3	5/11/15
PACE, J. W., Capt.	24th Battn.	14/2/17

Croix de Guerre (with Palms).

GORRINGE, SIR G. F., Major-Gen. ..	Divl. Commander. (Two awards)	
*MILDREN, W. F., Brig.-Gen. ..	(6th Bn.) 141st Inf. Bde.	25/4/18

Croix de Guerre.

PEARSE, E. W., Sec.-Lieut.	7th Battn.	9/2/17
*WHEELER, W. R., Capt.	22nd Battn.	7/4/19
WRIGHT, C. S. E., Capt. ..	R.A.M.C., att. 22nd Bn.	29/5/17
ANDERSON, C. B., L.-Cpl.	20th Battn.	20/1/16
BAKER, E., Sgt.	21st Battn.	9/2/17
BIANCHI, F. W., C.Q.M.S. ..	8th Battn.	29/5/17
*CHURCHMAN, W. B., Sgt. ..	2/3rd London Fd. Co., R.E.	25/4/18
GRAYSMARK, J. T., C.S.M. ..	6th Battn.	9/2/17
*HILL, F., Pte.	20th Battn.	5/11/15
*MIDDLETON, R. A., Rfn. ..	21st Battn.	25/4/18
MOORE, E. M., Rfn.	18th Battn.	1/11/18
*OXMAN, R. H., Sgt.	23rd Battn.	5/11/15
*TAYLOR, A. J., Sgt.	7th Battn.	5/11/15
*WOOD, J. W., Sgt.	4th Lon. Fd. Amb. ..	29/5/17
*JELF, A., C.S.M.	6th Battn.	5/11/15

Medaille Militaire.

*BURGESS, H. J., Cpl.	19th Battn.	9/2/17
*GLOVER, B. E., Cpl.	Sig. Co.	5/11/15
*HICKMAN, E. H., Sgt. ..	Z/47 T.M.B.	29/5/17
KNIGHT, F. C., C.Q.M.S. ..	6th Battn.	29/5/17
*NAPIER, C. G. D., Sgt. ..	Div. Cyclist Co.	5/11/15
*NOEL, W. P., Cpl.	6th Lon. Bde., R.F.A. ..	9/2/17
PAYNE, S., Pte.	22nd Battn.	1/11/18
*SHONK, E. G., Sgt.	22nd Battn.	25/4/18
*SMEED, F. A., Pte.	5th Lon. Fd. Amb. ..	9/2/17

Chevalier de l'Ordre de Merite Agricole.

GOLD, R. J. S., Capt. .. .. 15th Battn. 4/10/17

Medaille d'Honneur (avec glaives).

*HINTON, H., S.S.M. .. .. .. Div. Train, att. Div. H.Q. 15/12/19

BELGIAN.
Chevalier de l'Ordre de Leopold.

*WHEELER, W. R., Capt. .. .. 22nd Battn. 7/4/19

*FULLER, R., C.S.M. .. .. .. 18th Battn. 7/4/19
*TIDMARSH, S., Sgt. .. .. .. 21st Battn. 7/4/19

Croix de Guerre.

*GREEN, C. J. S., Lt.-Col. .. .. 7th Battn. 2/2/18
*SAUNDERS, C. J., Capt. .. .. 24th Battn. 2/2/18

BINGHAM, A. L., Spr. .. .. 517 Field Co., R.E. .. 2/2/18
BLAKE, J. C., Bdr. .. .. Div. Amm. Col. 2/2/18
*BOUGHTON, A., Sgt. .. .. 21st Battn. 2/2/18
*BRIGDEN, H. E., L.-Cpl. .. .. Signal Co. 2/2/18
BROOKS, H., Pte. .. .. .. 7th Battn. 2/2/18
BUTLER, R. W., Sgt. .. .. 21st Battn. 2/2/18
*CHESNEY, H., R.S.M. .. .. 20th Battn. 2/2/18
CHILDS, B. H., Cpl. .. .. 520 Field Co. 2/2/18
COLEMAN, R., Sgt. .. .. 7th Battn. 2/2/18
*DAVIES, S., Sgt. .. .. 4th R.W.F. 2/2/18
*DREWETT, G. H. A., S.M. .. .. 236th Bde., R.F.A. .. 2/2/18
*FLETCHER, S., L.-Cpl. .. .. 15th Battn. 2/2/18
GOMER, J., L.-Cpl. .. .. 20th Battn. 2/2/18
HALL, H., C.S.M. .. .. .. 19th Battn. 2/2/18
*HIRON, A. G., C.S.M. .. .. 17th Battn. 2/2/18
*HOUGHTON, H., Sgt. .. .. 6th Battn. 2/2/18
JONES, E., R.Q.M.S. .. .. 23rd Battn. 2/2/18
*LISHMAN, T. B., C.S.M. .. .. 18th Battn. 2/2/18
*OWENS, G., C.S.M. .. .. 4th R.W.F. 2/2/18
PEACOCK, W. J., C.S.M. .. .. 17th Battn. 2/2/18
RUSSELL, B. E., Gnr. .. .. 235th Bde., R.F.A. .. 2/2/18
RYE, C. H., Q.M.S. .. .. X/47 T.M.B. 2/2/18
*SCUDAMORE, N. R. W., L.-Cpl. .. 23rd Battn. 2/2/18
SHADGETT, G. A., Sgt. .. .. 24th Battn. 2/2/18
SMITH, J. H., L.-Cpl. .. .. Signal Co. 2/2/18
SULLIVAN, W. C., Rfn. .. .. 17th Battn. 2/2/18
*WADE, H., Sgt. .. .. .. 6th Battn. 2/2/18

Decoration Militaire.

BLICK, H., Sgt. .. .. .. 8th Battn. 2/2/18
*BOWERS, C. C., Sgt. .. .. .. 7th Battn. 2/2/18

ITALIAN.
Silver Medal for Valour.

TOTTON, A., Capt. .. .. .. 18th Battn. 11/3/17

Bronze Medal for Valour.

*JORDAN, C., Cpl. .. .. .. 18th Battn. 11/3/17
*MANTHORP, C., Sgt. .. .. .. 15th Battn. 26/4/18
*NOTTINGHAM, E. B., Sgt. .. .. 15th Bn., att. 140th T.M.B. 11/3/17
*RIDDLE, H. B., Sgt. .. .. .. 15th Battn. 11/3/17
 TIMON, F., Sgt. .. .. .. 24th Battn. 11/3/17

ROUMANIAN.
Officier—Crown of Roumania.

*READ, H. S., Major .. .. .. 20th Battn. 10/3/19

Chevalier—Star of Roumania.

*SHEPPARD, J. J., Major .. .. 19th Battn. 10/3/19

Croix de Virtute Militara.

*SKILTON, J. F., Sgt. .. .. .. 22nd Battn. 10/3/19

Medaille Barbatie si Credinta.

*HOCKING, P. F., C.S.M. .. .. 17th Battn. 10/3/19

RUSSIAN.
Medal of St. George.

*KEYWORTH, L. J., L.-Cpl. .. .. 24th Battn. 1/9/15

Appendix H.

THE DIVISIONAL SIGN.

Many of the divisions which came to France after divisional signs were already an established institution, adopted symbols which had some connection with the recruiting area or the number of the division or some personal reference to its commander. The sign of the 47th Division, a white star within a square blue border, had no such hidden meaning.

When the 47th Division went oversea in March, 1915, distinguishing marks were not officially recognised, and were used as a matter of convenience only on the vehicles of mechanical transport units. The eight-pointed star was originally chosen by the O.C., 47th Divisional Supply Column, as being a simplified form of the star in the Army Service Corps badge. The square border was coloured according to the sections of the column — blue for divisional troops, yellow for the 140th Infantry Brigade group, green for the 141st Infantry Brigade, and red for the 142nd Infantry Brigade.

In November, 1915, divisional trains were ordered to mark their vehicles with the same sign as was used by the supply column of the division. The sign was therefore adapted slightly so that it could be placed on the side of a G.S. wagon, the coloured border still indicating the brigade company of the Train to which the wagon belonged.

During the winter of 1916 the marks hitherto peculiar to divisional trains were placed by order of G.H.Q. on all vehicles of the Division, and registered officially as divisional signs. As variations for brigades were not allowed, the blue border previously used only by divisional troops was extended to the whole Division.

Appendix I.

THE COUNTY OF LONDON TERRITORIAL FORCE ASSOCIATION.

It is not generally realized, either by the general public or by the regimental officer, how important a part in the recruiting, equipping, and maintaining of the Territorial divisions of the British Army was played by the Territorial Force Associations. These bodies consisted of a number of ex-officio military members—commanding officers of units and so on—and of prominent local men of affairs, many of them old Volunteer and Territorial officers, who freely gave to their country's service the benefit of business and professional experience, for which they commanded high salaries in everyday life.

On the outbreak of war the establishment of the Territorial Force administered by the County of London Association, with Lord Esher as President, was 26,968 N.C.O's and men. Its actual strength was 20,691. This included the whole of the 2nd London Division and certain units of the 1st London Division, besides Army Troops. In Lord Haldane's scheme it was intended that on a general mobilization being ordered, the county associations should cease to function, but owing to the inability of the Army Ordnance Department and other military authorities to cope at once with the vast arrangements involved in a European war, the County of London Association was asked to continue its administrative services, and to supply as before all clothing, equipment, harness, saddlery, and other necessaries required for the units of the Territorial Force under its administration.

The County of London Association was the only one which carried out these responsibilities under a centralized scheme, which it was enabled to do only by the facilities provided at the Duke of York's Headquarters—the big building in King's Road, Chelsea, occupied by the Duke of York's School before its removal to Dover, and taken over soon after the inception of the Territorial Force as headquarters for the County Association, the 2nd London Division, and a number of the units administered by them.

From the beginning of the war in August, 1914, till the departure of the 47th Division for France eight months later, the Association fitted out and maintained with clothing and equipment, from supplies obtained under its own contracts, about 65,000 N.C.O's and men. From March onwards it continued to maintain in clothing and equipment about 35,000 N.C.O's and men till June, 1915, when the Royal Army Clothing Department took over these supplies, and the Association was responsible only for their issue to recruits. Transport had to be arranged for all these stores to units in stations so far apart as St. Albans, Edinburgh, Canterbury, Yorkshire, Reigate, Ipswich, Bishop's Stortford.

The County of London Association can fairly lay claim to having initiated the plan under which, after a Territorial Division had proceeded oversea, it was immediately replaced by the cadres of a second line, with a third line of depots behind it. The 2/2nd London Division afterwards became famous in Palestine as the 60th (London) Division.

Throughout this difficult period Lord Esher was the life and soul of the Association. In fact it may be said that he, with the small office staff of six officers and eleven clerks and storemen, *was* the Association. For the outbreak of war removed at once all the military members, who, by statute, were to form the majority of the Association, as well as many of the other members. Lord Esher, therefore, with the assent of the Chairman, Lord Nicholson, and the Vice-Chairman, Mr. R. M. Holland-Martin, C.B., informed the Army Council that during the period of the war it was not practicable to call the Association together and work on normal lines, and that he proposed, with the invaluable financial advice of Mr. Holland-Martin, to carry on the work of the Association by means of its appointed officers, together with such help, voluntary and other, as could be obtained.

No record of the war history of the 47th (2nd London) Division would be complete without some tribute also to the unceasing work done in the background on its behalf by the staff of the County Association, and especially by Colonel J..C. Oughterson, the former secretary, and Captain H. Mansbridge, O.B.E., his assistant and successor. The latter was personally responsible for contracts representing the purchase of over 750,000 articles of clothing, and an expenditure, during the first year of the war, of over a million pounds. Towards the middle of the war a special department, instituted under his control, was paying the weekly separation allowances to approximately 97,000 wives and dependents—many of them those of members of the 47th Division.

INDEX.

z

MAPS.

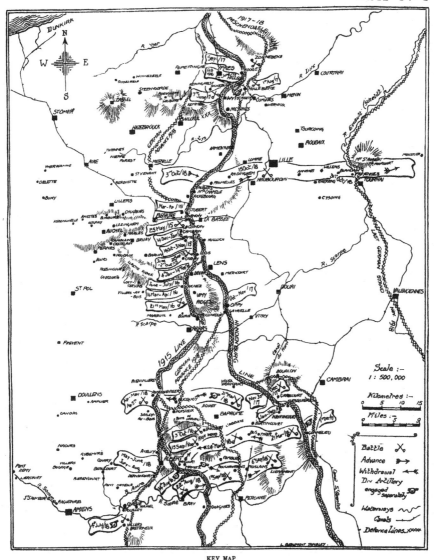

KEY MAP
Showing movements of the 47th Division from March, 1915, to the Armistice.

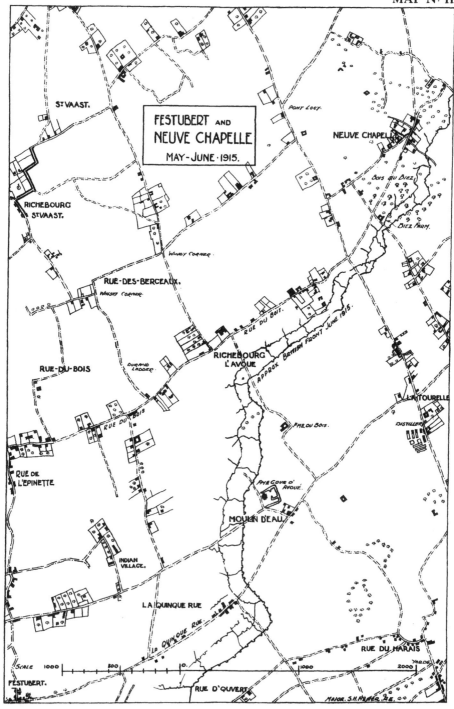

FESTUBERT AND
NEUVE CHAPELLE
MAY – JUNE · 1915.

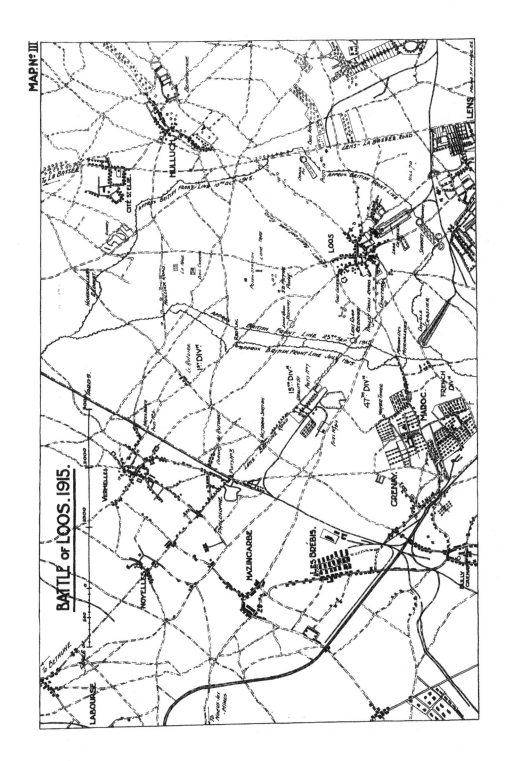

BATTLE of LOOS. 1915.

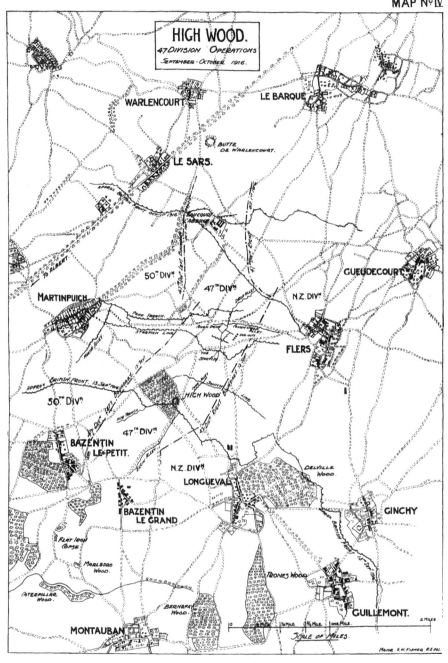

HIGH WOOD.
47 DIVISION OPERATIONS
SEPTEMBER - OCTOBER 1916.

BATTLE of MESSINES 7TH JUNE 1917.

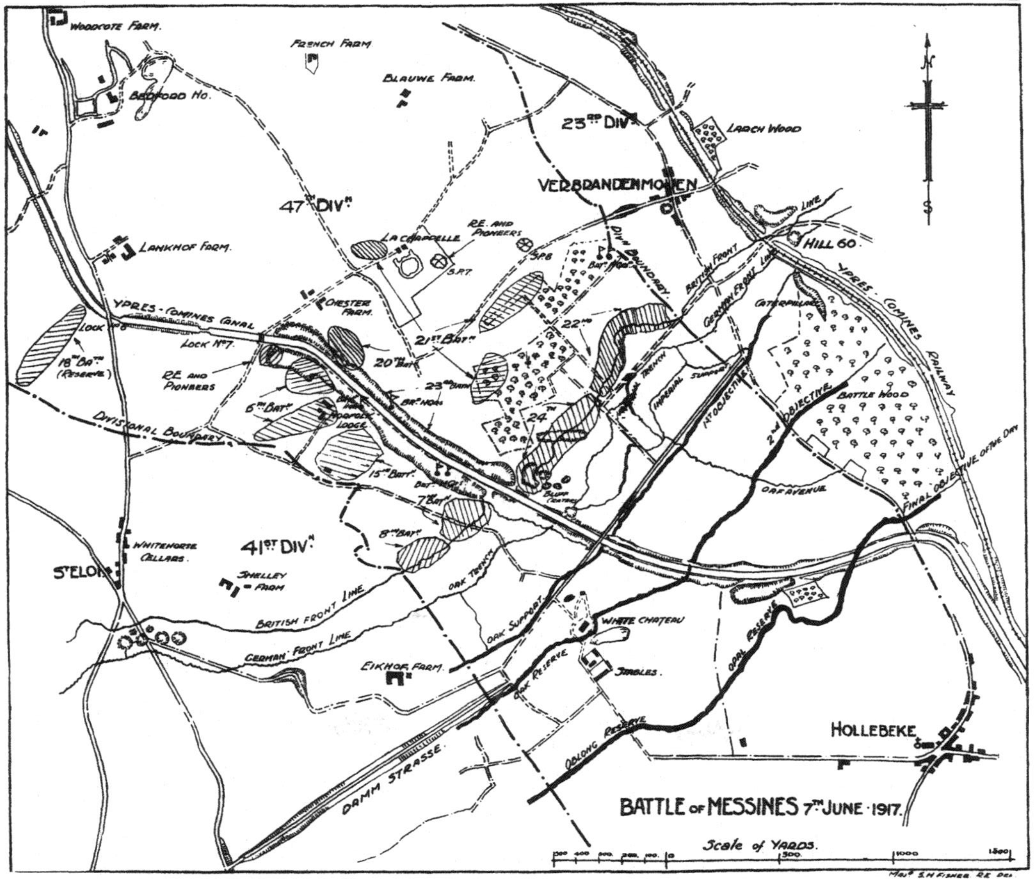

Scale of Yards.

YPRES - COMINES RAILWAY

HILL 60

LARCH WOOD

BATTLE WOOD

WHITE CHÂTEAU

HOLLEBEKE

VERBRANDENMOLEN

23RD DIV.

47TH DIV.

41ST DIV.

STEENBEEK

FRENCH FARM

BLAUWE FARM

HEDGE ROW

LANKHOF FARM

YPRES-COMINES CANAL

WOODCOTE FARM

STE ELOI

WHITESHEET CELLARS

GRAND STRASSE

DIV BOUNDARY

DIVISIONAL BOUNDARY

BRITISH FRONT LINE

GERMAN FRONT LINE

OOSTTAVERNE LINE

N.
S.
E.
W.

HOOGE-WESTHOEK. AUGUST-SEPT.1917

POLYGONEVELD
BLACK WATCH CORNER
NONNE BOSSCHEN
VEERBEEK FARM
GLENCORSE WOOD
FITZCLARENCE FARM
NORTHAM
INVERNESS COPSE
ST. JULIEN ON JUNCTION 1917
CLAPHAM JUNCTION
DUMBARTON LAKES
23ᴿᴰ DIVⁿ.
5ᵀᴴ DIVⁿ.
SURBITON VILLAS
STIRLING CASTLE
WESTHOEK
LINE ADVANCED BY 5ᵀᴴ DIVⁿ AUGUST 1917
APPROXIMATE BRITISH FRONT LINE AUGUST 16ᵀᴴ 1917
FAIRHOLM
RABBIT VILLA
RED LODGE
LAKE FARM
SIEBEN HAUSE
ETANG DE BELLEWARDE
BELLEWARDE FARM
CHATEAU WOOD
HOOGE
MENIN ROAD
THE CULVERT
BIRR CROSS ROADS
WING HOUSE
ZOUAVE WOOD
SANC
TORMANSY POST
VALLEY FARM
RAILWAY WOOD
YPRES-ROULERS RAILWAY
DIVISIONAL BOUNDARY
DIVISIONAL BOUNDARY
WIELTJE-ST.FISHER RD.

300 YARDS   500   1000 YARDS

BOURLON WOOD · Novʳ - Decʳ 1917.ˢ

Scale of Miles

MAP No. VIII

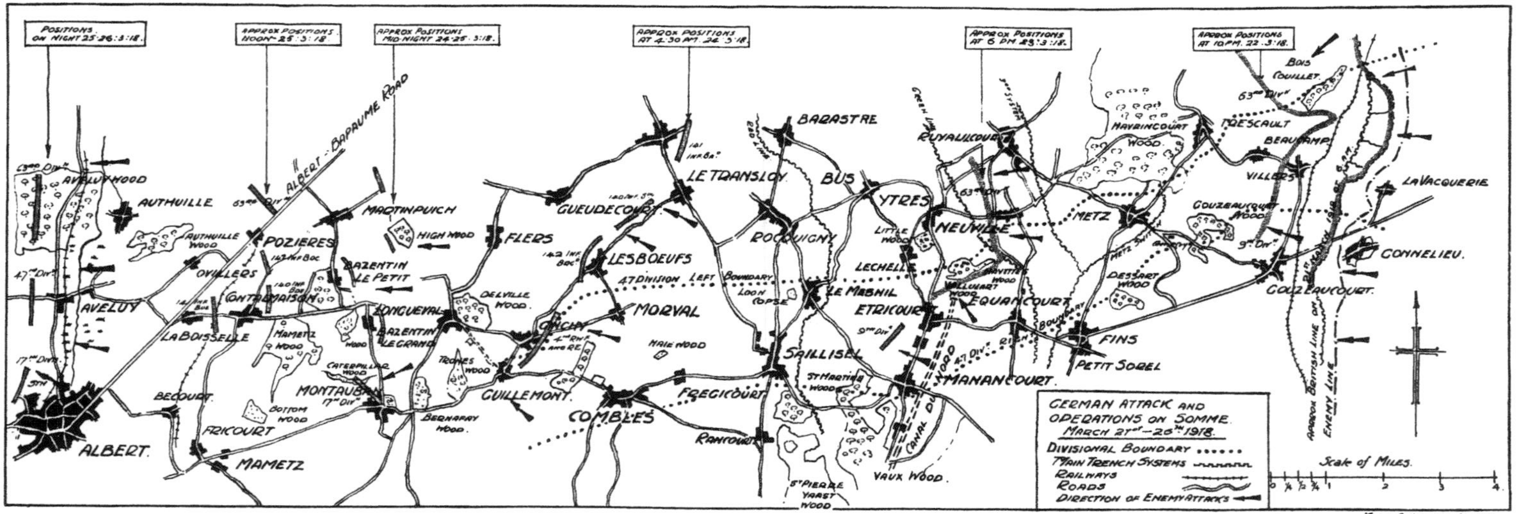

GERMAN ATTACK AND
OPERATIONS ON SOMME.
MARCH 21ST - 28TH 1918.

DIVISIONAL BOUNDARY ....
TRENCH SYSTEMS ~~~~~~
RAILWAYS ━━━━━━
ROADS ━━━━━━
DIRECTION OF ENEMY ATTACKS ➤

Scale of Miles

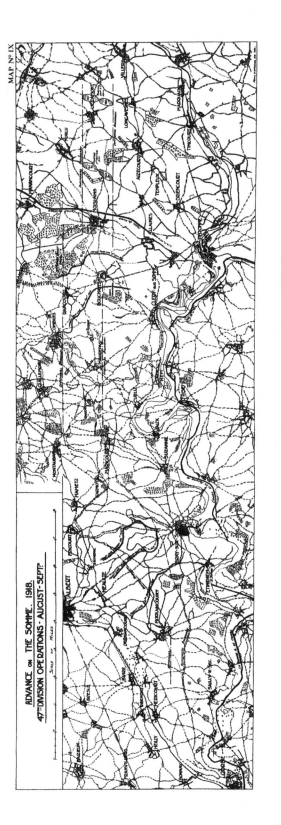

ADVANCE on THE SOMME. 1918.
47TH DIVISION OPERATIONS · AUGUST-SEPTR
Scale of Miles

MAP Nº X

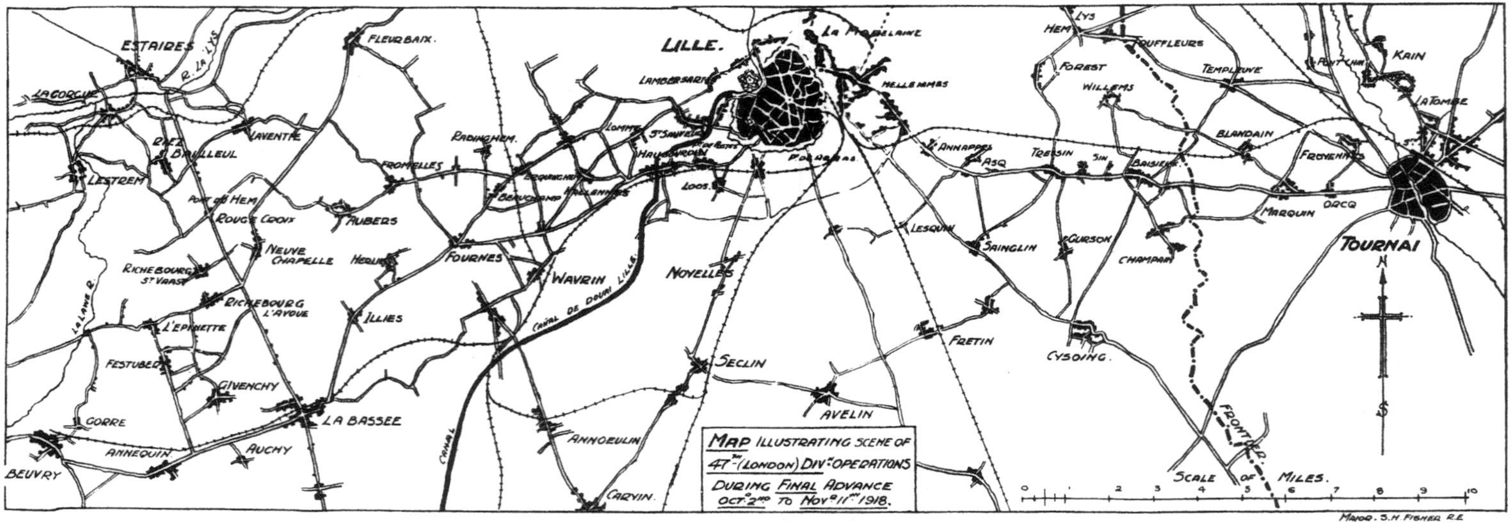
MAP ILLUSTRATING SCENE OF
47TH (LONDON) DIVN. OPERATIONS
DURING FINAL ADVANCE
OCT. 2ND TO NOV. 11TH 1918.
LILLE.
TOURNAI
ESTAIRES
R. LA LYS
LA GORGUE
LAVENTIE
LESTREM
FLEURBAIX.
RADINGHEM.
FROMELLES
AUBERS
FOURNES
WAVRIN
ILLIES
NEUVE CHAPELLE
RICHEBOURG ST VAAST
RICHEBOURG L'AVOUE
L'EPINETTE
FESTUBERT
GIVENCHY
LA BASSEE
GORRE
ANNEQUIN
AUCHY
BEUVRY
ANNOEULIN
CARVIN.
SECLIN
NOYELLES
LOOS.
HAUBOURDIN
LOMME
LAMBERSART
LA MADELAINE
HELLEMMES
ANNAPPES
ASQ
LESQUIN
SAINGLIN
FRETIN
AVELIN
CYSOING.
GURSON
CHAMPAIN
TRESSIN
BAISIEUX
MARQUIN
ORCQ
FROYENNES
BLANDAIN
TEMPLEUVE
WILLEMS
FOREST
HEM
LYS
TOUFFLEURS
KAIN
LA TOMBE
FRONTIER
CANAL DE DOUAI LILLE
CANAL
LA LAWE R.
SCALE OF MILES.
0 1 2 3 4 5 6 7 8 9 10
N
S
MAJOR. S.H. FISHER R.E.